Philosophy of Action

ROYAL INSTITUTE OF PHILOSOPHY SUPPLEMENT: 80

EDITED BY

Anthony O'Hear

CAMBRIDGE
UNIVERSITY PRESS

PUBLISHED BY THE PRESS SYNDICATE OF THE UNIVERSITY OF CAMBRIDGE
The Pitt Building, Trumpington Street, Cambridge, CB2 1RP,
United Kingdom

CAMBRIDGE UNIVERSITY PRESS
UPH, Shaftesbury Road, Cambridge CB2 8BS, United Kingdom
32 Avenue of the Americas, New York, NY 10013–2473, USA
477 Williamstown Road, Port Melbourne, VIC 3207, Australia
C/Orense, 4, planta 13, 28020 Madrid, Spain
Lower Ground Floor, Nautica Building, The Water Club, Beach Road,
Granger Bay, 8005 Cape Town, South Africa

Printed in the United Kingdom at Bell and Bain Ltd.
Typeset by Techset Composition Ltd, Salisbury, UK

A catalogue record for this book is available from the British Library

ISBN 9781108414890
ISSN 1358-2461

Contents

List of Contributors   v

Preface   vii

The Scope of Intention: Action, Conduct, and Responsibility   1
  ROBERT AUDI

Rational Planning Agency   25
  MICHAEL E. BRATMAN

Two Libertarian Theories: or Why Event-causal Libertarians
Should Prefer My Daring Libertarian View to Robert Kane's View   49
  ALFRED R. MELE

Are Character Traits Dispositions?   69
  MARIA ALVAREZ

Knowledge How in Philosophy of Action   87
  JENNIFER HORNSBY

The Doing and the Deed: Action in Normative Ethics   105
  CONSTANTINE SANDIS

Prichard on Causing a Change   127
  JONATHAN DANCY

Motor Skill and Moral Virtue   139
  ELLEN FRIDLAND

Forms of Rational Agency   171
  DOUGLAS LAVIN

Action as Downward Causation   195
  HELEN STEWARD

The Representation of Action   217
  ANTON FORD

Agency and Practical Abilities   235
  WILL SMALL

Actions as Prime   265
  LUCY O'BRIEN

Index   287

List of Contributors

Maria Alvarez – King's College London

Robert Audi – University of Notre Dame

Michael E. Bratman – Stanford University

Jonathan Dancy – University of Texas at Austin

Anton Ford – University of Chicago

Ellen Fridland – King's College London

Jennifer Hornsby – Birkbeck College, Centre for the Study of Mind in Nature, Oslo

Doug Lavin – University College London

Alfred R. Mele – Florida State University

Lucy O'Brien – University College London

Constantine Sandis – University of Hertfordshire

Will Small – University of Illinois at Chicago

Helen Steward – University of Leeds

Preface

This volume is based on the lectures given in the Royal Institute of Philosophy's annual London lecture series 2015–16. The subject was the philosophy of action and in it we were fortunate to be able to bring together an internationally distinguished team of lecturers. As befits the theme itself, a wide range of topics relating to action are covered. These include the nature of action itself and its relation to knowledge-how. There are a number of papers on issues relating to freedom and responsibility, and also to the relation between action and causation. Other papers consider the notion of planning in relation to agency, and the connection between agency and practical abilities. And there are also considerations of virtue and ethical concepts as applied to the notion of action.

The papers collected here will testify to the liveliness of discussions of action in contemporary philosophy, and will also demonstrate the way many ancient conceptions of action are being developed in contemporary philosophical thought.

On behalf of the Royal Institute of Philosophy I would like to thank all the contributors most warmly both for their lectures and for their written papers. I would also like to thank Adam Ferner for his work on compiling the index and also on the series more generally.

doi:10.1017/S1358246117000157   © The Royal Institute of Philosophy and the contributors 2017
Royal Institute of Philosophy Supplement **80** 2017   vii

The Scope of Intention:
Action, Conduct, and Responsibility

ROBERT AUDI

Abstract
Intention takes various forms. Must its objects be acts or activities? How much can be encompassed in the content of a single intention? Can intentions can have the content: *to A for R,* where '*A*' ranges over act-types and '*R*' over reasons for action, for instance *to keep my promise*? The question is particularly important on the widely accepted assumption that, for concrete actions (act-tokens) that are rational and have moral worth, both their rationality and their moral worth depend on the reason(s) *for* which they are performed. If intentions can have content of the form of 'to *A* for *R*', should we conclude that (contrary to the position of many philosophers) we have direct voluntary control of the reason(s) for which we act? If intentions cannot have such content, how can we intend to do, not just what we ought to do, but to do it with 'moral worth'? This question is also raised by the idea that we can be commanded to treat others as ends in themselves – which presumably has moral worth. If the commandable is intendable, then, to understand commands and other directives, we need a theory of the scope of intention. This paper explores kinds and objects of intention, outlines an account of its scope, and brings out some implications of the account for moral responsibility.

Intending is widely considered a "practical" attitude. It is so conceived because it has an essential connection to action. One basis of this conception is an intrinsic element in intentions: by their very nature they are, in content, in some way directed to action. A second basis of the conception is relational: intentions are conceived as bearing a special relation to actions that realize them. It is, however, quite difficult to see just how to understand these aspects of intention. The second aspect has received far more attention from philosophers than the first.[1] My concern here is mainly the first: the nature of intention and the scope of its content. Without understanding this, we cannot adequately understand what it is to intend, and, in ethics, we cannot fully account for imperatives, commands, promises, or decisions. These include Kant's categorical imperative, the famous

---

[1] Detailed discussions of intention have been profuse since G.E.M. Anscombe's *Intention* (Oxford: Blackwell, 1957; 2nd ed., Oxford: Blackwell, 1963), but the usual focus is on their role in explaining action and, especially in this century, in providing reasons for action or determining moral responsibility.

doi:10.1017/S1358246117000030   ©The Royal Institute of Philosophy and the contributors 2017
Royal Institute of Philosophy Supplement **80** 2017   1

Robert Audi

biblical love commandments, promises to love, and decisions to be less didactic. A fully adequate theory of obligation and moral responsibility must be supported by an account of what kinds of objects intention has; how its formation can be a response to commands, promises, and other intention elicitors in human experience; and what kind of control we have over its formation and realization.

1. Forms of Intention

It will help us to begin with intention-locutions. These indicate some of the variety of intentions themselves, though, as will soon be evident, we should not uncritically assume that every element in the locutions considered reveals an important aspect of intention itself. Some of the locutions are *infinitival*, e.g. '*to* send a letter'. Some designate umbrella intentions *to bring about something,* for instance an improvement in relations with certain in-laws. Some designate other indefinite intentions, e.g. to *try* to A, where A-ing is an act but no act constituting the would-be trying is specified. Some non-actions represented by verbs should also be included, say to forgive and to be a good friend.[2]

A different category of intention-ascriptions includes the *objectual,* for instance intending some object for a purpose or intending someone to serve on one's committee. I can intend a sharp carving knife for a Thanksgiving turkey. Such cases show that we cannot take intention-ascriptions at face value – as clearly indicating what is intended. The intentional object of this "object intention" is not the knife but some set of acts concerning it. As in other cases of intention-ascription, these (if true) require the agent to have a concept of *some* action, but – except where one intends an *agent* to be or do something – need not indicate a particular act or a specific agent. In the knife example, the action, carving, is specified, but no agent is

---

[2]   I have heard it said that forgiveness is an action, but I do not think so. I can say I intend to forgive, at least where I see why someone failed me and resolve to forgive the broken promise. But we can also say 'I intend to love', and surely 'love' here is not an action-reporting term (what intending to love one's neighbor comes to will be discussed below). Perhaps 'I intend to forgive' is typically a way of saying either that one will *express* forgiveness, which is readily understandable, or that one will try to achieve forgiveness, in which case 'try to' leaves open a number of possible forgiveness-related acts but does not designate forgiveness itself. An account of forgiveness is not possible here, but there is now much philosophical literature on the topic (including books by Charles Griswold and Glen Pettigrove).

indicated. If I intend a bottle of wine for my hostess, this leaves open both who hands it to her (say my companion or me) *and* just what, if anything, I intend her to do with it.

A less common and less often discussed intention-ascribing locution is *subjunctive*, for instance, 'intending *that* my students learn punctuation'. Normally one doesn't intend that something be so without having both a related intention *to* and a *tendency* to intend to do certain things which, in the case in question, are implicit in the intention or appropriate to fulfilling it. If I intend that my students understand why utilitarianism should not be described as the view that right acts are those that promote the greatest good for the greatest number, I likely have in mind and intend a series of explanatory acts. But suppose that in a prospective conversation with an old friend the latter says 'I intend that my children be well educated'. In a mood of identification with the friend, one could form a similar intention, say that one's children be freed of anxiety about tuition. At that moment one is of course disposed to form action-intentions, but one need not do so. If, however, this subjunctive intention persists, doing so is expectable.

We should also consider intending *to be*, for instance to be a friend to someone. This may be best understood in terms of a kind of intending *that*, say intending that one give the person support in stressful situations. This subjunctive construction is important in part because it can also encompass the content of a person's intentions to be of a certain character, say kind or more understanding. There may be still other intention-locutions best understood subjunctively, and later I will illustrate an important aspect of subjunctive intentions.

All of the cases considered are instances of intention conceived as a practical attitude, in a sense implying an essential connection with action (at least with some act-type). Even if, as with objectual and subjunctive intentions, no particular act is entailed by the concept of the intention in question, there remains a self-evident connection with action: the intention-ascription portrays the person as in some sense aiming at doing something. The ascription may not indicate, and the agent may not know, just what act-type(s) are intended or otherwise (if only in some implicit way) encompassed. Precisely for this reason, objectual and subjunctive intentions cannot be reduced to infinitival ones: they entail a readiness to form the latter but do not require a determinate set of such intentions. The same points hold for desire, to be sure, but desires need not imply the kind of commitment of the will implied by intending. Many of our desires even *to do* are far from committing us – and may be overwhelmingly opposed by our deepest plans.

3

Robert Audi

2. Sources of Intention

One of the routes to understanding intention is by way of its conceptually relevant sources. These are not just genetically informative, but indicative of elements in its nature. They are also important for understanding moral responsibility. We are responsible for intentions – in the sense that we are subject to praise or criticism for forming or harboring certain intentions – and so should do what we can both to form or nurture those that go with realizing desirable goals and to prevent formation, or at least, harboring, those directed to what is undesirable or wrong. Talk of responsibility for intentions may suggest their formation *prior* to action, but my concern with sources of intention extends to cases in which (as with actions as immediate responses) intentions are not formed before the intended action.

First, consider *volitional routes* to intention-formation. We often decide to do something. Deciding to A is a kind of manifestation of will, and as such it entails intending to A, even if not an awareness of intending to A. Resolving to A seems similar. But could there be hollow resolutions, as with some that one might list on New Year's day? Doubtless, but where resolution is volitional and not merely verbal, it is like decision (though 'decide' may also have "hollow" uses). The generic notion here is *willing*, which is familiar in at least some cases of trying as well as in some instances of achieving an aim. Here it suffices to note that we often consider options, decide on one, and thereby form an intention to do something or to try to do it. It of course does not follow, and is not true, that all intentions emerge from decision.

A second route to intention-formation is *doxastic*. A common case occurs when we form an intention upon forming an instrumental belief *given* predominant motivation to which the belief is relevant in a certain way. Suppose I am contemplating a prospect I don't see how to realize, say attending a favorite play. Then coming to believe that A-ing, say phoning a friend who has a subscription, will realize it can immediately lead to my forming the intention to A. Belief combined with trying constitutes another route to intention-formation. If one is trying to A, one already hopes or intends to A. If, however, there is some instrumental action, say B, that one intends as a way to bring about A-ing, one might suddenly realize that C-ing will definitely work and come to intend to C instead. Trying to open a jar by tapping its top may not be succeeding when one suddenly remembers an available pipe wrench. Straightaway one forms the intention to apply it.

4

A third case in which intentions are formed is phenomenologically less prominent. Suppose one has the habit of reaching for the right shoe first when dressing. In the morning, seeing it across the room, one might then intend to get it without even considering the option of reversing one's procedure. Reaching out a hand when introduced to someone is similar, though given certain cues one may be ready to form the intention to abstain. It is interesting to note here that habit need not imply any specific conceptualization of the action in question, say *to put on the right shoe first*. The intention might be simply *to put on that shoe now*, where 'that' designates the right shoe one is viewing. For some cases, moreover, an objectual intention might do; I might, as I take a pair of shoes from the rack, simply intend the right and left ones for the respective feet without the notion of order's figuring in the content of my intention.

In some of the cases illustrated, there is an event that *triggers* intention formation: either a belief forms and completes the sufficient conditions for intending, where there is already a desire to do the deed, or a habit is activated by ongoing activity or by circumstances. Perhaps we can also speak of a trigger where an obviously needed response is intended in suddenly encountered circumstances, say where an opportunity to A is suddenly seen. Walking in England, an American starting to cross a street might, having looked for traffic the wrong way, unexpectedly see an approaching car and form an intention to wait for the green light. In this fourth case there are standing beliefs connected with standing motivation to avoid getting hit. Yet the behavior is not mere reflex. Neither is withdrawing a hand from a hot stove, though some instances of the corresponding movement might be.

A fourth kind of case is a sudden attraction to doing something, as where it fits some overall purpose one has or even occurs as part of a plan or prospect one suddenly wants to realize. Planning a party, I may be reminded of Jack, perhaps by glimpsing a letter on the table. I immediately form the intention to invite him to the party.

In all four cases considered, there is some event in consciousness that yields an intention, something in consciousness that, even if not a trigger of intention, is a phenomenally perceptible element. There is a fifth case that does not entail such perceptibility. It occurs where standing motivation to A becomes predominant over competing motivation or, in another kind of case, over inertia. The agent may be torn between attending a play and attending a symphony scheduled for the same night. In time, one of the desires can become stronger than the other in such a way that, on being asked what one will do that night, one can find oneself truly saying one is

5

going to go to the symphony. One *might* have heard the composer's music and enjoyed it, which might, without one's realizing it, strengthen the desire to attend the symphony; but no such event is necessary for spontaneous motivational predominance.

3. The Range of Objects of Intention

Much about the range that the objects of intention can have is now apparent in outline; but there are important cases not so far identified. Here it will suffice to focus just on objects of intentions *to*. The 'to' is commonly followed by specifications of act-types, including activity-types. The usual paradigms of intention discussed in the literature are single-act intentions. But, in addition to intending, say, to shake someone's hand as a greeting, there are complex sequences we can intend, though the expected conditions for doing a deed need not all figure in the content of intending it.[3]

If we think of the objects of intentions *to* as limited to such acts and activities, we miss an important element that often comes into the scope of an intention. What we do is done in some *way,* and sometimes this *manner of action* is important and intended. To be sure, a manner of an intended action need not itself be intended. Intention is not closed even under believed consequences, including expected manners of performance: I can intend to phone someone at 7 a.m. and believe that this will wake a teenage child, yet not intend to wake the teenager; and we can intend to ask help of someone, believe that we will do it timidly, but not intend to do it timidly.

One might think that acts described by an adverb of manner are simply acts simpliciter and that therefore intending to A *M-ly,* where M is a manner of acting, reduce to intending to B, for some act-type B, identifiable without such an adverb. Suppose there is an at least approximately equivalent act-type, as in some cases of declining a request decisively and refusing it. It does not follow that *to B* is the content of the original intention. The intention may have a precise content lost by any but an exactly equivalent substitution. Moreover, in principle any act can be performed in more than one way, and to provide an act-name that absorbs the adverbial modifier

---

[3]   One can intend to find something out by consulting reference works, or intend to speak to someone who is visibly occupied with driving. Neither all that one believes is involved in consulting those works nor, of course, someone else's driving, is in the content of these intentions – of what one intends.

(as 'yelling' absorbs voicing in a certain loud tone) can be misleading, and even when it is not false, it may easily conceal an important dimension of behavioral assessment. It matters greatly *how* we do what we do, for instance whether we correct a child's speaking error gently or harshly.[4] Eliminating adverbs of manner in favor of "simpler" act-reports may both reduce clarity and impair normative appraisal.

A further dimension of complexity in the objects of intention is that of 'scripts'. These might be conceived as encapsulated complex intentional contents. Consider intending to play a piano piece that is memorized so well as to be second nature. When one plays it in fulfillment of the intention, one intends each note (that goes right), though the intention might be objectual; but one could not even describe the whole sequence, nor need one have the thought of each behavioral element in the script as the occasion to act occurs. A simpler case would be a script for leaving a message when one is issuing phone invitations to a party. Intending to invite Liz via her voicemail might encapsulate a series of sentences and even an intonation, speed, and volume. There is no sharp distinction between scripted content of an intention expressible without a detailed conception of an activity and, on the other hand, an unspecific, perhaps generically conceived, activity content, but at least this much is clear. A script is relatively determinate in that it expresses or prescribes a behavioral sequence that, at least in simple cases, can normally be described in some detail in advance, whereas some activities one can intend, such as talking with a friend about a film, are far from routine and are describable beforehand only in outline.[5]

Might the scope of intentions also include a purposive element, say a reason for the intended act as well as a conception of the act itself? To see the problem, consider intentions whose objects appear to be acts purposively described. Suppose I promise to help Clarence clean out his messy garage in the spring and by then he inherits a fortune and doesn't need my help. Asked why I'm taking the

---

[4]   For discussion of how adverbs figure in action theory see, e.g. Donald Davidson, 'The Logical form of Action Sentences', in *Essays on Actions and Events* (Oxford: Oxford University Press, 1980). Detailed discussion is found in ch. 3 of my *Means, Ends, and Persons: The Meaning and Psychological Dimensions of Kant's Humanity Formula* (New York and Oxford: Oxford University Press, 2016).

[5]   The variety of scripts is greater than here indicated. One possibility is a *de re* grasp of a complex kind of behavior, as where someone who hears and well remembers a tune forms the intention to sing *that*.

trouble when Clarence has hired someone to help and perhaps even forgotten my promise, I might say: 'I intend to help him because I promised to'. Note first that this is ambiguous. It might mean roughly (1) 'The reason why I intend to help him is that I promised to' or, by contrast, (2) 'I intend to help-him-because-I-promised-to', where this ostensibly specifies the *content* of the intention and not *why one has it*. Can an intention have such a content? We can also be said to intend to A in order to B, say to meet a friend in order to plan an event. This is not a case of intending-to-A-for-R but of attributing both an intention to A and a purposive explanation of it. The attribution indicates both what is aimed at and what motivates the aim.

There are perhaps circumstances in which I can intend *that* my helping be explainable by my promising. This intention might embody an intention to do something that causes that explanation relation to hold. I might, e.g., get my brain manipulated so that my making promises does in fact explain why I do the promised deeds. But do phrases of the form of 'A-ing for R', where R is a reason, report any act or activity? Surely this, like 'A-ing from a sense of duty' and 'A-ing for the purpose of helping her', is a double-barrelled report indicating items in two categories: an action, which is an event, and a reason as a motivational element (e.g. to live up to my duty), which is not an event. We must not let the difference between *what* is done and *why* it is done be obscured by our desire to act for the right kinds of reasons combined with the not unnatural thought that, being something we can say we intend, 'to A for R' simply designates doing something. We can also say we intend to be upright citizens, and this plainly does not imply that 'being an upright citizen' designates doing.

The considerations just noted are not the only possible explanations for misconceptions of locutions like 'I intend to do it because I promised to'. Ascriptions of intentions, especially 'further intentions' (and further aims in general) have considerable power in describing what people are doing. Consider the question 'What is he *really* doing?' This presupposes that (1) he is doing something more than the salient deed referred to, such as helping an elderly woman with her groceries, and (2) that this further action is supported by a significant reason (carried by some intentional element, such as a *hope* of financial gain, even if not necessarily by intention). An implication of such parlance is that one cannot tell what people are doing (intentionally) without knowing at least one appropriately governing reason for their doing it. Now suppose this is so. This does not entail anything about the question whether reasons can enter the content of the presumed underlying intention. The most important point it shows is that one (objectually) can intend one action to bring about another, say intend assisting with loading groceries to provide an opportunity to pickpocket their owner. This concerns the relation between intended acts, not between an action and a reason for it, and it does not imply that the agent has an intention whose content has the form of 'to A for R'. Similarly, expressions like 'intending to B by A-ing' are informatively double-barrelled: forward-looking (toward a desired result of A-ing) and instrumental. The 'by' indicates how – by what action(s) – the agent intends to achieve the result, not a reason for aiming at it. The scope of intention can also include behavioral consequences of the 'target', *focally* intended, act – one might loosely call these *penumbrally intended* – but it does not follow that it can include the (or a) reason for which the act is to be performed.

This case suggests how the role of intentions in framing act-descriptions can be understood without countenancing intentions with the kind of purposive content we are exploring. One might think that at least for basic acts for which two or more reasons we have are eligible grounds, we can intend to bring about, at will, their being performed *for* one of these reasons in particular. But is this so? Granted, we can immediately bring about A-ing for R provided that we can A *and* our only way to A is on the basis of R, as where my only reason to shake your hand is *to greet you*. But this is really bringing about A-ing for R *by* A-ing – there is only one reason available to yield the deed: A-ing is performed at will and its performance of course guarantees that the only route to that performance has been traversed. Suppose, however, that I have a reason of self-interest as well as a promissory reason to help someone with a task and each reason is strong enough to yield the deed. Can I at will bring about my doing it for the promissory reason? And does intending this even make good sense? I might do things that justify my expecting that I *will* do the deed for the preferred reason. But the expectable is not thereby intendable; and intending to *cause* oneself to A for R does require having an intention whose content is to-A-for-R.

It should be clear, then, that from the point that a further intention or further aim in A-ing, say to achieve G, can yield and often does yield, a better description of what the agent is doing in A-ing, we may not infer that descriptions of the form of 'A-ing for R' are act-reporting phrases. That acts can bear many descriptions on the basis of the agent's relevant intentions shows much about the number and scope of underlying intentional attitudes, but does not justify taking any act-description to be a combined report and explanation. We have also seen that one reason not to take 'A-ing for R' to be an action-report is that we do not have, and do not take ourselves to have, the needed control over the reason(s) for which we act, and we do not normally intend to do anything we do not take ourselves to be in general able to do. But there is a more important and perhaps better reason.

Questions and explanations are very important in individuation. Given different questions about the same phenomenon, where answering one, say 'Why did S A?', leaves open importantly different answers to the second, say 'For what reason(s) did S A?', an item cited in properly answering the former should not be identified with an item properly cited in answering the latter. This is especially evident where the answers specify entities in different ontological categories, such as events and desires. Now the question 'What did S do?' is not properly answered by 'S A-ed for R' – to that one might respond: Never mind *why* S did it – that is a further matter and for the jury to decide. Similarly, 'For what reason did S A?' is properly answered by 'For R' – that S A-ed is presupposed, and various reasons are eligible. Such erotetic individuation is important. When a statement constitutes a proper and direct answer to one question and not to a second, and the counterpart point holds for a second statement regarding the second question, this is a strong indication that the two statements report different kinds of thing.[6]

---

[6] Suppose, however, that 'What did S do?' could be properly answered by 'S A-ed for R', say A-ed in order to appear kind (where 'to appear kind' expresses the reason). If A-ing-for-R can *itself* be performed for a reason, we must apparently countenance the idea that, for reason R_1, S can-A-for-R. But that higher-order act can presumably also be for a reason, R_2. This is not to imply a vicious regress. That would arise if intentionally A-ing entailed intention to A-for-a-reason *and* the higher-order act this requires must itself be intentional. Still, this picture forces us to posit, for agents with finite comprehensional capacities, a kind of intentional action that – contrary to the most plausible conception of intentional action – *cannot* be for a reason. Call A-ing-for-R a double-barreled intentional act – double-barreled because there is both a report of a first-order intentional action and a specification of a higher-order explanatory condition, *for R*. A double-barreled intentional act, as intentional, is still for a reason; we thus need to posit further intentional acts involving R_1, R_2 ... etc. But, for every agent with finite capacity, there would be a kind of brute double-barreled intentional action, A-ing for R_n, where n is too large for the agent's comprehension in the relevant way, to which the idea of intentional action as action for a reason would not apply. This is an implication action theory can readily avoid. See ch. 2 of W.D. Ross, *The Right and the Good* (Oxford: Oxford University Press, 1930), on this point.

4. The Itinerary Conception of Intention

Both the constitution and the scope of intention can be clarified by fruitful analogies. Our belief systems are in some sense our maps of the world. But if, as intellectual beings – beings having theoretical reason – we have a map of our world, do we not, as practical beings, have an itinerary? Do we not, for instance, have plans and, usually, efforts afoot to realize them? Unpacking the itinerary metaphor might begin with reflection on the questions – posed, say, to a visitor, 'What do you hope to do today?' and 'What do you actually intend to do today?' Both presuppose stored "directional" information such as our internal maps express – routes indicated by our cartographic beliefs. One, the intention question, should elicit expectations that are roughly predictive and a basis for evaluation of the day's activities as successful or not. The hope question should elicit a kind of wish list, which may be much wider than the former list. An itinerary presupposes a map – or at least a need for one. When we have an intention to move to a destination on our map, we tend to have some subsidiary, instrumental intentions (though dispositions to form them will do). Whether we do have them is variable. The point is that without intention we could have a splendidly informative map but no itinerary.[7]

We can follow an itinerary for various reasons; and intending to go to a destination, though it requires a conception of getting there, does not require a conception of why one is or should be going there (though we normally have some such conception, even if we need not and are sometimes quite wrong about our motivation). This is to be expected if it is true that intentions do not have contents of the form of 'intending to-A-for-R'. Indeed, we commonly distinguish between where one is going and why one is going there. Of more direct relevance is that two people can share an itinerary though they are going to the various shared destinations for different reasons. Intentions carry the direction of behavior in their content and tend to energize and guide it. But that content should not be taken to include the reason (or a reason) for the intended action, and, if it can include it, then the content of such intentions is at odds with the capacities we take ourselves to have. It would be as if we could have

---

[7] Strictly speaking, without an appropriate conative attitude, since strong hopes can yield action toward the relevant end even when the agent thinks it likely unreachable. Granted, even for such hopes it is arguable that the agent must intend *some* act, such as trying to A (where A is roughly achieving the hope).

destinations on our itinerary that we do not and cannot reasonably expect to reach. Such aspirational goals could be objects of hope, but that is quite different. Objects of hope need not even be acts.

It might seem that the itinerary view of intention is too intellectualistic, requiring deliberation or at least reflection for intention-formation and precluding unconscious intentions. It does neither. An itinerary may be implicit. In certain cases, we would not form an intention without considering the prospect of its realization. Where there are competing desires, for instance, we may compare the prospects of satisfying each. But as we saw in considering sources, forming intentions does not require such comparison. Moreover, on the plausible view that intending to A (as opposed to hoping to A) entails some degree of expectation that one will A, so long as one has appropriate access to such expectations, the intentions undergirding them can play the role in our planning for the future – for our pursuit of our itineraries – that they normally do play. Granted, one can have intentions one would disavow; but even that, as with self-deception, does not entail that one does not take account of the relevant expectations in planning.

These points leave open not only the possibility of self-deception but also the belief-desire theory of intention, but our concern is with scope and other matters that are neutral with respect to that theory as against competitors. The more important point here is that the itinerary conception also helps us to see that from an act's being expected as a result of intending something, it does not follow that it is intended. Much that we expect to do in reaching our destination is of no concern to us and in no sense a destination. I expect to trample grass on a walk through a field, but this is not something I want and is incidental to my itinerary. That does not absolve me of responsibility for it: like collateral damage in targeting a munitions dump, it is foreseeable and I may be criticizable for doing it. Similarly, even seeing that one will do something, say vote for a candidate, *for* a selfish reason, does not imply an intention to-do-it-for-that-reason. Indeed, one might prefer to do it for the reason that the candidate is best. A meritorious reason we have may be important and we may be embarrassed at its not determining a vote. Causing "collateral damage" may be similar: one might hope to intend only to hit the target but be aware that the collateral damage has greater military value and act for that reason instead. One would be morally responsible either way; but the actions reflect differently on character depending on their grounding reason(s).

We have already made room for activities as objects of intention, but have not considered how much detail regarding them must figure in the content of intentions to perform them. The same holds for scripts. The degree of detail is variable and I leave it open. An important point about that openness is that, just as one can form specific beliefs and intentions in thinking about how one will follow a geographic itinerary, one can do the same for an intentionalistic itinerary. In either case, such reflection sometimes leads to a change in a destination on the itinerary or a change in planned routing to reach it, or in both. This must be kept in mind as we consider how intentions figure in realizing some major moral standards.

5. The Problem of Intended Conduct

Often people speak of conduct where they are referring to a single action or a single activity, usually one that is an object of evaluation. But the term can have wider reference. Consider the shameful conduct of a confidence man. In order to steal her purse, he helps an elderly woman load her car, gently placing her packages. This is immoral conduct, even if the arrival of her husband prevents the theft. The helpful deeds are motivated by concealed immoral desire, and their gentleness is hypocritical. Conduct can also merit criticism even when its motivation is admirable and it also fulfills an obligation, but is marred by a constituent act performed in the wrong way. Suppose that, annoyed by an unpleasant phone call, the boss, Jim, gruffly says to a new intern who has been slightly over-using lights, 'Turn off the lights when you leave'. Jim may be obligated to save power and saying this might be called for, but if Jim does it harshly and glaringly upon briskly closing the door, the intern is likely to feel hurt, and Jim is criticizable for this aspect of his conduct: acting hurtfully toward a junior employee.

These cases illustrate that 'conduct' can designate a three-dimensional behavioral phenomenon specified by act-type (ordering that the lights be turned off), motivation (to save electricity), and manner of performance (gruff). Once we clearly focus on conduct as a three-dimensional behavioral notion, we can better account for both the appeal and the elusiveness of Kant's categorical imperative in its humanity formula – a directive in which almost everyone finds something plausible and morally important.[8] It calls for treating persons as ends in themselves and never merely as means. With this in mind, recall our confidence trickster. His assisting his prey

---

[8] See Immanuel Kant, *Groundwork of the Metaphysics of Morals* (1785), Allen W. Wood, trans. (New Haven: Yale University Press, 2002), Sec. 422.

has the appearance of treating her as an end: he helps with loading the car. But his conduct, being partly constituted by a desire to rob her, is morally repugnant. As to the angry boss, his action – directing that the lights be turned off – and his motivation for his directive are appropriate, but his conduct is unacceptable as unduly harsh. He fails to treat the intern as an end.

If, as seems clear, treatment of persons as ends is a kind of conduct – since it involves doing an appropriate thing for an appropriate reason and in an appropriate manner – then we face a problem. If treatment, as having a motivational element, is not action, how is it commandable or otherwise an appropriate object of an injunction? Must not the commandable be intendable? Must we either give up the idea that intentions (at least when infinitival) are act-directed or take complexes of act-plus-its-motivator to be action after all? On the itinerary theory, we might conceive the problem as that of how treatment of persons can be on our itinerary. In outline, the answer is that it can be a destination without being an action. Even if there is no act of treating-someone-as-an-end, there can be acts of bringing this about. These take various forms and can be both commanded and contents of intention.[9] The notion of treating persons as ends an important challenge to understanding intention, and we should consider at least three approaches to a solution.

Take first the case of the boss and intern. I have already cited a boss-intern relationship in which the former should treat the latter as an end and not merely as means, say to an income. Suppose that the boss later realizes the objectionable conduct, and imagine that he is rather Kantian. How should we conceive his resulting resolution to treat the intern as an end? Certainly the intention to treat the intern as an end is not completely fulfilled unless any action constituent in the treatment – its *vehicle* – is motivated substantially by caring about the person's good intrinsically: for the sake of that person. The difficulty is to understand what counts as the content of the intention to treat as an end. A similar problem is to account for the content of the intention to love someone else as oneself, where motivation is implicitly part of the letter of the command. The challenge in both cases is to account for the intention in a way that does justice to its practicality by taking its content to be broadly a matter of action while also specifying conditions that normally yield, and can be conceived by the agent at least to tend to yield, the success of the relevant

---

[9]   Even if I should be mistaken in denying that 'treating as an end' expresses an act-type, the three kinds of intentions described in this section can be taken to indicate how such an "act" can be intended.

action(s) in achieving the conduct aimed at: roughly, to be brought about.

A natural way to approach the problem is to reflect on the point that – as is illustrated by intending to try – an intention can have a higher-order behavioral object. Treating others as ends is something one can surely intend to *bring about*. What one intends to bring about will in this case be conduct and thus entails acting for a reason, but it should not be thought that this implies that the intention to bring about something *embodying* action for a reason is thereby a case of intending to *bring-about-for-a-reason*. Bringing about is a kind of doing, and its objects can be simply acts or even *conduct*, conceived in terms of acts, their underlying motives, and their manner of performance. Applied to the imperative to treat others as ends, we might call this an *altruistic-pattern interpretation*. On this interpretation, the intention that is formed in fully accepting the imperative is roughly this: to do things having an altruistic pattern (though the agent need not use exactly this concept), where the agent has an expectation or at least hope of performing the relevant deeds for appropriate reasons and in appropriate ways.

In line with this interpretation, we might widen the kind of behavioral content the object of intention can have and take it to include at least mainly bringing about states of affairs of any sort within a broad range, such as, for a teacher, gently explaining imperfections in a student's paper. The behavioral focus of the intention is the acts that one sees as the vehicles of such treatment, acts like pointing out errors and omissions. But there is also an accompanying penumbral aim that differs from person to person in a way the focal aim does not. The penumbral aim is directed toward what one takes to support the motivational and manner requirements of conduct. For me, such supporting elements might be reminding myself of both the constructive aim of my relationship to students, recounting the good points to be mentioned, putting out of mind annoying deadlines that might sour my mood. For you, it might be more a matter of bearing in mind the needs and vulnerability of the student, which you know will strengthen your tendency to act toward the student for the right kinds of reasons – the end-regarding kinds of reasons that "aim" at some good for the student. These elements are less likely to figure in considering the content of one's intention, but might well be mentioned if one were to explain in detail how one will carry it out. To be sure, in explaining this, one might form new intentions. But just as elements in a script need not figure in forming or expressing an intention to do the thing in question, say recite a memorized poem, many elements that are, as it were, tacitly

15

Robert Audi

intended need not figure in forming or expressing an intention to bring about a complex end.

On the altruistic pattern view, then, the content of the intention to treat someone as an end is roughly the higher-order aim to bring about or to sustain (or both) the kind of pattern that characteristically manifests such end-regarding treatment. Since bringing about is action (though often not basic action, if it ever is), this interpretation accommodates the idea that the objects of intention are acts of some kind, and it also allows us to deny that 'intend to treat as an end' expresses an intention whose object is conduct conceived explicitly in the three-dimensional way I have described. In this way, we can leave open what is in the penumbral area of the intention. This openness helps in accommodating individual differences among agents.

Once it is seen that the content of an intention may be higher order and include in its content not just determinate focally intended acts but also penumbrally intended acts, we can see how a second interpretation might be developed. On this interpretation – call it *the conjunctive interpretation* – the expression 'to treat others as ends' can be taken to indicate (elliptically) not a single act-type but an open-ended conjunction of actions and activities of a beneficent kind.[10] The difference is that on the altruistic pattern interpretation a behavioral umbrella notion like *bringing about* expresses the content of the intention, whereas, on the conjunctive interpretation, 'to treat as an end' is conceived more concretely as a shorthand for a perhaps indefinite list of specific kinds of deeds, and the umbrella notion need not figure in the content. Something like it must figure, however, if the intention is to reflect the full content of treating as an end; the agent might have to have, for example, some at least penumbral aim to develop or sustain a tendency to be properly motivated in deeds toward the person(s) in question. No specific vocabulary is required, but the intentions should include deeds directed toward causing, or making likely, doing the intended things for the right kind of reason. Moral agents often do, and certainly should, have a sense of the appropriate range of actions here. That they usually do is illustrated by the ready

---

[10] A conjunction of intentions might also fit the psychology of the agent, sometimes better, and it may be that in different situations one or the other case better fits the agent. Certainly if what is, say, resolved, is a course of action that is constituted by doing dozens of discrete things that the agent in some sense foresees, it may be more plausible to take the agent to intend to A, and to B, and to C, etc., as opposed to having a single intention to A and B and C, etc. With certain possible exceptions, we would expect the same behavior with either of the corresponding ascriptions.

16

understandability of the morally criticizable treatment of the elderly lady by the confidence trickster. Compare the intention *to be* a better friend. This could bear an altruistic pattern or conjunctive interpretation, depending on the circumstances.

On both interpretations, intentional content may be quite vague, but vagueness is ineliminable in natural languages and, on some views, a property of concepts themselves. Vagueness may be expected to figure in any kind of content broad enough and flexible enough to capture our normal representations of our aims and our projected routes to attaining them – our itineraries. Still, even allowing for vagueness, not every agent thinks in terms of such an umbrella concept, at least in framing or considering the content of an intention. In practice, roughly the same conduct might be expected from people who internalize the end-regarding injunction on either interpretation. Moreover, for different people, or for the same person at different times, one or the other interpretation the agent's intentional state may be preferable.

These two understandings of the intention to treat another as an end are each applicable in different cases. To be sure, if we consider promises as raising similar questions about the scope of the intention formed through sincerely making them, then the second, conjunctive interpretation may accord better with the way many who promise to love would explain what they intend. Think of someone sincerely promising to love an adopted child. Such persons would describe themselves as intending to do nurturing deeds, to provide resources, to comfort during illness, and so forth, but more would be implicit in such a promise. Even if we can intend only acts and activities, either understanding of the content of promising – and correspondingly of the injunction to treat persons as ends – makes it possible to see how we can intend what we must if we are properly said to intend to *treat persons as ends*. That phrase is not an act-description, but the intention referred to does have the kind of intimately related behavioral content I have described, and such behavior can be commanded in a literal sense in which intention-formation is acceptance of a command and actions are its execution. Moreover, either kind of treatment-directed intention I have described is available to Kantian ethics in relation to the humanity formula and to the theory of deciding, promising, resolution, and other intentionalistic elements important for ethics and the theory of action.

The umbrella and altruistic pattern interpretations of intending to treat another person as an end are not the only options. There is a third interpretation, appealing to subjunctive intentions. These can be carried out by actions realizing either of the first two kinds of intention. They may provide for an interpretation of treating a person as an end superior to either of the other interpretations taken by themselves. As we have seen, intentions *that* may have indefinite content, at least regarding the acts one takes to realize the state of affairs one intends to bring about. Such subjunctive intentions always imply some intentions *to do*, including open-ended intentions *to bring about something*, but they do not require as detailed an agential conception of the acts in their scope, if indeed they require any specific act-type in that role. They are best conceived as *act-directed* but not *act-specific*, and they are instrumentally unified but not necessarily in any particular way. Intending *that* seems irreducible to intending *to*, but this leaves open a supervenience relation such that (allowing for differences due to self-reference) no two people who are alike in their intentions *to do* and dispositions to form these can differ in their intentions *that*, their subjunctive intentions. This supervenience relation may perhaps hold for intentions *to be* as well.

We could take injunctions to treat persons as ends to require for their fulfillment *that* one be, in a certain way, altruistic toward the person in question and *that* one achieve treating persons as ends, where these construals are understood in the open-ended way I have indicated, concerning act-type, motivation, and manner of action. Intentions *that* have indefinitely wide content, and the intention that one treat others as ends may imply intentions with the behavioral content indicated on either of the first two readings of this intention. Given these options, we can retain the idea that one cannot be commanded to do what one cannot intend, but we must clarify this by indicating the kind of intention and the elements and range of its content.

It should be stressed that none of these options for understanding an ethics that is like Kant's in emphasizing conduct as well as acting on principles implies that acting-for-a-particular-reason is itself an act-type or that *only* treatment-types (such as treating someone as an end) are genuinely objects of moral obligation. The assumption that, for Kant, they are the only genuine objects of obligation – perhaps a natural assumption given his taking his various formulations of the categorical imperative to be equivalent – may be one reason why he is sometimes taken to be committed to conceiving acting for a particular reason, as well as acting on a specific maxim, to be types of action.[11] But doing justice to Kant's overall view does not require this interpretation of him.

---

[11]   W.D. Ross may have so interpreted him. See, e.g. *The Categorical Imperative* (Oxford: Clarendon, 1954). Ross read Kant as thinking we can

It may be that some people can form intentions to do what is required to treat a person as an end only where they conceive the commitment as directed toward bringing about a certain range of deeds in a certain way, whereas others have a more concrete understanding of their commitment in terms of an open-ended list of kinds of acts that they can readily perform and that they take to be normally motivated in some appropriate way. Suppose that, in either instance or both – i.e. on the altruistic pattern or the conjunctive interpretation of the injunction to treat persons as ends – a case can be made that the content of commands and promises need not, even when properly formulated, be acts. They certainly need not be in cases wherein intentions *that* are the crucial elements whose content indicates commitment to the commands or promises. One can, for instance, intend that all one's acts toward a distressed child be gentle. Nonetheless, fulfilling commands and promises – at least fulfilling their spirit – is done *by* our actions under certain motivational and behavioral conditions.

On the assumption I favor, that what we are commanded to do is intendable, even if only implicitly, the content of the intention formed in accepting a command is constituted by act-types (including higher-order act- and activity-types), and we can still give a reasonably clear interpretation of the imperative to obey the humanity formula, to keep promises to love, and the like. But on any plausible interpretation of the injunction to treat persons as ends, we must suppose that complete fulfillment, as opposed to mere behavioral conformity, is not achieved not just by actions of an appropriate act-type, or even by those actions performed in appropriate ways. It is achieved only by the relevant deeds being based on end-regarding motivation *and* being done in an appropriate way; in short, by what I call *conduct*. Bringing about good conduct requires a measure of self-understanding and self-control. Achieving it may be difficult. The difficulty varies with different people and with different kinds of situation. Reducing that difficulty is one aim of moral education, though there is no formula for doing so and, in my judgment, no adequate substitute for good role modeling.

Conduct is not constituted by action alone, but most of our interpersonal actions manifest conduct, and action is its perceptible element. Given that conduct has action as its vehicle and as its

---

perform acts that harness actions to our ends. For discussion of this issue see my *Practical Reasoning and Ethical Decision* (London: Routledge, 2006), e.g. 59–60.

most commonly manifest element, it is no surprise that conduct – including the loving conduct intended in the commandment to love one's neighbor as oneself – can be commanded and required. If we can readily perform the relevant action(s), and especially if we have considerable control of the manner of our performance, we can at least *begin* to fulfill the requirement the command imposes by readily achievable doings. Moreover, we apparently can, at will, sometimes extinguish certain anti-social feelings, such as resentment or, at will, do for someone a deed that, beforehand, we are reasonably sure we will in fact do for an end-regarding reason when the occasion for action comes.

We now have the core of an account of the problem of how we can intend to fulfill conduct requirements, such as those of the humanity formula, even though we cannot at will bring it about that we have the right motivation, much less that if we act consistently with that motivation, our action will be *for* the reason expressed in the motivational content. Perhaps the first point to make here is that we sometimes can cause ourselves to do a deed for the right reason. We can, e.g., bear in mind not only doing the good we take to be possible in, say, treating someone as an end, but also the attractive elements, even if their realization is far off, in living up to the standard, and the rewards of enhancing the other's well-being. Such mental activity helps some people more than others – something one would expect to vary with empathy and with other-regarding elements in which people differ. Still, the point is not to provide a formula for treating persons as ends or even explain success in this, but, within a plausible theory of intention, to make sense of the attempt to achieve that conduct. By countenancing umbrella intentions, conjunctive ones that may include the former, and subjunctive intentions, we make room for numerous indirect strategies, variable from person to person, for increasing the likelihood of various kinds of conduct: treating persons as ends, acting from virtue, and perhaps even loving one's neighbor as oneself – or at least the elements in this that are constituted by conduct rather than emotion.

6. Responsibility for Action, Intention Formation, and Conduct

It is clear that we bear moral responsibility for our actions: on their account, we are subject to praise or blame and, more generally, to holistic appraisal. But once it is seen that conduct, including treatment of persons as ends or, negatively, merely as means, is an important behavioral type not reducible to an act-type, it is plain that our moral responsibility extends, in quite definite ways, beyond action. Here I want to consider moral responsibility in two cases already discussed: intention formation and treatment of persons.

Regarding intention formation – or preventing its formation – consider a case in which someone is obligated to make a promise to care for an ageing aunt, but makes a lying one, i.e., one accompanied by no intention to do the things promised. May we say that the person nonetheless ought to intend to keep the promise, and may we criticize the person for not having that intention? This seems correct, but there is no doubt about something related to it: one should abstain from promising to A if one cannot, or foreseeably will not, thereby form the intention to A. In this case, there is also reprehensibility for the act of promising. Note, however, that some people might not be able to tell that they will not intend to A, even when they make a promise to. This might imply some responsibility for failure to intend; but again, arguably the responsibility is for failure to recognize one's motivational incapacity or, perhaps, failure to revoke the promise after making it in the absence of the required intention.

A large question that arises here is the status of the *traceability thesis:* the view that moral responsibility ultimately traces to action, including omission, and in that sense to the will.[12] This thesis is consistent with my main point: that, whatever its ultimate *basis*, responsibility *applies* to intention in certain cases. If there is any doubt about this point about the scope of responsibility, consider two possibilities. One is forming an intention to do something morally wrong, as where an agent makes a plan to murder. A second is forming an incontinent intention, as where, against one's better judgment, one forms the intention to have another glass of champagne but never makes any attempt because every glass is taken before the waiter gets near. Self-criticism is appropriate here, whatever one's view about whether one could have done something to prevent this unfortunate failure.

The case of adversely criticizable intention is highly pertinent to the negative injunction of Kant's humanity formula: we are to avoid treating others merely as means. Such treatment is conduct and, as such, implies a kind of motivation, here merely instrumental motivation. But this conduct also requires action, and from this kind of action one can by and large abstain. Indeed, we should be able to

[12] Detailed discussion of the traceability thesis in given in my 'Responsible Action and Virtuous character', *Ethics* **101** (2)(1991), 304–321.

tell when we are even tempted to treat someone merely instrumentally, or, especially, when we have formed an intention to treat someone so, and we should try either to abstain from any act that would be a vehicle of such treatment or at least to prevent the treatment by eliciting in ourselves some end-regarding motivation. The former is a kind of negative control of conduct, the latter a kind of positive control – or at least positive influence. The latter may not always be possible, but it sometimes is.

Indirect control of conduct is clearly possible. We can, for instance, remind ourselves of what we care about; call to mind things about others that evoke empathy; and focus on our moral and professional commitments. Even such indirect and partial control of intention, motivation, and conduct is highly limited. But if we cannot always cause ourselves to form the right kinds of intentions and to avoid forming the wrong kind, we have some sense of how this is to be done. Philosophical reflection, combined with psychological investigation, can assist in this. People differ in their capacities and certainly in their opportunities to use these resources. Moral education is partly aimed at helping in such endeavors. There is, however, for most of us at least some of the time, a significant measure of moral luck in both our formation and our realization of intentions important for good lives.

———

Intentions have much more diverse content than is generally recognized. They may be not only *to* do, but also *to be*, and *that* something be the case. They may also be toward an ordinary object not specifiable in an infinitive or propositional clause at all: we may intend *an object* for a task, where the 'for'-clause carries the relevant intentionalistic content. Intentions are crucial in determining our life's itinerary; and, partly for that reason, how good or bad we are is to a significant degree a matter of what we intend. This applies not only to what we intend as a result of decision, but also to intentions that arise from combinations of desires and beliefs that, singly or in combination, may influence the will without our reflecting on the intended object or even being aware of our intending it. These major roles of intention are among the grounds for its moral importance, but it is also morally important as essential in making sincere promises and in carrying out directives. Both our promises and such important injunctions as Kant's categorical imperative and the commandment to love one's neighbor as oneself are properly accepted only if the addressee forms some appropriate intention – indeed, at least one intention whose realization is appropriate to yielding the sort of conduct describable as *treating persons as ends*.

The problem that emerges on analysis is that the kind of treatment central in the humanity formula, the love commandments, and promises to love is not an act-type but more complex: a kind of conduct. One of its dimensions is motivational, and this presents a problem insofar as we do not have direct voluntary control of our motivation, nor is either desiring something or acting on a reason the kind of thing that is an object of intention. We saw that it is only by appeal to umbrella intentions, conjunctive intentions, or subjunctive intentions that we can make good sense of the intention to achieve the morally required conduct. I have described the sorts of elements that constitute the content of such intentions. Those intentions are highly diverse, and their cultivation and maintenance requires not only determining what actions to perform, but also monitoring oneself and performing many kinds of acts aimed at eliciting appropriate motivation, reinforcing certain habits, resisting certain temptations, and controlling the manner of one's actions. The scope of our moral responsibility is thus very wide and extends to internal as well as external behavior. Even in the realm of thinking and planning, there is not only *what* we do, but also *why* we do it and *how* we do it. Responsibility for conduct reaches the domain of thought, including intention and even emotion, as well as the realm of overt action. There is much to be said for the view that a major moral responsibility of all of us is to treat others as ends. Such conduct is neither easily analyzed nor easily achieved. It cannot be achieved or even well understood apart from understanding intention and the range of its contents. This paper is meant to both enhance that understanding and to clarify some major dimensions of moral responsibility for conduct.[13]

University of Notre Dame
Robert.Audi.1@nd.edu

[13]   This paper has benefited from discussions following its presentation as a Royal Institute for Philosophy Lecture in October, 2015, and later at the Universities of Adelaide, California – Riverside, and Pennsylvania. Section 5 represents refinements and extensions of Sections 2 and 3 of Chapter 8 in my *Means, Ends, and Persons*. For helpful comments I thank Maria Alvarez, Claire Finkelstein, Peter J. Graham, the late Hugh J. McCann, Anthony O'Hear, Eric Schwitzgebel, and, especially, Garrett Cullity.

Rational Planning Agency[1]

MICHAEL E. BRATMAN

Abstract
Our planning agency contributes to our lives in fundamental ways. Prior partial plans settle practical questions about the future. They thereby pose problems of means, filter solutions to those problems, and guide action. This plan-infused background frames our practical thinking in ways that cohere with our resource limits and help organize our lives, both over time and socially. And these forms of practical thinking involve guidance by norms of plan rationality, including norms of plan consistency, means-end coherence, and stability over time.

But why are these norms of rationality? Would these norms be stable under a planning agent's reflection? I try to answer these questions in a way that responds to a skeptical challenge. While I highlight pragmatic reasons for being a planning agent, these need to be supplemented fully to explain the force of these norms in the particular case. I argue that the needed further rationale appeals to the idea that these norms track certain conditions of a planning agent's self-governance, both at a time and over time. With respect to diachronic plan rationality, this approach leads to a modest plan conservatism.

We are planning agents. In support of both the cross-temporal and the social organization of our agency, and in ways that are compatible with our cognitive and epistemic limits, we settle on partial and largely future-directed plans. These plans pose problems of means and preliminary steps, filter solutions to those problems, and guide action. As we might say, we are almost always already involved in temporally extended planning agency in which our practical thinking is framed by a background of somewhat settled prior plans.

In this plan-infused practical thinking we are guided by norms of plan rationality. These include norms of plan consistency, including plan-belief consistency and the possibility of agglomerating one's various plans without running into problems of consistency.[2]

---

[1]   This is a substantially revised version of my talk at the Royal Institute of Philosophy in October 2015. A version of this essay was presented at the April 2016 Conference on Practical Reason and Meta-Ethics at the University of Nebraska. The ideas in this essay are developed in more detail in my 2016 Pufendorf Lectures, delivered at Lund University in June 2016. (See http://www.pufendorf.se/sectione195f.html?id=2864)

[2]   For this way of formulating a norm of agglomerativity see Gideon Yaffe, 'Trying, Intending and Attempted Crimes', *Philosophical Topics* **32** (2004), 505–32, 510–12.

doi:10.1017/S1358246117000042

Michael E. Bratman

These consistency norms are in the background of the filtering roles of our prior plans. These norms also include a norm of means-end coherence – a norm, roughly, that mandates intending believed necessary means to ends intended.[3] This norm is in the background of the problem-posing roles of our prior plans. And these norms include a norm of stability of plans over time, one that is in the background of the default stability of our plans in the support of cross-temporal and social organization. While these norms admit of qualifications, we do not simply treat them as rules of thumb: we normally see their violation as a mistake/a breakdown. And guidance by these norms helps frame practical thinking in which we weigh pros and cons with respect to specific decisions that are on the deliberative table.

In other work I have developed these ideas as part of what I have called the planning theory of our human agency.[4] In this essay I want to reflect on the way in which the status of these norms can seem puzzling. After all, it is common to desire non-co-possible things, or to desire an end without desiring means. Why are intentions and plans different? Further, there seem to be cases in which we can better pursue our basic ends by adopting plans that are not consistent with each other.[5] And we can wonder what the problem is in failing to intend believed necessary means to an intended end if that belief is false, or if we have no good reason for our intended end.

These reflections point to a fundamental challenge: in giving these norms their own independent significance are we endorsing an unjustified fetish for 'psychic tidiness'?[6] We can think of this as a challenge

---

[3] For a more precise formulation see my *Intention, Plans, and Practical Reason* (Harvard University Press, 1987; reissued CSLI Publications, 1999), 31.

[4] Bratman, *Intention, Plans, and Practical Reason*.

[5] This is the structure of the video games example I discuss in Chapter 8 of *Intention, Plans, and Practical Reason*.

[6] An early version of this challenge is in Hugh McCann, 'Settled Objectives and Rational Constraints', *American Philosophical Quarterly* **28** (1991), 25–36. It is developed further in Joseph Raz, 'The Myth of Instrumental Rationality', *Journal of Ethics and Social Philosophy* **1**(1) (2005) and in Niko Kolodny, 'The Myth of Practical Consistency', *European Journal of Philosophy* **16** (2008), 366–402. Talk of 'psychic tidiness' is from Niko Kolodny, 'How Does Coherence Matter?' *Proceedings of the Aristotelian Society* **107** (2007), 229–63, 241. The worry about being 'fetishistic' is from Kolodny, 'Why Be Rational?' *Mind* **114** (2005), 509–63, 547.

to the reflective stability of these norms.[7] According to this challenge, a planning agent who accurately reflects on these structures of her practical thinking will reject these as norms with independent normative significance, since she will reject a brute appeal to the significance of mere mental tidiness. She will come to see that appeal to these norms as basic norms of practical rationality is an indefensible 'myth'. So these norms will not be stable under her critical reflection.

Such a failure of stability under reflection would pose a challenge to the descriptive and explanatory ambitions of appeals to our planning agency. If the norms involved in such agency would not survive a planning agent's critical reflection then it would be less plausible that thinking shaped by these norms is a basic feature of human agency.[8] And my aim in this essay is respond to this challenge.[9]

In doing this I assume that if we can show that these norms are both central to the basic structure of a planning agent's practical thinking and would survive a planning agent's critical reflection, then we can justifiably conclude that these are indeed norms of practical rationality for a planning agent. This is not yet to determine whether we should be in a strong sense realists about these norms. But for our purpose of defending the explanatory ambitions of the planning theory we need not settle that metaphysical question.

So how might we establish the reflective stability of these norms? Focusing at first on synchronic norms of plan consistency and coherence, an initial idea might be to see these norms as riding piggy-back on norms of theoretical rationality that enjoin consistency and coherence of associated beliefs. This is *cognitivism* about these aspects of plan rationality. In other work, however, I have argued that this is not going to work.[10] This is primarily (but not solely) because one

---

[7]   Cp. Christine Korsgaard: 'If the problem is that morality might not survive reflection, then the solution is that it might' – though my concern here is not with morality but with basic plan-theoretic norms. See Christine Korsgaard, *The Sources of Normativity* (Cambridge University Press, 1996), 49.

[8]   This is to some extent in the spirit of Niko Kolodny, 'Reply to Bridges', *Mind* **118** (2009), 369–376.

[9]   My hope is thereby also to respond further to trenchant challenges to my earlier treatments of these issues in J. David Velleman, 'What Good Is a Will?' in Manuel Vargas and Gideon Yaffe (eds), *Rational and Social Agency: The Philosophy of Michael Bratman* (Oxford University Press, 2014), 83–105, and in Kieran Setiya, 'Intention, Plans, and Ethical Rationalism' in Vargas and Yaffe, (eds), *Rational and Social Agency,* 56–82.

[10]   See Michael E. Bratman, 'Intention, Belief, Practical, Theoretical', in Simon Robertson (ed.), *Spheres of Reason: New Essays on the*

Michael E. Bratman

might believe one intends the necessary means to an end one intends and yet not in fact intend those means. In such a case one's beliefs might be theoretically coherent even though one's intentions do not conform to the norm of means-end coherence.

A second idea might be to say that our acceptance of these norms is inescapable for agents, so there is no real problem about their reflective stability. And, indeed, it is a central feature of planning agency, as understood within the planning theory, that one's intentions and plans are guided by one's (perhaps, implicit) acceptance of these norms. But this would only show that the acceptance of these norms is inescapable for agents if planning agency were inescapable for agents. But it isn't. One can be a goal-directed agent who acts purposively and for reasons but is nevertheless not a planning agent. This is an aspect of the *multiplicity of agency*.[11]

Granted, we may not have the capacity, just like that, to give up being a planning agent and become, instead, a non-planning agent. But even if there were this contingent incapacity, we would need to address the possibility that a planning agent would, on reflection, be alienated from these norms in a way that would threaten their longer-term stability and challenge their status as basic features of our agency.[12]

Donald Davidson's work on interpretation points to another kind of inescapability. Davidson treated norms of rationality as a single over-all package. With respect to that package he wrote:

> It is only by interpreting a creature as largely in accord with these principles that we can intelligibly attribute propositional

---

Philosophy of Normativity (Oxford University Press, 2009), 29–61; and 'Intention, Belief and Instrumental Rationality', in David Sobel and Steven Wall (eds), *Reasons for Action* (Cambridge: Cambridge University Press, 2009), 13–36.

[11] An idea built into the strategy of creature construction in H.P. Grice, 'Method in Philosophical Psychology (From the Banal to the Bizarre)', *Proceedings and Addresses of the American Philosophical Association* **48** (1974), 23–53. And see my 'Valuing and the Will', as reprinted in Michael E. Bratman, *Structures of Agency: Essays* (Oxford University Press, 2007), 47–67; and Jennifer Morton, 'Toward an Ecological Theory of the Norms of Practical Deliberation', *European Journal of Philosophy* **19** (2011), 561–584.

[12] For helpful discussion of related issues see Luca Ferrero, 'Inescapability Revisited', unpublished manuscript, April 2016, section 6.

attitudes to it …An agent cannot fail to comport most of the time with the basic norms of rationality.[13]

Broad conformity to certain basic norms of consistency and coherence is a fundamental feature of the attitudes we ascribe in interpreting an agent.

Something along these lines seems right. But it does not solve our problem about plan rationality. First, this would not explain why a violation of these norms in the particular case is a breakdown. At most what is claimed to be inescapable for a person with a mind is failing to 'comport most of the time' with relevant norms.[14] Second, Davidson sees the relevant norms of rationality as a single over-all package, one involved quite generally in interpreting minds. But once we note the multiplicity of agency we need to be alive to the possibility of a minded agent who is not a planning agent. So Davidson's idea about interpreting minds does not establish the inescapability, for a minded agent, of conformity with the norms of plan rationality.

A fourth idea would highlight the large benefits to us of our planning agency. Given general features of our minds and our environments, our pursuit of our most basic ends will normally be made more effective by our plan-shaped practical thinking, practical thinking that supports both cross-temporal and social organization and, as I will discuss, our self-governance. This fecundity of planning agency supports the idea that we have good reason to be planning agents. Since our planning agency involves the application of the cited norms to particular cases, we may then try to infer that we have good reason to conform to these norms in their application to particular cases. This would be a two-tier pragmatic justification of these norms.

But, as we have learned from J.J.C. Smart, there is a problem.[15] Even given the advantages of general patterns of thought guided by norms of plan consistency and coherence, there can be particular cases in which it is known that conformity to these norms would not be as effective, with respect to the very same benefits, as would divergence. Perhaps sometimes it is useful to have inconsistent or incoherent plans. But what we are seeking is not just a defense of a

[13] 'Incoherence and Irrationality', as reprinted in Donald Davidson, *Problems of Rationality* (Oxford University Press, 2004), 189–98, 196–7.

[14] Niko Kolodny makes this point in his 'The Myth of Practical Consistency', 386.

[15] J.J.C. Smart, 'Extreme and Restricted Utilitarianism', in Philippa Foot (ed.), *Theories of Ethics* (Oxford University Press, 1967), 171–83.

Michael E. Bratman

general tendency to conform to these norms. We are also seeking a justification of the application of these norms to the particular case.

There is an insight built into the two-tier pragmatic approach: the general capacity for planning agency is good in myriad ways. But what we learn from Smart is that we need also to provide a further rationale that, given that one is (as there is reason to be) a planning agent, supports the application of these norms to the particular case. Otherwise, we cannot be fully confident that the acceptance of these as norms with independent significance in application to the particular case will be reflectively stable.

Here we can learn from Gilbert Harman's suggestion that in theorizing about such norms we follow

> a process of mutual adjustment of principles to practice and/or intuitions, a process of adjustment which can continue until we have reached what Rawls (1971) calls a reflective equilibrium. Furthermore, and this is important, we can also consider what rationale there might be for various principles we come up with and that can lead to further changes in principles, practices, and/or intuitions.[16]

Our concern is with the stability under reflection of planning norms. Following Harman's suggestion, we can understand such reflection on the part of a planning agent as 'a process of mutual adjustment' and search for a 'rationale' that underlies the norms that guide one's plan-infused practical thinking. We can suppose that this rationale will involve some sort of two-tier pragmatic support. But it will need to go beyond that. So we ask: is there some further consideration appeal to which could supplement the two-tier pragmatic approach and enable the reflective planning agent to make good normative sense of her application of these norms in the particular case? This would enable the reflective planning agent to defend her norms by way of a kind of inference to the best normative explanation.

---

[16] Gilbert Harman, *Change in View: Principles of Reasoning* (Cambridge, MA: MIT Press, 1986), 9. Harman is here focusing on what he calls principles of reasoning, whereas our focus is on principles of plan rationality. We can nevertheless apply the spirit of Harman's comments to our concerns about plan rationality. This is also to some extent in the spirit of Nadeem Hussain's emphasis on a strategy of reflective equilibrium in his 'The Requirements of Rationality', vers 2.4. (unpublished manuscript, Stanford University), though Hussain would not be sympathetic to what I later call the reason desideratum.

In pursuit of such a best normative explanation I will frequently speak directly in my own voice. But in doing so I take myself to be speaking on behalf of a planning agent who is reflecting on her plan-infused practical thinking. It is the reflective stability for a planning agent of that practical thinking that is our main concern.

We can articulate three inter-related desiderata for a rationale that underlies these planning norms. First, and in partial response to the myth theorist's challenge, it should explain why the forms of coherence at stake in these norms are not merely a matter of mental tidiness. Second, it would be good if this rationale articulated a relevant commonality across these different norms, both synchronic and diachronic. And third, it should explain why there is a systematically present normative reason that favors conformity to these norms.[17]

How should we understand this talk about normative reasons? This is controversial territory. But I think that, given our concern with the stability of these planning norms in light of the agent's own reflection, it is reasonable for us to work with a model of reasons as anchored in ends of the agent where what those ends favor is desirable. Roughly: a consideration is a reason for S to A only if it helps explain why S's doing A is needed to promote relevant ends of S,[18] and only if what these ends favor is desirable. A planning agent reflecting on her own practical thinking will have a keen interest in what is needed to promote her ends and in whether these ends favor what is desirable. So it makes sense, for our present purposes, to work within this dual framework in exploring the reflective stability of the planning norms.

Let me briefly clarify my talk here of an agent's ends. Roughly: to have E as an end is to have a non-instrumental concern in favor of E. Not all such ends are intentions since, in contrast with intentions, not all ends tend to diminish when they are not co-realizable in light of one's beliefs. It is common in our complex lives to have ends that we know are not jointly realizable even while we believe that each is realizable. Further, one may intend X even if X is not in this sense

---

[17] For this broad issue see John Broome, *Rationality Through Reasoning* (Wiley Blackwell, 2013), ch. 11. Broome, however, does not work with the model of normative reasons to which I turn in the next paragraph. Further, talk of a 'systematically present' reason is mine, not Broome's; and I will have more to say about this idea below.

[18] A classic source of this idea is Bernard Williams, 'Internal and External Reasons', in his *Moral Luck* (Cambridge University Press, 1981), 101–113. My formulation follows, with important adjustment, Mark Schroeder, *Slaves of the Passions* (Oxford University Press, 2007), 59.

one of one's ends, since one's intention may favor X solely instrumentally. Nevertheless, an intention in favor of X solely as a means can still induce rational pressure for an intention in favor of a known necessary means to X. So we need to be careful to understand the idea of an intended end, as it appears in the norm of means-end coherence, in a way that does not require that what is intended is, strictly speaking, an end of the agent's.

The second desideratum seeks a commonality across synchronic and diachronic norms. What diachronic norm? The idea is that our planning agency involves a norm of stability of plans over time. What norm?

Note two preliminary ideas. First, a prior intention at t1 to A at t2 will frequently lead to change in the circumstances between t1 and t2 in ways that reinforce that intention. Think about buying, at t1, a non-refundable ticket in support of your intention at t1 to fly to London at t2. This is the snowball effect.[19] Second, having formed the prior intention it may not be rational to reconsider. After all, reconsideration has its own costs and risks, especially for resource-limited agents like us. And normally, if one does not reconsider one's rationally formed prior intention, then one continues rationally so to intend.

In my 1987 book I focused on these two aspects of the rational stability of intention over time. But I have come to think that there is more to say about this rational stability. My reasons for this primarily involve two cases of potential intention stability. I will focus first on a case involving potential willpower.[20] Later I will turn to a second case. In the end, a virtue of the account I will propose will be that it treats both cases within the same overall framework, one that also supports a significant commonality in the rationale underlying synchronic and diachronic plan rationality.

Suppose that you know you will be tempted to drink heavily tonight at the party. You now think that, in light of what matters to you, this is a bad idea. However, you know that at the party your evaluation will shift in favor of drinking more. You also know that if you did drink heavily your evaluation would later shift back and you would regret that. So this morning you resolve to drink only one glass tonight. The problem is that, as you anticipate, if you

---

[19]   *Intention, Plans, and Practical Reason*, 82.

[20]   See Richard Holton, *Willing, Wanting, Waiting* (Oxford: Clarendon, 2009). And see my 'Toxin, Temptation, and the Stability of Intention', as reprinted in my *Faces of Intention* (Cambridge University Press, 1999), and my 'Temptation and the Agent's Standpoint', *Inquiry* **57** (2014), 293–310.

were to stick with your resolve at the party, you would act against what would then be your present evaluation. And we normally suppose that action contrary to one's present evaluation is a rational breakdown. So how could you rationally follow through with your resolve?

As Sarah Paul has emphasized (in conversation), cases with this structure are ubiquitous in our lives.[21] We many times face temporarily shifted evaluations with respect to continuing with an ambitious project when, as it is said, the going gets tough. And even in the case of more modest temporally extended projects, we frequently face issues of procrastination. In following through with planned temporally extended activities one will frequently be tempted to procrastinate just a bit. It will frequently seem that one could get the benefits of the planned activity plus a small incremental benefit of, say, reading just one more email.[22] Problems of willpower and temptation pervade our planned temporally extended activities. If we are going to understand the deep ways in which our plans help support important forms of cross-temporal organization we will need to understand how those plan structures are responsive to such de-stabilizing pressures. So we will need to ask whether there is at work here a norm of diachronic plan stability that goes beyond snowball effects and issues of rational non-reconsideration.

I turn to this question below. But first we need to return to our general pursuit of a rationale that underlies the planning norms in a way that suitably supplements the two-tier pragmatic account.

Here I propose a *strategy of self-governance*: a basic rationale underlying these norms, one that supplements the two-tier pragmatic account, appeals to a planning agent's self-governance, both synchronic and diachronic.[23] Planning norms, both synchronic and diachronic, track forms of coherence that are essential to a planning

---

[21] For Paul's approach to these matters see her 'Doxastic Self-Control', *American Philosophical Quarterly* **52** (2015), 145–158, and her 'Diachronic Incontinence is a Problem in Moral Philosophy', *Inquiry* **57** (2014), 337–355. For a discussion of related phenomena see Jennifer Morton and Sarah Paul, 'Grit', (unpublished).

[22] See Sergio Tenenbaum and Diana Raffman, 'Vague Projects and the Puzzle of the Self-Torturer', *Ethics* **123** (2012), 86–112, esp. section III.

[23] A related idea is in David Copp, 'The Normativity of Self-Grounded Reason', in his *Morality in a Natural World* (Cambridge: Cambridge University Press, 2007), 309–53, 351. A somewhat related idea is Kenneth Stalzer's thought that a violation of these norms is a breakdown in 'self-fidelity'. See his *On the Normativity of the Instrumental Principle* (Ph.D. Thesis, Stanford University, 2004), ch. 5.

Michael E. Bratman

agent's self-governance, and such coherence is not merely mental tidiness. Further, a systematically present reason in favor of conformity to these norms is grounded in one's reason to govern one's own life. A planning agent with the capacity for self-governance will be in a position to conclude, on reflection, that the best rationale for her planning norms, one that supplements the two-tier pragmatic account, appeals in these ways to the significance of self-governance. And given this rationale, her acceptance of these norms will be reflectively stable. Or so I will argue.

This is to focus on planning agents with the capacity for self-governance. At some point we would need to consider planning agents who do not have the capacity for self-governance – 3-year old humans, perhaps. But I put this issue aside here.

The idea is not to see self-governance as a constitutive aim of agency.[24] As I see it, an appeal to such a substantive constitutive aim would overburden[25] our descriptive and explanatory theory of action: there are just too many cases of agency that seems not to be guided by such an aim. R. Jay Wallace gives us a lively sense of this point when he highlights 'sheer willfulness, stubbornness, lethargy, habit, blind self-assertion, thoughtlessness, and various actions expressive of emotional states'.[26] Just as the legal positivists distinguished between law as it is and law as it ought to be, we should distinguish between agency as it is and as it ought to be.

Again, the idea is not to appeal to self-governance to convince a purposive but non-planning agent to try to become a planning agent. To be sure, there are strong pragmatic reasons for making such a transition, if one can. But that is not the main focus of the strategy of self-governance. Its main concern is, rather, directly to address an agent who is already a planning agent, one whose reasoning

---

[24]   J. David Velleman sees the constitutive aim of action as self-intelligibility. However, I take it that on his account this constitutive aim is, in effect, an aim of autonomy. See J. David Velleman, *How We Get Along* (Cambridge University Press, 2009), chapter 5, esp. 131–5. See also 26–27. (In his 'The Possibility of Practical Reason', in his *The Possibility of Practical Reason* (Oxford University Press, 2000), 170–199, 193, Velleman appeals explicitly to a constitutive aim of 'autonomy' and notes the continuity of that appeal with his account in his *Practical Reflection* (Princeton, N.J.: Princeton University Press, 1989).)

[25]   Thanks to Jon Barwise and John Perry (in conversation) for this apt term.

[26]   'Normativity, Commitment, and Instrumental Reason', as reprinted in R. Jay Wallace, *Normativity and the Will* (Oxford University Press, 2006), 82–120, 91.

accords the cited planning norms an independent normative significance. In addressing such an agent the self-governance strategy aims
to articulate a rationale to which that agent can appeal to make good
normative sense of her plan-infused practical thinking.

Such a rationale would need to be responsive to our three desiderata: articulate relevant forms of coherence that are not merely
mental tidiness; articulate a relevant commonality across the different
norms; and identify a systematically present reason in favor of conformity. While this last desideratum – as I will call it, the *reason desideratum* – is fundamental, I will for now put it to one side and try
to articulate a structure of self-governance-based norms that is responsive to concerns with coherence and commonality. In this way
I will try to construct an initial, *prima facie*, though not yet conclusive
self-governance-based case for these norms. I will then return to the
reason desideratum.

A first step is to sketch a broadly naturalistic model of self-governance at a time (or anyway, during a small temporal interval). And here
we can learn from Harry Frankfurt's idea of 'where (if anywhere) the
person himself stands'.[27] Self-governance involves guidance of
thought and action by where the agent stands, by the agent's relevant
practical standpoint. Such a standpoint will need to be sufficiently
coherent to constitute a clear place where the agent stands on relevant
practical issues. It will need to guide choice. And choice will need to
cohere with that coherent standpoint.

So coherence of relevant standpoint and coherence of choice with
standpoint are elements in our model of self-governance at a time.
And now we can propose, as part of our pursuit of inference to the
best normative explanation, that there is a close connection between
these forms of self-governance-related coherence and practical rationality. In doing this we will want a somewhat qualified connection.
Incoherence of standpoint with respect to trivial choices, or with
respect to tragic conflicts,[28] may not be irrationality. And we will want
to leave room for a *pro tanto* or local rational breakdown that, while it
is not merely a potentially misleading, *prima facie* indicator of irrationality, nevertheless does not ensure all-in irrationality.[29] So consider:

[27]   Harry Frankfurt, 'Identification and Wholeheartedness', as reprinted in Harry Frankfurt, *The Importance of What We Care About*
(Cambridge University Press, 1988), 159–76, 166.   And see also Gary
Watson, 'Free Agency', *The Journal of Philosophy* **72** (1975), 205–220, 216.
[28]   E.g. William Styron, *Sophie's Choice* (Random House, 1979).
[29]   For a distinction between local and global rationality see Michael
Smith, 'The Structure of Orthonomy', in John Hyman and Helen

Michael E. Bratman

Practical Rationality / Self-Governance (PRSG): If S is capable of self-governance it is, defeasibly, *pro tanto* irrational of S either to fail to have a coherent practical standpoint or to choose in a way that does not cohere with her standpoint.

PRSG says that if S is capable of self-governance and yet fails to satisfy the cited coherence conditions of synchronic self-governance then, defeasibly, S is *pro tanto* irrational. The connection it articulates between a breakdown in self-governance-related coherence and irrationality is doubly qualified: it is a defeasible connection to *pro tanto* irrationality. But such a breakdown in self-governance-related coherence is not merely a potentially misleading *prima facie* indicator concerning what really matters.

As noted, this is so far only an initial, *prima facie* case for PRSG. I will turn later to the reason desideratum; but first, let's see how this initial case can be extended to, more specifically, a planning agent.

A planning agent will have a web of plans that settle – frequently in the face of conflict – on certain projects, as well as on certain considerations that are to matter in the pursuit of those projects. These plans will normally cross-refer to each other: one's plan for today will typically involve a reference to one's earlier and later plans; and vice versa. These issue-settling, cross-referring plans will frame much of one's practical thought and action over time. They will pose problems about how to fill in so-far partial plans with sub-plans about means and the like, sub-plans that mesh with each other. And they will filter options that are potential solutions to those problems. In playing these roles these plans will induce forms of psychological connectedness and continuity that are familiar from Lockean models of personal identity over time.

This leads to a proposal about self-governed planning agency.[30] Given the settling, cross-referring, framing, mesh-supporting, and Lockean-identity-supporting roles of her plans, a planning agent's practical standpoints will involve her web of plans concerning both projects and considerations that are to matter in her practical

---

Steward (eds), *Agency and Action* (Cambridge: Cambridge University Press, 2004), 165–93, 190.

[30] See my 'Three Theories of Self-Governance' as reprinted in my *Structures of Agency* (Oxford University Press, 2007), 222–253, and my 'A Planning Theory of Self-Governance: Reply to Franklin', *Philosophical Explorations* (forthcoming). For a deep challenge see Elijah Millgram, 'Segmented Agency', in Vargas and Yaffe (eds), *Rational and Social Agency*, 152–89.

thinking: her practical standpoints will be *plan-infused*. A planning agent's plans help constitute her practical standpoint at a time in part because of their roles in structuring her temporally extended practical thought and action over time. So the guidance of her thought and action by these planning structures will help constitute her relevant self-governance. In such self-governance, plan-infused standpoints will need to be both coherent and coherent with choice. And when we combine this point about a planning agent's self-governance with PRSG we arrive at

> *Practical Rationality/Self-Governance-Planning Agency (PRSG-P):* If S is a planning agent who is capable of self-governance it is, defeasibly, *pro tanto* irrational of S either to fail to have a coherent practical plan-infused standpoint or to choose in a way that does not cohere with her plan-infused standpoint.

Again, what we have so far is only an initial, *prima facie* case in favor of PRSG-P. Keeping this limitation in mind, however, we can explore the implications of PRSG-P concerning plan consistency and coherence. And the basic idea here is that inconsistency or incoherence in plan, given one's beliefs, normally baffles the coherence of plan-infused standpoint that is needed for there to be a clear place where the agent stands with respect to relevant issues. If you intend A and intend B, while believing that A and B are not co-possible, there is no clear answer to the question of where you stand with respect to this practical question. If you intend A but believe not-A then you will normally be buffeted by conflicting dispositions to plan on the assumption that A and to plan on the assumption that not-A.[31] In this way there will be no clear answer to the question of where you stand with respect to A. And if you intend E but do not intend believed necessary means to E even though you believe it has come time to (as we say) fish or cut bait, there will be no clear answer to the question of where you stand with respect to E. In each case there is a contrast with ordinary desire: desires for non-co-possible things, or for things one believes will not happen, or for ends in the absence of desiring the means, are a common feature of our lives and need not block relevant coherence of standpoint.

---

[31] See *Intention, Plans, and Practical Reason*, 38–9. Carlos Núñez develops a forceful challenge to a prohibition on intention-belief inconsistency. See Carlos Núñez, *The Will and Normative Judgment* (Stanford University PhD Thesis, 2016).

Michael E. Bratman

A complication is that there can be intention analogues of the preface paradox.[32] Perhaps one has a wide range of plans for one's vacation, but sensibly believes that one will not accomplish everything one plans. So it is not possible to realize all one's intentions in a world in which all of one's beliefs are true. Still, one may sensibly proceed to plan in the normal way with respect to each of one's intended ends.

This suggests that in certain preface-analogue cases plan-belief inconsistency may not induce a breakdown in coherence of plan-infused standpoint. So we have a double defeasibility. As noted earlier, coherence of plan-infused standpoint is, defeasibly, needed to avoid self-governance-grounded *pro tanto* irrationality. To this we add that plan-belief consistency is defeasibly needed for coherence of plan-infused standpoint. We thereby arrive at:

> *Plan consistency and coherence (PCC)*: If S is a planning agent who is capable of self-governance it is, doubly-defeasibly, *pro tanto* irrational of S to have plans that are inconsistent or means-end incoherent, given her beliefs.

What underlies this rational pressure against plan inconsistency or incoherence is not merely mental tidiness but the coherence of standpoint that is essential to a planning agent's synchronic self-governance.

Though this is so far only a *prima facie* case in support of PCC, we can go on to ask whether this approach to synchronic plan rationality could be extended to diachronic plan rationality. Does diachronic plan rationality track a kind of cross-temporal coherence that is central to a planning agent's diachronic self-governance?[33]

To explore this we need a model of a planning agent's self-governance not only at a time but also *over* time.[34] An initial idea is that a planning agent's self-governance over time involves her self-governance at times along the way while engaging in a planned temporally extended activity, where these forms of synchronic self-governance

---

[32] I note this complexity in my 'Intention, Practical Rationality, and Self-Governance', *Ethics* **119** (2009), 411–443 at note 7. It is the target of an extended discussion in Sam Shpall, 'The Calendar Paradox', *Philosophical Studies* **173** (2016), 801–825.

[33] In asking this question here I continue with my strategy of postponing the question whether there is, systematically, a reason that favors conformity with these norms.

[34] This is the focus of my 'A Planning Agent's Self-Governance Over Time' (unpublished).

are appropriately interconnected. But what interconnections are these?

Here I propose that they involve the interconnections between plan-infused attitudes that are characteristic of planned temporally extended activity, all in the context of self-governance at times along the way. These interconnections will include forms of continuity of intention, cross-reference between intentions, intended mesh in sub-plans, and interdependence between intentions and/or expectations of intention.[35] Further, though I cannot defend this here, I think such cross-temporal intention inter-connections within planned temporally extended activity will be significantly analogous to the inter-personal intention inter-connections highlighted in the account of shared intentional action I have developed elsewhere.[36] This is a version of an important parallel between the cross-temporal organization of an individual's activity and inter-personal, social organization. The idea that a planning agent's diachronic self-governance involves inter-connections characteristic of planned temporally extended activity, taken together with this parallel between the individual and the social, supports the metaphor that in her self-governance over time a planning agent is 'acting together' with herself over time.

Will willpower comport with a planning agent's diachronic self-governance, so understood? Well, in a temptation case involving evaluation shift, following through with one's prior resolution to resist the temptation, while it would involve the cited cross-temporal inter-connections, would conflict with one's then-present evaluation. It seems to follow that sticking with one's prior resolution would be incompatible with synchronic self-governance, and so with diachronic self-governance. But it also seems an important commonsense idea that willpower can be a central case of diachronic self-governance.

In responding, we do not merely seek some sort of causal mechanism in the psychology that can explain why one sometimes sticks with

[35] Given the hierarchical structure of plans, there can be such interconnections at a higher level despite a breakdown in interconnection at a lower level. If the lower level breakdown in interconnections is grounded in a sensible reassessment of lower-level plans, perhaps in light of new information, the higher-level interconnections will, in the context, normally support a judgment of diachronic self-governance. But in some cases a more complex judgment about the extent of diachronic self-governance will be apt.

[36] Michael E. Bratman, *Shared Agency: A Planning Theory of Acting Together* (Oxford University Press, 2014). I defend this analogy in my 'A Planning Agent's Self-Governance Over Time'.

Michael E. Bratman

one's resolve. We want to explain why, at least sometimes, sticking with one's resolve coheres with one's present standpoint and, in part for that reason, coheres with self-governance. And here we will want to appeal to some general feature of the agent's standpoint that helps explain how the prior resolve sometimes helps re-shift the standpoint in favor of willpower. But what feature?

We do not want simply to appeal to an end of constancy of intention,[37] since such an appeal would face familiar concerns about a fetish for (in this case, cross-temporal) mental tidiness. In a discussion of related matters, J. David Velleman proposes that we appeal to our interest in understanding ourselves: 'my intellectual drives ...favor fulfilling my past intentions'.[38] Given the commonality desideratum, however, this will lead to a general cognitivism about planning norms, with all its difficulties.

So let me propose instead that we appeal to the end of diachronic self-governance − where such self-governance is understood in terms of the model we are hereby developing. This is not an appeal simply to an end of constancy of intention; but it is also not an appeal that leads to cognitivism. This end would sometimes support willpower in the face of temptation, since such willpower would involve the cross-temporal continuity and interconnection of plan structures that is an element in diachronic self-governance.[39] In this way this end would be poised to help stabilize the agent's temporally extended, planned activities. Further, the presence of this end would help explain why a planning agent's diachronic self-governance is, at least frequently, intentional under that description.

Granted, this end of diachronic self-governance, even if present, may be overridden by other ends in the agent's standpoint at the time of temptation. And if it is overridden then sticking with one's prior resolution will not comport with synchronic self-governance; and so it will not comport with diachronic self-governance. But sometimes this end of diachronic self-governance can indeed help re-shift the agent's standpoint at the time of temptation to favor

---

[37] For ideas broadly in this spirit see Jordon Howard Sobel, 'Useful Intentions', in his *Taking Chances: Essays on Rational Choice* (Cambridge University Press, 1994), 237–254, and Wlodek Rabinowicz, 'To Have One's Cake and Eat It Too: Sequential Choice and Expected-Utility Violations', *Journal of Philosophy* **92** (1995), 586–620.

[38] J. David Velleman, 'The Centered Self', in his *Self to Self* (Cambridge University Press, 2006), 253–283, 272.

[39] A full story would also appeal to the agent's expected regret at giving into temptation, but I put that aside here. See my 'Toxin, Temptation, and the Stability of Intention'.

willpower. So this end can sometimes support the coordination of synchronic self-governance and diachronic continuity in such cases. In this way, willpower in the face of temptation may comport both with synchronic and with diachronic self-governance, given the end of diachronic self-governance. This does not explain how willpower always comports with self-governance; but we do not need to explain that, since it is not true.

So let's model a planning agent's diachronic self-governance as involving this end of diachronic self-governance. A planning agent's self-governance over time involves coordination of two kinds of coherence within planned temporally extended activity: the synchronic coherence involved in self-governance at times along the way, and the coherence involved in relevant cross-temporal continuities and interconnections of intentions over time. And this coordination of these two forms of coherence is to some extent supported by standpoints that include the very end of diachronic self-governance.

Return now to diachronic plan rationality. In discussing synchronic plan rationality I argued that a reflective planning agent with the capacity for self-governance would be led to the idea that there is, defeasibly, *pro tanto* rational pressure in favor of the coherence that is partly constitutive of synchronic self-governance. This would be an inference to the best normative explanation of her plan-infused practical thinking – though, as noted, the support for this is so far only *prima facie*, since we have so far not addressed the reason desideratum. So let us now, in the same spirit, ask whether a reflective planning agent with the capacity for diachronic self-governance would be led to the idea that there is, defeasibly, *pro tanto* rational pressure in favor of the forms of coordinated coherence that are partly constitutive of a planning agent's diachronic self-governance.

A basic thought here is that there is a natural generalization available to the reflective planning agent. Just as there is rational pressure for the coherence central to her synchronic self-governance, so there is rational pressure for the coherence central to her diachronic self-governance. In each case the underlying idea, supported by an inference to the best normative explanation of her plan-infused practical thinking, is that there is rational pressure for coherence that is partly constitutive of her self-governance. So there is, in particular, rational pressure in favor of the coordination of synchronic and diachronic coherence that is characteristic of a planning agent's diachronic self-governance. So consider:

Michael E. Bratman

Diachronic Plan Rationality (DPR): If S is a planning agent who is capable of diachronic self-governance then the following is, defeasibly, *pro tanto* irrational of S:

(a)   S is engaged in a planned temporally extended activity that has so far cohered with both synchronic and diachronic self-governance.

(b)   Given her present standpoint, a choice to continue with her planned activity would cohere with that standpoint and so cohere with her continued synchronic self-governance and, in part for that reason, with her diachronic self-governance. And yet

(c)   S makes a choice that blocks her continued diachronic self-governance.

Condition (a) is an historical condition: it matters whether the agent has been engaged in a relevant planned temporally extended activity. And condition (b) would not be satisfied if S's ends develop in a way such that a choice to continue with the planned activity would not cohere with then-synchronic self-governance.

Return to willpower. Suppose you resolve at t1 to have only one beer at the party at t2 while knowing you will at t2 at least initially think it better to have many beers, but also knowing that at t3 you would regret it if you did indeed have many beers at t2. How does DPR apply to this case?

Well, we do not yet know since we do not yet know whether at t2 condition (b) is satisfied. If the standpoint at t2 included the end of diachronic self-governance then perhaps it would favor willpower, and so (b) would be satisfied. Since abandoning the prior resolution would satisfy (c), DPR would then favor, instead, willpower. But we are not yet in a position to suppose that the standpoint at t2 does include this end of diachronic self-governance.

Granted, DPR focuses on a planning agent with the capacity for diachronic self-governance. This capacity includes the capacity for having the end of diachronic self-governance, since that end is involved in central cases of a planning agent's diachronic self-governance. But you could have the capacity for that end and yet not in fact have that end. So in order to understand how DPR would apply to cases of potential willpower we need to reflect further on the status of this end of diachronic self-governance.

But first we need to address a different issue about DPR. Let's assume that the end of diachronic self-governance is present, and so that at least some cases of willpower would cohere with both synchronic and diachronic self-governance and so be favored by DPR. The idea is that in such cases the end of diachronic self-govern-ance re-shifts the agent's standpoint at the time of temptation so that it now favors following though with her prior resolution. So a failure of willpower would now be a failure of synchronic plan rationality. But then we can ask whether we really need a distinctive norm of dia-chronic plan rationality, a norm along the lines of DPR. Why not simply work with a norm of synchronic plan rationality along the lines of PRSG-P? DPR does have the implication I have emphasized concerning temptation cases: given the end of diachronic self-govern-ance, it can explain why a breakdown in willpower in such cases can sometimes be irrational. But our question now is whether we need DPR for this. Why not just work with synchronic plan rationality, given the way in which the end of diachronic self-governance may shift the agent's standpoint at the time of temptation?

To respond to this challenge we need to consider, as anticipated earlier, a second kind of case that poses a problem of plan stability. These are cases in which one makes a decision in the face of non-com-parable temporally extended options and then, in the process of follow through, is later faced with continued non-comparability.[40] In Sartre's famous example, the young man needs to decide between staying with his mother and fighting with the Free French, where he (plausibly) sees this as a decision between non-comparable values.[41] Suppose he decides in favor of staying with his mother. Later he (sensibly) reconsiders and notes that the non-comparability remains. Is there any rational pressure for him to stick with his earlier decision?

One virtue of DPR is that it articulates a rational pressure in favor of constancy in such cases. Whether or not the young man has the end of diachronic self-governance, each option – the option of staying with his mother, as well the option of instead fighting with the Free French – is supported by his now-present standpoint. But what is crucial is that, if the young man does stick with his prior

---

[40]   For a seminal discussion of the case of Abraham and Isaac, see John Broome, 'Are Intentions Reasons? And How Should We Cope with Incommensurable Values?' in Christopher W. Morris and Arthur Ripstein (eds), *Practical Rationality and Preference: Essays for David Gauthier* (Cambridge University Press, 2001), 98–120, esp. 114–119. My earlier discussion of such cases is in Michael E. Bratman, 'Time, Rationality, and Self-Governance', *Philosophical Issues* 22 (2012), 73–88.

[41]   Jean-Paul Sartre, 'Existentialism Is a Humanism', in *Existentialism from Dostoevsky to Sartre*, edited by Walter Kaufmann. rev. and expanded. (New York: Meridian/Penguin, 1975), 345–69.

Michael E. Bratman

decision to stay with his mother, his intentions over the relevant time will have the inter-connections characteristic of a planning agent's diachronic self-governance. In contrast, if he changes his mind in favor of the Free French then his intentions over the relevant time will not have these inter-connections. So DPR will favor his sticking with his decision.

In this way DPR can help us understand the rational pressure for constancy in such cases of decision in the face of on-going non-comparability.[42] And once we are led in this way to DPR we can note that it promises to contribute to an overall treatment of the rational stability of plans in both such non-comparability cases and, to return to our earlier discussion, temptation cases. But, as noted earlier, the relevant implications of DPR concerning willpower depend on the presence of the end of diachronic self-governance. So we need to return to our question: what is the status of this end of diachronic self-governance?

In discussing synchronic plan rationality I argued that a reflective planning agent would be led to the thought that the best normative explanation of her plan-infused practical thinking draws on the significance of the coherence involved in her synchronic self-governance. I then generalized: the best normative explanation of her plan-infused practical thinking will draw on the significance of the coherence involved in her self-governance, both synchronic and diachronic. This led us to DPR. And this suggests yet a further generalization: we appeal to constitutive conditions of a planning agent's self-governance, where these include, but may not be limited to, coherence conditions. To this we then add our conjecture that diachronic self-governance, at least in (ubiquitous) cases of temptation, involves the end of diachronic self-governance. We thereby have an argument for a norm that supports an end of diachronic self-governance:

> *Rational End of Diachronic Self-Governance (REDSG):* If S is a planning agent who is capable of diachronic self-governance then it is *pro tanto* irrational of S to fail to have an end of diachronic self-governance.[43]

---

[42] This is to disagree with the Sartrean theme of 'the total inefficacy of the past resolution'. *Being and Nothingness* (Hazel Barnes translation) (New York: Washington Square Press, 1984), 70.

[43] I take it that concerns with trivial cases, tragic cases, and preface-analogue cases do not apply here; so we can express REDSG without the appeal to defeasibility that appears in our earlier principles.

The argument for REDSG involves three ideas. First, there is the general idea, in the spirit of inference to the best normative explanation, that there is rational pressure in favor of satisfying constitutive conditions of self-governance. Second, there is the idea that a planning agent's diachronic self-governance, at least in cases of temptation, involves her end of diachronic self-governance. And third, there is the idea of the ubiquity of forms of temptation as potential destabilizers of planned temporally extended activities.[44]

So, the self-governance-based rationale for norms of plan coherence, both synchronic and diachronic, leads, on further reflection, to a rationale for a rationally supported end. In reflecting on our planning agency we are led to the self-governance strategy in order to support norms of plan coherence, both synchronic and diachronic, and in response to the challenge that these norms express a fetish for mere mental tidiness. This promises a significant commonality of rationale underlying synchronic and diachronic norms. And it leads us to an argument for a norm that supports the end of diachronic self-governance.

REDSG is a weak principle in at least two ways. First, it does not require, even *pro tanto*, that the end of diachronic self-governance be pre-eminent within the agent's standpoint. Different agents might satisfy REDSG by way of ends of diachronic self-governance that have different relative weights within their standpoints. Second, REDSG does not address the issue of how to respond in cases in which there is a tension between what is called for by diachronic self-governance over different temporal intervals.[45]

Nevertheless, it remains true that REDSG, together with DPR, can sometimes induce rational pressure in favor of willpower; and DPR on its own induces rational pressure for constancy in non-comparability cases. So when we combine DPR with REDSG we arrive, *prima facie*, at a modest plan conservatism, one that includes but goes beyond the support of plan stability that is traceable to snowball effects and the rationality of non-reconsideration.

So we have an initial *prima facie*, self-governance-based case in favor of seeing PRSG-P, PCC, DPR, and REDSG as norms of plan rationality. These norms are, plausibly, central to the basic structure of a planning agent's practical thinking. They track forms

---

[44] This is an argument for rational pressure in favor of a certain end, given capacities for planning agency and diachronic self-governance; it is not an argument for rational pressure in favor of the introduction of a new basic capacity.

[45] A point made by Gideon Yaffe.

of coherence central to self-governance, both synchronic and diachronic, and – in the case of REDSG – a basic form of support for the coordination of such synchronic and diachronic coherence. So these norms do not merely track mental tidiness. And this self-governance-based case promises to provide a common justificatory framework for this package of norms of synchronic and diachronic plan rationality.

We can now return, as promised, to the question whether for a planning agent with the capacity for self-governance there is a systematically present normative reason that favors conformity to these norms. I take it that if we could defend an affirmative answer to this question we would then be justified in going beyond the cited initial case for these norms and concluding that they are indeed norms of practical rationality for a planning agent. But how can we defend such an affirmative answer?

An initial observation is that a planning agent will have such a reason if she has a reason for her self-governance and that self-governance is attainable. After all, these norms track necessary constitutive features of a planning agent's self-governance. And a reason for self-governance will transmit to a reason of self-governance for those necessary constitutive features if the self-governance is attainable.[46]

But why think that a planning agent with the capacity for self-governance has a normative reason for her self-governance? Given our approach to normative reasons, and given the plausible assumption that self-governance is a human good, she will have this reason for self-governance if, but only if, she has the end of her self-governance. But what is the status of this end?[47]

The key is to proceed in two stages. We note first that, as I have argued,

(1)   there is an initial self-governance-based, *prima facie* case for REDSG.

---

[46]   See Michael E. Bratman, 'Intention, Practical Rationality, and Self-Governance', *Ethics* **119** (2009). I here put aside complexities about this inference. For an insightful overview of related issues, see Benjamin Kiesewetter, 'Instrumental Normativity: In Defense of the Transmission Principle', *Ethics* **125** (2015), 921–46 (though Kiesewetter focuses on the transmission of what he calls the deliberative 'ought', whereas the issue here is the transmission of normative reasons).

[47]   I take it that the value of X does not by itself induce even *pro tanto* rational pressure to have the end of X: there are too many goods and, in our finite lives, not enough time.

We then note that

(2)   if a planning agent who is capable of diachronic self-govern-
       ance conforms to REDSG by having the end it supports,
       she will thereby have a normative reason (a reason of self-gov-
       ernance) to conform to this norm.

And my conjecture is that, given (1), (2) constitutes a sufficiently systematic connection to a supporting normative reason for REDSG to
satisfy the reason desideratum, appropriately understood.[48] Granted,
this does not show that there is normative reason to conform to
REDSG whether or not one does conform to REDSG. But it does
show that if one does conform to REDSG by having the end it supports then there is normative reason in support of this conformity.
And my conjecture is that, given (1), this suffices for REDSG to
satisfy the reason desideratum, appropriately understood. So we
can conclude that REDSG is indeed a norm of practical rationality
for such a planning agent. So the end of diachronic self-governance
is in this way rationally self-sustaining.

A planning agent with the capacity for diachronic self-governance
who conforms to REDSG by having the end it supports will have a
reason for her diachronic self-governance, and so for the synchronic
self-governance that is partly constitutive of that diachronic self-governance. We now note that this reason also supports conformity to
PRSG-P, PCC, and DPR, since each of these norms tracks a constitutive element of relevant self-governance. So we can conclude that
these norms also satisfy the reason desideratum, appropriately understood. So given the initial self-governance-based case for these norms
we can conclude that they too are norms of practical rationality for a
planning agent.

Return now to a planning agent who has the capacity for self-governance and is reflecting on basic norms involved in her planning
agency. She will see that the best rationale for these norms treats
self-governance, both synchronic and diachronic, as the basic consideration that supplements a two-tier pragmatic rationale. She will see
that given that she is, as there is reason to be, a planning agent, the
application to the particular case of the norms that are central to
her planning agency is supported by appeals to the significance of
her self-governance. She will thereby be in a position to see the rational dynamics of her planning agency as having a justifying rationale that involves both two-tier-pragmatic and self-governance-based

---

[48]   This is where my talk, in my formulation of the reason desideratum,
of a 'systematically present' reason is doing important work.

Michael E. Bratman

support. In this way her plan dynamics will make sense to her and be reflectively stable. And that is what we needed to show to defend the planning theory from the challenge posed by the myth theorists.[49]

Stanford University
bratman@stanford.edu

[49]   Many thanks to audiences at the Royal Institute of Philosophy, the University of Nebraska, and Lund University, and to participants in my winter 2016 seminar on plan rationality at Stanford University. Special thanks to: Ron Aboodi, Facundo Alonso, Gunnar Björnsson, Olle Blomberg, John Broome, David Copp, Jorah Dannenberg, Luca Ferrero, Amanda Greene, Carlos Núñez, Herlinde Pauer-Studer, Sarah Paul, Björn Petersson, David Plunkett, Johanna Thoma, Han van Wietmarschen, Gideon Yaffe, and an anonymous reviewer.

Two Libertarian Theories: or Why Event-causal Libertarians Should Prefer My Daring Libertarian View to Robert Kane's View

ALFRED R. MELE

Abstract

Libertarianism about free will is the conjunction of two theses: the existence of free will is incompatible with the truth of determinism, and at least some human beings sometimes exercise free will (or act freely, for short).[1] Some libertarian views feature agent causation, others maintain that free actions are uncaused, and yet others – event-causal libertarian views – reject all views of these two kinds and appeal to indeterministic causation by events and states.[2] This article explores the relative merits of two different views of this third kind. One is Robert Kane's prominent view, and the other is the 'daring libertarian' view that I floated in *Free Will and Luck*.[3] (I labeled the view 'daring' to distinguish it from a more modest libertarian view that I floated a decade earlier.)[4] I say 'floated' because I am not a libertarian. I do not endorse incompatibilism; instead, I am agnostic about it. But if I were a libertarian, I would embrace my daring libertarian view (or *DLV*, for short).

---

[1]   Determinism is 'the thesis that there is at any instant exactly one physically possible future' (Peter van Inwagen, *An Essay on Free Will* (Oxford: Clarendon Press, 1983), 3. There are more detailed definitions of determinism in the literature, but this one suffices for my purposes.

[2]   For overviews of the first two kinds of view, see Timothy O'Connor, 'Agent-Causal Theories of Freedom', in R. Kane, ed., *The Oxford Handbook of Free Will* 2nd ed. (New York: Oxford University Press, 2011), 309–28 and Thomas Pink, 'Freedom and Action without Causation: Noncausal Theories of Freedom and Purposive Agency' in R. Kane, ed., *The Oxford Handbook of Free Will* 2nd ed., 349–65.

[3]   See Robert Kane, 'Responsibility, Luck and Chance: Reflections on Free Will and Indeterminism', *Journal of Philosophy* **96** (1999), 217–40,'Rethinking Free Will: New Perspectives on an Ancient Problem', in R. Kane, ed., *The Oxford Handbook of Free Will* 2nd ed., 381–404, 'New Arguments in Debates on Libertarian Free Will: Responses to Contributors', in D. Palmer, ed., *Libertarian Free Will* (Oxford: Oxford University Press, 2014), 179–214, and Alfred Mele, *Free Will and Luck* (New York: Oxford University Press, 2006).

[4]   Alfred Mele, *Autonomous Agents* (New York: Oxford University Press, 1995).

doi:10.1017/S1358246117000108   © The Royal Institute of Philosophy and the contributors 2017

Alfred R. Mele

This article's thesis is that event-causal libertarians should prefer *DLV* to Kane's 'dual or multiple efforts' view.[5]

1. Kane's Concurrent-efforts View

Kane distinguishes among 'three freedoms'.[6] He asserts that 'Free acts may be':

(1)   acts done voluntarily, on purpose and for reasons that are not coerced, compelled or otherwise constrained or subject to control by other agents.

(2)   acts [free in sense 1 that are also] done 'of our own free will' in the sense of a will that we are ultimately responsible (UR) for forming.

(3)   'self-forming' acts (SFAs) or 'will-setting' acts by which we form the will from which we act in sense 2.[7]

Kane observes that free actions of type 1, as he conceives of them, are compatible with determinism and that free actions of types 2 and 3 are not.[8] All free actions of type 3, as Kane conceives of them, are indeterministically caused by their proximal causes, and only agents who perform free actions of type 3 can perform free actions of type 2.

Here, as in *Free Will and Luck*, I call any free *A*-ings that occur at times at which the past (up to those times) and the laws of nature are

---

[5]   See Kane, 'New Arguments', 209. The details of 'daring libertarianism' appear in my presentation of what I call 'daring soft libertarianism' (see *Free Will and Luck*, ch. 5). A *soft* libertarian is open to compatibilism in a certain connection, asserting that 'free action and moral responsibility [may be] compatible with determinism but ... the falsity of determinism is required for ... more desirable species of' these things (95). A *daring* libertarian maintains that there are free actions of such a kind that it is at no time determined that the action will occur. A daring soft libertarian endorses both of these theses. Eventually, I make the obvious point that the softness – that is, the openness to compatibilism – can simply be subtracted from daring soft libertarianism (that is, without modifying anything else), yielding what I call 'daring libertarianism' (202–3).

[6]   Robert Kane, 'Three Freedoms, Free Will, and Self-Formation: A Reply to Levy and Other Critics', in N. Trakakis and D. Cohen, eds, *Essays on Free Will and Moral Responsibility* (Newcastle upon Tyne: Cambridge Scholars Publishing, 2008), 142.

[7]   Kane, 'Three Freedoms', 143. The brackets are present in the quoted text. On senses 2 and 3, also see Robert Kane, *The Significance of Free Will* (New York: Oxford University Press, 1996), 77—78.

[8]   Kane, 'Three Freedoms', 143.

consistent with the agent's not A-ing then *basically free actions*.[9] My focus in this article is on basically free actions that are indeterministically caused by their proximal causes. If there are such actions, it is possible that all actual actions of this kind are self-forming actions. But whether an action is self-forming or not depends on its effects on the agent's 'will'; and if basically free actions are possible, we can imagine basically free actions that immediately precede the agent's death and therefore have no effect on the agent's will.

An agent performs a basically free action A at a time t only if there is another possible world with the same past up to t and the same laws of nature in which he does not do A at t.[10] In some cases, the A-ing is an action of deciding (or choosing) to do something or other – deciding to cheat right then, for example. And in many such cases, there is another possible world with the same past up to t and the same laws of nature in which, at t, the agent decides to do something else instead. Reflection on such pairs of worlds has led some philosophers to worry that what the agent decides to do is too much a matter of luck for the agent to be morally responsible for the decision and to have made it freely. In my own formulation of the worry, the cross-world difference in decisions at t is just a matter of luck, and, for example, the agent's deciding at t to cheat is partly a matter of luck.[11]

I have never claimed that the luck here is incompatible with basically free action or with the agent's being morally responsible for the action. Instead, I have offered a solution to the worry – a solution that acknowledges the presence of luck at the time of action.[12] Kane offers another solution.[13] His proposed solution also acknowledges the presence of luck: 'The core meaning of "He got lucky", which *is* implied by indeterminism, I suggest, is that "He succeeded

[9]   See Mele, *Free Will and Luck*, 6.
[10]   For complications introduced by Frankfurt-style cases and an associated notion of *basically** free action, see Mele, *Free Will and Luck*, 115–17, 203–5. A comment on time t is in order here. Some actions take more time than others to perform. In the case of a nonmomentary action A performed at t in W, the possible worlds at issue have the same laws of nature as W and they have the same past as W up to a moment at which the agent's conduct first diverges from his A-ing. This initial divergence can happen at a moment at which the agent is A-ing in W or at the moment at which his A-ing begins in W (see Mele, *Free Will and Luck*, 15–16).
[11]   See Mele, *Free Will and Luck*, 8–9, 54–55, 114, 132–33.
[12]   See Mele, *Free Will and Luck*, ch. 5.
[13]   See Kane, 'Responsibility, Luck and Chance', 'Rethinking Free Will', and 'New Arguments'.

Alfred R. Mele

despite the probability or chance of failure"; and this core meaning does not imply lack of responsibility, if he succeeds'.[14]

Elsewhere, I have explained how Kane's libertarian view evolved over the years in response to some worries about luck.[15] Here I cut to the chase more expeditiously. Kane's proposed solution to one such worry, in cases in which the actions at issue are decisions, features the idea that the agent simultaneously tries to make each of two or more competing choices or decisions.[16] In this article, to keep things relatively simple, I restrict attention to cases in which only two competing choices are in the running. Regarding such cases, Kane claims that because the agent is trying to make each choice, she is morally responsible for whichever of the two choices she makes and makes it freely, provided that 'she endorse[s] the outcome as something she was trying and wanting to do all along'.[17] If Kane is right, he has provided a successful answer to a certain challenge about luck) – at least in scenarios of a certain kind.[18]

Part of the inspiration for Kane's position is the observation that 'indeterminism [sometimes] functions as an obstacle to success without precluding responsibility' and free action.[19] In one of his illustrations, 'an assassin who is trying to kill the prime minister ... might miss because' his indeterministic motor control system leaves open the possibility that he will fire a wild shot. Suppose the assassin succeeds. Then, Kane says, he 'was responsible' for the killing 'because he intentionally and voluntarily succeeded in doing what

---

[14] Kane, 'Responsibility, Luck and Chance', 233.

[15] Mele, *Free Will and Luck*, 75–76.

[16] See Kane 'Responsibility, Luck and Chance'; also see Kane, 'On Free Will, Responsibility and Indeterminism: Responses to Clarke, Haji, and Mele', *Philosophical Explorations* 2 (1999), 105–21, 'Responses to Bernard Berofsky, John Martin Fischer, and Galen Strawson', *Philosophy and Phenomenological Research* 60 (2000), 157–67, 'Some Neglected Pathways in the Free Will Labyrinth,' in R. Kane, ed., *The Oxford Handbook of Free Will* (New York: Oxford University Press, 2002), 406–37, and 'Rethinking Free Will'. Readers who balk at the thought that an agent may *try to choose to A* (Kane, 'Responsibility, Luck and Chance', 231, 233–34, 'Rethinking Free Will', 391–92, 'New Arguments', 193–202, 208–9) may prefer to think in terms of an agent's trying to bring it about that he chooses to *A*.

[17] See Kane, 'Responsibility, Luck and Chance', 231–40. The quotation is from page 233.

[18] For the challenge, see Mele, *Free Will and Luck*, ch. 3.

[19] Kane, 'Responsibility, Luck and Chance', 227.

he was *trying* to do – kill the prime minister'.[20] It may be claimed, similarly, that the indeterminism in the scenario does not preclude the killing's being a free action. If these claims are true, they are true even if the difference between the actual world at a time during the firing and any wild-shot world that does not diverge from the actual world before that time is just a matter of luck.

Kane contends that 'libertarian views in general must try to show that whatever chance may be involved in undetermined choices need not undermine free agency and responsibility'.[21] He also contends that to show this one must go beyond my daring libertarian view (to be described in sections 3 and 4) and defend the claim that 'the agent *makes one set of reasons win out* over the other at the moment of choice, so that the agent can be fully responsible for causing it to be the case that one choice rather than the other is made, despite the indeterminism'.[22] Here he appeals to his *concurrent efforts* idea: 'the *agent makes* one set of reasons prevail over the other *by* making an effort to do so against the competing effort to make a contrary choice'.[23] The assassin succeeds at something he is trying to do, despite the luck involved. Similarly, Kane says, the person who makes dual efforts to choose may succeed – whichever of the two competing choices he makes – at doing something he is trying to do, despite the luck involved. And his succeeding includes his making one set of reasons prevail over the other.

2. Probing Kane's View

As I pointed out elsewhere, although Kane is ordinarily pretty sensitive to the phenomenology of agency, trying to choose to A while also trying to choose to do something else instead seems remote from ordinary experience.[24] We may occasionally have an experience of trying to bring it about that we choose to A. (For example, someone who knows that it would be best to quit smoking but who has not yet chosen to quit may try to vividly represent to himself the most important reasons for quitting, including the dangers of not quitting, with a view to bringing it about that he chooses to

---

[20]   Kane, 'Responsibility, Luck and Chance', 227.
[21]   Kane, 'New Arguments', 207–8.
[22]   Ibid., 208.
[23]   Ibid., 208.
[24]   Alfred Mele, 'Kane, Luck, and Control: Trying to Get by Without Too Much Effort', in D. Palmer, ed. *Libertarian Free Will*, 43.

Alfred R. Mele

quit.) But how many of us have experienced simultaneously trying to bring it about that we choose a particular course of action and trying to bring it about that we choose a competing course of action instead? If such dual efforts never occur, they never underwrite free choices.

Obviously, someone who grants that we never experience dual efforts to choose may wish to posit such efforts anyway in an attempt to solve a theoretical problem.[25] But alternative routes to a solution should also be explored. If concurrent efforts of the kind at issue never happen, is an event-causal libertarian unable to explain why some choices that are indeterministically caused by their proximal causes are free? I take up this question in sections 3 and 4.

In response to the phenomenological worry, Kane asserts that 'introspective evidence cannot give us the whole story about free will'.[26] But, of course, no one who expresses the worry claims that such evidence can give us the whole story. Instead, people like me have their doubts about whether normal human beings ever simultaneously try to make each of two (or more) competing choices or decisions, and phenomenological considerations are among the considerations we cite in support of the doubts.

I turn from this empirical issue to a theoretical question. Even if people sometimes do make dual efforts of the kind at issue, would that give Kane the result he wants? Consideration of some cases featuring dual efforts of some other kinds will prove useful.

Here is a warm-up case. Ann knows that either of a pair of targets will suddenly disintegrate before a bullet fired at it hits it and that it is undetermined which target will do this. She is promised a prize of ten dollars for hitting target 1 and twenty dollars for hitting target 2. Ann is ambidextrous and an expert with firearms. She fires simultaneously at each target, shooting at target 1 with the pistol in her right hand and at target 2 with the pistol in her left hand. As luck would have it, target 2 disintegrates and Ann hits target 1.

This story differs from stories about Kane-style dual efforts to choose in three potentially noteworthy ways. It is not a story about alternative choices, the agent's efforts end before success is achieved (Ann's efforts end when she pulls the triggers), and the efforts do not hinder one another.

Here is a story in which the second difference is eliminated. Beth is promised a prize of ten dollars for fully depressing the v key on a

---

[25] See Kane, 'Rethinking Free Will', 391–92; 'New Arguments', 193–202, 208–9.

[26] Kane, 'New Arguments', 197.

computer keyboard with her left index finger and twenty dollars for fully depressing the m key on the same keyboard with her right index finger. She knows that one key or the other will stick (and so will not fully depress) and that it is undetermined which. She also knows that if she opts to press both keys she must press them simultaneously in order not to be disqualified. Her plan is to press each key simultaneously. She tries to press the v key all the way down with her left index finger while also trying to press the m key all the way down with her right index finger. As luck would have it, the v key sticks and Beth fully depresses the m key.

The next story eliminates two of the three differences. Cathy's situation is like Beth's except that her index fingers are linked together by a fancy collection of plastic strings and pulleys. Moving either finger downward makes it harder to move the other finger downward. Her fingers are an inch above the keys, and her plan is to try to press each key at the same time. As luck would have it, the m key sticks and she fully depresses the v key.

Here is an obvious point about these cases. It is not up to the agent which target she hits or which key she fully depresses. Is it up to agents what they choose in Kane-style cases of dual efforts to choose? Or is what happens pretty well understood on the model of my third case? In that case, we have two simultaneous attempts, each of which hinders the other, and one of them happens to succeed while the other one happens to fail.

Recall Kane's claim that 'the *agent makes* one set of reasons prevail over the other *by* making an effort to do so against the competing effort to make a contrary choice'.[27] One might try to do justice to this claim by representing the agent as trying to make reasons R1 prevail over reasons R2 while also trying to make reasons R2 prevail over reasons R1. But this does not capture the idea that the agent is making the former effort 'against' the latter effort, if what is being claimed is that the agent represents the former effort as being undertaken against the latter.[28] If that is what is being claimed, we can say the following: the agent is trying to make reasons R1 prevail over reasons R2 and to prevent his contrary effort from making R2 prevail over R1 while also trying to make reasons R2 prevail over reasons R1 and to prevent his contrary effort from making R1 prevail over R2.

---

[27]   Ibid., 208.

[28]   Even if actual people never consciously represent the efforts at issue in this way, Kane can claim that they unconsciously do so.

Alfred R. Mele

My third case can be modified accordingly. This time, Cathy performs her task while in a brain scanner. She is told that one thing she must do to win either prize is to represent what she is trying to do in a certain way and that the scanner will reveal how she represents her attempts. The relevant part of her instructions read as follows:

> One thing you must do to win either prize is to represent yourself as trying to make your reason for fully depressing the v key (that you will get $10 for doing so) prevail over your reason for fully depressing the m key (that you will get $20 for doing so) and to prevent your contrary effort from making the latter reason prevail over the former while also representing yourself as trying to make your reason for fully depressing the m key prevail over your reason for fully depressing the v key and to prevent your contrary effort from making the latter reason prevail over the former.

After thinking about this for a while and then trying to represent her options to herself in terms of making one reason prevail over another, Cathy reports that she is almost ready. After a bit more thinking – specifically about the idea of her trying to prevent an effort of hers from being successful – Cathy reports that she is ready. According to the scanner, she represents what she is up to in the specified way and, as luck would have it, the m key sticks and Cathy fully depresses the v key.

In this case, as in the earlier story about her, it is not up to Cathy which key she fully depresses. Which key she fully depresses depends on which key gets stuck, and she has no say at all about which key gets stuck.

Here, Kane may say, we have hit on an important difference between Cathy's story and a case of Kane-style dual efforts to choose. In Cathy's story, the outcome hinges on an external event over which she has no control; but in a Kane-style story, all the work is done by the agent's own activity – his dual efforts. How much mileage can one get out of this difference?

Considering the following story from my *Free Will and Luck* will help answer this question.[29] Bob lives in a town in which people make many strange bets, including bets on whether the opening coin toss for football games will occur on time. After Bob agreed to toss a coin at noon to start a high school football game, Carl, a notorious gambler, offered him fifty dollars to wait until 12:02 to toss it. Bob was uncertain about what to do, and he was still struggling

---

[29]   Mele, *Free Will and Luck*, 73–74.

with his dilemma as noon approached. Although he was tempted by the fifty dollars, he also had moral qualms about helping Carl cheat people out of their money. He judged it best on the whole to do what he agreed to do. Even so, at noon, he chose to toss the coin at 12:02 and to pretend to be searching for it in his pockets in the meantime.

Imagine, if you can, that Bob is trying to choose to toss the coin at noon, as promised, while also trying to choose to cheat and that these efforts are or include efforts to make pertinent reasons prevail over other pertinent reasons and are made 'against' each other. In possible world W1 Bob's attempt to choose to cheat succeeds at t. But there is another possible world, W2, with the same past up to t and the same laws of nature in which, at t, Bob's attempt to choose to toss the coin on time succeeds. We get two very different outcomes with no antecedent difference at all.

In W1, what is the status at t of Bob's attempt to choose to toss the coin on time? One possibility is that it has not yet stopped. It is still underway at t, but it is not successful. Another possibility is that this attempt stopped just then. We can say, if we like, that Bob's attempt to choose to cheat rendered this competing, persisting attempt ineffective in the former scenario without stopping it and that it stopped the competing attempt at t in the latter scenario. (Recall Kane's claim that 'the agent makes one set of reasons prevail over the other by making an effort to do so *against the competing effort* to make a contrary choice'.)[30] But we should not lose sight of the point that what is going on is such that, in another possible world with the same laws of nature and the same past right up to t, exactly the opposite happens. There is no difference in the efforts – or anything else, for that matter – before t; and, even so, in W2 Bob's attempt to choose to toss the coin on time succeeds (and, if you like, stops the competing attempt at t or renders it ineffective at t without stopping it then). The difference at t between W1 and W2 seems to be just a matter of luck. And readers would understandably have doubts about claims that the following things were up to Bob: which of his two efforts to choose succeeded; which reasons prevailed; what he wound up choosing when his dual efforts to choose ran their course.

As I see it, to assert that the difference at issue is just a matter of luck is not to assert that Bob's decision is not a basically free action or not something for which he is morally responsible. In fact, one plank in my response to the problem about luck at issue is the

---

[30]   Kane, 'New Arguments', 208; italics altered.

following thesis: (*LD*) Even if the difference between what an agent decides at *t* in one possible world and what he decides at *t* in another possible world with the same past up to *t* and the same laws of nature is just a matter of luck, the agent may make a basically free decision at *t* in both worlds.[31] In *Free Will and Luck*, I present what I called the problem of 'present luck' in the same spirit that someone who hopes for an adequate explanation of why a perfect God would allow all the pain and suffering that exists may vividly present the problem of evil, and I do it without formulating any argument for a conclusion that is incompatible with *LD*.[32] Part of what I asked for, in effect, was a plausible explanation of the truth of *LD*. Kane has offered the answer that I have been discussing. I will get to the alternative answer that I offered pretty soon.

LD resembles the following thesis about actions in general: (*LG*) Even if the difference between what an agent does at *t* in one possible world and what he does at *t* in another possible world with the same past up to *t* and the same laws of nature is just a matter of luck, the agent may perform a basically free action at *t* in both worlds. Recall my stories about Ann, Beth, and Cathy. It is not up to Ann whether she hits target 1 or target 2, and it is not up to Beth and Cathy whether they fully depress the v key or the m key. Even so, readers who believe that basically free actions are possible may well regard the actions at issue – Ann's hitting target 1, Beth's fully depressing the m key, and Cathy's fully depressing the v key – as basically free. And, of course, if these actions are basically free, the same goes for Ann's hitting target 2, Beth's fully depressing the v key, and Cathy's fully depressing the m key in worlds with the same laws and past in which that is what happens.

There are versions of my stories about Ann, Beth, and Cathy in which their actions have moral significance. For example, we can imagine a version of the keyboard stories in which key presses are means of administering painful shocks to kittens. Fully depressing the m key administers a shock to an adorable gray kitten, and fully depressing the v key does the same to an equally adorable white kitten. Beth and Cathy press the m key in an attempt to shock the gray kitten, and they press the v key in an attempt to shock the white kitten. If the kitten-shocking actions are performed freely, might the agents be

---

[31]   For a critical discussion of an objection to a version of *LD*, see Alfred Mele, 'Is What You Decide Ever up to You?' in I. Haji and J. Caouette, eds, *Free Will and Moral Responsibility*. (Newcastle-upon-Tyne: Cambridge Scholars Publishing, 2013), 84–95.

[32]   The quotation is from Mele, *Free Will and Luck*, 66.

morally responsible for them? In Kane's view, as I mentioned, the assassin with an indeterministic motor control system is morally responsible for killing the prime minister, something he was voluntarily trying to do. Beth and Cathy also voluntarily try to do what they succeed in doing (but while also trying to shock the other kitten). So when Beth and Cathy shock the gray (or white) kitten, Kane may be happy to say that they are morally responsible for doing that. But what he should not – and presumably would not – say is, for example, that Cathy is morally responsible for the fact that she shocked the gray kitten *rather than* the white kitten. She lacks moral responsibility for this contrastive fact.[33] Her being morally responsible for that fact would require that she is morally responsible both for the fact that she shocked the gray kitten and for the fact that she did not shock the white kitten. And although Cathy's attempt to shock the white kitten failed, she is not morally responsible for its failing nor for her not shocking this kitten. I return to this matter in section 4.

3. Comparing the Competing Views

Libertarianism has a negative and a positive side. The negative side is incompatibilism, and the positive side is the claim that at least some human beings sometimes exercise free will. The positive claim is not merely that free will is possible; it is that free will is actual and actually exercised by real people. Now, any typical libertarian view makes it a necessary condition for a directly free action that there is no time at which it is determined (in the 'deterministic causation' sense of determined) that the action will occur.[34] And any typical *event-causal* libertarian view holds that although directly free actions are caused, they are not deterministically caused by their proximal causes. Given the positive side of libertarianism, we have here a commitment about actual human beings: namely, that at least some of us sometimes

---

[33] The assertion that Cathy is morally responsible for the fact that she shocked the gray kitten rather than the white kitten – that contrastive fact – should be distinguished from the assertion that Cathy is morally responsible for the fact that she shocked the gray kitten rather than for the fact that she shocked the white kitten.

[34] *Directly* free actions are to be distinguished from, for example, free actions of Kane's type 2 that are deterministically caused by their proximal causes. On a typical libertarian view, all directly free actions are basically free.

Alfred R. Mele

perform actions that are not deterministically caused by their proximal causes. Because, in any case of action, at least some of the proximal causes of actions are internal to agents, the commitment here for typical event-causal libertarians is to there being indeterminism in some action-producing causal streams right up to the time of action (including choice or decision).

Kane certainly seems to hold that dual (or multiple) efforts of the kind he posits are *required* for directly free choices. This adds a second commitment about actual human beings – at least, those who make directly free choices. This commitment is not merely to what is possible. It is a commitment about what some actual human beings actually do. Kane mentions evidence about dual processing in perception; but, to the best of my knowledge, there is no direct evidence of Kane-style dual attempts to choose in normal human beings.[35]

Two things have kept me from being a libertarian. First, I have not been persuaded by any argument for incompatibilism. Second, for reasons I have set out in *Free Will and Luck*, I take (a naturalistic) event-causal libertarianism to be the most promising brand of libertarianism, and I do not know of strong evidence that human brains work as they would need to work if a theoretically attractive event-causal libertarian view is true.[36] Both of these things stand in the way of my endorsing the daring libertarian view that I floated. But, as I observed, all I want to argue here is that event-causal libertarians should prefer that view (*DLV*) to Kane's view.

My *DLV* (in *Free Will and Luck*) is similar to Kane's view. The main difference is that where Kane postulates concurrent competing indeterministic efforts to choose, I postulate an indeterministic effort to decide (or choose) what do. That effort can result in different decisions, holding the past and the laws of nature fixed. For example, in Bob's story, as I tell it, there are no concurrent competing efforts to choose. Instead, there is a possible world in which Bob's effort to decide what to do about the coin toss issues at t in a decision to cheat, and in another world with the same past up to t and the same laws of nature, that effort issues at t in a decision to toss the coin right then. Bob has competing reasons at the time, and the decision he makes – whether it is to cheat or to do the right thing – is made for the reasons that favor it. The cross-world difference at t in what Bob decides seems to be a matter of luck. But it does not seem to

---

[35]   See Kane, 'New Arguments', 197.

[36]   For discussion of the evidential issue, see Alfred Mele, 'Libertarianism and Human Agency', *Philosophy and Phenomenological Research* **87** (2013), 72–92.

be any *more* a matter of luck than a cross-world difference that I identified in a version of Bob's story in which he is trying to choose to
cheat while also trying to choose to do the right thing: namely, the
difference between the former effort succeeding and the latter
effort succeeding.

Kane contends that choices of the sort at issue – choices that issue
from one member of a pair (or group) of competing efforts to choose –
'are "up to the agent" in the strong sense that the agents have plural
voluntary control over whether or not they are made'.[37] He comments
on the nature of plural voluntary control earlier in the same article:

> we are interested in whether [agents] could have acted voluntarily
> and intentionally in *more than one way*, rather than in only one
> way, and in other ways merely by accident or mistake. I call
> such conditions of more than one way voluntariness and inten-
> tionality *plurality conditions* for free will, and the power to act
> in accordance with them *plural voluntary control*.[38]

As Kane grants, when an agent satisfies the conditions set out in
DLV, 'we can ... say that the choice that results is made by the
agent; and we can even say it is voluntary (since uncoerced) and intentional (since knowingly and purposefully made)'.[39] Moreover, we can
correctly say these things both about the choice the agent makes at *t* in
the actual world and about a competing choice he makes at *t* in
another possible world with the same laws of nature and the same
past up to *t*.[40] And from this we can infer that *DLV* accommodates
'plural voluntary control' over choice making. If, as Kane says,
plural voluntary control in this connection is sufficient for the
choice the agent makes to be up to the agent, then *DLV* also accommodates it sometimes being up to agents what they choose in scenarios of the sort at issue. The point is that, given Kane's own
account of plural voluntary control and his own claim about what is
sufficient for an agent's choice to be up to the agent, an agent
whose making of a particular choice fits my *DLV* makes a choice
that it was up to him to make.

Even so, Kane finds fault with *DLV*. He writes: 'The agent will
indeed make one choice or the other at *t*, but which choice the
agent makes depends on which reasons "win out"; and this is

---

[37]   Kane, 'New Arguments', 202.
[38]   Ibid., 185.
[39]   Ibid., 207.
[40]   Here, taking my lead from Kane, I do not treat 'voluntary' as entail-
ing 'basically free'.

Alfred R. Mele

undetermined. That the agent decides to do A at t in one world and B in another seems therefore to be a matter of luck or chance'.[41]

A pair of observations are in order. The first is about victorious reasons. Call Bob's reasons for cheating RC and his reasons for tossing the coin at noon RT. In the present context, what it is for RC to win out is for Bob to choose for those reasons; and if that happens, then, of course, Bob chooses to cheat. Now, in order for Bob's choice to cheat to be basically free – according to Kane's view and my DLV – there must be no time at which it is determined that he will choose to cheat and so no time at which it is determined that he will choose for RC.[42] So Kane cannot, given his own view, treat the point that which reasons will win out is undetermined as incompatible with Bob's making a basically free choice to cheat. The upshot, of course, is that he cannot consistently claim that this point falsifies DLV. If the point falsifies DLV, it falsifies Kane's view too.

My second observation is predictable, given some remarks I have already made. When Bob's choice-making occurs in a way that fits my DLV, the cross-world difference in what he chooses is, in Kane's words, 'a matter of luck or chance'.[43] But when Bob's choice-making occurs in a way that fits Kane's concurrent-efforts view, the cross-world difference in which of his efforts to choose wins out is no less a matter of luck or chance. Picture Bob's dual efforts to choose as (mutually interfering) processes aimed at targets or goals.[44] The target at which his effort to choose to cheat aims (T1) is his choosing to cheat, and the target at which his effort to choose to do the right thing aims (T2) is his choosing to do the right thing. In W1 the former process wins out at t: T1 is hit then and T2 is not. And in W2, which has the same past all the way up to t and the same laws of nature, the latter process wins out: T2 is hit then and T1 is not. This difference is no less a matter of luck than the featured cross-world difference when Bob's choice-making accords with DLV. More is going on in Kane's vision of things than in mine: He represents the agent as trying to make each of two different competing choices, and I represent him as simply trying

---

[41]   Kane, 'New Arguments', 207.
[42]   On DLV, an analogue of a basically free choice is possible in some Frankfurt-style cases. See note 10 for references.
[43]   Kane, 'New Arguments', 207.
[44]   On prospective choices as goals, see Kane, 'New Arguments', 193–94.

to decide what to do. But the more that is going on in Kane's concurrent-efforts picture does not yield less cross-world luck.

I will say more about *DLV* shortly, and I will compare the main costs of the two views at issue. But I would like to linger for a while over Kane's idea that, in a dual-efforts scenario, the agent makes some reasons prevail over others.

In my story in which Cathy is in a brain scanner, readers may have a hard time imagining her trying to make her ten dollar reason prevail over her twenty dollar reason. Such an attempt would be perverse, and it seems that all she is really up to is simultaneously trying to fully depress the ten dollar key and trying to fully depress the twenty dollar key while also attempting to represent what she is doing in a certain reason-featuring way. So consider the following case. Donna replaces Cathy in the scanner, each full key press is worth fifteen dollars, and the two keys assign money to two different charities – one for stray dogs and the other for stray cats. The representation instructions that Donna receives reflect this fact, of course. Further details: Donna is very fond of cats and dogs and very interested in helping them, and she believes that the two charities are equally proficient at achieving their aims.

Donna attempts to follow her instructions about representations. The strategy that she endeavors to implement includes her vividly imagining the plight of an adorable stray kitten in an attempt to make her reasons for helping stray cats prevail and vividly imaging the plight of an equally adorable stray puppy in an attempt to make her reasons for helping stray dogs prevail. Her former attempt also includes rehearsing reasons for helping stray cats and the latter includes rehearsing reasons for helping stray dogs. Donna simultaneously presses both keys. In the actual world, she fully depresses the cat key at t, and in another possible world with the same laws and the same past up to the sticking point, she fully depresses the dog key at t. We can say, if we like, that in fully depressing the cat key, Donna made her reasons to help cats prevail. And this claim can be counted as true, if we do not read too much into it. But the truth of the claim is utterly compatible with the difference in the two worlds at the time at issue being just a matter of luck. And, in a Kane-style dual-efforts scenario, the same is true of the difference between Bob's making his reasons to cheat prevail in choosing at t to cheat and his making his reasons to do the right thing prevail in choosing at t to toss the coin. Bear in mind that Bob does not make either set of reasons prevail *before* he makes his choice. Which reasons prevail is up for grabs until he makes his choice, and the prevailing of a collection of reasons is precisely a matter of Bob's

Alfred R. Mele

choosing for those reasons – that is, his choosing for reasons RC to cheat or his choosing for reasons RT to do the right thing. Again, in one world one set of reasons prevails at t, and in another world a competing set of reasons prevails at t – and there is no cross-world difference in the reasons, Bob's efforts, or anything else before t.[45]

As I observed, Kane contends that his view secures the making of choices that 'are "up to the agent" in the strong sense that the agents have plural voluntary control over whether or not they are made'.[46] And, as I explained, my own *DLV* fares no less well in this regard: Agents who fit the latter view can satisfy Kane's sufficient conditions for plural voluntary control over what they choose. Kane can reply that exercising plural voluntary control over what one chooses is not, after all, sufficient for acting freely because an additional requirement for choosing freely is that the agent was trying specifically to choose what he chose.[47] But what contribution does a choice's satisfying this requirement make to its being a free choice? Kane might, by way of analogy, point to the contribution that the assassin's trying to kill the prime minister (in an example mentioned earlier) makes to the killing's being a free action. However, the contribution here seemingly consists in the support the occurrence of the trying offers for the claim that the assassin *intentionally* killed his victim, presumably as a means to an end;[48] and it is commonly recognized that choosing to A is *essentially* intentional.[49] Agents do not need to try to choose to A nor to try to bring it about that they choose to A in order to choose to A; and the nature of choosing is such that, whenever they choose to A, they intentionally do so: there are no nonintentional choosings to A. If trying to choose to A is supposed to make a contribution to

---

[45]   A novice may suggest that Kane can dramatically improve his view by claiming that one collection of reasons or the other prevails before the choice is made. Imagine a scenario in which Bob's effort to choose to cheat has the result that at 200 milliseconds (ms) before t it is determined that he will choose at t to cheat. Imagine also that in another possible world with the same laws of nature and the same past up to t-200 ms, Bob's effort to choose to do the right thing has the result that at t-200 ms it is determined that he will choose at t to toss the coin straightaway. The problem of present luck has not disappeared; it has been moved back 200 ms.

[46]   Kane, 'New Arguments', 202.

[47]   I am grateful to Helen Beebee for recommending that I consider this reply.

[48]   Kane, 'Responsibility, Luck and Chance', 227.

[49]   See Hugh McCann, 'Intrinsic Intentionality' *Theory and Decision* **20** (1986), 247–73 and Alfred Mele, 'Agency and Mental Action,' *Philosophical Perspectives* **11** (1997), 231–49.

freely choosing to A that goes beyond its contribution to exercising plural voluntary control over what one chooses, Kane has not said what that contribution is.

4. The Two Views: Relative Costs

I have made two main points that bear directly on this article's thesis.

1. *On cross-world luck*. When an agent's choice-making occurs in a way that fits my *DLV*, the cross-world difference in what he chooses is, in Kane's words, 'a matter of luck or chance'.[50] When the agent's choice-making occurs in a way that fits Kane's concurrent-efforts view, the cross-world difference in which of his efforts to choose wins out is no less a matter of luck or chance.

2. *On empirical burdens*. Kane's concurrent-efforts view requires more for basically free decisions than *DLV* does. It requires that the agent simultaneously makes competing efforts to choose. Ordinary experience supports the claim that normal human agents sometimes make an effort to decide what to do. The same cannot plausibly be said for the claim that agents sometimes make concurrent efforts to choose of the kind featured in Kane's view. And, to the best of my knowledge, there is no direct evidence of any kind that normal agents ever make Kane-style concurrent efforts to choose.

The conjunction of 1 and 2 is motivation for this article's thesis – that event-causal libertarians should prefer *DLV* to Kane's concurrent-efforts view. Kane's view has a significantly heavier burden – and therefore carries a significantly higher cost – on the empirical front, and, as far as I can see, it has no advantage over *DLV* on the issue of cross-world luck at the time of choice or decision.

Regarding point 1, some people may worry that *DLV* leaves more room for wildly improbable choices than Kane's view does. But the worry is unfounded. Presumably, a typical Kane-style agent's character, values, beliefs, learning history, and the like constrain the options that it is open to him to choose, and there is nothing to prevent these factors from being equally constraining in an agent who fits *DLV*.

Regarding point 2, I have heard it said that Kane is not seriously claiming that agents make simultaneous competing efforts to choose – that all he really has in mind is that the agent has reasons

---

[50]   Kane, 'New Arguments', 207.

Alfred R. Mele

or motives for two or more competing choices and chooses for reasons. Quotations from Kane's work that I have provided here should make it clear that this interpretation is far off the mark, as should a little reflection on the use to which Kane puts his assassin analogy (discussed earlier).[51] Moreover, on *DLV*, agents have reasons or motives for two or more competing choices and choose for reasons in cases of the kind at issue; and Kane makes it clear that he is not willing to settle for this, as I have observed.

Another difference between *DLV* and Kane's concurrent-efforts view merits mention. Kane tries to find a solution to a worry about present luck in what is happening at and around the time of a decision. According to *DLV*, not everything that is needed for a solution to the worry can be found there; we should also look back in time. A detailed discussion of what a daring libertarian hopes to find in agents' histories is beyond the scope of the present article. My *DLV* finds in reflection on agents' pasts a partial basis for an error theory about why *some* people may view cross-world luck at the time of decision as incompatible with making a basically free decision.[52] Brief attention to this issue is in order.

My error theory is for a limited audience – people who are attracted to libertarianism and reject agent-causal and non-causal libertarianism. When some such people reflect on stories like that of Bob and the coin, they may ignore the sources of the antecedent probabilities of Bob's choosing to cheat and his choosing to do the right thing. If it is imagined that these probabilities come out of the blue, Bob may seem to be adrift in a wave of probabilities that were imposed on him, and, accordingly, he may seem not to have sufficient control over what he chooses to be morally responsible for his choices. But, as I have explained elsewhere, it is a mistake to assume that 'indeterministic agents' probabilities of action are externally imposed' or that such agents 'are related to their present probabilities of action roughly as dice are related to present probabilities about how they will land if tossed'.[53] If it is known that Bob's pertinent probabilities shortly before noon are shaped by past intentional, uncompelled behavior of his, one may take a less dim view of Bob's prospects for being morally responsible for the choice he makes and his prospects for making it freely.

---

[51] Also see Kane's table-shattering example: 'Responsibility, Luck and Chance', 227, 'New Arguments', 194, 200.
[52] See Mele, *Free Will and Luck*, 111–34.
[53] Ibid., 124–25.

This is a long story that carries us all the way back to candidates for young agents' earliest basically free actions, and I cannot do justice to it here.[54] I will touch upon just one further issue and then wrap things up.

Recall my observation at the end of section 2 that Cathy is not morally responsible for the contrastive fact that she shocked the gray kitten *rather than* the white kitten because she is not morally responsible for the fact that she did not shock the white kitten. Cathy deserves no moral credit for the failure of her effort to shock the white kitten. What about Bob in a story in which what goes on is captured by my *DLV*? Might he be morally responsible for deciding to cheat *rather than* deciding to do the right thing. Well, if, past intentional, uncompelled behavior of his played a significant role in shaping his character and the antecedent probability that he would decide to cheat, and if better behavior was open to him on many relevant occasions in the past, behavior that would have given him a much better chance of deciding to do the right thing on this occasion, then maybe so. But this, as I say, is a long story that I have spun elsewhere.[55]

I mentioned that my error theory is for a limited audience. Some people who regard *DLV* as lacking the resources to provide what is needed for basically free action may require something for free action that no event-causal theory can give them: luck-excluding control over what they choose in a scenario in which it is at no time determined what they will choose.[56] But Kane is not such a person. He means to get by with an event-causal view of action (including choice) production, and he acknowledges the presence of luck in cases of basically free actions.[57] What I have argued here is that anyone with Kane's aspirations – and any event-causal libertarian –

---

[54] See Mele, *Free Will and Luck*, 111–34.

[55] It merits mention that, in a range of typical cases, in deciding to *A* an agent decides *against* some alternative course of action. For example, in deciding to cheat, Bob decides against tossing the coin at noon (for more on this, see Mele, 'Is What You Decide Ever up to You?' 93–94).

[56] I am not suggesting that some other theory can accomplish this trick.

[57] Kane, 'Responsibility, Luck and Chance', 233; quoted earlier.

Alfred R. Mele

should prefer my daring libertarian view to Kane's concurrent-efforts view.[58]

Florida State University
amele@fsu.edu

[58] This article was made possible through the support of a grant from the John Templeton Foundation. The opinions expressed here are my own and do not necessarily reflect the views of the John Templeton Foundation. Material from this article was presented at Dartmouth College, the University of Manchester, and the Royal Institute of Philosophy. I am grateful to my audiences and Mirja Perez de Calleja for feedback.

Are Character Traits Dispositions?

MARIA ALVAREZ

Abstract
The last three decades have seen much important work on powers and dispositions: what they are and how they are related to the phenomena that constitute their manifestation. These debates have tended to focus on 'paradigmatic' dispositions, i.e. physical dispositions such as conductivity, elasticity, radioactivity, etc. It is often assumed, implicitly or explicitly, that the conclusions of these debates concerning physical dispositions can be extended to psychological dispositions, such as beliefs, desires or character traits. In this paper I identify some central features of paradigmatic dispositions that concern their manifestation, stimulus conditions, and causal bases. I then focus on a specific kind of psychological disposition, namely character traits, and argue that they are importantly different from paradigmatic dispositions in relation to these features. I conclude that this difference should lead us to re-examine our assumption that character traits are dispositions and, by implication, whether we can generalize conclusions about physical dispositions to psychological dispositions, such as character traits and their manifestations.

1. Dispositions: physical and psychological

Disposition terms, such as 'cowardice', 'fragility' and 'reactivity,' often appear in explanations. Sometimes we explain why a man ran away by saying that he was cowardly, or we explain why something broke by saying it was fragile. Scientific explanations of certain phenomena feature dispositional properties like instability, reactivity, and conductivity.[1]

As this quotation states, we often explain why something happened by reference to 'dispositional properties' or dispositions. For instance, we explain why the poison dissolved by reference to the fact that it is water-soluble, or why the glass shattered by reference to its fragility. And, as the quotation suggests, this is not just true of what I shall call 'paradigmatic dispositions', that is, physical dispositions such as fragility, solubility or conductivity. It is also true of 'psychological' dispositions: human actions, especially intentional actions, are often explained by citing psychological factors that are

---

[1]   J. McKitrick, 'A Defence of the Causal Efficacy of Dispositions', *Sats: Nordic Journal of Philosophy* **5** (2004) 110–130, 110.

doi:10.1017/S1358246117000029   ©The Royal Institute of Philosophy and the contributors 2017

generally thought of as dispositions. Consider the following examples of psychological explanations:

(a)   Alison went to the Police because she thought that her car had been stolen and wanted to get a certificate for the insurance company.
(b)   Tom sits at the back of the classroom because he is shy.
(c)   I exercise in order to keep fit.
(d)   James shouted because he was angry.

Statements (a)–(c) explain by reference to psychological factors: (a) explains by reference to Alison's beliefs and desires; (b) explains by reference to a character trait: shyness. (c) explains by giving my aim or goal in exercising: to keep fit; and (d) explains by reference to an emotion: anger. These explanations are quite different from each other. But many philosophers think that they are all explanations that cite dispositions: mental or psychological dispositions. So wanting and believing something are said to be psychological dispositional states of the person that has the relevant wants and beliefs:[2] they dispose the person to act in certain ways; for instance, in our example, the belief and desire combined dispose Alison to go to the Police. Being shy is a character trait that disposes those who have it to act in certain ways, ways conducive to their not being noticed by others, etc.[3] Aims and goals are also regarded as dispositional concepts: having the aim of, say keeping fit, disposes one to do things that one thinks conducive to fitness. And anger is an emotion that disposes people to react and behave in certain ways.

As the above suggests, it is generally thought that physical and psychological dispositions feature in explanations of inanimate phenomena and of human actions respectively. Citing the fact that an object has a disposition can explain an occurrence or an action by

---

[2]   C.B. Martin, for example, writes: 'The fact that belief and desire states are dispositional is both familiar and obvious', C.B. Martin, *The Mind in Nature* (Oxford: Oxford University Press, 2008), 184. This is a widespread view in the literature on dispositions, see e.g. S. Mumford, *Dispositions* (Oxford: Oxford University Press, 1998).

[3]   See C.B. Miller, *Character and Moral Psychology* (Oxford: Oxford University Press, 2014), fn 41 for a representative list of philosophers who conceptualise character traits as dispositions. John Doris, in his *Lack of Character* (Cambridge: Cambridge University Press, 2002), along with other 'situationists', expresses scepticism about character traits. I can put aside that debate because their target is 'robust' rather than 'local' character traits and my argument requires accepting merely the latter.

characterising the latter as a *manifestation* of the corresponding disposition.[4] But what exactly is a disposition?

The past few decades have seen a lot of work on the nature of dispositions or powers among philosophers. But before saying more about that, I need to put a side a possible complication. Many authors treat the terms 'power' and 'disposition' as equivalent;[5] while others restrict the use of the term 'disposition' on the grounds that, they say, not all powers are dispositional: one can have the ability to wash the dishes without having any disposition to do so; or the ability, but not the disposition, to murder, or to speak Russian.[6] To some extent, this is a terminological choice, although the second practice accords more closely with ordinary usage, while the first reflects the fact that the term 'disposition' has become a semi-technical term in philosophy, partly because powers are often characterised as 'dispositional' properties and contrasted with 'categorical' properties. As a result, powers of any kind get to be called 'dispositions'.[7] I shall have something to say about this issue towards the end of the paper but, for the moment, I needn't concern myself with this difference in use because in the immediate sections my discussion will focus on phenomena that both parties

---

[4] The precise character of these explanations is a controversial issue. For a discussion see McKitrick, 'A Defence of the Causal Efficacy of Dispositions' and 'Are Dispositions Causally Relevant?', *Synthese* **144** (2005), 357–371.

[5] Mumford and Anjum, for example, claim that 'we have different terms for dispositions with different features, for instance, "tendency" (for dispositions with a frequent or reliable manifestation); "ability" (dispositions that it is an advantage to have); "liabilities" (a disadvantage)'. (S. Mumford and R. Anjum *Getting Causation from Powers*, Oxford: Oxford University Press, 2011: 4).

[6] See e.g. M. Fara, 'Dispositions and Habituals' , *Noûs* **39** (2005), 43–82 and P. Hacker, *Human Nature: The Categorial Framework*, (Oxford: Wylie Blackwell, 2007), esp. ch.4 Vetter says that 'is disposed to' is a sort of technical sense in these debates, and we should not to be misled by its ordinary connotations which is either something like 'is willing to' or, 'has a passing tendency to' with no grounding on the individual's intrinsic features. With plural subjects, she adds, it also expresses 'statistical correlation' (Vetter, *Potentiality. From Dispositions to Modality*, Oxford: Oxford University Press, 2015, 67).

[7] As Molnar, following Elizabeth Prior (1985), says '"disposition" and "potential" (in Aristotle's sense) are philosophers' artefacts' (Molnar, *Powers. A Study in Metaphysics* Oxford: (Oxford University Press, 2003), 57).

agree are powers that do not merely enable but *dispose* their possessors to display certain forms of behaviour.

Although there is disagreement among philosophers on various issues concerning dispositions, there is also a degree of consensus about which are paradigmatic dispositions and specially about some of their defining features. I shall give a brief sketch of four such features. I start with two which I shall introduce using George Molnar's terms and characterisations: 'Directedness' and 'Independence'.

A power has **Directedness** 'in the sense that it must be a power for, or to, some outcome' or '*for* some behaviour, usually of their bearers';[8] the same idea, roughly, is sometimes expressed by saying that a power is defined by its exercise, or a disposition by its manifestation: what it is a power or disposition to do.

The second feature, **Independence**, consists in the fact that powers are ontologically independent of their manifestations: an object can have a power that is not being manifested, has never been manifested and will never be manifested. This feature is widely accepted to be defining of dispositions in general. For instance, a recent discussion of dispositions opens as follows: 'It's important to note that neither the activation conditions nor the manifestation conditions need ever actually occur in order for an object to have the disposition in question'.[9] And the authors of the entry on 'Dispositions' for the *Stanford Encyclopaedia of Philosophy* agree: 'In general, it seems that nothing about the *actual* behaviour of [the possessor of the disposition] is ever necessary for it to have the dispositions it has'.[10] This seems intuitively very plausible: there are plenty of things that have the disposition to break, to dissolve, expand, to poison humans etc. that never have broken,

---

[8] Molnar, *Powers*, 57, 60. Molnar lists five features which he says are defining of what he calls 'the family of dispositional properties'; the remaining three being: 'Actuality', 'Intrinsicality' and 'Objectivity'. See Molnar, *Powers*, chs 3–7 for further details. I shall put aside Molnar's somewhat controversial claim that we should understand directedness as a kind of physical intentionality, i.e. that 'something *very much like* intentionality is a pervasive and ineliminable feature of the physical world', Molnar, *Powers*, 62.

[9] Cross, 'What is a Disposition' *Synthese* **144** (2005) 321–341, 322.

[10] Sungho Choi and Michael Fara, 'Dispositions', *The Stanford Encyclopedia of Philosophy* (Spring 2016 Edition), Edward N. Zalta (ed.), URL = <http://plato.stanford.edu/archives/spr2016/entries/dispositions/>. See also Mumford, *Dispositions*, 21; and Mumford and Anjun *Getting Causes from Powers*, 5: 'a disposition or power ... may nevertheless still exit unmanifested'.

dissolved, expanded or poisoned and never will break, dissolve, expand, or poison anyone.

There are two further notions central to understanding paradigmatic dispositions, namely stimulus conditions and causal basis.

Dispositions in general require conditions for their manifestation. Most current literature on dispositions characterises these in term of stimulus conditions. **Stimulus conditions** or triggers are generally occurrences that change the extrinsic circumstances or the intrinsic properties of the disposition's possessor *other than* those that constitute the disposition.[11] Not all dispositions need have triggers: some may manifest spontaneously and/or continuously. For instance, radioactive material may start the process of decaying spontaneously, without there being an occurrence that triggers the manifestation. But we can put those possibilities aside for the moment.

An object may have a disposition but not manifest it because of the absence of the stimulus or trigger event. But the occurrence of the trigger is consistent with a thing's having a disposition but not manifesting it because of the presence of 'masks' or 'antidotes', which prevent the manifestation of the disposition:[12]

> Consider a fragile glass cup with internal packing to stabilize it against hard knocks. Packing companies know that the breaking of fragile glass cups involves three stages: first a few bonds break, then the cup deforms and then many bonds break, thereby shattering the cup. They find a support which when placed inside the glass cup prevents deformation so that the glass would not break when struck. Even though the cup would not break if struck the cup is still fragile.[13]

---

[11] Occurrences that change those intrinsic properties of a thing that constitute the relevant power are 'finks'. There are also 'reverse'-finks (see Martin, *The Mind in Nature*.)

[12] For discussion see, A. Bird, 'Dispositions and Antidotes', *The Philosophical Quarterly* **48** (1998), 227–234; S. Choi, 'Improving Bird's Antidotes', *Australasian Journal of Philosophy* **81** (2003) 573–580; M. Johnston, 'How to Speak of the Colours', *Philosophical Studies, **68**(3) (1992): 221–263; Lewis, 'Finkish Dispositions'; Martin, *The Mind in Nature*; Molnar, *Powers*, 83ff.; D. Manley & R. Wasserman, 'On Linking Dispositions and Conditionals', *Mind* **117** (2008), 59–84 and 'Dispositions, Conditionals, and Counterexamples', *Mind* **120** (2011), 1191–1227; and Vetter, *Potentiality*, 35ff. – to give just a representative sample of the debate.

[13] Johnston, 'How to Speak of the Colours', 233.

Maria Alvarez

The final concept I wish to introduce is that of a disposition's **categorial** or **causal basis**. The categorial base of a disposition can be characterised as a property (or property complex) that is conceptually distinct from, and grounds, the disposition – that is, it's a property, conceptually distinct from and in virtue of which the bearer has the disposition.

The concept of a categorial basis is at the heart of the Molière's famous joke about opium in the *Imaginary Invalid*. Molière ridicules scholastic doctors who say that opium puts people to sleep because it has 'a *virtus dormitiva*', i.e. the power (in our terms 'disposition') to induce sleep.[14] But note that the joke depends on the fact that the question *presupposes* that opium has that power, and so the answer that it has it because it has a 'soporific power', even if said in Latin, is not remotely informative. If the question had been 'Why did the man fall asleep after taking opium?', the answer that opium has the power to put people to sleep *would be* informative, at least for someone who didn't know it.[15] This is the kind of thing we discover when, for example, we discover that tobacco smoke is carcinogenic: we learn that tobacco smoke has the power to cause cancer. But of course the question in Molière's play is about the *categorial* basis of opium's power to do so: what is it in opium that gives it this power? What explains the fact that opium has this power? The beginning of an answer, which the doctors didn't know but we do is that opium has certain chemical compounds, such as morphine and codeine. That is only the beginning of an answer because in turn we need to understand how these compounds work so that opium has the effects it does: we investigate what dispositional properties these substances have, and in virtue of what categorial bases, if any. And if they do, the same questions can be asked about those. And so on.[16]

---

[14]   Quia est in eo /Vertus dormitiva,/ Cujus eat natura/ Sensus assoupire (*Le Malade Imaginaire*).
[15]   See Mumford, *Dispositions*, 136ff. for further discussion.
[16]   Which raises the question whether 'science finds dispositional properties all the way down', Blackburn, S., 'Filling in Space', *Analysis* **50** (1990), 62–65, 63, quoted by Vetter, *Potentiality* 8. See also Mumford *Dispositions*; Molnar *Powers* and Bird *Nature's Metaphysics: Laws and Properties* (Oxford: Oxford University Press, 2007); and, relatedly, the question whether all dispositions have categorial basis, on which, see, e.g., J. McKitrick 'The Bare Metaphysical Possibility of Bare Dispositions', *Philosophy and Phenomenological Research* **66** (2003), 349–369 and S. Mumford, 'The Ungrounded Argument', *Synthese* **149** (2006), 471–489.

The last two concepts introduced help explain Independence. First, we attribute dispositions to particular objects even when they've never manifested them because of the kind of object or stuff they are (or are made of). So it makes sense to say of *this tumbler* that it is fragile because it is made of glass and *glass* is fragile, even though the tumbler has never broken; and it makes sense to say this piece of copper wire has the property of conductivity because *copper* (or copper wire) has that property, even though this piece has never conducted electricity. And so on. And the reason is, partly, that things that belong to the same (relevant) kind have the same constitution, so that there is a categorial basis in virtue of which they have the disposition and, on account of that, it makes sense to attribute it to them, independently of their manifestations. Second, a thing may have a disposition but have never manifested it because it is never subject to the stimulus conditions or because the disposition is being masked.

Debates about dispositions have focused on whether it is possible to provide an analysis of the concept of disposition and, in particular, whether the conditional analysis associated with Gilbert Ryle – or an improved version of it – succeeds. On this, the consensus seems to be that it isn't possible to provide non-circular accounts of the manifestation conditions for any disposition precisely because of the myriad possibilities of masking, antidotes, finks, etc. Philosophers have also debated the relationship between dispositions and causation and, relatedly, between dispositions and their underlying basis. Further, they have disagreed about whether dispositions have causal efficacy and whether they genuinely contribute to explaining their manifestations.[17]

To sum up the received view of paradigmatic dispositions I have sketched: a disposition is a property of an object, defined by its manifestation but ontologically independent of its ever being manifested. Many, though perhaps not all, dispositions have stimulus conditions, which trigger their manifestation. And many, though perhaps not all, dispositions have a categorial base, which are properties in virtue of

---

[17] Some of the main contributions to these debates are Bird, *Nature's Metaphysics:* Fara, 'Dispositions and Habituals' D. Lewis, 'Finkish Dispositions', *The Philosophical Quarterly* **47** (1997), 143–158; Martin, *The Mind in Nature*; Molnar, *Powers*; Mumford, *Dispositions*; E.W. Prior, R. Pargeter, F. Jackson, 'Three Theses about Dispositions', *American Philosophical Quarterly* **19**(3) (1982), 251–57; Vetter, *Potentiality*. See also A. Marmodoro (ed.), *The Metaphysics of Powers* (Oxford: Oxford University Press, 2010).

which the object has the disposition in question. I now turn to character traits.

2. Character traits as psychological dispositions

In this section I examine the extent to which character traits, which as we saw above are thought of as psychological dispositions, fit this received view of paradigmatic dispositions. I start with their manifestations.

2.1 Character Traits and their Manifestations

How is a character trait defined? What are its typical manifestations? In *the Concept of Mind*, Ryle distinguishes two kinds of dispositions. First, what he calls 'single-track' or 'determinate' dispositions, that is, dispositions whose manifestation takes one form. So for example, dispositions like 'fragile' are manifested in the object's breaking or shattering. Then there are 'multi-track' or 'determinable' dispositions, whose manifestation can take many forms. For example, the disposition 'elastic' can be manifested in the object's expanding, contracting, etc. Although some have questioned whether there are any single-track dispositions, the idea that psychological dispositions are multi-track seems plausible. Ryle illustrates his point about character traits as follows:

> When Jane Austen wished to show the specific kind of pride which characterised the heroine of 'Pride and Prejudice', she had to represent her *actions, words, thoughts and feelings* in a thousand different situations. There is no one standard type of action or reaction such that Jane Austen could say 'My heroine's kind of pride was just the tendency to do this, whenever a situation of that sort arose' (*The Concept of Mind*, 32. My italics).

So as Ryle notes, a character trait such as pride is multi-track in two important respects. First, it is a disposition to engage in a variety of 'overt' behaviour (including e.g. omissions and failures), such as (not) talking, (not) dancing with certain people, etc. And, second, it is also a disposition to certain 'inner' phenomena such as thinking, judging, reasoning, desiring and feeling in certain ways. And this complexity of possible manifestation does not seem peculiar to Elizabeth Bennet's type of pride, nor even to pride in general, but to character traits in general. For instance, cowardice is a disposition to avoid danger or pain when it behoves the person to face the danger or pain – which will result in very different forms of behaviour (even if these forms can all be brought under the label 'pain-' or 'risk-aversion behaviour'); but it is also a disposition to have certain thoughts, to reason in certain ways, to have emotional reactions, to feel certain sentiments, etc. which are characteristic of cowardice.[18]

So character traits are manifested not just in action and omission (behaviour) but also in thoughts, desires, feelings and emotions. In other words, we may say that character traits have *external* manifestations (i.e. manifestations that can be perceived and are typically changes, though refrainings, i.e. absence of change, should be included too), which may be behavioural, whether purposive, e.g. intentional actions, including linguistic behaviour; or merely expressive behaviour: laughing, cringing, etc. And they also have *internal* manifestations (i.e. purely mental phenomena): thoughts, which may be unbidden or the result of intentional mental acts and include practical reasoning; imaginings, and also emotional reactions, feelings and sensations: sadness, joy, fear. These internal manifestations can be expressed externally by behaviour of either kind, or they may be kept private, unexpressed.

But, it might be objected, is it right to think of thoughts, emotional reactions, sensations, etc. as *manifestations* of a psychological disposition? Aren't manifestations things that are externally available – available to an observer, so that only overt behaviour should count as the manifestation of a psychological disposition? I cannot see why we should accept this restricted view. First, although the manifestation of physical dispositions may always be observable in principle – though perhaps not always directly – this seems no reason to apply the same restriction to the manifestation of a psychological disposition such as a character trait. It seems perfectly plausible that character traits are dispositions not just to act overtly in certain ways, but also to think, reason, feel, etc., certain things, and that all these are characteristic manifestations of a trait.

Besides, as I noted above, many of the internal manifestations can be expressed, so that they are then observable: my feelings of joy, fear, compassion, etc. may be visible in my face, gestures, posture, expressive behaviour etc. And I may speak my thoughts aloud, instead of

---

[18]   For an analysis of character traits that is consistent with this view and sees them as 'patterned dispositions distinct from garden-variety, instrumentally bundled sets of beliefs and desires' see D. Butler, 'Character Traits in Explanation', *Philosophy and Phenomenological Research* **49**(2) (1988), 215–238.

keeping them to myself. So it is hard to see why the fact that these phenomena may be unexpressed or concealed should undermine their status as genuine manifestations of a character trait.

Finally, it is true that external manifestations (i.e., overt behaviour, and in particular intentional actions) are often criteria that determine whether the inner phenomena are genuine, rather than, say, expressions of sentimentality or wishful thinking. Pious thoughts and feelings about the plight of those in need unaccompanied by deeds to provide help may be rightly judged as only bogus manifestations of compassion, pity or generosity. This, however, does not show that inner phenomena of the right kind cannot constitute genuine manifestations of a character trait. Moreover, external behaviour also counts as a manifestation of a character trait only if it is genuine: for something to be an act of kindness, or generosity it must be done for the right reason and 'in the right spirit'.[19] If I donate money to a worthy cause but do so grudgingly, or do it to further my interests, then my act of donating may still be helpful but is not a manifestation of generosity.[20] Thus, there is reason to treat both the internal and external phenomena (which, for ease of exposition I shall call 'behaviour broadly understood') as potentially manifestations of character traits; even though there are constraints on when each constitutes genuine manifestations – and whether it does depends, largely, on the interrelation between the two.

I shall now turn to the second feature, Independence.

[19]   I should say the behaviour must be 'permeated' by the right inner phenomena. However, I am here trying to remain neutral on whether the interrelations between inner and outer manifestations should be understood causally: the inner causes the outer; or – as I think is right – in terms of internal, non-contingent relations.
[20]   On what seem the most plausible conceptions of virtue, in order for you to act virtuously, it is not just enough to do the right thing but you must to do it for the right reasons and having the appropriate desires, feelings and emotions. As Aristotle puts it, 'moral excellence is a state concerned with choice, and choice is deliberate desire, therefore both the reasoning must be true and the desire right, if the choice is to be good, and the latter must pursue just what the former asserts' (Aristotle, *Nicomachean Ethics*, 1139a 22–25). I shall have to leave aside the complications introduced by Aristotle's highly demanding conception of virtue and of the unity of the virtues.

2.2 Character traits and Independence

The first thing to note about character traits is that, in general, their attribution seems to require *actual* manifestation in some form: a character trait is attributed to someone only if the person to which it is attributed behaves, thinks, reacts emotionally, etc., in ways that are typical of the character trait.

This could be merely an epistemic point: the only way we know whether someone has a character trait is whether they manifest it in any of the possible ways just outlined. That is right, but my contention is that the point about attribution is not merely epistemic but rather constitutive. In other words, it is not simply about how we establish whether someone is a generous, cowardly or shy person but what *it is* to be a generous, cowardly or shy person. Manifesting the character trait in the relevant circumstances is *constitutive* of what it is to have the character trait. In order to be generous one must manifest generosity, to be punctual one must manifest punctuality, to be greedy one must manifest greed, and so on. So a person does not have a character trait unless she has manifested it in some way, at some time: someone who has never had a generous thought, feeling, reaction or action is not a generous person; and someone who has never had a malicious, courageous, or timid thought, feeling, or has acted accordingly does not have the corresponding character trait.[21]

If this is right, then character traits, at least some of them, seem to violate *Independence*; in fact they are characterised by **Dependence**: they are dispositions whose possession requires (ontologically) that the object display the sort of behaviour (broadly understood) that is characteristic of the disposition.[22]

This may appear to be false because it may seem possible for a person to have a character trait that she has never manifested. Surely, there may be people who are malicious, or greedy, deceitful, or generous, courageous or kind but who have not manifested those character traits: perhaps they haven't had the opportunity to manifest those traits. Indeed, Dependence is rejected on this grounds by

---

[21]   This view is defended by S. Hampshire in 'Dispositions', *Analysis*, **14** (1953), 5–11, esp. 6. It is also endorsed, though expressed differently by Hacker, *Human Nature*, ch.4.

[22]   In my paper 'Desires, Dispositions and the Explanation of Action' in *The Nature of Desire*, J. Deonna and F. Lauria (eds) (Oxford: Oxford University Press, forthcoming 2016), I argue that desires are also manifestation-dependent dispositions.

Maria Alvarez

Christian Miller, for whom 'it seems conceivable that someone could have a trait such as heroism, but never be presented with an opportunity to actually exhibit it in either thought or action'.[23] And so it might seem that someone can have a character trait even though they have never manifested it. But is this right?

First, a brief clarification: of course someone may conceal the inner manifestations of their character traits, in the sense that they may repress any external expression of them. This possibility does not, however, undermine Dependence because in that case the character trait would have been manifested – albeit only internally. Indeed, it is those internal manifestations that give substance to the claim that the person is *concealing* the manifestation of the trait.

More importantly, although Miller asserts that the possibility he describes is conceivable, it is not clear that it is. If having a trait such as heroism means that one is heroic, we can ask what it would mean to say that someone who has never displayed heroism either in thought, word or deed *is* heroic: what would her being heroic consist in? Unless that can be given an answer, the claim that she is heroic seems an empty claim. Perhaps the thought is that certain counterfactuals are true of this person, for instance, that were she to be faced with a situation that requires heroism, she *would* act heroically. Let us suppose that such a counterfactual is true of Annie. Does this mean that Annie *is* heroic? I do not see that it does. What it means is that, in that counterfactual situation Annie *would act* heroically, perhaps even that she *would be* heroic. It also means that Annie is now *capable* of being heroic. But those are different from the claim that Annie, who has not betrayed any hint of heroism to date, *is* heroic.[24]

---

[23] C. Miller, *Character and Moral Psychology*, 19ff. Miller is criticising the so-called 'summary view' of character traits which shares the claim of Dependence with my view. I do not, however, endorse the reductive account that some defenders of that view seem to endorse – for details and references see Miller, 18ff. In this context, if should be noted that Dependence is not the claim that you only have the trait *while* you manifest it; it is, rather, that you don't have it *unless* you've manifested it in some way, which is consistent with thinking of character traits as dispositional.

[24] Mumford *Dispositions*, 8, considers the possibility described by A Wright in 'Dispositions, Anti-Realism and Empiricism', *Proceedings of the Aristotelian Society* **91** (1988), of someone who has never been in the circumstances to act bravely, or has but was 'drunk or affected by food additives'. Mumford admits that there would be a question as to what 'such a person's bravery consists in' and asks rhetorically whether there is a fact of the matter in this case. I think that the answers is that the person is not

Richard Brandt seems to trade on this modal thought in his argument against Dependence:

> Is it contradictory to affirm that a person is T, or, on the evidence probably T, and at the same time to say that certainly or probably he has never acted in a T-like way in the past? I fail to see that it is, at least for the traits of moral character with which we are concerned (...) take 'courageous.' Suppose we knew a given person had lived a very sheltered life and had never been required to act in the face of a serious threat. (...) Would we infer of such a person that he cannot be courageous? Surely not.[25]

But even putting aside the fact that Brandt's argument is restricted to 'acting', it misses its target. For his opponent's claim is not that the person Brandt describes *cannot* be courageous, if that means that he would be incapable of acting courageously if faced with a serious threat. The claim is, rather, that he *is not* courageous. Perhaps Brandt's point depends on taking the 'can' of 'he cannot be courageous' as expressing epistemic possibility: although a person has never displayed courage in any way he may, for all we know, be courageous.[26] But if that is Brandt's claim, then his argument also fails. For, while there is nothing wrong with the claim that a person who has never manifested courage is, for all we know, capable of acting courageously, the claim that someone who has never manifested courage in any way whatsoever is, for all we know, a courageous person is a claim that is, if not contradictory, at least in search of meaning. For if we know that he's not ever manifested any courage we know that he's not courageous (though we don't know that he's not capable of being courageous, or that he won't be when the moment comes- nor, for that matter, do we know that he is cowardly!).

---

brave although it may be true that she *would* have been brave, had she not been incapacitated or had she found herself in the right circumstances.

[25] Brandt's target is certain related claims made by W.P. Alston in 'Toward a Logical Geography of Personality: Traits and Deeper Lying Personality Characteristics', in H.E Kiefer & M.K. Munitz (eds), *Mind, Science and History* (Albany: State University of New York Press, 1970) 59–92.

[26] It is worth asking what evidence Brandt thinks would be relevant here. And it seems that the only relevant evidence would be manifestations of characteristics that the person has displayed whether in action or in psychological tests, such as fearlessness, independence, integrity, etc., that are suitably related to courage, which again supports Dependence.

A somewhat different reason why one might think that Dependence is false is the following. Surely it is possible to *discover* that one has a character trait. Suppose I find myself in a dangerous situation and react with great courage: I risk my life in order to save others from serious danger even though I have no duty to do so and even I am surprised at my behaviour. In such a situation it seems plausible to say that I would have discovered that I have a character trait, courage, that I'd never manifested before. And, if this is right, it would follow that some character traits are not manifestation-dependent. But is this right? Is this a good objection to Dependence?

To deal with this point we need to distinguish between acting with a motive and having and displaying a character trait. Consider the statement

'Jim ran away because he is a coward.'

This statement explains Jim's action of running as being motivated by cowardice. But as well as saying what motivated him on that occasion, the statement attributes a character trait to Jim, namely, cowardice, and says that Jim's action was a manifestation of that character trait. In other words, this statement says that Jim's *motive* to run away on that occasion was cowardice, and also that he has a *disposition* to be motivated by cowardice – a disposition that, on the occasion at issue, was manifested in his running away then.[27]

But the fact that we can distinguish between being motivated by an emotion such as cowardice or courage, and *having* the corresponding character trait suffices to bring out the point that it is possible to act out of a motive now and then even though one does not have the corresponding character trait. This is something that Ryle famously appears to deny in *The Concept of Mind*, where he says that 'the statement that a man boasted from vanity' should be construed as

> He boasted and his doing so satisfies the law-like proposition that whenever he finds a chance of securing the admiration and envy of others, he does whatever he thinks will produce the admiration and envy of others (89).[28]

Ryle has been criticized for implying that it is not possible to act out of a motive, such as vanity or greed, only once – which is clearly false: a person can act out of vanity or greed once without being a vain or

---

[27]   For a discussion of motives and their role in action explanation, see my *Kinds of Reasons* (Oxford: Oxford University press, 2010), sections 3.1.1 and 6.4.
[28]   Ryle, *The Concept of Mind*, 89.

greedy person:[29] there's a difference between acting once or twice in a mean or courageous way (acting with the motive), and being a mean or courageous person (having the character trait). Indeed, the possibility is conceptually necessary given that having a character trait is precisely having a tendency to be motivated by the corresponding motive. In other words, to have the character trait of, say, malice, is to often be motivated by malice. But one can act out of character: be motivated by compassion even though one is malicious (and *vice versa*).

Still, one might say that some acts are *so* courageous, or magnanimous, or treacherous that they suffice to attribute the corresponding trait to the person. So the fact that a particular action or thought is the first need not imply that the act so motivated is not a manifestation of a character trait.[30] Perhaps so. Nonetheless, the one act of courage, however impressive, does not imply that the person *had* the disposition beforehand, independently of this first manifestation. For it is plausible to say that what I discover in that sort of case is that I *have* the disposition and not that I *had* it all along. It may be that particular act of courage that generates the disposition: perhaps the situation helps me to, as it were, see the point of courage, or of generosity, etc. And, similarly, with negative character traits like being treacherous or corrupt, where the one act of betrayal may be the act that sets one off on the path of treachery or corruption – the disposition is acquired through the treacherous or corrupt act. Though it is more likely that, in these cases, what we discover is that we were capable of acting courageously, contrary to what we thought; or that we are *more* courageous (or generous or *more* treacherous or corrupt than we thought): we have already in the past manifested those character traits and we discover that we have the disposition to a higher degree than we suspected (I come back to degrees of disposition below).

Thus, it seems that character traits are characterised by Dependence: behaviour (broadly conceived) within the range typical of a character trait is *necessary* for one to have the character trait. On the other hand, we have seen that occasional behaviour

---

[29] For further discussion, see Alvarez 'Ryle on Motives and Dispositions', *Ryle on Mind and Language*, D. Dolby (ed.), (Basingstoke: Palgrave MacMillan, 2015), 74–96.

[30] Although it is also true that if, after the incident, the person doesn't ever again display any signs of courage, then it is doubtful that they really are courageous, rather than that they *were* courageously on that occasion, which reinforces dependence. For an interesting discussion of these issues see, B. Powell, 'Uncharacteristic Actions', *Mind* **68** (1959), 492–509, where she also endorses Dependence though not under that name.

characteristic of a trait may not be enough to have the trait: it is possible to act and react meanly or generously now and again without thereby being a generous or mean person.

If this is right, there's the question what degree or extent of manifestation is necessary and sufficient for an attribution of the trait to be meaningful. The answer is complex because, as is the case with many dispositions, having a character trait admits of degrees: that is, one may be very or a little generous, slightly or quite greedy, terribly or just a little vain, etc. Partly because of this, and partly for other complications that limitations of space prevent me from examining, there cannot be a general answer to how often or in what conditions one must manifest a character trait or what form the manifestation must take, in order for someone to have the character trait.[31] The possibility of degrees is, however, consistent with Dependence, which says that total absence of manifestation implies (constitutes) absence of character trait.

Still one may wonder whether Dependence, even if true, is a feature that cuts as deep as I am claiming: are character traits as different in their logical features from paradigmatic dispositions as I am claiming? After all, we could in the future discover the categorial basis of certain character traits, so that we might know someone has a trait because she has the categorial basis, even though she's never manifested it. Indeed, the absence of manifestation might be explained, as in the case of paradigmatic dispositions, by the absence of enabling conditions or stimulus for the manifestation of the dispositions. So really a person may have a trait she's simply been unable to manifest due to lack of propitious conditions.

This suggestion raises several issues that require much more careful treatment than I am able to give them here. However, I shall say two things in response to it. One is that, as we saw, paradigmatic dispositions may be attributed sensibly to an individual on account of its belonging to a kind or its having certain categorical basis. But this is not so with character traits for, even if we discovered reliable correlations between certain character traits and, say, genetic make up, or neural features, or upbringing, or nationality, etc., we still could not attribute the trait to the person independently of whether she had manifested it. Note: I do not mean we could not do so with confidence or certainty; the claim is that it would *not make sense* to attribute it in the

---

[31] See Vetter *Potentiality*, §2.4 for a discussion of the issue of degrees of dispositions in general. Aristotelian 'virtues' do not seem to admit of degrees as I am suggesting – an interesting complexity that I cannot examine here.

absence of some kind of manifestation, for the reasons given above.[32] Second, character traits do not seem to need very special circumstance to be manifested, and often don't seem to need any triggers. For even someone in solitary confinement can have malicious thoughts, generous intentions or mean reactions even if only to imagined scenarios; moreover, failure to have certain thoughts, images, etc. may also, given certain conditions, constitute manifestation of a character trait. It seems that being conscious and having basic mental abilities is all that is required to be able to manifest one's character traits.[33]

3. Conclusion: Are character traits dispositions?

If character traits are, as I have argued, characterised by Dependence, should we conclude that character traits are not really dispositions? The question cannot be answered without revisiting the issue about kinds of powers and terminology mentioned in section 1.

As I noted above, it is widely held that Independence is defining of dispositions. If it is, then character traits are not dispositions and we would need a different term for them, one that still connotes that they are dispositional powers – that is, they are powers that their possessors have a tendency to manifest, like paradigmatic dispositions and unlike abilities; but which cannot be attributed to their possessors merely on account to their belonging to a kind. As I said above, Dependence is consistent with thinking of character traits as dispositional: attributing a character trait is partly a record of past and present behaviour, broadly understood, but it also provides grounds (albeit defeasible ones) for predictions of future behaviour. Perhaps the term 'tendency' captures this feature of character traits. But we should remember that the decision to call character traits 'tendencies' rather than 'dispositions', though reflecting a real difference between them and 'paradigmatic dispositions', would to some extent be a terminological choice that introduces a degree of regimentation relative to our ordinary use of these words. We could, therefore, instead chose to continue

---

[32] This is an important reason why relying on national, gender, racial, ethnic, etc. stereotypes concerning character traits in order to judge individuals is at best perilous. It is not just that the statistical regularities on which the stereotypes are based are often deeply flawed but also that, even if they were accurate, attribution of a trait to a particular person still requires manifestation of the trait *by the person*.

[33] A different question is what conditions are needed for the acquisition of character traits but I cannot discuss that here.

to call character traits 'dispositions' but deny that Independence is defining of all dispositions: it would then become defining of a special kind of disposition.[34]

Whatever terminological choice we make, we can draw some conclusions that go beyond it. We have seen that we can explain both human action and the behaviour of inanimate things by reference to their so-called dispositions. I have argued that (at least some of) the psychological dispositions that explain human actions have quite distinctive features.[35] I have also claimed that, because of Dependence, character traits cannot be attributed to particulars on the basis of their belonging to a kind, or their being (made of) a certain kind of stuff, as is the case with paradigmatic dispositions. These considerations raise many issues about what psychological dispositions are, whether they have causal bases, and if so, what these might be. And, importantly, they also suggest that we ought to re-examine whether the model of how paradigmatic dispositions explain their manifestations is the best model to understand how character traits explain *their* manifestations, which include intentional actions. But these are issues that are beyond the scope of this paper.[36]

King's College London
maria.alvarez@kcl.ac.uk

[34] It is interesting to note in this context that Hampshire takes Dependence and related features of character traits to be grounds for arguing that they *are* dispositions, unlike what he calls 'descriptions of the causal properties of things – e.g. "electrically charged", "magnetised", "soluble in *aqua regia*"' ('Dispositions', 7), that is, the paradigmatic dispositions of contemporary philosophers!

[35] I do not mean that character traits, or psychological dispositions in general, are the only dispositions that display all or some of these features. At least some of the dispositional terms applied to some artefacts, such as being unreliable or 'temperamental', are similar in this respect but I do not have space to explore this here.

[36] Versions of this paper were presented at research seminars at Edinburg, King's College London, Essex, Zurich, the May 2016 'Ascription, Causation and the Mind Workshop' at the University of Utrecht, and at the 2016 UNC/KCL Workshop on Explanation, as well as at the RIP Lecture Series on 'Action', 2016–17. I thank organisers and participants for their very helpful comments. Work on this paper was carried out during my tenure of a Leverhulme Trust Major Research Fellowship and I thank the Trust for the award of the Fellowship.

Knowledge How in Philosophy of Action

JENNIFER HORNSBY

Abstract
I maintain that an account of knowledge how to do something – an account which might be supposed to uncover 'the nature' of such knowledge – can't be got by considering what linguists tell us is expressed in ascriptions of knowing how. Attention must be paid to the knowledge that is actually being exercised when someone is doing something. I criticize some claims about ascriptions of knowledge-how which derive from contemporary syntactic and semantic theory. I argue that these claims can no more provide an understanding of what it is to *intend* to do something than of what it is to *know how* to do something. Philosophy, not linguistics, must be the source of such understanding.

Gilbert Ryle said that his opponents, the intellectualists, had 'for the most part ignored the question what it is for someone to know how to perform tasks'. Ryle blamed their lack of attention to this question on their holding a mistaken view of what it is to act rationally.[1] Anti-Rylean intellectualists of today don't ignore the question that Ryle said his opponents ignored. Indeed they advance a definite thesis about the nature of knowing how to do something (of how to perform tasks, as Ryle put it). If their understanding of knowing how commits them to a view about acting rationally, then they find no problems with it.

I'm going to be concerned with connections between the questions what it is to *know how to do* something and what it is to act rationally (as Ryle put it[2]). My focus will be on work by Jason Stanley and Timothy Williamson. Their joint paper, 'Knowing How',[3] makes

---

[1] *The Concept of Mind*, 1949. At page 15 in the 2009 edition published by Routledge.

[2] I take Ryle's 'acting rationally' as meant to locate the kind of action in which rational beings participate as such – intentional action as most people nowadays would probably say. Ryle's 'perform tasks' carves out an area smaller than what's at issue, given that 'task' is not naturally applied to much of what we do as agents. I settle here for 'do something' although it has an opposite sort of fault, carving out a larger area that what's at issue specifically in philosophy of action. (See further n.9.)

[3] Jason Stanley and Timothy Williamson, 'Knowing How', *Journal of Philosophy* **98**(8) (2001), 411–44.

doi:10.1017/S135824611700008X   ©The Royal Institute of Philosophy and the contributors 2017

Jennifer Hornsby

use of resources from linguistic theory to put in place the thesis that 'knowledge-how is simply a species of knowledge-that' – is knowledge of propositions. What it is to *do* something is not at issue in that paper; but Stanley's elaboration and book-length defence of the thesis[4] makes contact with philosophy of action. And when it comes to Williamson's paper, 'Acting on Knowledge'[5] – the last of the pieces in my sights – philosophy of action is firmly in the frame; although *knowing how to* is absent from it. Williamson relies there upon an an understanding of 'intend to' which (as I shall explain) is caught up with the understanding of 'knowing how to' derived from the theory which was the basis of the joint paper. I think that such understandings are inimical to a correct philosophy of action. My overall aim is to show that contemporary linguistic theory is no basis for a credible story of action in which *knowing how* could belong.

1.

I start from a generalization about knowing how to do something which Stanley and Williamson themselves endorse. As I see things, Stanley and Williamson's single-minded attention to questions about the syntax and semantics of sentences used to attribute knowledge how ensures that the significance of their own generalization is lost on them. It is given expression by Stanley when he formulates the following schema.[6]

(IAK) If x intentionally φ-s, then x knows how to φ.

(IAK) seems right. One is apt to say that a person could not have done something intentionally if she didn't know how to do it. And a further connection between the ideas of *intentionally doing* and *knowing how*

---

[4] J. Stanley, *Know How* (Oxford, Oxford University Press, 2011).

[5] T. Williamson, 'Acting on Knowledge', to appear in J.A. Carter, E. Gordon, and B. Jarvis (eds), *Knowledge-First Approaches in Epistemology and Mind* (Oxford, Oxford University Press). Quotations here are from a draft available at: http://old.philosophy.ox.ac.uk/__data/assets/pdf_file/0005/35834/KfirstCarter.pdf

[6] (IAK) is a consequence of what Stanley and Williamson say (pages 414–5 in 'Knowing How'). I quote it from J. Stanley, 'Knowing (How)', *Nous* **45**(2) (2011), 217 (although I have replaced Stanley's 'F' with 'φ' in order to signal that instances of the schematic letter are verbs).

to do can also be agreed on all hands.[7] The only things which are candidates for things which a person could know how to do are those that
she might intentionally do.

I'll come back to the relation between the schema (IAK) as it stands
and the sort of intuitive justification for it that I've just given. But
first I bring out its implications for what knowing how to do something may involve.

It is often assumed that the word 'intentionally' or 'intentional' can
serve to pick out what needs to be treated in an account of human
agency. A certain line of thought may put this assumption in place –
that a particular kind of explanation is proper to cases of human
agency, namely *reason* explanation; and that that which, and only
that which, someone has done by virtue of having a *reason* to do it,
she has intentionally done.[8] What (IAK) suggests is that a different
line of thought could lead to the same place: that which and only
that which someone has done by virtue of *knowing how* to do it she
has intentionally done. Insofar as the two lines of thought converge,
knowing how to have done appears to go hand in hand with *having had a
reason to do*. One might account for this by pointing out that when a
person's having done one thing *rationally explains* her having done
some other thing, then doing the one was *how* she did the one.
Thus: that she φ-d explains why she Ψ-d, and Ψ-ing was *how* she
φ-d – she φ-d by Ψ-ing.

This little account of the manner in which *knowing how* to do connects with the *having of reasons* to do can hardly be adequate as it
stands, however. For one thing, it simply passes over the '*know*' of
'know how to do'. For another thing, the 'by' of 'φ by Ψing' falls
short of the 'how' which introduces the idea of the means employed
in getting something done. You may have broken the eggs because
you were making a cheese omelette; but you didn't make the omelette
simply by breaking eggs. If you made a cheese omelette, then you did
so by breaking eggs and whisking them, grating the cheese in readiness, pouring the mix into a hot pan, and ... – by doing all of these
things, each in turn.

---

[7]   See 'Knowing how', page 415, where it is said that what makes it
clearly false that if Hannah digests her food, then she knows how to digest
her food is that 'digesting food is not the sort of action that one knows
how to do'.
[8]   The line of thinking is present in much philosophy of action taking off
from Donald Davidson's paper 'Actions, Reasons, and Causes', *Journal of
Philosophy* **60**(23) (1963), 685–700. Davidson held that any *action* has as
reason explanation – a 'rationalization' in his sense.

The two points – about knowledge, and about the need to do a series of things in order to get done what one has reason to do – are connected. When someone has φ-d (intentionally[9]) by first doing one thing, then another, then a third, a fourth ..., the fact that she has φ-d is not a matter merely of her having done each of the things in turn. She knew what sort of things to do because she knew how to φ. Certainly her doing any of the things she did in sequence can be reckoned a part of her φ-ing. But she had no reason to do any of the specific things she actually did except insofar as, in appropriate conjunction with doing other things, doing them would subserve her end.

When one thinks of an agent as setting off with knowledge of how to φ, and as knowing that there are steps to be taken, it becomes easy to imagine that her φ-ing must be a matter of her carrying out a plan or programme whose details were settled at the start. But an agent's question *how* to do something doesn't lapse as soon as she starts on doing it. It is not as if someone who made a cheese omelette had first thought out how that was to be done, and then, having determined how, set her body onto automatic pilot so that the several intentions she had formed would be executed in turn. No. One's intentions themselves take on new specifications even in the course of their being fulfilled. She knew to get the frying pan out, but in practice how to do so depended upon where it had last been put. She had intended to scatter the cheese she had grated ahead of folding the omelette, but only at the point of introducing the cheese did determinacy attach to how much of the cheese to use. Of course someone who knows how to make an omelette will have no need, in the course of making it, to dwell upon such questions as are implicitly answered by an agent who keeps track. Still, one's knowledge how to make an omelette ensures that one can be alive to what one is doing if ever one engages in omelette making. So the series of particular steps someone took in exercising her knowledge on some actual occasion is not matched to any inflexible routine.

---

[9]   I leave the word 'intentionally' out in what follows, taking it to be everywhere implicit. Williamson avails himself of a means of ensuring it is implicit when he announces 'Here and henceforth, 'action' is to be read as 'intentional action''. It can help to see why it should be possible to leave the word out if one accepts, with G.E.M. Anscombe, that 'the term 'intentional' has reference to a form of description of events' so that 'descriptions of events effected by human beings' may be *formally* descriptions of executed intentions'. See *Intention* (Oxford, Basil Blackwell, 1957), pages 84 and 87.

Knowledge How in Philosophy of Action

It is hard to say much of a general sort about what goes on when someone puts her knowledge how to do something into practice. And there is a danger, consequent on needing to be explicit about what an agent must have known, to falsify the phenomenology, making it seem that she must *consciously* have known it all. At any rate, I won't try to say more than starts to show up in the particular mundane example. The point of the example is only to draw attention to the fact that when an agent has done that which she intended to do, a much more detailed story could in principle be told about the knowledge how which actually she had used. For the agent herself, the question what to be doing next is always the question how to proceed as things now stand. In thinking close up about a particular example, one sees how much more has been going on when someone has done something than would come to attention in any explanation of her doing it which would ordinarily be given. (IAK), in portraying knowing how to as co-ordinate with intentionally doing, may remind one of just how much knowledge of how to act is in play in action. In order to bring this out, one needs to advert to the perspective of the one who knew what was going on – who, in exercising her knowledge of how to do what she did, knew what she was doing so long as she was doing it.

I have relied on (IAK), taken from Stanley and Williamson, in order to motivate thinking about the knowledge how that is actually exercised when someone does something. But I should note two discrepancies between Stanley's (IAK) and what I have tried to make from it. They used the schematic letter 'φ' whereas I have relied on the 'something' present in the ordinary language of 'do something'.[10] And whereas I have stuck to the past tense, for the sake of explaining why one might endorse (IAK) and for thinking about an example,

---

[10]   When P.F. Strawson argued that fear of Platonism should not be a reason to disallow that quantification into predicate-position is a feature of natural language, his examples were taken from the language of agency. (See 'Positions for quantifiers', *Semantics and Philosophy*, ed. M.K. Munitz and P.K. Unger (New York: New York University Press), 63–79, 1974.) It will be evident that I welcome Strawson's view that 'staying close to the surface structure of natural language sentences [is] .. always to be aimed at if we seek to understand our own understanding of the structure of our language' (For this, see the Introduction to *Entity and Identity: And Other Essays* (Oxford: Oxford University Press, 2000), in which the 1974 essay is reprinted.) But it will be important that the things we speak as if there were when we say that someone did this that or the other 'thing' are not properties (as Strawson seems to have supposed they were). See further the Appendix.

their schema on the face of it is present tensed: 'She ϕ-s'. Well, I take it that so far as tense is concerned, they actually mean something generic: one imagines the conditional, 'x intentionally ϕ-s, ...' as falling in the scope of an implicit 'At any time'. But if so, then the use of a schematic letter in making a connection between 'intentionally' and 'know how to' might encourage one to focus on some single verb phrase as providing the whole of an answer to the question what someone is now intentionally doing. One would then be bound to fail to appreciate that at any time, the answer to the question what someone is doing may be 'many things'. She is now pouring egg mix into a pan, and she is now making an omelette, and she is now preparing dinner. She knows how to do all these things if (IAK) is correct. Indeed if she's doing these things now, then there must be other things she knows how to do than any she is now doing.

2.

Stanley 's interest in what he calls 'the folk notion of knowing how to' leads him to confine his attention to *ascriptions* of knowledge how. Here are some of the things knowledge of how to do which are ascribed to the agents in Stanley's book: field a fly ball, do the Salchow, swim, ride a bicycle, change a light bulb, get to Boston, grasp a door knob, post a card into a slot.[11] There is certainly variety here, ranging from kinds of know-how which it requires a skill to possess, kinds which perhaps need no skill but may need to have been learnt, and a more mundane kind which most able-bodied people in our social circumstances can be expected to have, or readily to come to have, without any special instruction. The variety goes hand in hand with differences as to what might be at issue if it were in question whether someone knew how to do something. Depending on the sort of know how in question, different sorts of interest will attach to whether someone has it. If one learns that X knows how to swim, then one comes to know that there are things X might do which a non-swimmer would never do. If one has been told a walkable route to the museum, which no doubt can be told by rehearsing some facts, then knowing already how to walk, one may use what one's been told in getting to the museum oneself. Any ordinary ascription of know how to X is made on the

---

[11] The examples are scattered throughout Stanley's *Know How* (2011). I've imposed a sort of ordering, starting from things that require some skill.

assumption that X has plenty of other knowledge, both of the knowledge-that and the knowledge-how kinds.

An application of (IAK) revealed that in the actual business of getting things done, a person makes use of much more knowledge how than would come to attention in thinking about what it might be *said* that she knew how to do (§1). And consideration of the actual use of sentences in which it is said that a person knows how to do something, now reveals that an interest in the truths conveyed in such sentences is not in the first instance an interest in knowing what states a person is in.

At one point Stanley asks 'Why should one expect it to be a virtue of an account of knowing how that it is plausibly taken to be what is expressed by ascriptions of knowing how in natural language?'. He then imagines a challenge from someone who thinks that 'science could show us that states of knowing how are very different in kind from what ordinary speakers use sentences like 'Ana knows how to swim' to express'.[12] But in order to put it in question whether an account of knowing how can be confined to uncovering the structure of sentences in which knowledge how is ascribed, there is no need to speculate about whether scientists might postulate a kind of knowing how unfamiliar to the folk. Stanley and Williamson themselves say that 'intentional actions are ... employments of knowledge-how'.[13] If that is right, and if one aims to provide an account of the nature of knowledge-how, then one surely needs to think about its *employment*. Stanley has a view about its employment. Employing one's knowledge how to do something, Stanley thinks, is a matter of *being guided by* one's knowledge how to do it. His claim against Ryle is not only that knowing how to do something amounts to knowing a fact, but that someone's acting amounts to her being guided by her knowledge of facts. (See e.g. page 175 of *Know How*. That we are 'guided by our knowledge' of how to do things is a recurrent theme in his and Williamson's paper.)

3.

Let me turn to the argument Stanley and Williamson gave for saying that knowledge how to do something is propositional knowledge. It starts from the thought that the word 'how' of 'know how', belongs with question words, including 'when', 'where', 'what', 'who', ... ,

[12]   J. Stanley, *Know How*, 143.
[13]   J. Stanley and T. Williamson, 'Knowing How', 442–3.

Jennifer Hornsby

etc. In such sentences as 'A knows [how —]', 'A knows [when —]', 'A knows [where —]' ... , the '[how —]'s and the '[when —]'s and the '[where—]'s are treated as embedded questions in standard semantics. So the knowledge attributed to A in such a sentence is knowledge of the answer to a question – the question 'How —?', 'When —?' ... A sentence may goes into the slot '—' following the question word (as in 'She knows how alcohol affects the body'). But in sentences that are of particular interest in a debate about knowing how to, there will be a verb in the infinitive in that slot (as in 'She knows how to set the thermostat' and, for that matter, 'She knows what to do next').

Where an infinitive comes after the question word, a sentence has to be constructed from the infinitive if something propositional is to be got. That means that the verb φ has to be supplied with a subject, and it has to be made finite so as to be predicable of the subject. Take as example 'Hannah knows how to swim'. Stanley and Williamson use the linguists' unpronounced pronoun 'PRO' as its subject, inheriting its reference from its antecedent ('Hannah' here); and they make the verb finite using a modal auxiliary such as 'could'. Thus for 'Hannah knows how to swim' Stanley at one point has 'Hannah knows how she could swim', which he says is 'a natural paraphrase of "Hannah knows how to swim"'.[14] The putative paraphrase does away with the infinitive, but it still contains the 'how'. So there is more work to do in linguistic theory. The idea then is that Hannah's knowing how she could swim is a matter of her being acquainted with some specific way or ways of swimming w, and knowing that w is a way she herself can or could swim – a way that will give her counterfactual success in swimming.[15]

[14] J. Stanley, *Know How*, 114.
[15] Here I've put together some different formulations in Stanley. It is unclear when he means to expose linguistic structure merely, when to provide the sort of analysis a philosopher may seek, when give full dress semantics. The idea of counterfactual success is present in the propositions which he claims are known by someone who knows how to do something. But I take it that his account of linguistic structure would require the introduction of a modal verb (with a meaning somehow slightly differently from that of plain 'can' or plain 'could'), which a philosopher might want to explain in terms of counterfactual success. (I note that accepting that so-called counterfactual success is a necessary condition of knowledge-how in itself does nothing to favour the idea that knowledge-how is propositional. The 'counterfactual success' condition might be spelt out saying: 'If S knows how to φ in circumstances C, then S would φ if she tried to φ in C.' When Katherine Hawley introduced the condition in her 'Success and knowledge how' (*American Philosophical Quarterly* **40**(1), 19–31 (2003)),

94

One might wonder why someone who knows ways of doing something should need, if she is to know how to do it, also to know *propositions* concerning those ways. It is as if Stanley thought that in addition to knowing ways, one needs to know something else knowledge of which will guide one in doing it. Stanley appears to think that knowing propositions follows somehow from knowing ways. He says:

> What we assert when we assert of a skilled outfielder that he knows how to field fly balls is that he knows *all* of a range of relevant ways that give him counterfactual success in fielding fly balls. Hence, to say of an outfielder in baseball that he knows how to catch a fly ball is to impart [*sic.*] to him knowledge of *many* propositions of the form 'w is a way for him to field a fly ball'.[16]

The 'hence' here effects a transition from knowledge of ways of fielding fly balls to knowledge of propositions, or facts, about those ways. In explication, Stanley says:

> That the acquisition of a skill is due to the learning of a fact explains why certain acts constitute exercises of skill, rather than reflex. A particular action of catching a fly ball is a skilled action, rather than a reflex, because it is guided by knowledge [sc. of facts].[17]

But why should an explanation be needed of why certain acts constitute exercises of skill?[18] If intentional actions are .. employments of knowledge-how (to quote Stanley and Williamson once more), then

---

she was quite explicit that endorsing it 'leaves open the question whether knowledge-how is distinct from propositional knowledge' (20).)

[16]   J. Stanley, *Know How*, 183.

[17]   Ibid., 130.

[18]   Stanley often writes as if doing anything required skill. He sets out saying that 'an action manifests skill in virtue of being a manifestation of the agent's knowledge how to do it' (*Know How*, 5); and he sums up his view saying that 'knowing how to do something is a kind of propositional knowledge that guides skilled actions' (ibid., 150). It may be that Stanley's focus on skilled action is owed to his imagining an opponent who, save for cases of skill, would make no objection to his treatment of 'know how to'. But objections to the idea that a person's knowing how to do something amounts to her possession of knowledge of propositions which guide her actions need not derive from any particular view of skill. (It is true, however, that Stanley is committed to a view about the *acquisition* of a skill – that it's a matter of gaining evidence providing one with the

Jennifer Hornsby

X's catching a fly ball was X's employment of X's knowledge how to catch a fly ball. No more is needed to see X's catching of a fly ball to be the exercise of a skill. Someone who knows how to do something, whether or not this is something she knows by virtue of having acquired a skill, may, when she is in a position to do it, simply *exercise* her knowledge how to. She is in no need of further knowledge which will guide her. (I note that 'exercise' is the word which Ryle used wherever Stanley would have 'is guided by'. And Ryle spoke of knowledge how as a *capacity*. It may be that Stanley's speaking of knowledge how always as a *disposition* ensures that he has no use for the idea that it may simply be exercised, despite his occasionally allowing that it may be 'employed'.[19])

4.

When Stanley introduces knowledge of propositions about ways, the idea that the infinitive 'to φ' of 'know how to φ' gives way to a sentence having 'PRO' as its subject rather gets lost sight of. But the idea recurs. For in Stanley's theory, the unpronounced element PRO is assumed to be the subject of infinitival clauses *generally*; Stanley speaks of 'the widespread consensus that infinitival constructions .. are expressions of *de se* attitudes'.[20] Thus a theorist of the linguistics to which Stanley subscribes will say that a 'PRO' is present in

---

realization that certain propositions are true of oneself. This has been found objectionable in its own right.)

[19] Ryle must take some of the blame for Stanley's assumption that someone's knowing how to do something can happily be called a disposition. For Ryle himself subsumed capacities in an overarching category of dispositions. When Ryle said that 'there is at our disposal an indefinitely wide range of dispositional terms' (op. cit. n.1, 109), he took the range to be as wide as he did because among his 'dispositional terms' were some of the terms he applied to what he called capacities. Ryle's terminology is owed to his thinking that he could account for capacities as 'multi-track dispositions'. Still, Ryle never spoke of anything both as a disposition and as exercised.

[20] J. Stanley, *Know How*, 72. A *de se* reading of a pronoun is one which 'involves a first-person way of thinking'. So when *de se* pronouns make an appearance in linguistic theory, the first personal character of ascriptions of intentions is unearthed from the structure of sentences. I hope that §1 above made it plain that an account of action must be an account of a sort of first person thinking – that someone who intends to so-and-so is someone who could (in principle) knowingly say '*I* intend to so-and-so'. I

96

the underlying syntax not only where an infinitive is preceded by a question word – as in 'John knows how to hit a ball hard' or 'Mary knows when to add the cheese' – but also where there is a simple infinitive, as in 'John tried to win the race' or 'John wants to become a doctor'. Inasmuch as Stanley and Williamson's treatment view of 'know how to' goes hand in hand with a view about sentences containing 'try to' and 'intend to', it will evidently have repercussions for philosophy of action beyond any I have so far touched on. The repercussions are worth exploring. There is no need to subscribe to any particular theory of infinitives to think that the same sort of construction is found following 'know how' and such words as 'try', 'want' and 'intend'. Even from the standpoint of superficial syntax, connections between such infinitives are evident. These infinitives can co-occur in sentences, apparently in construction one with another. Consider: 'Someone who did something that she intended to do knew how to do it.' Or: 'If someone knows how to do something, then it will be no accident if her trying to do it should be her actually doing it.'[21]

When Stanley argues that a full sentence must stand in place of an infinitival construction following 'tries' or 'wants' 'or 'intends', he takes 'try' as his test case. In accordance with the consensual view, 'John tried to win the race' is to be written 'John tried PRO to win the race', and according to the propositional theory which Stanley endorses, this is to be understood as saying 'John stands in the trying relation to a proposition about John'.[22] Really? It is hard not to notice that 'stands in relation to' is mismatched for tense with 'tried': perhaps Stanley meant to write 'John *stood* in the trying relation to'. But how are we to understand the putative proposition to

---

take the representation of first person thought to be a topic in its own right which can be explored otherwise than by fathoming English syntax.

[21]   Stanley says that 'No commitments about the meaning of infinitivals are needed to defend the view that knowing how to do something is a species of propositional knowledge' (*Know How*, 71). In order to separate his defence of his view about infinitivals from his defence of his propositionalism about knowing how to, Stanley presents a schema whose validity he claims suffices for demonstrating that knowing how to do something is knowing something to be the case. But he does not say how the schema – which has 'knows how to ф' on one side, 'knows that' on the other, and 'iff' between – might itself be defended. (I note that however the schema might be supposed to be supported, it relies upon the idea that if a way to do something is known, then a proposition about that way is known.)

[22]   J. Stanley, *Know How*, 76.

which John stands, or stood, in relation? It is about John, and it is expressed with a sentence whose subject is 'PRO' referring back to John. One wants to know what is *predicated* in the sentence. The only clue Stanley gives as to how 'win the race' is to be inflected for tense or otherwise made finite is given when he treats a different sentence and speaks of 'assuming that the meaning of the infinitive "to win" … is equivalent to the modal "will"'.[23] But suppose now that John *has* won the race: that which he tried to do, he did. In that case, it would seem that the proposition about John to which John stood in 'the trying relation' is one to which he also stood in a 'doing relation'. But 'John won the race' surely does not say that John stands in relation to a proposition about John.

It is not surprising that we are at a loss to know what proposition it could possibly be to which someone stands in relation by virtue of trying, or having tried, to do something. There are no intelligible sentences of the form 'She is trying that—' or 'She tried that—' from which to seek illumination. It might be thought that 'try to' is somehow to be exempted from the usual treatment of infinitives. 'She intends that—' is intelligible; and so perhaps is 'She wants that—' (or at least 'She wants it that—'). Perhaps then a philosopher can join the linguists' consensus about infinitival constructions but set 'try to' aside as somehow exceptional.

It is true that English (even if not other languages) allows the construction 'intends that —'. Still, the view about 'intending to —' which is the counterpart view of Stanley's view of trying can hardly be in better standing than Stanley's view of trying. For 'intend to' and 'want to' share with 'try to' the feature that makes a difficulty for the idea that there is some proposition to which one stands in relation by virtue of one's trying to do something. That which one may intend to do or want to do, like that which one may try to do, one may also simply do. Mary, who intends to eat the whole pie, is doing what she intends if she is eating the pie, and she will have done what she intended when she has finished it off. But eating the pie, even eating it until it's finished, is surely not a proposition. ('Mary ate the whole pie' expresses a proposition. But *that* Mary ate the whole pie is not what Mary did.) The fact that one may do what one intends to do apparently makes a problem about taking the 'to do' of 'intend to do' as holding a place for a proposition.

I think that this is a genuine problem. I want to show that it infects the view of intention held by Williamson. Williamson's view is present in a paper which explores an analogy between knowledge

---

[23]   J. Stanley, *Know How*, 76.

and action by pursuing an analogy between belief and intention. I shan't here be concerned either with the analogies or with Williamson's general view of the practical: I attend exclusively to the account of intention there. The account evidently derives from views about sentence structure found in the sort of contemporary linguistic theory he first applied to the case of 'knowing how' in his paper with Stanley. This is the theory which I think can only lead a philosopher of action astray.

5.

On the face of it, Williamson's analogy between belief and intention is hindered by the fact that declarative sentences ordinarily follow the word 'believe' but don't ordinarily follow the word 'intend'. On the face of it, to compare the contents of beliefs with the contents of intentions is not to compare like with like. The point is slightly obscured, thanks to Williamson's giving the name of verb phrases both to phrases that contain finite verbs such as 'melted the butter' and to infinitival verb phrases such as 'to melt the butter'. But however that may be, Williamson thinks that there is no real hindrance. He says that if 'intend' is followed by a verb phrase, 'the verb phrase still needs a subject'. And '[I]n "one intends to ɸ", the unpronounced implicit subject of "to ɸ" is mandatorily co-referential with "one"'. Here word Williamson shows himself as signed up to the consensus that infinitival constructions following such words as 'intend' are expressions of *de se* attitudes. Thus Williamson takes the syntax of the sentence 'John intends to have a drink' to be given when it is written 'Joe$_i$ intends PRO$_i$ to have a drink'. The English version of this is: 'Joe intends himself to have a drink'.

Williamson acknowledges that one might be bothered by a mismatch between the words we actually use in attributing intentions and those we should use if we stuck to the letter of his account. We simply don't say 'She intends herself to so-and-so' when she intends to so-and-so. Williamson's response is to provide an explanation of the difference between the normal sounding 'Joe intends to have a drink' and the abnormal sounding 'Joe intends himself to have a drink'. He says that the difference between them 'is a non-semantic conversational effect, predictable on quite general grounds... If a speaker envisaged a normal case of Joe intending to have a drink, then going to the trouble of adding the redundant word "himself" would be pointless and prolix, thereby violating Grice's conversational maxim of manner.' Well, this obviously cuts no ice with

Jennifer Hornsby

someone who questions the syntactic theory, and who thinks that 'to have a drink' as it follows 'intends' lacks a subject. Doubting that infinitival verb phrases always need a subject, she thinks that 'himself' is simply absent from 'Joe intends to have a drink'.

Williamson speaks of finding no evidence against the 'assumption that the objects of intentions are as propositional as the objects of belief'. But he needs more evidence in its favour. If the assumption were correct, then not only would a subject be implicit in 'to have a drink' but something would be predicated of that subject. Yet Williamson, no more than Stanley, tells us how 'to have a drink' is to be made into something predicable of 'PRO'/'himself'. A simple way to move from 'intend to have a drink' to 'intend himself that —' would be to say Joe intends that himself have a drink'. But insofar as 'have a drink' is here subjunctive, no proposition is expressed by 'Himself have a drink'.[24] Is it then that Joe intends that himself be having a drink, or that himself will be having a drink, or that himself will have had a drink? Less implausible than any of those perhaps is that Joe intends that himself *will* have a drink. But suppose that Joe has just now finished having a drink: he intended to have one, his intention didn't lapse, and it is just now fulfilled. That which he intended can hardly now be that he himself *will* have a drink (although I suppose Joe might already have decided to have another drink).

And there is more at issue than whether ordinary ways of talking count against his assumption that intentions have propositional objects. Williamson writes as follows about the success conditions for intentions:

> [T]he success condition for an intention to bring it about that P is that one brings it about that P, not merely that somehow or other P. If you intend to open the door, but the wind blows it open before you can get there, your intention failed, because you did not do what you intended to do.

Two points about the 'to bring it about that *p*' here are striking. (1) It is infinitival, so that Williamson has departed from his official view, perhaps because of the difficulty there is about manufacturing a propositional intention out of one expressed with an infinitive. (2) It introduces 'bring about', so that 'to open the door' is equated with 'to bring it about that the door is open'. Of course there is

---

[24]   I assume that one needs a truth-evaluable sentence, with an indicative verb, to express a proposition. That assumption appears to be in place in Williamson when he seeks 'a declarative sentence' in place of a verb phrase so as to have intentions' contents match those of beliefs.

something right about what Williamson says. Very certainly if the door *is* open (at a time) you cannot fulfil an intention you have to open it (then). And if the wind blows the door open, then the wind's action is very likely to put a stop to your intention. If *you* intend to open the door, there can be no question of the wind fulfilling *your* intention. Indeed when Williamson allows that you may or may not do what you intended to do, he seems to recognize that you will fulfil your intention to open the door only if you open the door. And if you are able simply to open the door, then you would have no need to intend *to bring it about that* the door is open. When it comes to an intention to bring it about that *p*, it seems impossible to say anything general about what might need simply to be done in order for the intention to have succeeded. The certain thing is that no-one can intend to bring anything about unless she is able to simply do some things intentionally. It seems impossible then that someone should ever have intended to bring anything about unless there were things she could both intend to do and was able simply to do. So the fact that propositions are not the kind of things one is able simply to do matters. It ensures that 'intend that —' could not possibly always record what is said with 'intend to ɸ'.

6.

I want finally to come full circle. I haven't gone into very much detail about the treatment of sentences containing 'know how' and 'intend' that Stanley and Williamson provide on the strength of current linguistic theories. But I've only meant to put aspects of their treatment in question. In §1, I suggested that when one attends to the knowledge how which is actually exercised in doing something intentionally, one won't think that an account of such knowledge could be got from attending to the grammar of sentences used when knowledge how to do something is ascribed to someone. And so I think it is for an account of intention. Williamson writes 'Sometimes, even though one ɸs and intends to ɸ, one does not intentionally ɸ. A would-be assassin may accidentally run over and kill the man he intends to kill, without intentionally killing him.' Indeed. It could be that the explanation why the would-be assassin did not intentionally kill his intended victim is that the knowledge how he exercised when he accidentally ran him over was not knowledge how to kill *him*. This explanation is in keeping with Stanley and Williamson's own (IAK).

Jennifer Hornsby

Appendix

I've raised questions both for Stanley and for Williamson about how verbs are supposed to give way to predicates when infinitival clauses are transmuted into something propositional. One reason, I suspect, why we don't find an answer to these questions is that no consideration is given to the behaviour of the *verbs* whose infinitives occur in sentences they wish to treat. This comes out, I think, when Stanley considers a rival to his own propositionalist approach to 'intend to' 'try to' and 'want to'.[25]

The rival Stanley considers he calls a predicational approach. On that approach, 'try', 'want' and 'intend' are 'essentially relations to *properties*'. And Stanley thinks that there is something going for the predicational approach *prima facie*. He says that it explains why a certain inference should be 'intuitively valid' – an inference he sets out as follows:

> (P1) John tried PRO to win the race.
> (P2) Everything John tried, Sue tried.
> (C) Sue tried PRO to win the race.

The first question must be whether we do have something *intuitive* here at all. Do we even understand (P1), which purports to contain a sentence following 'tried' lacking any predicate? Might we be allowed to consider the English sentence 'John tried to win the race', which we do understand? When this is allowed, the sentence which in conjunction with it will deliver the conclusion that Sue tried to win the race will be 'Sue tried to do everything that John tried to do'. And here we've surely recorded the inference that Stanley took to stand in need of explanation.

There is a different sort of inference for which Stanley's own (P2) is well suited. It's an inference exemplified in the move from (B1) and (B2) to C**.

> (B1) John tried the Pecorino.
> (B2) Everything [on the cheeseboard] John tried, Sue tried.
> (C**) Sue tried the Pecorino.

Stanley evidently fails to distinguish 'try' as it is followed by (e.g.) 'to win the race' and 'try' as it is followed by (e.g.) 'the Pecorino'. It appears that he fails to see that 'try' takes complements of two different sorts. Not only that: he relies upon his readers failing to see that 'want' likewise takes two (at least). When he makes his case for his own propositionalism, Stanley says that it alone can explain the invalidity of the argument from (1C) and (2C) to (3)

> (1C) John wants to become a doctor.
> (2C) John's mother wants everything John wants.
> (3) John's mother wants to become a doctor.

---

[25]   J. Stanley, *Know How*, 76–80.

But this argument is very obviously invalid. And its invalidity is easily explained: (1C) has an infinitive; but (2C) cannot be heard as saying that John's mother wants *to do* everything that John wants to do: in (2C) the 'everything' would never be understood as quantifying over things that are such as to be *done*.

On the predicational approach that Stanley treats as a rival to his own, the 'everything' of his (P2) quantifies over *properties*. (P1) is then supposed to amount to 'John stands in the trying relation to the property λx(x wins the race)'. Well, a property is surely not the object of 'try' in 'Someone tried to do something'. It is true that someone might be said to try *to have* a property. If Sammy tried to be quiet, for instance, then the property of being quiet (*had* by one who is quiet) might be said to be something that Sammy tried to have. Stanley, however, was not dealing with 'to be quiet' but with 'to win the race'. And *win the race* is not something one might try *to have*, although it is something one might try *to do*.

Even though the idea that an 'everything' might introduce quantification over anything except for properties is not on Stanley's horizon, he nonetheless acknowledges the need to insert an elided 'to do' in his (P2). He says that both his own propositional approach and the predicational approach need 'special pleading' to justify the introduction of 'to do'. But no special pleading is needed when it is recognized that properties, unlike things that may be done, are such as to had, and that things a person may do, unlike properties, are such as to be done. Stanley follows the linguists in speaking only of properties. But a difference between properties and things that may be done has to be recognized if it's allowed that the tense and aspectual behaviour of what is predicated must be brought into account.

One starts to see a difference between properties and things people do when one appreciates that whereas a property is such that the following can be said of how it stands to an object: will be had by (in the future), is had by (presently), was had by (in the past), a thing a person may do is such that all of the following can be said of how it stands to a person: will be being done by **or** will have been done by (in the future), is being done by (presently), has been being done by **or** has been done by (in the past). (I note that I don't suggest that predication should be explained in terms of the having of properties or the doing of doable things, but only that differences in possibilities of predication should be recognized.)

Thanks to what he takes to be special pleading, Stanley allows himself to write (P2) as (P2*):

(P2*) Everything John tried PRO to do, Sue tried PRO to do.

And at the end of the day, it is (P2*) which is supposed to reveal John as 'standing in the trying relation' to a proposition about John. Which proposition is never specified, as I said in the text. When one finds oneself at a loss to discover anything predicable of PRO, one can't help but wonder why 'PRO' should have made an appearance at the start, in Stanley's (P1). At any rate, the 'PRO's which Stanley introduced magically disappear when Stanley comes to his evaluation of the predicational approach.

When the 'PRO's disappear from the account, one is bound to wonder why they should ever have been introduced. Consider Stanley's argument for a propositional, rather than predicational reading of his (15).

(15) 'John wants [PRO to become a doctor], but his mother doesn't want that'.

Stanley says 'what John's mother doesn't want is that John becomes a doctor, where the 'that'-clause clearly denotes a proposition about John'. But suppose that the 'PRO' had never been inserted. Instead of (15), one would have "John wants to become a doctor, but his mother doesn't want him to'. This would be the natural thing to say, I take it. And Stanley makes no case for the *de se* pronouns independently of subscribing to the theories in which they are introduced.

Williamson claims that any difference between his 'Joe intends himself to φ' and the English 'Joe intends to φ' is explained in pragmatics (§5). Will he say that 'Joe believes himself to be clever' means the same as the unsayable sentence 'Joe believes to be clever'?

In the matter of 'knowing how', Stanley also recognizes a rival to his own propositionalism. He says 'The alternative view of knowing how treats knowing how to do something as a relation to an activity rather than as a relation to a question meaning' (141). Here he forgets that one might be said not only (e.g.) to know how to swim (an activity) but also (e.g.) to know how to swim to the far shore (an act). An 'activity', Stanley says 'is presumably just a property' (146). I think that Stanley's assimilation of verbs to predicates expressing properties stands in the way of his seeing what the possible viable treatments of 'know how to —' might be. But there is another reason why Stanley fails to take seriously what he thinks of as 'the' alternative to his own propositionalism. He thinks that an account of 'know how to' must go hand in hand with an account of 'know when to', 'know where to', etc., and he imagines that someone who wanted to defend any alternative to his own account would confine themselves to an account specifically of 'know *how* to'. But someone who thought that 'How to φ?' could be so to speak a subject-less question (a question one could put to oneself without making actual mention of oneself) would want to allow that there are other such questions: 'Whom to show this to?', 'When to stop arguing?', 'Where to go next?'.

Birkbeck College, University of London
Centre for the Study of Mind in Nature, Oslo
j.hornsby@bbk.ac.uk

The Doing and the Deed: Action in Normative Ethics

CONSTANTINE SANDIS

Abstract

This essay is motivated by the thought that the things we do are to be distinguished from our acts of doing them. I defend a particular way of drawing this distinction before proceeding to demonstrate its relevance for normative ethics. Central to my argument is the conviction that certain ongoing debates in ethical theory begin to dissolve once we disambiguate the two concepts of action in question. If this is right, then the study of action should be accorded a far more prominent place within moral philosophy than previously supposed. I end by considering an extension of the above to aesthetic evaluation and, *mutatis mutandis*, that of our lives in general.

Prologue

There exists a contested distinction within the philosophy of action which entails that the correct evaluation of what one does or creates may part ways with that of one's act of doing or creating it.[1] Drawn correctly, this distinction is of utmost importance to questions in ethical theory, and how we generally evaluate our actions and lives. Or so I shall be arguing.

Attempts to relate philosophy of action to ethics have tended to focus on agency, responsibility, free will, and other questions in moral psychology, the latter now treated as a separate and increasingly empirical branch of ethics. This is not that project. There are additional ethical questions which the philosophy of action is in a position to address, not least debates in normative and practical ethics about the nature of right action.[2] A particular case in point is the interminable debate between consequentialists, deontologists, and

---

[1] One might additionally distinguish between acts and actions but this wouldn't affect anything I have to say here. For a puzzling attempt to map the act/action distinction onto that between doing and thing done see David Wiggins, *Ethics: Twelve Lectures on the Philosophy of Morality* (Cambridge, MA: Harvard University Press, 2006), 97, n.8.

[2] For complications that need not detain us here see Brad Hooker, *Ideal Code, Real World* (Oxford: Clarendon Press, 2000) 1, n.2.

doi:10.1017/S1358246117000121 ©The Royal Institute of Philosophy and the contributors 2017
Royal Institute of Philosophy Supplement **80** 2017

Constantine Sandis

virtue-theorists on the potential relevance of person's motives and intentions to the rightness or wrongness of her acts.

The questions of action, intention, and motive I shall focus on are usually identified as belonging to moral psychology. To this extent, it is regrettable that the latter has branched off in a way that has encouraged philosophers to think that such questions do not belong in normative ethics. This is one of two unintended and unforeseen consequences of Anscombe's revolutionary paper 'Modern Moral Philosophy', published in this journal almost sixty years ago.[3] The second involves the creation of normative virtue ethics as a separate position within moral theory, one to be adopted by *all and only* those who think that questions of character matter to right action.[4]

In what follows I resist both trends by relating conceptual and ontological questions about action to normative ethics. We may characterise this method as *applied* philosophy of action, so long as such a thing leaves space for a kind of analytic deconstruction of moral theory.

1. Ambiguity in Action

Someone interested in action might wish to explore a number of distinct things such as how the word 'action' is used, our concept(s) of action, different conceptions of action, and empirical findings about actions themselves. In each case there are numerous distinctions to be made and different ways of carving things up. I shall focus on just one of these, namely the conceptual distinction between *what* one does and one's *doing* (of) it. There are radically different ways of understanding this distinction. Indeed, those who appeal to it, myself included, express such a wide range of competing conceptions of each of the two things distinguished that it is legitimate to wonder whether they are really all making the same distinction. I begin by quoting from three influential approaches, in chronological order.

John Macmurray writes the following in an *Aristotelian Society* exchange with A.C. Ewing on the nature of actions:

---

[3] G. E. M. Anscombe, 'Modern Moral Philosophy', *Philosophy* **33** (124) Jan (1958), 1–9. Anscombe's own failure to distinguish between doings and things done is a topic for another paper.

[4] See Rosalind Hursthouse, 'Normative Virtue Ethics', in (ed.) R. Crisp, *How Should One Live?* (Oxford University Press, 1996), 19–33.

The term 'action' is involved in the same ambiguity [as] terms like 'perception' or 'conception'. It may refer either to what is done or to the doing of it [...] either 'doing' or 'deed'. When we talk of an action we are normally referring to what is done.[5]

Leaving aside the final claim about ordinary language, the idea here is that the word 'action' is not in any way special for being ambiguous in this regard. Macmurray's distinction is presented as a formal one that may presumably also be extended to additional psychological phenomena such as those of belief, desire, fear, suspicion, thought, etc. In effect, it is a basic logical distinction between a kind of process or activity on the one hand, and its product, content, or object on the other (things which should themselves resist conflation). We don't do our own doings anymore than we fear our own fearings or suspect our own suspectings.[6]

Paul Ricœur extends this scope of interest to speech and writing:

What in effect does writing fix? Not the event of speaking [...] it is speech itself insofar as it is *said* [...] To what extent may we say that what is *done* is inscribed? [...] in a metaphorical way, some actions are events that imprint their mark on their time.[7]

In the case of writing, the distinction comes closer to that between a *process* and its resulting *product*. Ricœur is suggesting that we might, by extension, hold the same to be true of the speaking and the thing said and, *a forteriori*, the doing and the thing done.[8] He is aware that his suggestion contains the difficulty that, when all is said and done, these things do not remain in the world in the literal way that things written might; they are not carved in stone, or even paper. And yet, Ricœur reminds us, our events of acting – a subset of which are speech-act events – may nonetheless leave imprints or traces of a biographical, psychological, historical, cultural, or empirical nature.[9]

[5]   John Macmurray, 'What is Action?', *Proceedings of the Aristotelian Society*, Supp. Vol. **XVII** (1938), 74–6.
[6]   See Alan R. White, 'What We Believe' in (ed.) N. Rescher, *Studies in the Philosophy of Mind* (Oxford: Blackwell, 1972), 69–84.
[7]   Paul Ricœur, *From Text to Action*, trns. K. Blamey & J. Evanston (London: Continuum, 2008 [1986]), 142–9.
[8]   For the philosophy of what we are doing when we say things, see Jennifer Mather Saul, *Lying, Misleading, and What is Said: An Exploration in the Philosophy of Language and Ethics* (Oxford: Oxford University Press, 2012).
[9]   For Ricœur's development of Levinas and Derrida's theories of the trace see his *La Mémoire, l'Histoire, l'Oubli* (Paris: Éditions du Seuil, 2000).

Constantine Sandis

This thought of actions as *events* connects with Jennifer Hornsby's way of framing the distinction as one between (i) the spatio-temporally located events of our doing things and (ii) the things we do, the second admitting to being done by different agents across more than one location or occasion, including the possible future as in Lenin's *What is to be Done?*:

> The word 'action' is ambiguous. Where it has a plural: in ordinary usage what it denotes, nearly always, are the things people do; in philosophical usage, what it denotes, very often, are events, each one of them some person's doing something.[10]

Like Macmurray, Hornsby takes our ordinary talk of action to typically denote things done. My own view is that in everyday language the term 'thing done' is itself multiply ambiguous, much as we might use the expression 'soup' in any of the following assertions: 'the soup is always great at *Gino's*'; tonight's soup is very good'; and 'your soup looks nicer than mine (even though they presumably come from the same kitchen batch)'. Such ambiguities account for much conflation in the philosophy of action, if not that of Donald Davidson who, misled by the Quinean dream of desert landscapes, provides a systematic argument for why all action statements quantify over events.[11] The trouble is that there exists conceptual space for a distinction that is only partially mirrored in our ordinary use of the terms 'doing' and 'thing done', the latter frequently being used rather liberally, as in 'the hardest thing I ever did'.

All analogies sooner or later come to an end, of course. What I do is neither the *product* nor the *content* of my doing. Nor is it an object in the way that the things I perceive, such as the records on the table, are. Deeds are not entities of any kind, be they type or token. Accordingly, we must take my soup comparisons with a pinch of salt: what I do is not the same sort of thing as what I ate or hope to eat[12], not even in the Proustian sense in which I might lament that the rusty bicycle in the garden shed is not as bright or green as the one in my memory.[13]

[10]   Jennifer Hornsby, *Simple Mindedness* (Cambridge, MA: Harvard University Press, 1997), 142.
[11]   Donald Davidson, 'The Logical Form of Action Sentences' (1967); reprinted in his *Essays on Actions & Events*, 2nd ed. (Oxford: Clarendon Press, 2001), 105–21.
[12]   See Hans-Johann Glock, 'Truth Without People?', *Philosophy* **72** (1997), 98. I discuss the individuation of things done in *The Things We Do and Why We Do Them* (London: Palgrave Macmillan, 2012), 34 & 150.
[13]   As the narrator of *In Search of Lost Time* puts it in the volume's closing passage, '[t]he places we have known do not belong only to the

Moreover, it is at best contentious to assume that the 'of' in 'the event of my doing x' is one of identity (as in 'the county of Hertfordshire') as opposed to, say, relation (as in 'the University of Hertfordshire').[14]

Unsurprisingly, we find competing ontologies of doings and things done in the literature, with little consensus on whether the former are particulars, events, processes, instances of relations etc., and the latter universals, types, results, products, and so on.[15] For now, however, I merely wish to highlight a more general agreement on the basic distinction between particular doings and repeatable things that you and I might both do.[16] We might, for example, both listen to Leonard Cohen's *You Want it Darker* again and again, with each of our singular, spatio-temporally located, acts of doing so differing in their properties: you play the MP3 as background on your iPod during your morning jogs and in the afternoons as you drive home from work; I listen to the LP attentively in the evenings by my fireplace at home, a glass of burgundy in hand.[17]

---

world of space on which we map them for our own convenience. They were only a thin slice, held between the contiguous impressions that composed our life at the time [...] houses, roads, avenues are as fugitive, alas, as the years', Proust, *Swann's Way* [1913], 513.

[14] *The Things We Do*, 8 & 33.

[15] Just as there are different conceptions of the basic distinction between doings and things done, so there are different conceptions of each of the two things distinguished; the latter may differ even when there is agreement on the former.

[16] Not everybody conceives of the doing/thing done distinction in even these general terms. For example, H.A. Prichard, G.H. von Wright, and David Charles all think of the thing done as the bodily event that action results in; see Prichard's 'Duty and Ignorance of Fact' (1932) as reprinted in his *Moral Writings*, (ed.) J. MacAdam (Oxford: Clarendon Press, 2004, 85), G.H. von Wright *Norm and Action* (London: Routledge & Kegan Paul, 1963, 39) and D. Charles 'Processes, Activities and Actions' in (ed.) R. Stout, *Process, Action and Experience* (Oxford University Press, forthcoming).

[17] We could, of course, contract sets of things done to include such details, but not beyond the bounds of generality. For complications to do with properties and descriptions see Davidson, 'The Logical Form of Action Sentences', 106 & 'Adverbs of Action' (1985), reprinted in his *Essays on Actions & Events*, 293–304.

Constantine Sandis

2. Right and Wrong Action

Despite the relative prevalence of the above distinction in the philosophy of action, it is all but completely ignored in normative theories concerned with right action. These are typically in the business of offering necessary and sufficient conditions of the form 'an action is right if (and only if) it...' where the blanks may be filled by statements such as 'promotes the greatest good', 'maximises pleasure', 'stems from a good will', 'is what the virtuous agent would (advise you to) do', 'is prescribed by divine command', and so on.[18] But moral theorists rarely stop to ask conceptual questions about action, sticking to the bare minimum needed to deal with the act/omission distinction and the doctrine of double effect.[19] The unvoiced assumption is that one can simply plug in one's favoured account of action, the dominating consensus having largely been that actions are events. I maintain that this assumption lies at the core of what renders debates within normative ethics irresolvable.

To illustrate, I present some concise claims about right action, chosen randomly from across the normative spectrum. The first comes from Jesse Prinz's defence of sentimentalism about moral rightness and wrongness:

> An action has the property of being morally right (wrong) just in case it causes feelings of approbation (disapprobation) in normal observers under certain conditions.[20]

Notice how actions are here understood as the sorts of things that can have moral properties, but there is no mention (and you will have to trust me that this is so throughout his book) about whether he is here thinking of a doing or a thing done. The sentence gives us some clues: it is the sort of thing that may be observed and 'cause feelings'; to this extent sound more like a *doing* than a thing done. Either way, the view is meant to be in competition with other accounts of right action which also fail to disambiguate.

---

[18]   Andreas Lind has convinced me that the employment of such biconditionals is often confused with regard to whether they are picking out meanings, right-makers, truth-conditions, etc.

[19]   Neglected exceptions include E. D'Arcy's *Human Acts: An Essay in their Moral Evaluation* (Oxford: Clarendon Press, 1963) and D.G. Brown's *Action* (London: George Allen & Unwin, 1968).

[20]   Jesse Prinz, *The Emotional Construction of Morals* (Oxford University Press, 2007), 20.

Writing about moral obligation, H.A. Prichard claims that:

An obligation is always an obligation *to do* some action.[21]

So long as I *do* the action in question, I have fulfilled my obligation, whatever my motive. This is why W.D. Ross, following Prichard, will ultimately claim that moral rightness should be distinguished from moral goodness.[22] The question remains, however, whether I can be said to be acting wrongly merely by virtue of doing the wrong thing. Jonathan Bennett seems to not only think that this is so but that it is a basic semantic truth:

When we say that *what he did* was wrong we mean that *he acted wrongly*.[23]

Yet *acting wrongly* is at best itself ambiguous between doing the wrong thing and doing some thing (right or wrong) for the wrong reasons or out of a wrong motive.[24] One might think that killing, lying, cheating, or murder are all wrong. Such thoughts seem to be about act-types to the extent that it entails that all particular acts of killing etc. are wrong. If Eevee kills Jolene and we think that *what she did* was wrong in the sense of 'thing done' delineated in §1 (*viz.* kill someone) then the wrong thing done is something that Ceddy could have also done. Indeed, Ceddy could have even killed the very same person (Jolene), though it is too late now that Eevee has done so.

If this is so, then it cannot matter what Eevee or Ceddy's motives are for it cannot be the case that 'kill someone' is a wrong thing done when Eevee does it but not when Ceddy does it, at least not systematically so according to any of the normative theories on offer.[25] By contrast, Eevee's killing of Jolene on Monday morning may be a vicious act motivated by jealousy, whereas Ceddy's possible killing

---

[21]   H.A. Prichard, 'Duty and Ignorance of Fact', 95, my emphasis. Prichard's view of what sorts of things we are obliged to do would later change radically upon his embracing the conclusion that to act is to perform a mental activity of some kind (*viz.* to will something); see 'Acting, Willing, Desiring' (1945) in his *Moral Writings*, 272–81.
[22]   In §5 I argue that Ross makes this point in a strikingly paradoxical manner precisely because he lacks the doing/thing done distinction.
[23]   Jonathan Bennett, *The Act Itself* (Oxford: Oxford University Press, 1995), 46, my emphasis.
[24]   Both are, of course, to be distinguished from doing something in the wrong way or manner, such as when one goes about doing something without the appropriate skill or know-how.
[25]   Moral particularism might be an exception here, at least if the particularist is willing to distinguish between type and token things done (see §4).

Constantine Sandis

of her on Monday evening (say after Simon's botched attempt) would have been an act of mercy.

Similarly, for right actions: Eevee and Ceddy may both give the same amount of money and/or the percentage of their income (two different things which may coincide to the British Hen Welfare Trust). But suppose that Eevee's doing so *just is* her trying to impress Simon, whereas Ceddy does so in order to help rescue battery hens. In such a case. Eevee and Ceddy each do two things, only one of which is the same (give money to the British Hen Welfare Trust). Eevee's doing this one thing just *is* her showing off and, similarly, Ceddy's doing it is identical to his trying to help rescue battery hens. Whilst the thing done may or may not be the right thing to do, it would seem that Ceddy is acting rightly (or at least well)[26] whereas Eevee is not.

There seems, then, to be a huge difference between claims concerning a person's doing something, and claims about the rightness or wrongness of *what* they did. Once we become attuned to this, certain disputes within normative theory begin to dissolve. Recall the debate over whether or not intention matters to right action. If two or more people can do the same thing with different intentions, it is unclear how intention could possibly matter to the rightness or wrongness of the thing that they both do.[27] Conversely, it is highly implausible that intention doesn't matter to the moral evaluation of each individual's *doing* of this thing. It is hard not to conclude from this that the notion of right action most amenable to virtue ethics is different from that which is of interest to consequentialists.

While I have chiefly been focusing on motive and intention, the moral appraisal of our doings will also depend upon biographical information relating to upbringing, ability, education, circumstance, and more. Such facts may individually or collectively reveal that a person was acting rightly or (at least justifiably)[28] when they did the wrong thing, and wrongly (or unjustifiably) when they did the right thing.

None of this is to say that there is no connection between descriptions of our doings and the things that we do. On the contrary, one can act with the best of intentions and still be acting wrongly even if the action is not intentional under the negative description. An

---

[26]   I return to the evaluative/deontic distinction in §5.

[27]   The case of speech-acts in which two people utter the same words but with different meanings highlights a wider truth concerning the significance of *all* the things we do.

[28]   See §5.

act intending to pay tribute to another culture, for example, may nonetheless be an instance of cultural appropriation. For everything one does unintentionally, there will be a relevant description of their doing it. But there are no hard and fast rules by which we can decide which doings remain praiseworthy, permissible, or excusable, and which do not.

Often, it can take years or centuries before we are in a position to fully understand what had been done. In such cases, we must be lenient on the doing without becoming relativists about the thing done. Consider the well-trodden debates on whether or not it would be anachronistic to judge 19th century racism and slavery from a 21st century standpoint. The answer, I contend, is that while *things done* centuries ago were as wrong then as they would be if done now, past *doings* may be more forgivable, and at times even justified (precise judgements of past *doings* would need to be formed on a case by case basis).[29]

3. Inner and Outer Lives

I have been arguing that there is an important but neglected difference between what it is for *a thing one does* to be right or wrong and for *one's doing* it to be right or wrong. This lends itself to the response, alluded to in my Prologue, that those interested in the doing, motive, intention, etc. subscribe to virtue theory, thereby embracing just one normative position among many, and that other views – in competition with it – simply deny the importance of such things to right action, if not to morality altogether.[30] Such points are sometimes put forward as criticisms of virtue ethics being *agent*-centred (as opposed to *action*-centred) and thereby either failing to provide a theory of right action or offering one whose focus is misplaced. Thus, even someone as sympathetic to the concerns of virtue ethics as Martha Nussbaum criticises Iris Murdoch for being too obsessed with the agent's psychology to care about action:

---

[29]   Hence Luke 22:33–4, which could be alluding to multiple actions, from killing the son of God to giving birth to the Christian religion: 'And when they came to the place that is called The Skull, there they crucified him, and the criminals, one on his right and one on his left. And Jesus said, "Father, forgive them, for they know not what they do."'

[30]   The latter view is implicitly endorsed in Derek Parfit's *On What Matters* (Oxford: Oxford University Press, 2011).

> Murdoch is so preoccupied with the goings-on of the inner world
> that she seems almost to have forgotten about the difference that
> action can make [...] commitment to action can make the differ-
> ence to people who are suffering, no matter whether the agents'
> intentions are pure.[31]

Nussbaum is here completely separating action from intention,
thereby implicitly running with a 'thing done' notion of action.
The move is akin to thinking that since Eevee gave 20% of her
salary to the British Hen Welfare Trust, we should not be morally
distracted by the fact that she only did it to show off in front of
Simon. What matters, on this outlook, is *what* she did. In the case
at hand, the thing that Eevee did was right since, unlike her inner
motives, it made a good difference in the world. Nussbaum's worry
is that concerns with another's inner world are overly precious and,
in the case of one's own actions, narcissistic. Virtue ethicists such as
Christine Swanton have responded to such criticisms with the following sort of reasoning:

> Rightness, it may be claimed, has nothing to do with an agent's
> motives or reasons, but has exactly to do with success in the ex-
> ternal realm [...] on my view, an act which mimics the action of
> a virtuous agent may be wrong, because *in the hands of the actor*
> it is unvirtuous [...] uncaring or racist.[32]

This response is on the right track, but unless we can enrich it with a
suitable version of the doing/thing done distinction it shall remain as
question-begging as Nussbaum's original objection. The correct
thing to say, I believe, is that while *what* the vicious agent is doing
can be no more (or less) uncaring than what the virtuous agent
does, *her doing it* may well be. Indeed, things done are, in this technical sense the wrong sorts of thing to be caring or uncaring, rash
or prudent, and so on for only an individual person's doings may
be described adverbially.

There is, of course, an ordinary sense of 'what she did' in which we
might say that she did a kind or unkind thing, but all this amounts to
is that her doing of x was unkind, or that she was unkind to do it.[33] If

---

[31] Martha C. Nussbaum, *Philosophical Interventions: 1986–2011*
(Oxford: Oxford University Press, 2011), 269.

[32] Christine Swanton, *Virtue Ethics: A Pluralistic View* (Oxford:
Oxford University Press, 2003), 245.

[33] Macmurray and Hornsby are right to claim that in everyday language
we typically talk of things done, but as noted in §1 this way of speaking is
very loose.

we ignore the conceptual space for this distinction and simply talk of things done as if *they themselves* are re-describable as virtuous or vicious, we will have saved the truth of virtue ethics at the cost of masking the truth of consequence-based views and deontologies (such as some forms of divine-command theory) which appeal to the intrinsic goodness of act-types (as opposed to motives). The truth of these views is that the rightness of what is done does not (indeed *cannot*) depend on the psychology of the agent.

4. Ontologies of Action

At this juncture it might help to delve a little into some of the onto-logical questions I remained neutral upon earlier. Is there any sense in which an event can itself be deemed to be morally right or wrong? And what, if anything, would it be for a universal to be right?

One answer to the first question appeals to Donald Davidson's notion that an action is an event that is intentional under some de-scription. I shall not critique this here, save to say that while it is in-nocuous to say that the event of someone's doing one thing (e.g. playing music) intentionally may be identical to the event of their doing something else (waking up the neighbours) unintentionally, this does not reduce to the far more baffling claim that it is the event *itself* that is intentional under some description(s).

In a rare paper attempting to relate action theory to normative ethics Matthew Hanser resists Davidsonian simplicity as follows:

> We may think of the 'things people do', [...] as act – or behavior – types. A particular person's throwing of a particular baseball on a particular occasion, by contrast, is not an act – or behavior – type. It is a token action, an unrepeatable, particular instantiation of the act-type *throwing a baseball* [...] 'What he did was wrong' concerns some unspecified act-type instantiated by the agent, whereas 'He acted wrongly in doing what he did' concerns the agent's particular instantiation of that act-type.[34]

Hanser's metaphysics seem implausible to me for a number of related reasons: the things we do are not types of action but actions that fall under types. The relation between doings and things done is thus not

[34] Matthew Hanser, 'Actions, Acting, and Acting Well', in (ed.) Russ Shafer-Landau, *Oxford Studies in Metaethics* **3** (2008), 272–3. Cf. Romane Clark, 'Deeds, Doings and What is Done', *Noûs* **23** (2) (1989), 199–210.

Constantine Sandis

one between types and tokens. A doing is not an instance of a thing
done anymore than a believing is an instance of a thing believed,
and there are type and token doings (just as there are type and
token events and processes[35]) as well as type and token things done.
If A kills B this may or may not fall under the type 'killing an adoles-
cent' or 'killing an innocent human'.

A different way of resisting Hanser's approach is to deny that there
is any morally relevant distinction to be made between doings and
things done. An explicit defence of it has been made by Jonathan
Dancy, who writes:

> There should be less of action in our moral metaphysics, not
> more....'he did the right thing for the wrong reason' [...]
> means something like 'he acted rightly, but for the wrong
> reasons'[...]'he V-ed, and in the situation he was right to V,
> but the reasons why he V-ed were not the reasons he was
> right to V' [...] rightness is not a way of acting [...] there is no
> room for the combination of blameless agent and wrong action
> that might force us towards some notion of an action as a distinct
> bearer of evaluative properties.[36]

On Dancy's account, we so conduct all the theoretical work we need
to do with one notion of action, coupled with a narrative about the
agent's reasons. While there is much to agree with in the above
passage, it won't do to say that the person who does the right thing
for the wrong reason(s) is acting *rightly*. After all, she isn't acting virtuously, for it is merely by chance that she is doing the right thing at
all. This point is brought out well in the following passage by
Rosalind Hursthouse:

> [A]ct honestly, charitably, generously; do not act dishonestly,
> etc. [...] the adverbs connote not only doing what the virtuous
> agent would do, but also doing it 'in the way' she would do it,
> which includes 'for the same sort(s) of reason(s)' [...] What is
> misleading about this phrase is that it obscures the fact that, in
> one way, the agent is not 'doing the right thing'. What she is

---

[35] It should already be clear by now that I don't maintain that doings *are*
processes and/or events.

[36] Jonathan Dancy, 'Action in Moral Metaphysics' in (ed.) C. Sandis,
New Essays on Action Explanation (London: Palgrave Macmillan, 2009),
396ff. Cf. his 'Action, Content and Inference' in (eds) H-J. Glock &
J. Hyman, *Wittgenstein and Analytic Philosophy* (Oxford: Oxford
University Press, 2009), 278–98.

doing is, say, trying to impress the onlookers, or hurting someone's feelings, or avoiding punishment.[37]

Hursthouse makes her point without appealing to any form of the doing/
thing done distinction and, *pari passu*, concludes that *what* the vicious
agent is doing is wrong. And indeed, *one* of the things that she has
done is wrong (namely showing off), but she has also done something
quite right (donating to the the British Hen Welfare Trust), albeit for
the wrong reason, as Dancy puts it. Yet the idea that the agent has
done anything right has all but disappeared from Hursthouse's narrative.
Assuming that two people can do the same thing for different reasons, it
can be true that the person acting wrongly is still doing the right thing.
When two or more people do the same thing for different reasons, there
will be huge discrepancies in our evaluation of their doings. We need look
no further than the 69,456,897 people voted for Obama in 2008, and the
plurality of reasons in the offing.

5. Moral Appraisal

Consider the following claim by Thomas Nagel, which forms a
crucial assumption behind his understanding of moral luck:

> We judge people for what they actually do or fail to do [...] a
> person can be morally responsible only for *what he does*.[38]

Implicit in this remark is the identification of all action with the
things we do, as made explicit by Swann in Proust's *In Search of
Lost Time*, a novel fixated with the relation of fleeting particulars to
repeatable universals:

> 'It's not for nothing', he now assured himself, 'that whenever
> people pass judgements on their fellows, it's always for their
> *actions*. It's only *what we do* that counts, and not at all what we
> say or think...'[39]

---

[37] Rosalind Hursthouse, *On Virtue Ethics* (Oxford: Oxford University
Press, 1999), 29 & 125.

[38] Thomas Nagel, 'Moral Luck', in his *Mortal Questions* (Cambridge:
Cambridge University Press, 1979), 146, my emphasis. Nagel explicitly
conflates things done with events in *The View From Nowhere* (Cambridge:
Cambridge University Press, 1986, 114) an observation first made in
Hornsby, *Simple Mindedness*, 143–48.

[39] Marcel Proust, *Swann's Way* [1913], trns. C.K.S. Moncrieff &
T. Kilmartin, rev. d.J. Enright (London: Chatto & Windus 1992), 430,
my emphasis. The set of things we do, of course, includes speaking.

Here we encounter, once more, the idea that we judge others simply by being provided with a list of the things they did. We might call this the obituary view of moral appraisal. It is no wonder that actions so conceived – without mention of the doings that reveal our reasons, motives, and intentions – are so readily susceptible to moral luck.[40] But it would be pretty extreme to deny that we are not to judge them for this. Perhaps this is not Nagel's view and he thinks, with Anscombe, that action descriptions reveal intention. If so, he is conflating the things we do with our doings of them.[41]

Moving further back into the history of deontology, we find the following pronouncement in Kant's second *Critique*:

> Most lawful actions would be done from fear, only a few from hope, and none at all from duty; and the moral worth of actions – on which alone, after all, the worth of the person and even that of the world hinges in the eyes of the highest wisdom – would not exist at all.[42]

It is no surprise that all law, be it divine, social, or moral should primarily focus on things done rather than doings, for it is the fact that one did something that we can provide evidence for in any kind of court.[43] So it is that in Romans 2:6 of the the *New International Version* of the Bible, we are told in God 'will repay each person according to what they have done' (see also Matthew 16:27 and Corinthians 11:15).[44] Kant's insight is that one could do the right

---

[40] It is noteworthy that simple descriptions of things done (e.g. 'lying') may reveal the agent's intention but not their motive.

[41] For independent reasons for thinking that Nagel is guilty of such conflations see Hornsby, *Simple Mindedness* and Sandis, *The Things We Do*.

[42] Immanuel Kant, *Critique of Practical Reason* [1788]; trns & ed. M.J. Gregor & A. Reath (Cambridge: Cambridge University Press, 1997), 5:147. Yet it is events that have consequences (even if we might ordinarily speak of 'the things we do' having consequences).

[43] A complication here is that we can of course find evidence for the occurrence of *events*, which J.L. Austin famously brings close to facts in 'Unfair to Facts' (1954), reprinted in his *Philosophical Papers* (Oxford: Clarendon Press, 1961), 154–74. Those who follow Austin in this critique of P.F. Strawson may prove more inclined to identify things done, and not doings, with events of some kind (see note 15). It should by now be clear that I think that while this temptation should be resisted, we would do equally well to avoid conflating one's doing x with the *event of* one's doing x (it only being sensible to apply moral properties to the former).

[44] Other translations have variants of judge, reward, or render to everyone according to their 'deeds' (*King James*) or 'works' (*English Standard*

thing and yet one's action might still lack moral worth, if done from the wrong motive. Suppose we knew for certain that heaven and hell existed: many of us might then make sure that we did all the right (morally lawful) things, but we would do them from an unethical motive (fear or hope, but never duty).[45] This appreciation of the fact that the moral worth of actions is completely separable from the rightness or wrongness of the things they do, a view shared by his most famous opponent in moral philosophy, John Stuart Mill:

> He who saves a creature from drowning does what is morally right, whether his motive be duty or the hope of being paid for his trouble [...] A right action does not necessarily indicate a virtuous character and [...] actions which are blameable often proceed from qualities entitled to praise.[46]

Kant and Mill form a sharp contrast to the view from Nagel, according to which we are to appraise people for *what* they do, and nothing else.[47] The clash cannot be resolved in either party's favour, for it stems from muddled conceptions of action. In the above passages, Kant and Mill separate the worthiness of actions from their rightness and wrongness, whereas Nagel wishes to align the two.[48] A third solution, proposed by Robert Audi, is that we 'should distinguish the moral worth of an act from its creditworthiness'.[49] But this just

---

Version), the latter being the more accurate translation of the Greek 'ἔργα' and the Hebrew 'שַׂהֲמַעֲ' found in many of the Old Testament Parallels (Job 34:11, Psalm 62:12, Proverbs 24:1, Ecclesiastes 3:17, Jeremiah 17:10, and Ezekiel 18:20 & 36:19; cf. Exodus 32:34).

[45] For a deflationist interpretation of what Kant means by the motive of duty see Onora O'Neill, 'Kantian Ethics' in (ed.) P. Singer, *A Companion to Ethics* (Oxford: Blackwell, 1991), 183.

[46] J.S. Mill, *Utilitarianism*, 1863 (London: Parker, Son & Bourn), 18–20. This is in tension with those aspects of Mill's philosophy that seem to require actions to be events with causes and effects.

[47] Hegel famously talks of the history's progress from the ancient ethical concern with pure objective deed (*Tat*) to the modern interest in the subjective element of action (*Handlung*). For how this relates to my concerns in this paper see my 'The Man Who Mistook his Handlung for a Tat', *Bulletin of the Hegel Society of Great Britain* **62** (2010), 35–60.

[48] Cf. T.M. Scanlon *Moral Dimensions: Permissibility, Meaning, Blame* (New Jersey: Harvard University Press, 2008), esp. 122–7 & 151–9.

[49] Robert Audi, *The Good in the Right: A Theory of Intuition and Intrinsic Value* (Princeton, NJ: Princeton University Press, 2004), 133.

digs deeper into the same conceptual pit. The way out is not to pile on further distinctions but to understand that between the things we do and our acts of doing them.[50]

A neat way of proceeding is to attempt to map the distinction onto that between evaluative and deontic concepts and norms, the former being concerned with praise or blame (good and bad), the latter with duty and obligation (right and wrong).[51] So conceived, the doing would be the bearer of moral worth and the things done that of rightness and wrongness.[52] While not an altogether unhelpful move, it leaves one wondering why our doings cannot be morally right or wrong and, conversely, whether there might be things done that are in themselves good or bad (e.g. acts of kindness of charity).[53]

No discussion of the distinction between the right and good would be complete without mention of the pluralistic deontology of Ross, who brings out the extremely paradoxical nature of maintaining, alongside Kant, that the right action may be morally worthless:

> [N]othing that ought to be done is ever morally good [...] the only acts that are morally good are those that proceed from a good motive...If, then, we can show that action from a good motive is never morally obligatory, we shall have established that what is morally good is never right...That action from a good motive is never obligatory follows from the Kantian principle [...] that 'I ought' implies 'I can'. It is not the case that I can by choice produce a certain motive [...] if we contemplate a right act alone, it is seen to have no intrinsic *value* [...] however carelessly I pack or dispatch the book, if it comes to hand I have done my duty, and however carefully I acted, if the book does not come to hand I have not done my duty. Of course I should deserve more praise in the second case than in the first [...] we must not mix up the question of right and wrong with that of the morally good and the morally bad [...] if the carelessly dispatched book comes to hand, it is not my duty to send another

---

[50]   I don't claim that this way of carving things up is the only one true to the facts, just that it does a better explanatory job than its competitors.

[51]   Cf. Kevin Mulligan, 'From Appropriate Emotions to Values', *The Monist* **81** (1) (1988), 161–88, and Christine Tappolet, 'Evaluative Vs. Deontic Concepts', *The International Encyclopedia of Ethics* (2013).

[52]   Peter Geach argues that we should jettison the concept of right action and make do with talk of good and bad acts, which was good enough for Aquinas (P.T. Geach, 'Good and Evil', *Analysis* **1** (7) (1956), 41ff.) His illustrations, however, betray a conflation of deeds with doings.

[53]   But see note 33 above.

copy, while if the carefully dispatched book does not come to hand I must send another to replace it.[54]

This is all well and good, but the paradox of the first line occurs precisely because the evaluative and deontic properties are being applied to one kind of thing called 'action'. The same holds true of the added claim that 'what is morally good is never right'. How could it possibly be true that the right and the good can never coincide? Ross holds that motives belong in the world of evaluation and actions in that of obligation. But this distinction is ill equipped to do the work required from it. Ross' aims would have been better served by one between the doing and the thing done.

As noted earlier, the doing/thing done distinction is in some respects analogous to many others, including that between what one believes and one's believing it. Suppose I believe something that's true and which I ought to believe, but I do so for very bad reasons. You may wish to criticise my believing it without criticising the belief I have (which you and I might, after all, share). Conversely, I may be perfectly justified in having a belief that turns out to be false. Hence the initial divide of intuitions about whether Edmund Gettier's famous examples were indeed ones of justified true belief, for what was justified was the thing believed, not the believing. Clayton Littlejohn's diagnosis of the situation offers the following trifecta of ascriptions:

> Ascriptions of personal justification tell us something about a believer – whether *she* is justified in believing. An ascription of doxastic justification tells us something about a belief – whether *the belief* is justifiably held. An ascription of propositional justification tells us something about a proposition – whether the proposition is such that there is sufficient justification for someone to believe it.[55]

---

[54] W.D. Ross, *The Right and the Good* (Oxford: Clarendon Press, 1930), 132ff.
[55] Clayton Littlejohn, *Justification and the Truth Connection* (Cambridge: Cambridge University Press, 2012), 5. Cf. White, 'What We Believe', & Catherine Lowy, 'Gettier's Notion of Justification', *Mind* **87** (1978), 105–8. A further question (an analogue of which appears in my discussion of Harman further below) is whether the person's being justified to have the belief that p is identical to her believing that p being justified.

Constantine Sandis

Gilbert Harman makes a parallel disambiguation in relation to action:

> I do want to distinguish between using the word 'wrong' to say that a particular situation or action is wrong from using the word to say that it is wrong of someone to do something.[56]

This is the idea that what a person did was right but it was wrong of them to do it or, conversely, that what they did was wrong but it was right of them to do it. But what is it for something to be right or wrong *of* someone? Nothing that is worryingly relativistic or subjective. It is simply the thought that a person may be right or wrong to do something given all the evidence available in some further specifiable sense. Helpful as Harman's distinction is, it doesn't get us all the way. The problem, to return to the charity example, is not that it was wrong of me to make a donation to the British Hen Welfare Trust in the case where my doing so is vicious. The difficulty is not that some people ought to give to the British Hen Welfare Trust, but not me, it is that my giving to them was unethical despite the fact that it *would have been* right of me to make a donation.[57] This should not be confused with those of blameless wrongdoing as understood by either Bernard Williams or Derek Parfit, both of whom fail to distinguish between doing and thing done, thereby rendering their examples hostage to unnecessary paradoxes concerning luck and belief, respectively.[58]

Acting rightly does not amount to doing the right thing, nor vice versa. Philosophers who stop shy of making this distinction find themselves having to make up for it by concocting new distinctions elsewhere. And yet these never seem quite capable of doing the work required. Without losing track of the fact that even Oedipus' tragic deeds are imputable to him,[59] we should not praise or blame people solely on the ground of *what* they did or didn't do.

In an obituary what one typically finds is a list of achievements and failures. The sorts of things listed here are *things done* e.g. she founded a charity, fought in the second world war, directed two Oscar-winning films, or wrote an influential book. Indeed, the very chronology of peoples' life is typically offered as a sort of list of

---

[56] Gilbert Harman, *Explaining Value and Other Essays in Moral Philosophy* (Oxford: Oxford University Press, 2000), 6–7.

[57] Perhaps it neither was nor wasn't right of me to do so.

[58] Bernard Williams, *Shame and Necessity* (Cambridge: Cambridge University Press,1993), 68–70 & Derek Parfit, *Reasons and Persons* (Oxford: Clarendon Press, 1984),34.

[59] See my 'Motivated by the Gods', in (eds) A. Buckareff, C. Moya, & S.Rosell, *Agency and Responsibility* (Basingstoke: Palgrave Macmillan, 2015), §3.

things done: she went to school A. studied subject x at university B, took a job as y at firm C, and so on. What is much rarer is an attempt to reveal the person's acts of doing these things, as a serious biography might. Without this crucial feature any attempt at praise and blame will be half-blind and paradoxical. This holds true across moral theory as a whole. Normative ethics must leave space for both our deeds *and* doings.

Epilogue

John Macmurray, whose distinction between doing and deed we began with, would some decades later complain that art 'is treated not as a form of reflective activity, but as a set of "works" to be apprehended and appreciated'.[60] Around the same time, art critic Harold Rosenberg baptised a non-cohesive group of artists, the most famous of which was Jackson Pollock, as 'action painters'. Rosenberg's central idea – later taken up by David Davies[61] – was that the real work of art is not the the painting or building (noun) but the act of painting or building (verb). We might equally, if not entirely analogously, distinguish between the dancing and the dance, the composing of a song, and the song composed, the photographing and the photograph taken and subsequently developed. Thus, Bob Dylan's 'Girl from the North Country' may be a superior song to 'Scarborough Fair', even if the composition of the former involved stealing both melody and line from the latter.

Rosenberg's theory is coupled with the additional thought that the painting on the canvas represents the act of painting it, not the way in which one might draw a self-portrait of the artist at work but by being a residue of the act of painting which bears the gesture traces of the brush strokes that produced it:

---

[60] John Macmurray, *Persons in Relation* (London: Faber & Faber, 1961), 11.

[61] David Davies, *Art as Performance* (Oxford: Blackwell, 2004). For insightful critical overviews of attempts to capture something similar by distinguishing the phenomenology of making art from that of spectating see Steven Crowell, 'Phenomenology and aesthetics; or why art matters' in (ed.) J. Parry, *Art and Phenomenology* (London: Routledge, 2011), 31–53 and Kate Kirkpatrick, 'Beneath the Surface: Whose Phenomenology? Which Art?', in (eds) L. Nelstrop & H. Appleton *Mysticism and Art* (London: Routledge, 2017).

> A canvas is [...] an arena in which to act [...] A painting is an
> action [...] that becomes its own representation [...] An act can
> be prolonged from a piece of paper to a canvas.[62]

This echoes Ricœur's metaphor of acting as the thing done as a kind
of trace (of the event of acting) left in the world; a mark in history or
memory. The mark or imprint is a reminder or at best a kind of sou-
venir of the artistic event of painting (verb). Hence the famous videos
of Pollock painting his massive canvasses; this was not intended to
just be a portrayal of the artist at work but a document of the art
itself unfolding, with or without performance. What is subsequently
hung on the wall being nothing but the marks which have been left
behind; the ashes of an event long-gone.[63]

Rosenberg undoubtedly took his own metaphor too seriously, thus
prompting Mary McCarthy to quip 'you can't hang an event on the
wall, only a picture'.[64] But while it may be nonsense to say that a
painting is an action or that it represents itself, the movement
teaches us that art presents us with two objects of aesthetic evaluation:
the creating and the thing created. As with right action, I have no
interest in offering any theory of art here (let alone one which highlights one of these things over the other). I merely wish to point
out that it is the act of creating which expresses the author's
motives or intentions. After all, the thing created could have been
made by a different person with a different aim.[65]

We are now in a position to appreciate Nietzsche's intriguing conception of life as art:

[62]   Harold Rosenberg, 'The American Action Painters' in his *The
Tradition of the New* (New York, NY: Da Capo Press, 1960), 26–8. In his
Preface to the book Rosenberg nonetheless talks of art in terms of 'things
made' which he contrasts with 'deeds done'.

[63]   Marks which sell for grotesque amounts of money, but this arguably
only serves to illustrate our fetishistic attachment to unique souvenirs such
as the original reels of music or film. See Constantine Sandis 'An Honest
Display of Fakery', in (eds) Harrison, V., Kemp, G. & Bergqvist, A.,
Philosophy and Museums: Ethics, Aesthetics, and Ontology (Cambridge:
Cambridge University Press, 2017), 1–9.

[64]   As quoted in Rosenberg's Preface referring to 'her generous review of
this book'.

[65]   Victor Dura-Vila reminded me that aesthetics places no value in the
artistic analogue of a 'pure will'. To this extent, all art theory is on Mill's
side. There remains, nonetheless, the Collingwoodian understanding of
art as the imaginative creation, *Principles of Art* (Oxford: Clarendon Press,
1938), 128–34. Cf. Benedetto Croce, *Aesthetic: As Science of Expression
and General Linguistic*, trns. D. Ainslee (London: Macmillan).

Art is the real task of life, art as life's metaphysical activity.[66]

Nietzsche does not have the life of an artist in mind here. Rather, the task of any life is the *creating* of the life lived. The art in question, here, is not the life ones creates for oneself, but the life-long activity of creating it: the living of the life and not the life lived. In his magisterial work *Nietzsche: Life as Literature*, Alexander Nehamas parses Nietzsche's motto in terms of things done instead of doings:

Everything we have done actually constitutes who each one of us is.[67]

This is no misinterpretation of Nietzsche but a reflection of the fact that our ordinary term 'thing done' is itself ambiguous in ways that can be philosophically troubling. A case in point is Sartre's existentialist retelling of Nietzsche's tale:

Man is nothing other than his own projects. He exists only to the extent that he realizes himself, therefore he is nothing more than the sum of his actions, nothing more than his life.[68]

If this view is to capture the roundedness of human life, the sum of our actions had better include the totality of both our deeds *and* doings. It is in this spirit that Ronald Dworkin writes:

The final value of our lives is adverbial, not adjectival. It's the value of the performance, not anything that is left when the performance is subtracted.[69]

Dworkin models his distinction between having a good life and living well to that between art products and artistic acts of creation. The argument runs parallel to that of Rosenberg and Davies who claim that artistic value is adverbial though, like myself, Dworkin is not

---

[66]   Friedrich Nietzsche, *The Will to Power* [1886], trns. Walter Kaufmann (New York: Vintage Books, 1966), §853, IV.
[67]   Alexander Nehamas, *Nietzsche: Life as Literature* (Cambridge MA: Harvard University Press, 1985), 188. See also Zachary Simpson, *Life as Art: Aesthetics and the Creation of the Self* (London: Roman & littlefield, 2012).
[68]   Jean-Paul Sartre, *Existentialism is a Humanism*, trns. C. Macomber (New Haven, CT: Yale University Press, 2007 [1945]),37.
[69]   Ronald Dworkin, *Justice for Hedgehogs* (Boston, NJ: Harvard University Press, 2011), 197. Note the allusion to Wittgenstein's famous rhetorical question, 'what is left over if I subtract the fact that my arm goes up from the fact that I raise my arm?', *Philosophical Investigations*, trns. G.E.M. Anscombe (Oxford: Blackwell, 1953), §621.

Constantine Sandis

committed to any views about what art *is*. For my own part, I have merely sought to show that there is value to be found in both the living and the life lived, the doing and the thing done, the creating and the thing created.[70] In sum, we should be dualists about the objects of both moral and aesthetic evaluation.[71]

There is much that normative ethics can learn from the the once fashionable 'death of the author' view of art. Its insight is not that the author has no say *tout court* but only that, *pace* intentionalism about art products, our aesthetic evaluation of their creation must, unlike that of their creative acts, ultimately carry on without them.[72] As with creations, our deeds are but the ashes of our acts in time. To evaluate our lives solely by these would be a grave mistake.[73]

University of Hertfordshire
c.sandis@herts.ac.uk

[70]   The theological implications are nicely brought out in Kirkpatrick, 'Beneath the Surface'.

[71]   As with soup and things done, we can talk of things produced as either repeatables or particulars. P.F. Strawson writes: 'We should be able to speak of the same painting being seen by different people in different places at one time, in just the same way in which we now speak of the same sonata being heard by different people at different times in one place'. Strawson, 'Aesthetic Appraisal and Works of Art', *The Oxford Review*, no.3 (1966], reprinted in his *Freedom and Resentment and Other Essays*, 2nd ed. (London: Routledge, 2008), 202. I concur, but leave it for another day to quibble over whether Pierre Menard's *Don Quixote* could have ever been an identical work to that of Cervantes.

[72]   This does not preclude the possibility of better understanding the things we do and create by situating them within the normative contexts of their production. For the convoluted question of what, if anything, it is to understand an act or artwork, see my 'If an Artwork Could Speak', in (ed.) G. Hagberg, *Wittgenstein on Aesthetic Understanding* (London: Palgrave Macmillan, 2017).

[73]   I have subjected audiences in Cardiff, Grenoble, London, Helsinki, Hertfordshire, Montréal, Norwich, Oxford, Tartu, Turku, Wolverhampton, and Valencia to earlier versions of this material and am grateful to all of them for their comments and questions. I'd like to also thank Joseph Almog, Louise R. Chapman, Rémi Clot-Goudard, Meena Dhanda, Victor Dura-Vila, James Garvey, Naomi Goulder, Kate Kirkpatrick, Andreas Lind, Elijah Millgram, Danièle Moyal-Sharrock, Henry Mulhall, Luke Mulhall, Sarah Stroud, Christine Tappolet, and Susanne Uusitalo for helpful suggestions and discussions.

126

Prichard on Causing a Change

JONATHAN DANCY

Abstract
This paper starts by considering an interesting argument of H.A. Prichard's against the view that to act is to cause a change; the argument is that causing is not an activity. The argument is important because of the recent emergence of an 'agent-causation' view according to which actions are the causing of changes by agents. I suggest a way of responding to Prichard's argument, and then, profiting from one of his own conclusions, turn to consider the relation between neurophysiological changes and the causation of bodily movement by the agent. I make a suggestion about the proper way to understand the relation between the neurophysiological changes, the bodily movements and the action.

1.

This paper assumes without argument a certain view about the nature of action. This will limit its interest for those who do not accept that view. But the second half of the paper discusses a difficulty which arises for them just as much as for anyone else. So there should be something here for everyone.

The view that I assume is a view about the nature of action. It is an agent-causalist view, but not *the* agent-causalist view. Traditionally, agent-causalism has been the view that actions are events caused by agents. But this is not the view I assume (and which I in fact accept). The view I assume is one which I first learnt from an article by Maria Alvarez and John Hyman, 'Agents and Their Actions'.[1] It holds that to act is to cause a change, and an action is an agent's causing a change. The action is not the change caused; that change, which is an event, is (in Alvarez and Hyman's terms) the 'result' of the action. We need to respect here the distinction between the causing of a change and the change that is caused by, and so the result of, that causing. The cause of the change is the agent. So here we have a form of causation where the cause is not an event, but an agent. The result, the thing caused, is an event (probably). Is the causing of that result an event? Alvarez and Hyman say

---

[1] M. Alvarez and J. Hyman, 'Agents and their Actions', *Philosophy* **73** (1998), 219–45.

doi:10.1017/S1358246117000054

not, and I agree with them, but not for the reason they offer. They effectively try to prove that this must be so; but I only want to suggest that nobody should think that a causal relation is an event. Anybody who holds the more standard view that causal relations are relations between events should avoid saying that the relation between those events when one causes another is another event, to be added to the cause-event and the effect-event. Otherwise they will face the question what is the relation between the cause-event and the causing-event, and I don't see a plausible answer to that question – any more than there is a plausible answer to the question what the relation is between the causing-event and the effect-event. So I suggest that there is a considerable incentive for all of us to avoid thinking of causings as events.

To come at the matter another way, causal relations are too thin to count as events. The sort of thinness I am getting at here might be what is in the mind of those who think of causal relations as essentially explanatory. An explanatory relation is not the same sort of thing as a 'making-happen' relation. The latter might be thought of as a sort of forcefulness in nature, and such a relation looks as if it should be thick, rather than thin. But even if causal relations are not themselves merely relations of explanation, they will still be thin. On the form of agent-causalism that I accept, the relation between an agent and an effect caused by that agent is not itself another event somehow interposed between the agent and the effect. The exercise of a causal power should not itself be understood as a happening. For if so, we would want to ask how the agent manages to get that happening to happen; and if the answer is that she does it by causing it, we are back where we started, or, rather, off on a regress. And on a traditional Humean approach, relations of causation are relations of regular succession, and those relations are not themselves events in addition to the events in that succession. My conclusion is that we should all avoid thinking of causings as events.

2.

I said that the view that to act is to cause a change is one that I learnt from an article published in 1998. But it appears that this view was around 100 years earlier, since Harold Prichard ascribes it to John Cook Wilson. In his 'Acting, Willing, Desiring', Prichard writes: 'We should at first say that to do something is to originate or to bring into existence, i.e. really, to cause, some not yet existing state either of ourselves or of someone else, or, again, of some body.'

And he ascribes this view explicitly to Cook Wilson. But the relevant paper seems (like so much of Cook Wilson's oeuvre) to be lost. So we cannot be sure whether Cook Wilson actually tied himself to the thought that to do something is to cause some not yet existing *state* to come to exist. After all, there is the alternative possibility that some actions, at least, are the causings of a process rather than of a state; I mention this alternative now because it will become relevant later. So I think we should not take Prichard's talk of a state as committing him to any divisive metaphysics. Still, he mentions this view of Cook Wilson's in order to criticise it, and it is that criticism that originally intrigued me. Prichard continues thus:

> Now, so far as I can see, this account of what an action is, though plausible and having as a truth underlying it that usually in acting we do cause something, is not tenable.

> Unquestionably the thing meant by 'an action' is an activity. ...And if we ask ourselves: 'Is there such an activity as originating or causing a change in something else?', we have to answer that there is not. To say this is, of course, not to say that there is no such thing as causing something, but only to say that though the causing a change may require an activity, it is not itself an activity.[2]

Now in a way I should be sympathetic to this complaint, because it looks as if Prichard is here supporting the view I have already propounded, namely that causing is too thin a relation to be an activity. Still, the present paper is concerned with the rights and wrongs of this issue, and with those of another remark of Prichard's in the same paper, together with something that Alvarez and Hyman say on a related topic. Prichard, having announced that, though the causing a change may require an activity, it is not itself an activity, still wants to know what activity is required for causing a change, and he decides that this activity is that of willing. And he suggests without further ado that:

> Where we have willed some movement of our body and think we have caused it, we cannot have directly caused it. For what we directly caused, if anything, must have been some change in our brain.[3]

So it is by willing that we cause the changes we cause, and although we may thereby manage to cause other changes such as movements of

[2]   H.A. Prichard, 'Acting, Willing, Desiring', in *Moral Writings* (ed.) J. MacAdam (Oxford: Oxford University Press, 2003), 272–81, at 272–3.
[3]   'Acting, Willing, Desiring', 277.

the body, the changes we cause directly are all changes in our brain – neural changes, as I will say. This second suggestion is the topic of the second half of my paper. My interest in it derives from a remark on the same topic by Alvarez and Hyman:

> We do not wish to deny that when an agent causes a bodily movement, an event – perhaps in the agent's nervous system – causes the same bodily movement; but the agent's action is not identical with this event.[4]

I found this remark very puzzling. It seems to allow that the bodily movement can have two causes, one a neural event – as one event causing another – and one that is not an event at all but an agent. And the question is whether this suggestion is both compulsory and coherent. If it is indeed coherent, then it doesn't matter whether it is compulsory; but if it is both compulsory and incoherent, we agent-causalists are in trouble.

The general topic of this paper, then, is how to capture the role of neural events in one's account of an action as the causing of a change by an agent. And there is a question along the way, namely: is there something that drives us to the view that all our basic activities are acts of the will? Prichard supposes that when one causes a change, there must be some activity by which one does so, and that this activity can only be willing. So when I raise my hand, my raising of my hand is my causing my hand to rise, and such a causing is not itself an activity, but requires *another* activity – which he announces can only be an act of the will. Evidently we are not supposed to press the question how I do that act. We would have thought that I cannot 'just cause' the relevant volitional change in me, because there is 'no such activity as originating or causing a change'. Prichard's own suggestion, that what we 'directly cause' is a change in our brain, seems to be an account of what sort of a change we can 'just cause', since 'directly causing' seems hard to separate from 'just causing'.

There is one terminological issue that needs to be brought out here. I return to Prichard's remark first quoted above:

> Where we have willed some movement of our body and think we have caused it, we cannot have directly caused it.

To understand this remark, we need to disambiguate the potentially ambiguous phrase 'some movement of our body'. In the now standard way that we owe to Jennifer Hornsby, we need to distinguish

---

[4]   'Agents and their Actions', 230.

between transitive and intransitive senses of this phrase. When I move my body, I cause my body to move. The first occurrence of 'move' in this sentence is transitive, and the second is intransitive. When I move my body, I cause a change in the location of my body; this is transitive moving. When my body moves, its location changes, and nothing is said about what causes that change; this is intransitive moving, like the moving of the moon – mere motion. We say that when I move my body, I cause my body to move, and this does not mean that when I move my body, I cause my body to move itself. It only means that I cause a motion of my body. Though my body then moves, it does not cause that motion – I do. To render this distinction perspicuous as we go along, we mark it by subscripts: when I move my body, there is me, the mover, and the body, the thing moved, one thing moving another and this is transitive moving – bodily movements$_T$ – where the subscript T stands for 'transitive'. When the body moves – perhaps because I move it – we are thinking of bodily movements$_I$ – with the subscript I standing for 'intransitive'. I will also use the phrase 'bodily motion' for this intransitive sense. So when I move my body, I cause a bodily motion.

Now in which sense should we understand Prichard's remark about willing some movement? Am I willing a bodily motion to occur, or willing to move my body? The point of this question is to raise doubt about the idea that when I move my body, I do it either by willing some bodily motion or by willing to move my body. Neither of these things seems to be what I do. I do not will (one act) to move my body (another act), nor do I will a mere event (a change in my body's location). We seem to need a third possibility; and if none can be found this casts doubt on the whole idea of willing a bodily movement.

3.

Bruce Aune writes: 'the principle behind Prichard's claim is ...'Statements of the form 'Thing or person S causes event E' are to be understood as elliptical for statements of the form $\exists A(A$ is an activity by S and A causes E)'.[5] But Prichard does not challenge the idea that agents cause changes in favour of the view that causing is always done by activities. He only wants to identify the activity

---

[5]   B. Aune, 'Prichard, Action, and Volition', *Philosophical Studies* **25** (1974), 97–116, at page 98.

by which agents cause the changes they cause, because he thinks that, though there is such a thing as causing a change, still causing a change, though it requires an activity, is not itself an activity. The activity we are looking for is willing.

But we might wonder why Prichard should suppose that causing a change requires the same activity each time. For he could be right in his claim that causing a change is not an activity, but requires an activity, but wrong to suppose that it must be the same one each time. Perhaps I cause my arm to rise by raising it, and cause my hand to turn (when opening the door) by turning it. So I am suspicious of Prichard's apparent assumption that whenever we cause a change, there is one and the same activity involved each time. If it were, then perhaps the only candidate activity would be that of willing. But we need reason to believe this assumption.

What is more, Prichard himself is wary of such assumptions elsewhere. He famously compared the question 'Why should we obey the law?' with the question 'Why should we read books?'. It is clear that there are lots of different reasons to read books, depending on the book (and on us); and similarly there are different reasons to obey the law, depending on the law and the circumstances (and on us, again). So why should there not be different activities involved in the causings of different changes? I see no reason why.

So a Prichardian response to Prichard's challenge is to allow that there is indeed no activity of causing a change, but to insist that every causing of a change is an activity of some (other) sort, and every activity is the causing of a change. So: walking is causing a change by walking; it is an activity by doing which the agent causes a change in her location. Writing is causing a change by writing: and so on. So the general form of action is: causing a change in one way or another. This reminds me of Jonathan Lowe's suggestion[6] for the basic form of an agent-causal statement: Agent A caused event E by V-ing.

Could this be what Prichard meant by saying that though causing requires an activity, it is not an activity? No, because for him it must be the same activity every time. Lowe, by contrast, is happy – so far as the form of the causal statement goes – to allow that it might be a different V-ing for each causing. He argues, however, that all our *basic* actions are acts of will. A basic action can be understood for these purposes as a doing which is not done by doing something else. So I draw your attention by causing my arm to rise; and I cause my arm to rise by raising it (rather than in some other way). I raise it by an act of will.

---

[6]   J. Lowe, *Personal Agency* (Oxford: Oxford University Press, 2008), 7.3.

(I do not recommend this train of thought, and mention it only because of its relevance to what is to come later.)

Lowe's account of the form of an agent-causal statement allows that nothing can *just cause* anything. If an action is the causing of a change by an agent, there must be some way in which the agent causes that change. I cause my arm to rise by raising it – that is one way – but I could also do it by lifting it with the other arm, or by getting you to lift it. It is the way in which one does it that gives the causing its substance, its thickness (to revert to the idea that causing is itself a thin relation).

This returns us to the idea that causings are not events. If I write, I cause a change by writing, and the change caused is an event, but the causing of it is not. Causal relations do not have enough substance, enough thickness, for their instantiations to be events. So as an agent I cannot just exert a causal power and get something to happen. I have to act in a certain way if I am to cause a change. But whether this is compatible with the claim that I can just will, and that by willing I can do other things, such as raise my arm, is dubious.

If, when I cause a change, I do so by engaging in some activity, are we to say that it is the activity that is the real cause of that change? This is not the way the story is supposed to go. The ground idea is that the cause of the change is the agent, and the activity involved is the agent's causing that change in a certain way. Is there some danger that this response to Prichard generates a regress? I doubt it. If it does, the regress will derive from two thoughts: that one causes B by doing something else A, and that all doings are themselves causings. But the view above does not maintain that one causes B by doing something else A. It just holds that every change caused is caused in a certain way.

Furthermore, if there were a genuine regress here, how is it that willing would be able to stop it when nothing else can? Willing is an activity (if it happens at all), and there is no activity by doing which one wills. But why should one not say the same about causing one's fingers to move? If I can *just will*, why cannot I *just move* my fingers? To move one's fingers is to cause one's fingers to move by acting in a certain way, namely, by moving them. If we point out that there are various ways of causing one's fingers to move, the answer is that in this case one did not move one's finger by doing something else of which the motion of the finger is an effect. So understood, one's moving one's finger is a basic action.

Jonathan Dancy

4.

The notion of a basic action which I used in the previous sentence is taken from Alvarez and Hyman. More fully expressed, a basic action is the causing of a change whose result is not the effect of some other action by the same agent. (Remember that the 'result' of the action is the change of which the action is the causing.) An ordinary bodily movement$_I$, or motion, can be the result of a bodily movement$_T$, and such movements$_T$ are basic actions. An ordinary bodily movement$_T$ consists in the moving$_T$ of the body by the agent.

As far as this goes, we don't need to introduce considerations of neurophysiology. But Alvarez and Hyman complicate things enormously by maintaining (or perhaps one should simply say pointing out) that on their story there are two causal relations, event-causation and agent-causation, and one and the same event can be caused both by an agent and by a prior event. If we reserve the term 'causer' for an agent-cause, and restrict the noun 'cause' to event-causes, a bodily motion can have both a cause (perhaps neural) and a causer (agent). If that bodily motion is the result of the agent's causing (that is, the result of the exercise of a causal power by that agent) and not the effect of some other action by the same agent, it is a basic action of that agent's.

Now when I move my body, the relevant bodily motion is an effect of neural events. If I cause those events, my causing those events would be my basic actions. And if I don't cause those events, how is it that I can be the causer of their effects? I seem to be unnecessary, and we would be forced to conclude that no bodily movement$_T$ is a basic action.

We might optimistically suppose that the answer to this is that the two causal relations, event-causation and agent-causation, are so distinct that they do not compete. If they do not compete, the fact that our bodily motions are the effects of neural changes in our brain is not in tension with the fact that they are the results of our causings. The latter causings are ones done by causers rather than by causes. So we can have both causal relations in play simultaneously without either interfering with the other. We do not need to deny that those bodily motions that are the results of our agency are also the effects of neural changes in our brains. Those motions can be our doings (they are not our actions, of course, but the results of those actions) even though they have causes other than us.

I fear, however, that this suggestion has only to be understood to be rejected. It renders agent-causation epiphenomenal. As it represents things, there is the causal system (the event-causal system, that is) going on remorselessly in its own sweet way, and we somehow plaster agent-causation on top of that, to get ourselves into the story as agents. But we might reasonably notice that the bodily motion is going to happen anyway, once the relevant neural changes are under way, and there remains nothing really for us to do. Our role as causers is mere window-dressing.

Matters would be different if we could claim to be the causers of the neural changes whose effects are the relevant bodily motions. But if we were, those causings of neural changes would be our basic acts, for the bodily motions are the effects of those neural changes, and though we can be said to be the causers of events that are the effects of the results of other causings of ours, our basic acts will be the causings of neural changes.

I do not want to raise it as an objection to this picture, that our neural changes have other neural events as causes. This is true, but if we are to retain any sense of ourselves as agents, rather than as the conduits of extraneous causal forces, we have to find some point at which we do something – and, I would say, at which we do something for a reason.

Consider, in this connection, what Alvarez and Hyman have to say. They allow that the bodily motions that are the results of my basic actions are also the effects of certain neural events in my brain. And they allow that I do not cause the neural events to occur. What I do, according to them, is to ensure that those neural events have oc-curred by performing an action whose result is sure to be the effect of such a neural event. But what does cause them then? Three answers are possible: nothing, me, and something else. If something else, we seem to be locked into the causal nexus. The only way out of this impasse is to allow a plurality of causal relations, so that though an event is already perfectly well explained causally, there is room for a second causal explanation of that same event, but of a different sort. One might hopefully suppose that since the two causal explanations at issue are of very different sorts, there can be no competition between them. The technical term for this sort of approach is insouciance.

5.

But even the insouciant might prefer to tie the two causal relations to-gether in some way, if that were only possible. So the suggestion I am going to consider is that we think of the agent as causing a causal process, or a series of causally linked events: the neural at one end

Jonathan Dancy

causing the overt physical motion at the other, with the muscular in between. On this account, the basic action is not well understood as the causing of a bodily motion such as the rising of an arm; it is the causing of a process of which that motion is the terminal point.

What we cause when we act, on this account, is not a sort of causing to cause. We do not cause neural events to cause muscular ones, and we do not cause those muscular ones to cause arms to go up. These things are not up to us. What we cause is a causal complex, and we cause every part of that complex, but we do not cause the causal relations that bind it together. It is one thing to cause an event to occur, one that will have certain effects, and another to endow that event with causal powers. Similarly, it is one thing to cause a process to occur, and another to endow some element of that process with causal powers.

An immediate worry about this proposal is that it thinks of the agent as causing a process, when there are parts of that process of which the agent is more or less entirely ignorant. In fact, the only thing the agent really knows about is the final stage. But this epistemological reason for focusing on that final stage and thinking of the basic action in such terms applies just as well to the muscular as to the neural. We already knew that we are largely ignorant of the way in which we get our arm to rise. That the same applies to the neural events which are such an important part of the process should not disconcert us. The focus on the final stage had already to be abandoned, despite the fact that the sort of agentual knowledge that Anscombe tried so hard to understand is never of neural changes and only rarely of muscular ones.[7] So what I cause is not just, or really, the first stage of the neural/muscular/physical process, nor the last stage, particularly, but the whole thing, of which I may know only the later stage, and aim only at that.

One's basic action, on this approach, is the causing of the whole process. And this may seem to lead to immediate difficulties. Do I cause the neural events which are the first stage in the process? If so, how do I do that? The answer has to be that at the most I did that by causing the process of which those neural events were the first and the bodily motion the last stage. I suppose that one could try to suggest that I cause whatever neural changes are required for my hand to rise. But I prefer to stick to the letter of the 'process view' and maintain that I cause the whole process, and that my relation to that process is not identical to my relation to any of its stages. It is outside in rather than inside out.

[7] See her *Intention* (Oxford: Blackwell, 1957), §30.

Still, there is enough awkwardness about this for us to scout for possible alternatives. A different account might have it that the occurrence of the neural events is part of the story of how I cause the bodily motions. Not everything that is part of that story is itself a doing, or a causing, of mine, or the result of such a causing. This supposes that my action is *really* the causing of the bodily motion, and that is what I am trying to deny; so this new account is definitely different. But it still faces the familiar problem, which is that if I don't cause the neural changes, something else does, and this locks us into the causal nexus.

A better suggestion might be the the neural events are not part of the story of how I cause the bodily motions; they are part of the story of how those motions get to happen. It is not about how I do it. It is about how it works that the body moves$_I$. After all, there is no story of how I raise my hand – I just raise it, that's all. But if the neural events are part of how it works, must I not also cause them, in causing the process of which they are a part? Well, perhaps not. I do not necessarily cause to happen everything that needs to happen if some event of which I am the causer is to happen. I do not cause the absence of traffic jams that is required if I am to arrive in London by lunchtime. And I do not necessarily cause to happen everything that needs to happen if I am to cause that event – e.g. that I stay alive until the end of the process.

But this suggestion too runs up against the question what does cause the neural events if I don't. Again we face the fact that if the neural changes are not caused by me, they must be caused by something else, and the causal nexus looms.

So it seems that the best resort is to stick to the view that I cause the process of which the neural events are stages – a process which consists in a causal relation between neural changes at one end and bodily motion at the other. I don't cause the neural events in any other sense than this – and by the same token I don't cause the bodily motions in any other sense than this either.

There seems to me that the way in which children learn to control their bodily movements$_I$ might chime rather well with the account I have been trying to promote. Very young children move around haphazardly. A process occurs at the end of which they can coordinate hand and eye, and move intentionally. What is it that they are learning during this process? They are not learning to make happen those neural events that are necessary for their hand to move towards the toy in front of them. Perhaps what they are learning is how to make happen a process which consists in neural changes leading to bodily motions. As I have suggested several times now, they don't need to

Jonathan Dancy

be aware of every stage of that process in order to acquire the ability to execute it. And they don't need to be aware of it as a process either. It is a routine, but not one whose several stages will ever be present to consciousness. Nobody can say how it is done, but it might be possible to say what it is that we do.

The University of Texas at Austin
jdancy@austin.utexas.edu

Motor Skill and Moral Virtue

ELLEN FRIDLAND

Abstract
Virtue ethicists often appeal to practical skill as a way of understanding the nature of virtue. An important commitment of a skill account of virtue is that virtue is learned through practice and not through study, memorization, or reflection alone. In what follows, I will argue that virtue ethicists have only given us half the story. In particular, in focusing on outputs, or on the right actions or responses to moral situations, virtue ethicists have overlooked a crucial facet of virtue: namely, that through practice, virtuous agents develop a cache of perceptual skills that allow them to attend to, detect, and identify the relevant features of a perceptual array, the selection of which is central to recognizing and categorizing a situation as a moral situation of a particular type. In order to support this claim, I will appeal to empirical studies of motor expertise, which show that an expert's capacity to attend to and recognize relevant perceptual inputs differs in important respects from the layperson's. Specifically, I will argue that performing the right action in the right circumstances improves an agent's ability to attend to and identify the morally relevant features of a moral situation.

Virtue ethicists often appeal to practical skill as a way to clarify the nature of virtue.[1] An important commitment of a skill account of virtue is that virtue is learned through practice and not through study, memorization, or reflection alone. This commitment has its roots in the *Nicomachean Ethics*, where Aristotle's states that, 'What we need to learn to do, we learn by doing; for example, we become builders by building, and lyre players by playing the lyre. So too we become just by doing just actions, temperate by doing temperate actions and courageous by courageous actions' (NE 1033 a 32-b2).

The way in which most virtue ethicists explain the requirement to practice is by considering the way in which right actions or right responses to moral situations are learned or acquired. That is, most virtue ethicists hold something like the following view: learning which reaction or response to a moral situation is correct requires

---

[1]   See, for instance, Aristotle, *Nichomachean Ethics* (Oxford: Oxford University Press, 2009); J. Annas, *Intelligent Virtue* (Oxford: Oxford University Press, 2011); J. McDowell, *Mind Value and Reality* (Cambridge, MA: Harvard University Press, 2001); M. Stichter, 'Ethical Expertise: The Skill Model of Virtue', *Ethical Theory and Moral Practice* **10** (2007), 183–194; M. Stichter, 'Virtues, Skills, and Right Action', *Ethical Theory and Moral Practice* **14** (2011), 73–86.

doi:10.1017/S1358246117000078

Ellen Fridland

regularly performing the right actions in the right situations in childhood and beyond. This is because in order to know how to respond appropriately, one has to learn how to respond appropriately, and this is learned by regularly instantiating the appropriate actions in the appropriate situations, rather than, say, just thinking or reflecting on or deliberating about what the right action in that situation may be. In functionalist or cognitive science terms, we might say that virtue ethicists appeal to practice in order to explain how agents are able to select the appropriate output given a particular input.

In what follows, I will argue that framing things in this way only gives us half the story. In particular, I will argue that focusing on outputs, or on the right actions or responses to moral situations, ignores a crucial facet of moral expertise. Namely, that through practice, virtuous agents develop a cache of perceptual skills that allow them to attend to, detect, and identify the relevant features of a perceptual array, the selection of which is central to recognizing and categorizing a situation as a moral situation of a particular type. In order to support this claim, I will appeal to empirical studies in sports psychology, which show that an expert's capacity to attend to and recognize relevant perceptual inputs differs in important respects from the layperson's. Specifically, I will argue that performing the right action in the right circumstances improves an agent's ability to attend to, identify, and make predictions based upon the morally relevant features of a moral situation.

In the first section of this paper, I will consider four explanations given by virtue ethicists in order to justify the claim that virtue is acquired through practice. I will emphasize that each of these explanations focus almost exclusively on the selection of outputs and ignore how developing the right attention to and selection of inputs is relevant to a full account of virtue. In the second section of the paper, I will present evidence from sports psychology strongly suggesting that experts locate, attend to, recognize, and make predictions based upon the relevant features of domain-specific perceptual arrays in ways that significantly differ from non-experts. In section three, I will argue that if we take seriously the analogy between virtue and practical skill, then it is likely that performing virtuous actions tunes an agent's attention to the morally relevant features of an ethical situation. That is, I will claim that performing the right action, at the right time, in the right way, directed at the right person, etc., is required for an agent to develop the capacity to detect a situation as a moral situation, to classify it as a moral situation of the right type, and to make accurate predictions based on the features that one detects. I will end by providing some cursory remarks about the kind of perception that I propose may be involved in the selection of inputs by morally virtuous agents.

1. A look at the literature

As we turn to the literature on virtue ethics, we don't need to look very far to see that most virtue ethicists focus almost exclusively on the way in which agents respond to ethical situations. That is, virtue ethicists (along with other ethicists) are concerned primarily with explaining how an agent is able to determine and do the right thing, given the particular moral context in which the agent finds herself. Not many theorists are concerned with accounting for how agents attend to or recognize a situation as a moral situation in the first place.[2] This seems to me to be an important oversight.

In the following section, I will present four examples of discussions where virtue ethicists focus on one side of the perception-action divide. To be clear, I will not attempt to provide a comprehensive overview of the literature but simply point to a few illustrative instances of the problem that I am attempting to identify.

1.a. Virtue and 'giving an account'

Julia Annas, like most virtue ethicists, holds that virtue is acquired through practice. She states, 'Aristotle is right here: virtue is like building in that learning to be brave is learning to do something, we learn by doing it (not just by reading books about it)'.[3] For Annas, while virtue is acquired by performing virtuous deeds, the performance of such deeds is by no means sufficient for virtue.[4] At the heart of Annas's account is a distinction between a sub-rational knack and a practical skill, of which virtue is an instance of the latter and simply performing virtuous actions is an example of the former. For Annas, skilled agents not only have the ability to perform virtuous actions, that is, the right action, directed at the right person, at the right time, in the right circumstance but they also understand *why* that action is the right action in a particular set of circumstances. Possession of this understanding thereby

---

2   I will discuss exceptions to this generalization below. See especially: I. Murdoch, *Sovereignty of Good* (New York: Schocken Books, 1970) and L. Blum, 'Moral Perception and Particularity', *Ethics* **101** (1991), 701–725.
3   Annas, *Intelligent Virtue*, 22–23.
4   'From the start then, the child will learn by copying the role model... But this will not lead to bravery, as opposed to foolish repetition' (Annas, *Intelligent Virtue*, 23) and 'virtue cannot be adequately understood just as a disposition to perform actions: the virtuous person is a person whose actions are performed for certain reasons' (Annas, *Intelligent Virtue*, 28).

allows the virtuous agent to provide an explanation of why a particular action is the right action in a given context.

As Annas explains, the virtuous agent has 'the ability to convey why what is done is done'.[5]

> Indeed, just this serves to mark off skill (*techne*) from an inarticulate 'knack' (*emperia*); the skilled person can 'give an account' of what he does, which involves being able to explain why he is doing what he is doing…that virtue has these features, and that they are centrally important to what virtue is, is one of the main claims of the book (20).

For my purposes, the most important thing to notice about Annas's account is that moral expertise turns out to be exclusively about reactions or responses to moral situations. After all, both doing the right thing in a particular context and being able to explain why that action is the right action in that context address only the output side of moral agency. For Annas, virtue is a practical skill that does not seem to involve refining one's ability to attend to and identify the morally relevant features of a moral situation. As with so much of ethics, the input side of morality is taken as given.

1.b. Virtue and the particularity of right actions

A related suggestion for justifying the role of practice in moral expertise is that performing virtuous actions is required for the acquisition of virtue because identifying the right action cannot be articulated or organized into general principles. Rather, it is thought that virtue requires knowledge of what to do in particular situations, something that general rules or principles cannot capture.[6] As Daniel Jacobsen writes, 'the skill model implies that ethical expertise cannot be codified in principles'.[7] And as John McDowell explains,

> [T]here need be no possibility of reducing virtuous behavior to rules. In moral upbringing what one learns is not to behave in conformity with rules of conduct, but to see situations in a special light, as constituting reasons for acting; the perceptual

---

[5]   Annas, *Intelligent Virtue,* 20.
[6]   Likewise, Annas writes that, 'the need to learn does justice to the fact that virtues are always learned in particular embedded contexts' (Annas, *Intelligent Virtue,* 25).
[7]   Jacobsen, D. 'Seeing by feeling: Virtues, skills, and moral perception', *Ethical Theory and Moral Practice* **8** (2005), 387–409.

capacity, once acquired can be exercised in complex novel circumstances, not necessarily capable of being foreseen and legislated for by a codifier of the conduct required by virtue, however wise and thoughtful he might be.[8]

We should notice that these accounts are concerned only with the impossibility of codifying rules for behavior or for translating reasons for action into general principles. That is, these accounts, like Annas's above, are concerned with the impossibility of giving general rules for selecting appropriate outputs. But even if it's true that the appropriate response to a given situation is impossible to codify into general principles, when it comes to moral expertise, this is only half the story.

Standard accounts of virtue do not address the possibility that there's likely another part of virtue that may be equally difficult or impossible to codify into general principles and that is also likely refined through practice – namely, the ability to detect, attend to, recognize, identify, and make predictions based upon the morally relevant features of a moral situation. Such attention to and identification of the morally relevant features of situations seems crucial for recognizing that one is confronted with a moral situation in the first place and also for categorizing or classifying that moral situation as a moral situation of a particular type. If this kind of identification and classification is necessary for moral expertise, as I will argue that it is, then we should conclude that accounts of virtue that focus primarily on outputs or responses to moral contexts, the nature of which is assumed to be given in one way or another, focus only on one half of what is required for a full account of moral virtue.

1.c. Virtue as a sensitivity to reasons for action

Another suggestion for why practice is necessary for virtue comes from John McDowell.[9] According to McDowell, virtue amounts to a sensitivity to reasons for action.[10] On his view, this sensitivity or

---

[8] McDowell, *Mind, Value and Reality,* 85.

[9] J. McDowell, 'Virtue and Reason', *The Monist* **62** (1979), 331–350; J. McDowell, *Mind Value and Reality* (Cambridge, MA: Harvard University Press, 2001).

[10] 'So the deliverances of this sensitivity constitute, one by one, complete explanations of the actions which manifest the virtue. Hence, since the sensitivity fully accounts for its deliverances, the sensitivity fully accounts for the actions. But the concept of the virtue is the concept of a

Ellen Fridland

sensibility is akin to a perceptual capacity[11] but, importantly, it is not a perceptual capacity in the intuitionist sense. That is, the perceptual capacity that McDowell is concerned with is not a moral property or moral fact detector.[12] Rather, according to McDowell, the features that the ethical sensibility detects are reasons for action or ways of recognizing the demands that a situation places on us.[13] Such an ethical sensitivity is like a perceptual capacity insofar as it detects features of the world and, when it does, it delivers knowledge. So, on McDowell's view, as we develop virtue, we develop the capacity to see what action is called for in a particular situation. Insofar as this seeing is the detection of a reason, it also motivates one to perform the action that one sees as appropriate.

As with the cases above, McDowell emphasizes how an agent selects the appropriate outputs or responses to moral situations. The perceptual sensitivity that McDowell is concerned with delivers the ability to immediately sense what the right response to a given situation is. Importantly, this perceptual capacity is not identical to the ability to detect or identify features of moral situations. After

---

state whose possession accounts for the actions which manifest it. Since that explanatory role is filled by the sensitivity, the sensitivity turns out to be what the virtue is' (McDowell, 'Virtue and Reason', 332). See also, 'the position I am describing aims... at an epistemology that centres on the notion of a susceptibility to reasons' (McDowell, *Mind, Value and Reality*, 162).

[11]   'The deliverances of a reliable sensitivity are cases of knowledge; and there are idioms according to which the sensitivity itself can appropriately be described as knowledge: a kind person knows what it is like to be confronted with a requirement of kindness. The sensitivity is, we might say, a sort of perceptual capacity' (McDowell, 'Virtue and Reason', 332).

[12]   'Moreover, the primary-quality model turns the epistemology of value into mere mystification. The perceptual model is no more than a model; perception, strictly so called, does not mirror the role of reason in evaluative thinking; which seems to require us to regard apprehension of value as an intellectual rather than a merely sensory matter. But if we are to take account of this, while preserving the model's picture of values as brutally and absolutely *there,* it seems we need to postulate a faculty – intuition – about which all that can be said is that it makes us aware of objective rational connections; the model itself ensure that there is nothing helpful to say about how such a faculty might work, or why its deliverances might deserve to count as knowledge' (McDowell, *Mind, Value and Reality,* 132–3).

[13]   'In moral upbringing what one learns is not to behave in conformity with rules of conduct, but to see situations in a special light, as constituting reasons for acting; the perceptual capacity, once acquired can be exercised in complex novel circumstances...' (McDowell, *Mind, Value and Reality,* 85).

all, on McDowell's account, detecting that a situation has some morally relevant features is not sufficient for making that situation a reason for action. This is clear since, as McDowell explains,

> If a genuine virtue is to produce nothing but right conduct, a simple propensity to be gentle cannot be identified with the virtue of kindness. Possession of the virtue must involve not only sensitivity to facts about others' feelings as reasons for acting in certain ways, but also sensitivity to facts about rights as reasons for acting in certain ways; and when circumstances of both sorts obtain, and a certain stance of the second sort is the one that should be acted on, a possessor of the virtue of kindness must be able to tell that that is so. So we cannot disentangle genuine possession of kindness from the sensitivity, which constitutes fairness.[14]

Now, it may be argued that a sensitivity to reasons for action requires a prior or simultaneous sensitivity to identifying and categorizing moral situations accurately – this seems reasonable and it's a position that I'll defend in section 3. However, for now, I'd like to highlight that accounting for how a sensitivity to moral situations develops is not equivalent to accounting for how a sensitivity to reasons for action develops. And it is the latter sensitivity that McDowell gives an account of. My aim is to develop a plausible account of the former.

1.d. Virtue as automatic response

A fourth reason that virtue theorists seem to have for holding that the acquisition of virtue requires practice and not just study or reflection is that the virtuous agent sees and does the right thing automatically. That is, the virtuous agent perceives what is required of her immediately, without having to consult rules or deliberate about general principles. So, though in the beginning stages of moral education, the virtuous agent is usually provided with general rules or heuristics that act as training wheels, through the process of acquiring ethical expertise, those general rules fall away. What is left is an internalized framework that transcends general principles and allows the agent to respond effectively and automatically to both the nuance and novelty of particular moral situations.

As J. Jeremy Wisneiwski writes:

> through repeated exposure to situations that involve moral action, even when these situations initially involve deliberation

---

[14]   McDowell, 'Virtue and Reason', 333.

and judgment, we can develop the ability to respond immediately to the situation we perceive. The situation becomes 'unitized' or 'chunked', and what once required cognitive effort becomes automatic and immediate. …This is perhaps just another way of pointing out that repeated experience matters – that we learn – but what we learn to do is sometimes to perceive immediately the essential nature of particular situations, and this can involve immediate recognition of the kind of action called for by the situation.[15]

And as Jacobsen writes,

> The novice is given some handy rules, such as: 'think how you would feel if someone said that to you'. As one learns to be kind, though, these heuristics eventually give way to something like a perceptual capacity.[16]

And Annas, too, agrees that this as relevant aspect of virtue: She writes

> [T]he reasons have left their effect on the person's disposition, so that the virtuous response is an intelligent one while also being immediate and not one that the person needs to consciously figure out.[17]

But as with the above considerations for why practice is required for the acquisition of virtue, what becomes automatic and immediate, according to these theorists, is the right response or the selection of the appropriate output in a moral situation. That is, the rules that a novice is given are rules about right actions. Accordingly, the proposal is that those rules are internalized in such a way as to guide, in a subtle and flexible manner, responses to particular, embedded moral circumstances. However, as we've already seen in previous examples, nothing is said about how practice develops automatic, perceptual skills for attending to and identifying moral situations in the first place. That is, the input side of selecting the morally relevant features of a moral situation is almost completely overlooked. And even when perceptual capacities are invoked, as they are by Wisneiwski and Jacobsen, they are perceptual skills of the McDowell variety: that is, capacities to perceive appropriate responses.

Just to be clear, my claim here is not that the above accounts of virtue are incompatible with a view that emphasizes the importance

[15] J.J. Wisniewski, 'The case for moral perception', *Phenomenology and the Cognitive Sciences* **14** (2015), 129–148.
[16] Jacobson, *Seeing by feeling: Virtues, skills, and moral perception*, 393.
[17] Annas, *Intelligent Virtue*, 30.

of practice for acquiring the perceptual skills needed for selecting and identifying the morally relevant properties of particular situations. Rather, I am simply illustrating that standard accounts of virtue miss this feature of moral expertise and, as such, provide us with an incomplete picture of virtue and its acquisition. That is, by focusing on outputs or responses alone, standard accounts of moral expertise overlook the importance of practice in refining an agent's ability to select and identify appropriate moral inputs. Selecting appropriate inputs and identifying them veridically, as I'll argue below, is required if an agent is going to be able to respond to those inputs appropriately. After all, if one is unable to detect and categorize a situation as a moral situation in the first place, then it is unlikely that she'll be able to respond to that situation at all, never mind have the ability to respond to it appropriately.

2. Expertise and Motor Skill

In this section, I will present empirical evidence from sports psychology strongly suggesting that experts differ from non-experts in at least three ways when it comes to the selection of perceptual input: (1) experts and non-experts differ in the ways in which they attend to the same perceptual array, (2) Experts and non-experts recognize and thus recall different domain-specific patterns or properties of a perceptual array, and (3) experts and non-experts differ in the way in which they use information. That is, experts are able to use early visual cues to make quicker and more accurate predictions than non-experts.

The reason that these differences are important comes down to how seriously we want to take the analogy between virtue and practical skill. At the very least, it seems reasonable to hold that if virtue really is a kind of practical skill, then what studies of motor expertise prove is that experts select and organize inputs in categorically different ways from non-experts. This should force us think about how moral experts may attend, identify, and make predictions based on perceptual information in ways that differ significantly from those who lack moral expertise. In short, on the account that I am recommending, we need to take seriously the possibility that moral experts perceive the world differently from moral novices. This applies not only to expert decision-making or the selection of appropriate responses (the perception of affordances for moral action, one may say), but when it comes to the expert's abilities to detect, recognize, and categorize situations as moral situations in the first place.

147

What I am suggesting is that experts and non-experts literally see the world differently and it is this difference that we must take into consideration of if we are to have a complete account of virtue.

2.a. Expert attention

In examining the sports psychology literature on motor expertise, one feature that emerges across multiple domains and decades of research is that experts develop the capacity to effectively allocate attention for efficient information pick-up in ways that differ systematically from non-experts. Specifically, differences have emerged in the visual search strategies that experts employ when looking at a perceptual array. The plausible background assumption here is that looking to a particular location is importantly connected to attending to that location and retrieving information from the location where one looks. Before presenting the evidence from studies on motor skill and attention, I'd like to note that though attention is a complex phenomenon, the way in which I am using the term here, very generally, is to refer to the cognitive process responsible for selection. That is, I am concerned with attention as a process of filtering or highlighting features or targets of an action space insofar as they that are relevant for guiding, controlling, or otherwise contributing to a task or activity.[18]

It's important to notice that attention can be very roughly divided into two kinds: top-down and bottom-up. As Wayne Wu explains, top-down attention is endogenously deployed; it is attention that 'can be intentionally directed as when one looks for a missing object' whereas bottom-up attention is stimulus-driven. It is 'attention that is captured as when a loud sound pulls one's focus to it'.[19] Though bottom-up attention may be relevant to expertise, at least insofar as one can conceive of an expert's attention being captured by an unexpected event or stimulus relevant for successful task instantiation while the novice fails to notice the same event or feature, the studies that I will consider below will be concerned with top-down attention. That is, the studies will consider how an agent,

[18]   W. Wu, *Attention* (New York: Routledge, 2014), 11.
[19]   Wu, *Attention*, 11. More formally: 'S's attention to X is *top-down* if and only if S's attention to x involves the influence of non-perceptual psychological state/capacity for its occurrence' and 'S's attention to X is *bottom-up* if and only if S's attention to X did not involve a non-perceptual psychological state/capacity for its occurrence' (Wu, *Attention*, 30).

herself, directs her attention in various ways to the relevant features of a perceptual array. In what follows, I will sometimes refer to top-down attention as selective attention.[20]

Over the past three decades, evidence concerning motor expertise has converged on the fact that experts attend to sports-specific perceptual arrays in ways that differ in significant and systematic ways from non-experts. As Mann et al. write in their meta-analytic review, it has been found that 'experts differ from non-experts... on sport specific measures of attention allocation and information pick-up'.[21] Specifically, it has been found that experts employ fewer visual fixations than non-experts (*inter alia* they attend to fewer locations) and those fixations last for longer periods of time than the visual fixations of non-experts. As such, we can say that the selective attention of experts differs from that of non-experts along at least three dimensions: frequency, location, and duration.[22,23]

Evidence of attentional differences between experts and non-experts has accumulated for decades. For instance, in studying basketball, Bard and Fleury[24] found that:

The eye movement data indicated that significantly fewer fixations were used prior to a response by expert basketballers

[20] Selective attention can be defined as: the 'preferential detection, identification and recognition of selected stimulations' (D.L. Woods, 'The physiological basis of selective attention: Implications of event related potential studies', in J.W. Rohrbaugh, R. Parasurasman and R. Johnson (eds), *Event-Related Brain Potentials* (New York: Oxford University Press, 1990), 178.

[21] D. Mann, A.M. Williams, P. Ward, & C.M. Janelle, 'Perceptual-Cognitive Expertise in Sport: A Meta-Analysis', *Journal of Sport & Exercise Psychology* **29** (2007), 457–478, 459.

[22] Mann et al., 'Perceptual-Cognitive Expertise in Sport: A Meta-Analysis', 460

[23] In these studies, it is assumed that visual fixation is a sign of attention. For instance, as Just and Carpenter write: 'The more information which has to be processed, the longer the fixation duration.' (M.A. Just and P.A. Carpenter, 'Eye fixations and cognitive processes', *Cognitive Psychology* **8** (1976), 441–80). Though, not without its problems, this interpretation seems plausible. For problems see chapter 5 of A.M. Williams, K. Davids, and J.G. Williams, *Visual perception and action in sport* (New York: Routledge, 1999).

[24] C. Bard & M. Fleury, M. 'Analysis of visual search activity during sport problem situations', *Journal of Human Movement Studies* **3** (1976), 214–22.

(M = 3.3) than novices (M = 4.9). Also, differences were found in the distribution of visual fixations to selected areas of the display. Novices fixated primarily on a receiving team-mate when deciding to pass, while experts fixated additional sources of information such as the position of the nearest defender and the space available between the defender and basket.[25]

And when studying expert soccer players, the results of Tyldesley et al.[26]

showed that the experienced players responded significantly faster than the inexperienced players to the soccer-specific stimuli. Moreover, visual search data revealed that when viewing a right-footed player strike the ball, the experienced players did not fixate on either the supporting leg or any part of the left side of the body. Their scanning behaviour was more structured and consistent than the novices with fixations being restricted to the right side of the body and the shooting leg.[27]

The above observations have been confirmed across a range of sports domains including basketball,[28] soccer,[29] fencing, and table

[25] Williams et al., *Visual perception and action in sport*, 157.
[26] D.A. Tyldesley, R.J. Bootsma, & G.T. Bomhoff, 'Skill level and eye movement patterns in a sport orientated reaction time task', in H.Rieder, H. Mechling and K. Reischle (eds) *Proceedings of an International Symposium on Motor Behaviour: Contribution to Learning in Sport* (Cologne: Hofmann, 1982).
[27] Williams et al., *Visual perception and action in sport,* 158.
[28] C. Bard, & L. Carriere, 'Etude de la prospection visuelle dans des situations problèmes en sports', *Mouvement* **10** (1975), 15–23; C. Bard, & M. Fleury, 'Analysis of visual search activity during sport problem Situations', *Journal of Human Movement Studies* **3** (1976), 214–22; C. Bard. & M. Fleury, 'Considering eye movement as a predictor of attainment', in I.M. Cockerill & W.W. MacGillvary (eds) *Vision and Sport* (Cheltenham: Stanley Thornes, 1981); C. Bard, M. Fleury, & L. Carriere, 'La stratègie perceptive et la performance motrice: Actes du septième symposium canadien en apprentissage psychomoteur et psychologie du sport', *Mouvement* **10** (1976), 163–83.
[29] Tyldesley et al., 'Skill level and eye movement patterns in a sport orientated reaction time task'; W. Helsen, & J.M. Pauwels, 'A cognitive approach to visual search in sport', in D. Brogan and K. Carr (eds) *Visual Search* vol. II (London: Taylor and Francis, 1992); W. Helssen, & J.M. Pauwels, 'The relationship between expertise and visual information processing in sport', in J.L. Starkes and F. Allard (eds) *Cognitive Issues in Motor Expertise* (Amsterdam: Elsevier Science, 1993); A.M. Williams, &

tennis.[30] In sum, as Williams et al. write in their review of the literature on motor expertise and visual search:

> Finally, many other studies have identified differences in visual search strategy using film-based methods. For example, proficiency-related differences have been noted in tennis,[31] volleyball,[32] baseball,[33] and French boxing.[34] These studies have demonstrated differences in the allocation of fixations to selected areas of the display and, generally, have indicated some disparity in search rates between skill groups.[35]

K. Davids, 'Eye movements and visual perception in sport', *Coaching Focus* **26** (1994), 6–9; C. Bard, Y. Guezennec & J.P. Papin, 'Escrime: Analyze de l'exploration visuelle', *Medicine du Sport* **15** (1981), 117–26; H. Hasse, & H. Mayer, 'Optische orientierungsstrategien von fechtern' (Strategies of visual orientation of fencers) *Leistungssport* **8** (1978), 191–200.

[30]   H. Ripoll, H. 'Uncertainty and visual search strategy in table tennis', *Perceptual and Motor Skills* **68** (1989), 507–12.

[31]   R.N. Singer, J.H. Cauraugh, D. Chen, G.M. Steinberg, S.G. Frehlich, & L. Wang, 'Training mental quickness in beginning/intermediate tennis players', *Sport Psychologist* **8** (1994), 305–18; M. Fleury, C. Goulet & C. Bard, 'Eye fixations as visual indices of programming of service return in tennis', *Psychology of Motor Behaviour and Sport* (Champaign IL: Human Kinetics, 1986); C. Goulet, C. Bard, & M. Fleury, 'Expertise differences in preparing to return a tennis serve: A visual information processing approach', *Journal of Sport and Exercise Psychology* **11** (1989), 382–98; V. Ritzdorf, 'Antizipation in sportspiel-dargestelt am beispiel des tennisgrundschlangs' (Anticipation in sport: investigation of the tennis ground stroke), *Leistungssport* **13** (1983), 5–9.

[32]   C. Handford, & A.M. Williams, 'Expert-novice differences in the use of advance visual cues in volleyball blocking', *Journal of Sports Sciences* **9** (1992), 443–4; A. Neumaier, 'Untersuchung zur funktion des blickverhaltens bei visuellen wahrnehmungsprozessen im sport' (An investigation of the function of looking in visual perception processes in sport), *Sportswissenschraft* **12** (1982), 78–91; H. Ripoll, 'Analysis of visual scanning patterns of volleyball players in a problem solving task', *International Journal of Sport Psychology* **19** (1988), 9–25.

[33]   M.D. Shank, & K.M. Haywood, 'Eye movements while viewing a baseball Pitch', *Perceptual and Motor Skills* **64** (1987), 1191–7.

[34]   H. Ripoll, Y. Kerlirzin, J.F. Stein, & B. Reine, 'Analysis of information processing, decision making, and visual strategies in complex problem solving sport situations', *Human Movement Science* **14** (1995), 325–49.

[35]   Williams et al., *Visual perception and action in sport*, 166.

Ellen Fridland

It seems reasonable to interpret the above evidence in the following way: first, when it comes to understanding why experts fixate on fewer locations than non-experts, we can attribute this to the fact that experts know where to look. That is, experts know where the most rich and relevant sources of information in a perceptual array are to be found and, accordingly, they turn their attention directly to those areas. This allows experts to fix their attention to fewer places than novices who search for relevant information throughout a perceptual array and, as such, are less efficient in their capacity to allocate attention to only the most relevant visual locations for detecting task-relevant stimuli. In short, we can say that experts look to different locations than non-experts – experts look only to the most relevant, information-rich locations. And experts look to fewer places than non-experts, that is, they ignore the irrelevant or information-poor locations or features of domain-specific visual arrays.[36]

Further, once experts have developed efficient search strategies, focusing their attention only on the most relevant perceptual locations given their aims, they also spend more time looking at those locations. That is, expert visual fixations have been found to be, in general, longer than non-expert visual fixations.[37] It seems reasonable to interpret this fact as indicating that experts fixate for longer so that they can pick-up more information from those task-relevant, information-rich areas. As such, we see that experts are extracting more information from the task-relevant areas of a visual presentation than their non-expert counterparts.

It seems that these features of expert attention and perception are likely relevant for feeding into the successful follow-on processes of decision-making and action selection that experts employ. Presumably, these processes are relevant not only in allowing the expert more time for decision-making (because visual fixation is efficient) but also for providing the expert with the information she needs for selecting an appropriate response (because visual fixation is effective).

These finding are doubly important because they apply across skills and domains of expertise.[38] That is, at least when it comes to motor skill, it appears that 'all contexts require athletes to focus

---

[36] For further support for the claim that expert perceptual skills are domain-specific, see section 2.b.

[37] Mann et al., 'Perceptual-Cognitive Expertise in Sport: A Meta-Analysis'.

[38] Though there are task relevant differences depending on the nature of the sport. See Mann et al., 'Perceptual-Cognitive Expertise in Sport: A Meta-Analysis' for more.

attention on the most appropriate cues so as to perform effectively'.[39] And what the studies on selective attention show, very generally, is that the 'skilled performer knows the important information within the display and can focus attention on relevant and ignore irrelevant sources of information'.[40] Though the skilled performer excels only within her domain of expertise, across domains, the differences between experts and non-expert in sport are more or less consistent.

These differences in the attentional capacities of experts and non-experts are instructive since it seems at least possible that we'll be able to generalize from motor expertise in particular to expertise in general. Surely, this kind of extrapolation requires empirical support, but if one thinks, as the virtue ethicist does, that virtue is a species of practical skill and we have seen consistently, across a wide-range of practical skills, that there are dramatic changes in a skilled athlete's ability to attend appropriately to domain-specific regions of a perceptual array, then it would seem reasonable to hypothesize that such a capacity develops in moral expertise as well.

2.b. The identification/recognition of patterns

A second important difference between expert and non-expert input selection is reflected in the fact that experts are able to recognize and recall complex domain-specific perceptual patterns more quickly and effectively than non-experts. This is thought to be due to the experts superior abilities of encoding (organizing and storing) and retrieving (accessing) domain-specific information.[41] Studies in the 'recall and recognition' paradigms have shown consistent differences in perceptual recognition and recall across a wide array of domains of expertise from chess to gymnastics, volleyball, basketball, American football, snooker, and others.[42]

The seminal study in this paradigm was conducted by DeGroot in 1965.[43] Studying chess players at various level of skill from Grand Master to club player, DeGroot showed that:

> When chess masters were shown a game configuration for intervals of 5 to 10 seconds, they were able to recall the position of

---

[39] Mann, et al, 'Perceptual-Cognitive Expertise in Sport: A Meta-Analysis', 458.

[40] Williams et al., *Visual perception and action in sport*, 32.

[41] See Williams et al., *Visual perception and action in sport*.

[42] Ibid.

[43] A.D. DeGroot, *Thought and Choice in Chess* (The Hague, Netherlands: Mouton, 1955).

chess pieces almost perfectly from memory. In contrast, this ability dropped off very rapidly below the master level, from a recall accuracy of 93% to a value of 51% for club players.[44]

Of course, from this finding alone it is unclear which capacities expert chess players possess that non-experts lack. And based on this evidence alone, one might guess that Grand Masters have generally superior powers of perception or memory. However, this possibility was ruled out by Chase and Simon,[45] who improved on DeGroot's study by including 'a control condition where chess pieces were arranged randomly on the board rather than in a structured fashion. In this condition, there were no differences between a Grand Master, A-level and Club player'.[46]

What this shows, and what many studies in various domains have since replicated, is that the expert chess players possess neither superior perceptual nor mnemonic abilities. That is, Grand Masters are no better than novices at recognizing or recalling perceptual patterns, in general. Their superior skill comes from their ability to recognize and recall meaningful, chess-related configurations. As such, we can conclude that the superior memory of the Grand Master is domain-specific. That is, the Grand Master has domain-specific knowledge or skill that allows him to effectively encode and retrieve chess-related information more efficiently than more novice players. This is not a general skill that applies to perceptual pattern-recognition or recall at large.

From the recognition and recall paradigm alone, it is difficult to isolate where exactly the perceptual-cognitive advantage of the expert lies. That is, we can be certain that the advantage is domain-specific, but it is unclear whether the domain-specific superiority is in information retrieval or in information encoding or in both. Sports scientists usually interpret the results as indicating more efficient encoding and retrieval (as I do above).[47] As Williams et al. write in their review of the recall and recognition studies:

[44]   Williams et al., *Visual perception and action in sport*, 98.
[45]   W.G. Chase, & H.A. Simon, 'The mind's eye in chess', in W.G. Chase (ed.) *Visual Information Processing* (New York: Academic Press, 1973a); W. G. Chase, & H.A. Simon, 'Perception in chess', *Cognitive Psychology* **4** (1973b), 55–81.
[46]   Williams et al., *Visual perception and action in sport*, 98.
[47]   For instance: 'It appears that skilled basketball players encode task-specific information to a deeper and more meaningful level, thus facilitating the recognition of particular patterns of play. Similar findings have been obtained in American football (D.J. Garland, & J.R. Barry, 'Cognitive

Findings showed that experts are able to take in more information in a single glance than less skilled players because their knowledge allows them to chunk or group information into larger and more meaningful units. Grouping the discrete stimuli in this manner can result in emergent features that are not evident if the stimuli are viewed in isolation. That is, their ability to chunk items (i.e. players' positions) into larger and more meaningful units (i.e. patterns of play) enables them to recognise a developing pattern of play early in its initiation, thus facilitating anticipation.[48]

This interpretation seems reasonable since in the absence of a generally superior memory capacity it would seem that the way in which information is encoded is key to making it easily accessible for retrieval. Further, given the systematic difference in visual fixation that I reviewed in the previous section, it seems unlikely that the novice encodes and stores the same information as the expert but only fails to recall it. This is doubly unlikely since studies of perceptual learning show that with training and practice, individuals become able to detect perceptual patterns that are unitized into meaningful components.[49] For instance, with training, the radiologist detects patterns of visual information that the layperson misses.[50]

---

advantage in sport: The nature of perceptual structures', *American Journal of Psychology* **104** (1991), 211–28), gymnastics (C.H. Imwold, & S.J. Hoffman, 'Visual recognition of a gymnastics skill by experienced and inexperienced instructors', *Research Quarterly for Exercise and Sport* **54** (1983), 149–55), snooker (B. Abernethy, R.J. Neal, & P. Koning, 'Visual-perceptual and cognitive differences between expert, intermediate, and novice snooker players', *Applied Cognitive Psychology* **8** (1994), 185–211), and soccer (A.M. Williams, K. Davids, L. Burwitz, J.G. & Williams, 'Visual search and sports performance', *Australian Journal of Science and Medicine in Sport* **22** (1993), 55–65; A.M. Williams, & K. Davids, 'Declarative knowledge in sport: a by-product of experience or a characteristic of expertise?', *Journal of Sport and Exercise Psychology* **17** (1995), 259–75), Williams et al., *Visual perception and action in sport*, 98.

[48] Williams et al., *Visual perception and action in sport*, 99.

[49] For a recent review of visual perceptual learning, see: Z. Lu, H. Tianmiao, C. Huang, Y. Zhoue, & B.A. Dosher, 'Visual Perceptual Learning', *Neurobiology of Learning and Memory* **95** (2011), 145–151.

[50] See, for instance: P. Snowden, I. Davies, & P. Roling, 'Perceptual learning of the detection of features in X-ray images: A functional role for improvements in adults' visual sensitivity?', *Journal of Experimental Psychology: Human Perception and Performance* **26** (2000), 379–390; and

And the skilled reader becomes able to perceive words and not simply letters on a page. For example:[51]

> Aoccdrnig to a rseearch sduty at Cmabrigde Uinervtisy, it deosn't mttaer in waht oredr the ltteers in a wrod are, the olny iprmoetnt tihng is taht the frist and lsat ltteer be in the rghit pclae. The rset can be a toatl mses and you can sitll raed it wouthit porbelm. Tihs is bcuseae the huamn mnid deos not raed ervey lteter by istlef, but the wrod as a wlohe.

In short, training allows patterns to emerge that would otherwise remain undetectable to the unpracticed individual. As such, combining (1) the plausible assumption that the way in which information is stored effects the ease with which it is accessed with (2) evidence that expert's attend to perceptual arrays in ways that are systematically different from non-experts and adding (3) evidence that through perceptual learning, individual's refine their capacity to detect complex patterns or properties, it seems safe to conclude that experts differ from non-experts both in their ability to recognize various significant features or patterns of a domain-specific perceptual array and also excel at retrieving those relevant perceptual configurations from memory efficiently.

Returning to virtue, as above, if we want to take the parallel between practical skill and virtue seriously, then it seems that we should attribute to the moral expert the capacity to recognize and recall perceptual features or patterns that remain undetectable to the layperson. This may go for recognizing that one is in a moral situation in the first place, for instance, recognizing that one is encountering injustice or wrongdoing of some kind or other. Or it may go for detecting and identifying that one is in a moral situation of a particular type, for instance, encountering a situation of racism or sexism. Or, perhaps, it may contribute to the recognition and classification of a moral situation by allowing one to recognize various morally relevant properties, for instance, that a person is in pain or discomfort. The latter interpretation is the one I favor and about which I will say more below. For now, we should simply keep in mind that because recognizing and categorizing situations seems relevant for

---

B. Parolini, G. Soardi, G. & Panozzo, 'Do radiologists develop perceptual learning contrast sensitivity?' *Radiology Medicine* **88** (1994), 852–6.

[51] Georgetown University Medical Center, 'After learning new words, brain sees them as pictures', *ScienceDaily* (2015), <www.sciencedaily.com/releases/2015/03/150324183623.htm>

influencing follow-on deliberation and appropriate response selection, it would behoove us not to overlook this important stage of moral expertise.

2.c. Experts and early detection of perceptual cues

A third distinction between experts and non-experts that becomes apparent when reviewing the literature on motor expertise is that experts are able to use earlier perceptual cues than non-experts in order to anticipate the movements or actions of sport-relevant objects and persons. Studies across the board have shown that experts are quicker at detecting various sport-specific movements and more accurate at predicting the results of those movements. An illustrative example recounted by Williams, et al. reveals the expert capacity to detect and use early cues in tennis. In any early study,

> Jones and Miles (1978)[52] initially used this paradigm to investigate whether tennis players and non-players could successfully anticipate the direction of an opponent's serve. Three different temporal occlusion periods were used: 336 ms after the impact of the ball on the racket (condition A), 126 ms after impact (condition B) and 42 ms before impact (condition C). Subjects included county or international tennis players, club level players and undergraduate students with no tennis experience. Subjects reported their perceptual predictions by indicating where they thought the ball would land on a diagrammatic representation of the service court area which was divided into three sections. The results showed that there were significant differences between the players and non-players in conditions B and C, whilst no differences were found in condition A... Differences between groups were greater in condition C, when more potential information was withheld. Furthermore, the results indicated that the players scored significantly better than chance (i.e. 33.33% success rate) in condition C, signifying that skilled tennis players are able to effectively use information available prior to ball/racket impact in the tennis serve.[53]

---

[52]   C.M. Jones, & T.R. Miles, 'Use of advance cues in predicting the flight of a lawn tennis ball', *Journal of Human Movement Studies* **4** (1978), 231–5.
[53]   Williams et al., *Visual perception and action in sport*, 106.

The capacity to rely on early cues has been widely established in a wide variety of sporting domains. As Mann et al. write:

> Both temporal and spatial occlusion techniques have been employed to systematically demonstrate expert/nonexpert differences in the use of information presented early in the visual display across a variety of sports, including tennis, badminton, squash, cricket, baseball, and volleyball.[54] A summary of these experiments suggests that (1) experts are better able to predict the direction and force of an opponent's stroke based on kinematic information that maintain subtle clues (such as the dominant arm of a tennis player)[55] and (2) experts are more adept than nonexperts at using early flight cues to predict the ball's end location. These findings have been relatively consistent, signifying the attunement of expert-level performers to advance cues otherwise neglected by nonexpert performers.[56,57]

When we return to thinking about virtue as a kind of practical skill, then it becomes clear that the early and accurate detection of morally relevant cues will be important for responding appropriately to situations in real time. In sport, 'perceptual anticipation is essential... because inherent limitations in the performer's reaction time and movement time would result in decisions being made too late to provide an effective counter'.[58] Though some moral situations

---

[54] B. Abernethy, & D.G. Russell, 'Expert-novice differences in an applied selective attention task', *Journal of Sport Psychology* **9** (1987a), 326–345; B. Abernethy, & D.G. Russell, 'The relationship between expertise and visual search strategy in a racquet sport', *Human Movement Science* **6** (1987b), 283–319; E. Buckolz, H. Prapavessis, & J. Fairs, 'Advance cues and their use in predicting tennis passing shots', *Canadian Journal of Sport Science* **13** (1988), 20–30; J. Starkes, P. Edwards, P. Dissanayake, & T. Dunn, 'A new technology and field test of advance cue usage in volleyball', *Research Quarterly for Exercise and Sport* **66** (1995), 162–167.

[55] B. Abernethy, 'Expertise, visual search, and information pick-up in squash', *Perception* **19** (1990), 63–77; D.L. Wright, F. Pleasants, & M. Gomez-Meza, 'Use of advanced visual cue sources in volleyball', *Journal of Sport and Exercise Psychology* **12** (1990), 406–414.

[56] Abernethy & Russell, 'Expert-novice differences in an applied selective attention task'; Buckolz, et al. 'Advance cues and their use in predicting tennis passing shots'; Jones & Miles, 'Use of advance cues in predicting the flight of a lawn tennis ball'

[57] Mann, et al, 'Perceptual-Cognitive Expertise in Sport: A Meta-Analysis', 463.

[58] Williams et al., *Visual perception and action in sport*, 104.

are such that time-pressure exerts very little force (i.e., correcting a historical wrong-doing), others require, like in sport, 'thinking on one's feet' or reacting on the spot.

As an example of the kind of situation that requires a real-time response, we can think of something familiar to us all: sitting in a café or restaurant or bar and overhearing someone being verbally abused. Let's say that the appropriate response to this situation is to intervene on behalf of the less powerful individual.[59] If this is the right response, then one has to implement it in a timely manner. One cannot wait around until after the two leave to do something. Or, for a situation that may hit closer to home: one may find oneself at a conference dinner where a senior academic is making racist or sexist or other off-color remarks to a table full of junior scholars. Or, one may find oneself at drinks where the keynote speaker is making sexual advances towards a younger colleague, who clearly looks uncomfortable with the attention (I know, in philosophy, never!). These situations not only call for intervention but the intervention needs to be implemented in a timely manner. In such situations, one doesn't have the luxury of going home, calling friends for advice, deliberating about all the options, and then reflecting some more. The particular situation calls for an appropriate response at that particular moment. As such, the better one is at using early cues for assessing and predicting the likely unfolding of events, the more time one will have for choosing an appropriate response and the more time this will leave one to implement one's decided course of action.

2.d. Taking stock

To close, As Pylyshyn writes:[60]

[the] skill to direct attention in a task-relevant manner is documented in what is perhaps the largest body of research on expert perception – the study of performance in sports. It is obvious that fast perception, as well as quick reaction, is required

[59] See for instance, programs like Step Up (http://stepupprogram.org), which conduct 'bystander trainings' that provide individuals with the skills to able to intervene in difficult situations, when appropriate. See the Washington Coalition of Sexual Assault programs (http://www.wcsap.org/bystander-intervention-programs) for a list of bystander intervention programs.
[60] Z. Pylyshyn, *Seeing and Visualizing: It's not what you think* (Cambridge, MA: MIT Books, 2003).

for high levels of sports skill. Despite this truism, very little evidence of faster visual information processing has been found among athletes.[61] In most cases the difference between sports novices and experts is confined to the specific domains in which the experts excel—and there it is usually attributable to the ability to anticipate relevant events. Such anticipation is based, for example, on observing initial segments of the motion of a ball or puck or the opponents gestures.[62] Except for a finding of generally better attention-orienting abilities,[63] visual expertise in sports, like the expertise found in the Chase and Simon studies of chess skill, appears to be based on the nonvisual abilities related to the learned skills of identifying, predicting and therefore attending to the most relevant places.[64]

Generalizing these findings to thinking about virtue as a practical skill puts pressure on the virtue ethicist to consider seriously how it is that moral experts detect and use relevant perceptual inputs in order to organize and understand the situations they encounter. Further, it is important to think about how moral experts use their abilities at identifying, categorizing, and predicting in order to facilitate the selection of the most appropriate response to an encountered moral situation. It seems to me that if the analogy between virtue and

---

[61]   B. Abernethy, R.J. Neal, & P. Koning, 'Visual-perceptual and cognitive differences between expert, intermediate, and novice snooker players', Applied Cognitive Psychology **8** (1994), 185–211; J. Starkes, F. Allar, S. Lindley, & K. O'Rielly, 'Abilities and skill in basketball', *Special Issue: Expert-novice differences in sport, International Journal of Sport Psychology* **25** (1994), 249–265.

[62]   B. Abernathy, 'Visual search strategies and decision-making in sport', *Special Issue: Information processing and decision making in sport, International Journal of Sport Psychology* **22** (1991), 189–210; L. Proteau, (1992). 'On the specificity of learning and the role of visual information for movement control', in L. Proteau and D. Elliot (eds), *Vision and Motor Control, Advances in Psychology* **85**, 67–103 (Amsterdam: North-Holland, 1992).

[63]   U. Castiello, & C. Umilta, 'Orienting attention in volleyball players', *International Journal of Sport Psychology* **23** (1992), 301–310; P. Greenfield, P. deWinstanley, H. Kilpatrick, & D. Kaye, 'Action video games and informal education: Effects on strategies for dividing visual attention', *Special Issue: Effect of interactive entertainment technologies on development, Journal of Applied Developmental Psychology* **15** (1994), 105–123; V. Nougier, H. Ripoll, & J. Stein, 'Orienting attention with highly skilled athletes', *International Journal of Sport Psychology* **20** (1989), 205–223.

[64]   Pylyshyn, *Seeing and Visualizing: It's not what you think*, 85.

skill is going to be informative, then it is vital that this aspect of virtue be addressed. Of course, the virtue ethicist may double-down and claim that moral situations are presented to experts and novices alike and that the only difference is in the action selection or recognition of reasons for action. However, if this is the position that one chooses, then it must be acknowledged that the similarity between virtue and practical skill begins to break down. And it should also be acknowledged that moral perception would be a very strange kind of perception indeed, since even simple visual arrays admit of an infinite number of interpretations.[65]

3. Is the detection and identification of moral situations really important for virtue?

Though, for the most part, theorists have overlooked the importance of perceptual input selection, detection, identification and categorization for moral expertise, there are a few exception who have made the case that moral perception, insofar as it is addresses how 'a situation come[s] to have a particular character for a particular moral agent' is central to questions of ethics. This position was advocated by Iris Murdoch in *The Sovereignty of Good*[66] and it has since been defended by Lawrence Blum.[67]

Blum writes:

Moral philosophy's customary focus on action-guiding rules and principles, on choice and decision, on universality and impartiality, on obligation and right action have masked the importance of moral perception to a full and adequate depiction of moral agency. An agent may reason well in moral situations, uphold the strictest standards of impartiality for testing her maxims and moral principles, and be adept at deliberation. Yet unless she perceives moral situations as moral situations, and unless she perceives their moral character accurately, her moral principles and skill at deliberations will be for nought and may even lead her astray. In fact, one of the most important moral differences between people is between those who miss and those who see various moral features of situations confronting them.[68]

[65]   D. Marr, *Vision* (Cambridge, MA: MIT Books, 1982).
[66]   I. Murdoch, *Sovereignty of Good* (New York: Schocken Books, 1970).
[67]   L. Blum, 'Moral Perception and Particularity', *Ethics* **101** (1991), 701–725.
[68]   Blum, 'Moral Perception and Particularity', 701.

Ellen Fridland

The take-away point here is that even the best deliberator or decision-maker will not be a moral agent if she does not recognize the times at which she ought to deliberate, make decisions, or respond to a moral situation. That is, if one goes about one's life barely noticing when one is confronted with a moral situations then no amount of diligence in following principles (even internalized, automatic, situational ones) and no ability to articulate why a given action is the right action can be sufficient to guarantee that the agent will actually employ these principles or abilities in the situations in which they are called for. That is, if one does not have the capacity to detect that one is confronted with a moral situation and if one is unable to accurately identify the character of that situation when one is confronted with it, then even the most astute moral deliberator will not be able to respond appropriately to that moral situation.

To see how ubiquitous the need for accurate perception of moral situations is, we can look to the following mundane situation that Blum introduces:

> John and Joan are sitting riding on a subway train. There are no empty seats and some people are standing; yet the subway car is not packed so tightly as to be uncomfortable for everyone. One of the passengers standing is a woman in her thirties holding tow relatively full shopping bags. John is not particularly paying attention to the woman, but he is cognizant of her.

> Joan, by contrast, is distinctly aware that the woman is uncomfortable. Thus, different aspects of the situation are 'salient' for John and Joan. That is, what is fully and explicitly present to John's consciousness about the woman is that she is standing holding some bags; but what is in that sense salient for Joan is the woman's discomfort.[69]

One can see that even if one has internalized a more or less general principle that one ought to, when one can, offer help to someone who is in discomfort but one also lacks the ability to detect when another person is in discomfort then this kind of internalized principle, even if it is automatic and nuanced, will be useless. That is, if the appropriate response is not triggered by the identification of a matching situation, then one will not act morally.[70] After all, as Blum explains of Joan and John:

[69] Blum, 'Moral Perception and Particularity', 703.
[70] The same goes if we think of the capacity developed through learning and training as a refined sensitivity to reasons for action – that is, a sensitivity capable of distinguishing when it is right to and when it is not right to take

the deficiency lies not only in[John's] failure to act. For we can contrast with John someone who does perfectly clearly perceive other people's discomfort but is totally unmoved by it: he simply does not care and this is why he does not offer to help. John, as I am envisioning him, is not callous and uncaring in this way. We can imagine him as someone who, when other's discomfort is brought to his attention, is as sympathetic and willing to offer help as a person of average moral sensitivities. His failure to act stems from his failure to see (with the appropriate salience), not from callousness about other people's discomfort.[71]

I take it that we all know this kind of person: the one who doesn't notice things that she should and then apologizes profusely for not doing the right thing. In some ways, I have to admit that I find this person even more infuriating than the individual that just doesn't care. This is because, somehow, this 'John' kind of person has let himself off the hook for being unaware of what's going on around him but feels totally secure in his moral standing – that he *would* do the moral thing, had he noticed. Clearly, however, noticing the right things, that is, being sensitive to the right features of the world, is central to being a moral agent in the first place. In this way, moral education and moral virtue requires that agents not only do the right thing, if one notices that that thing is required, but to pay attention properly: to become aware of one's own surroundings, to notice others, to be properly engaged with the world. Without this kind of attunement, without the proper situational awareness real moral virtue is unattainable.

Another facet of detecting and identifying moral situations that seems relevant for moral expertise is identifying moral situations accurately. It seems clear enough that if one is confronted with a

---

steps in alleviating another person's discomfort. That is, if one has the ability to distinguish which reasons are legitimate reasons for action and which are not but one has not developed the ability to detect and identify when those reasons obtain, then one will not be poised to engage in moral situations appropriately.

It seems to me that McDowell's theory is the closest theory to getting this right – since we can naturally find a place for attending, recognizing and identifying moral situations on his account. Nevertheless, the features that one becomes sensitive to in order to detect moral situations and how that sensitivity develops needs to be added to the account that McDowell presents.

[71] Blum, 'Moral Perception and Particularity', 704.

Ellen Fridland

situation that one identifies as having morally-relevant features of S experiencing fear (let's say, as the result of another's speech acts) when in fact the situation is one in which S is experiencing humiliation then when one responds to this situation (let us suppose that the situation warrants a response), it will be very difficult to respond appropriately. After all, the proper reaction to a person who has been made to feel scared, presumably, is different from the proper reaction to a person who has been humiliated. As such, once again, we see that identifying and categorizing moral situations appropriately is crucial for responding to those situations appropriately. In this way, we see a natural parallel in moral expertise to the recognition and recall paradigm of motor skill discussed above.

Lastly, it appears to be a straightforward constraint on moral expertise that the virtuous agent not only act when a response is warranted and act in the right way, but also, act at the right time.[72] The early detection of morally relevant cues is implicated in this latter requirement. This should be obvious since, as I indicated above, there is at least an important set of moral situations (arguably, *the* most important set of moral situations), which involve real-time responses. They require saying or doing the right thing *en situ*. This may require intervention on behalf of a more vulnerable individual or, for instance, signaling that certain speech acts or behaviors are unwelcome and will not be tolerated. Such intervention and early signaling require predicting another's intentions and responding before a harm has been committed. In this way, early detection of cues is central to moral expertise. That is, detecting in advance the likely unfolding of a potentially volatile situation gives one the opportunity to diffuse that situation before it occurs. And, surely, having the ability to avoid or minimize potential harm must be an important feature of moral skill.

As such, we can find a natural place for attending to, identifying, and making predictions based upon relevant moral features of a situation in our theory of moral expertise. By considering, in a holistic way, what is required for moral action, we can see that accurate input selection is required for moral agency. Further, given the empirical evidence from sport psychology, we now have a framework for thinking about how perceptual skills relating to attention, pattern recognition and identification, and early detection of

---

[72] Think of Aristotle on virtue here: 'To be virtuous is to feel [passions] at the right times, with reference to the right objects, towards the right people, with the right motive, and in the right way' (Aristotle, *Nichomachean Ethics*, 1106b, 21–23).

perceptual cues might be relevant for moral expertise. This means that we not only have reason to think that the selection of perceptual input is central to moral action but we also have reason to think that the development of perceptual skills is the result of practice.

4. Some important clarifications and directions for future research

Of course, moral expertise, even if it is a practical skill, will differ from motor expertise in all sorts of ways. In this section, I will forward some cursory suggestions for how one ought to think about the kind of perception involved in the selection of relevant inputs for moral expertise, and the kinds of features that this perception detects. This section is meant to be a preliminary indication of how a theory of moral expertise might develop and not a complete theory in itself. It strikes me that the below proposals are worth refining and pursuing to see if their initial plausibility can withstand scrutiny.

One difference between motor expertise and moral virtue that has likely already alerted itself to the reader is that in studying sporting skill and input detection, the above studies focus almost entirely on visual perception: they measure visual fixation, duration, eye-gaze, etc. One worry, then, is the sensory modality of perception that is studied in motor expertise may not translate easily or straightforwardly to moral expertise. After all, though vision is likely relevant for the detection and identification of many moral situations, it is by no means necessary or sufficient. It is clear that, on the one hand, a visually blind individual need not be morally blind and, on the other, perfect vision does not guarantee accurate moral perception – a child may have 20/20 vision and still fail to detect the relevant features of a moral situation.

That said, it does seem that various kinds of sensory perception will be relevant for detecting moral situations. For example, visually perceiving a particular facial expression or gesture often bears on the proper detection and identification of moral situations. And the same goes for audition; for example, hearing a particular tone of voice or decibel level of speech is often important for the detecting and identifying the unfolding moral situation of a particular kind. However, as I noted above, moral perception is more than visual or auditory perception. I propose that we think of the detection, identification, and anticipation of morally relevant features as a kind of multi-modal perception. The primary sensory modalities may include vision or audition or touch (maybe others, too) but what makes moral perception different from more familiar kinds of perception is that moral expertise also typically involves emotional perception. This proposal is very much in line with recent theories in moral psychology, which insist that emotions play a central role in moral judgments. Such theories have been advocated by philosophers such as Peter Railton,[73] Sean Nichols[74] and Jesse Prinz.[75]

According to Nichols, if we examine the genealogy of norms and moral restrictions/principles, what we'll find is that those norms that are supported or accompanied by affect, are much more likely to persist. The basic implication of this anthropological/historical approach to morality is to show that emotions play a crucial role in the propagation and sustainability of morality. That is, the moral principles that we accept are very likely underpinned by an affective or emotional component. Moreover, it is this component that makes these principles effective either in encouraging or discouraging various kinds of behaviors such as helping and avoiding harm.

In a bolder proposal, Prinz argues that moral judgments not only involve or become sustained by emotions but that moral judgments simply are emotional attitudes.[76] In order to support this claim, Prinz appeals to, among other things, empirical evidence that emotions are both necessary and sufficient for moral judgments. In support of the necessity claim, Prinz appeals to studies of psychopathy. As Prinz explains,

> Psychopaths are the perfect test case for the necessity thesis, because they are profoundly deficient in negative emotions, especially fear and sadness. They rarely experience these emotions, and they have remarkable difficulty even recognizing them in facial expressions and speech sounds (Blair et al. 2001, 2002). Psychopaths are not amenable to fear conditioning, they experience pain less intensely than normal subjects, and they are not disturbed by photographs that cause distress in us (Blair et al. 1997). This suggests psychopathy results from a low-level deficit in negative emotions. Without core negative emotions,

[73] P. Railton, 'The Affective Dog and Its Rational Tale', *Ethics* **124** (2014), 813–859.

[74] S. Nichols, 'On The Genealogy Of Norms: A Case For The Role Of Emotion In Cultural Evolution', *Philosophy of Science* **69** (2002), 234–255.

[75] J. Prinz, 'The Emotional Basis of Moral Judgments', *Philosophical Explorations* **9** (2006), 29–43; J. Prinz, *The Emotional Construction of Morals* (New York: Oxford University Press, 2007).

[76] Prinz, 'The Emotional Basis of Moral Judgments'

they cannot acquire empathetic distress, remorse, or guilt. These emotional deficits seem to be the root cause in their patterns of antisocial behavior.[77]

Importantly, empirical studies have shown that psychopaths are incapable of distinguishing moral from merely conventional principles. That is, 'Psychopaths treat the word "wrong" as if it simply meant "prohibited by local authorities"'.[78] So, for example, a psychopath would treat a claim like 'killing innocent individuals is wrong' as if it were a judgment of the same nature as 'in setting a table, it is wrong to put the spoon to the left of the plate'. If we insist that being able to distinguish merely conventional rules from moral ones is essential to making authentic moral judgments then we should conclude that psychopaths are incapable of making moral judgments.[79] Further, since this inability to distinguish merely conventional from moral principles presumably stems from the emotional impairments characteristic of psychopathy, Prinz concludes that emotions are necessary for moral judgments.

To argue that emotions are sufficient for moral judgments, Prinz appeals to empirical evidence showing that an arbitrary emotional connection between a word like 'often' and an emotional response of disgust can trigger a negative moral judgment or appraisal in individuals who have been hypnotized to associate the two. As Prinz explains, in their study,

> Wheatley and Haidt (2005) hypnotized subjects to feel a pang of disgust when they heard the emotionally neutral word 'often'. They then presented these subjects with vignettes that either contained the word 'often' or a synonym. Some of these scenarios describe morally reprehensible characters, but others describe characters who are morally admirable. Subjects who are hypnotized to feel disgust when they hear the word 'often' judge that the morally admirable characters are morally wrong when that word appears in the vignettes! This suggests that a negative feeling can give rise to a negative moral appraisal without any specific belief about some property in virtue of which something is wrong.[80]

---

[77] Prinz, 'The Emotional Basis of Moral Judgments', 32.
[78] Ibid.
[79] As Prinz writes, 'Psychopaths acknowledge that their criminal acts are 'wrong' but they do not understand the import of this word', Prinz, 'The Emotional Basis of Moral Judgments', 32.
[80] Prinz, The Emotional Basis of Moral Judgments', 31.

Prinz goes on to generalize from the finding that the emotion of disgust has been shown to be sufficient for moral judgment to the claim that emotional attitudes, in general, are sufficient for moral judgments.

The position that I'd like to endorse here is more minimal than the one that Prinz recommends. I claim that the evidence above makes it clear that typical moral judgments involve an emotional component. However, I'd like to stop short of committing to the identity claim that Prinz endorses. This is because I see nothing wrong with allowing that certain moral judgments may be rooted in a purely rational basis and, as such, may lack an emotional component. So, for example, one may lack the emotional attitude of disgust even if one considers child marriage to be morally wrong. Moreover, I see nothing wrong with allowing that one may experience a certain emotional reaction and fail to form the typical moral judgment that corresponds to that emotion. One can think of a person raised in a racist culture trying to overcome her racism as an example of this. She may feel the emotions that usually cause racist judgments (disdain, disgust, etc.) but catch herself feeling those emotions and intervene so as not to form the typical judgment about the minority group member who has caused this reaction in her. We should notice that cases like these are not ruled out by the empirical evidence that Prinz uses to support his own view and, as such, I'd like to remain open to the possibility that such cases are possibilities. So, whereas Prinz insists that moral judgments just are emotional attitudes, I am relying on the evidence to support the more minimal but plausible position that moral judgments generally involve emotional attitudes.

Further, I see nothing in the above evidence that entails that we must accept that moral judgments are always nothing but emotional attitudes. As such, I'd like to admit that, typically, moral judgments involve an emotional component but keep open what seems to me both a plausible and attractive position that moral judgments also involve non-emotional components. For example, it seems likely that moral judgments also involve intellectual components that can be provided by a moral theory, a set of moral principles, or an understanding of moral concepts. It strikes me as likely that mature adults will often form moral judgments that have both emotional and intellectual components and that the intellectual component is not merely one that tracks the causal etiology of the emotional attitude involved in the moral judgment.

Despite this qualification, I believe that Prinz's position regarding the nature of emotional attitudes is illuminating and useful for the purposes of exploring moral expertise as a kind of refined emotional perception. According to Prinz, emotional attitudes are non-cognitive perceptions of bodily changes that are caused by certain events, actions or traits. Following Dretske,[81] Prinz claims that insofar as these bodily changes track certain determinate features of the world, they have representational content. That is, emotional states are non-cognitive perceptions of the body that represent those events, traits or actions that cause them. So, for instance, as Prinz offers, sadness is an emotional attitude that detects loss. And fear is an emotional attitude that tracks danger. Insofar as sadness is caused by loss and fear caused by danger, these emotions represent loss and danger. The representations that regularly cause bodily changes, on Prinz's account, are collected into mental files, or, more precisely, what he calls, 'calibration files'.

This way of thinking about emotional attitudes neatly allows for the refinement and development of emotional perception. This is because, according to Prinz, emotional perception is evolutionarily rooted but it is not fixed or brute. That is, emotional attitudes can be 'calibrated' to track the relevant features of the world more or less accurately. As Prinz writes, 'Calibration files contain a wide range of representations, both cognitive and non-cognitive, and these representations can change over the course of cognitive development'.[82]

In endorsing the view of emotional perception as a component of moral judgment, my claim is that as one practices performing the right actions, at the right time, directed at the right persons, etc. what one develops (at the very least) is a refined capacity to track morally relevant features of the world via emotional perception. That is, through practice, one develops emotional attitudes that are calibrated to the relevant moral features of a situation. Refined emotional perception of this kind gives us a natural way to think about the improvements in attention, identification, and prediction that come with moral expertise.[83]

To end, by endorsing a view of moral judgment as typically involving an emotional component and by relying on Prinz's view of emotional attitudes as both non-cogntitive and representational states that can be calibrated, it should become clear how the detection and

[81]   F. Dretske, *Explaining Behavior: Reasons in a World of Causes* (Cambridge, MA: MIT Press, 1988).

[82]   Prinz, *The Emotional Construction of Morals*, 63.

[83]   See Railton, 'The Affective Dog and Its Rational Tale' (*Ethics* **124**(4) (2014)) for more on how affective intuitions are best construed as attuned competencies.

Ellen Fridland

identification of morally-relevant inputs are refined, tuned, honed or calibrated through learning and development. Since we now have a way of conceiving of emotional perception as a kind of perception that can be refined through practice, this allows us to draw a parallel between motor skill and moral expertise. In motor skill, the ability to attend to, detect, locate, identify and make predictions on the basis of domain-specific visual features develops through practice and is central to motor expertise. Likewise, in moral skill, the ability to attend to, detect, locate, identify and make predictions on the basis of domain-specific emotional features of moral situations develops through practice and is central to moral expertise. As such, we can draw a parallel between refining visual perceptual capacities in motor expertise and refining emotional perceptual capacities in moral expertise. And this, I hope, gives us a cursory way to frame the kinds of suggestions that I've been gesturing to throughout the paper.

King's College London
ellen.fridland@kcl.ac.uk

Forms of Rational Agency

DOUGLAS LAVIN

Abstract

A measure of good and bad is *internal* to something falling under it when that thing falls under the measure in virtue of *what it is*. The concept of an internal standard has broad application. Compare the external breed standards arbitrarily imposed at a dog show with the internal standards of health at work in the veterinarian's office. This paper is about practical standards, measures of acting well and badly, and so measures deployed in deliberation and choice. More specifically, it is about the attempt to explain the unconditional validity of certain norms (say, of justice and prudence) by showing them to be internal to our agency and the causality it involves. This is *constitutivism*. Its most prominent incarnations share a set of assumptions about the nature of agency and our knowledge of it: *conceptualism*, *formalism* and *absolutism*. This essay investigates the merits and viability of rejecting *all* of them while still seeking the ground of practical normativity in what we are, in our fundamental activity.

1. Introduction: reason and will

We all know Hume says,

> the impulse [to pursue a certain object] arises not from reason, but is only directed by it... Reason is, and ought only to be, the slave of the passions[1]

whereas Kant says,

> the true vocation of reason must be to produce a will that is good, not simply as a means to other purposes, but *in itself*.[2]

Thanks especially to Matthew Boyle. I am indebted as well to Matthias Hasse, Christine Korsgaard, Sergio Tenenbaum and Michael Thompson. I have benefited from discussion at the Institute of Philosophy, Leeds, Leipzig, LMU, and the DFG-Netzwerk on Praktisches Denken und gutes Handeln. I am grateful to the Alexander von Humboldt-Stiftung for generous financial support.

[1] David Hume, *A Treatise of Human Nature*, ed. D. F. Norton and M. J. Norton (Oxford: Oxford University Press, 2003), II.3.iii.

[2] Immanuel Kant, *Groundwork of the Metaphysics of Morals*, ed. and trans. Mary Gregor (Cambridge: Cambridge University Press, 1998), 4:396.

doi:10.1017/S1358246117000091   ©The Royal Institute of Philosophy and the contributors 2017

They are commonly taken to be in a dispute about the role of reason in practice: whether this consists merely in determining means suitable to ends given from elsewhere, or also, and more fundamentally, in determining what ends to be pursued. How do we adjudicate such a dispute? When one party claims that rational reflection can and should play only an instrumental role in deliberation, while another claims that it can and should determine what ends are to be pursued, where do we look to figure out who is right?

An influential body of work in contemporary ethics and practical reason proposes that the dispute can be resolved by reflecting the nature of agency. The idea is that we might establish the authority of certain practical requirements – perhaps only conditional requirements between ends and means, or perhaps unconditional requirements on our ends themselves – by deriving them from the the very idea of agency. Seen through this lens, the dispute between Hume and Kant is about whether an agent, considered simply *as such*, is subject only to requirements to take means conducive to its ends, or whether it must also be subject to further, substantive requirements on the ends it pursues. The dispute, in other words, concerns what standards of correctness in practical thought, or measures of acting well, belong *internally* or *constitutively* to the power to act.

On one widespread conception, *constitutivism* is the project of defending a thesis of precisely this sort: a thesis that basic practical requirements are grounded in the nature of action.[3] Constitutivists typically argue, in addition, that fundamental practical principles can *only* be validated in this way – that an agent could shrug off without inconsistency any requirement that could not be traced back to the very nature of agency. Even in the absence of such an argument, this way of understanding the authority of a standard of action has obvious appeal. If it could be shown that any agent is, by nature, subject to certain requirements, this would elegantly clarify why we, who know ourselves to act intentionally, must (in some sense) know ourselves to be bound by them. And if there were such a proof, it would provide a particularly attractive sort of vindication: it would show them to be objective, while at the same

---

[3] Thus in an article summarising the current discussion, Elijah Millgram writes '[c]onstitutivist arguments move from the premises that anything you *do* will inevitably be an action, and that an action is such-and-such, to the conclusions that whatever you *do* will be a such-and-such' Elijah Millgram, 'Pluralism About Action', in *A Companion to the Philosophy of Action*, ed. Timothy O'Connor and Constantine Sandis (Oxford: Wiley-Blackwell, 2010), 90.

time illuminating why they are such as to immediately engage the will of each (perhaps not always, but when we deliberate without interference). It would thus avoid a familiar dilemma: the apparent need to choose between views which vindicate the objectivity of standards of action in a way that leaves a residual mystery about how they might make a dent on the will, and views which explain the immediate bearing of normative thought to move us to act on motivation, but in a way that deprives them of objectivity. Even if some philosophers have given up one or the other, they have done so under the pressure of the difficulty. The natural first response is to seek an account that shows the incompatibility to be merely apparent.

Can the concept of action bear the theoretical weight constitutivists place on it? One ground for skepticism is that different constitutivists come to such strikingly different conclusions about which requirements are built into the structure of agency. Humeans insist that only hypothetical requirements to take appropriate means to one's actual ends, whatever they may be, can be part of this structure.[4] Kantians maintain, on the other hand, that being subject to categorical requirements on ends is a condition of the possibility of being an agent at all.[5] There is reason to worry that intuitions about the requirements contained in the concept of agency simply reflect substantive convictions about the normative requirements to which we are subject, and cannot supply an independent point of leverage on the latter question. Moreover, even if it were shown that, on some

[4]   James Dreier, 'Humean Doubts About the Practical Justification of Morality', in *Ethics and Practical Reason*, ed. Garrett Cullity and Gaut Berys (Oxford: Clarendon Press, 1997), 81–100; Sharon Street, 'What Is Constructivism in Ethics and Metaethics?' *Philosophy Compass* **5**(5) (2010): 363–84; Sharon Street, 'Coming to Terms with Contingency: Humean Constructivism About Practical Reason', in *Constructivism in Practical Philosophy*, ed. Jimmy Lenman and Yonatan Shemmer (Oxford University Press, 2012); Candace A. Vogler, *Reasonably Vicious* (Harvard University Press, 2002).

[5]   Christine M. Korsgaard, *Self-Constitution: Agency, Identity, and Integrity* (Oxford University Press, 2009); Christine M. Korsgaard, *The Constitution of Agency: Essays on Practical Reason and Moral Psychology* (Oxford University Press, 2008); Sebastian Rödl, *Self-Consciousness* (Harvard University Press, 2007). Michael Smith, 'The Magic of Constitutivism', *American Philosophical Quarterly* **52**(2) (2015); Michael Smith, 'A Constitutivist Theory of Reasons: Its Promise and Parts', *Law, Ethics and Philosophy* **1**(0) (2013): 9–30; David J. Velleman, *The Possibility of Practical Reason* (Oxford University Press, 2000), and *How We Get Along* (Cambridge University Press, 2009).

Douglas Lavin

conception of agency, being an agent involves being bound by certain principles, it might still be asked *what reason there is to be an agent in the relevant sense*. A number of critics have argued that, in the absence of an answer, a putative derivation of normative requirements from the concept of agency cannot show them to be *unconditionally* binding. And, the critics add, answering this question requires appealing to a source of normativity other than, or external to, agency itself, and so the constitutivist program simply cannot succeed.[6]

2. Three assumptions about constitutivism

The aim of the present essay is to raise some questions about a set of assumptions accepted by all the parties to this dispute – Kantians, Humeans and their rationalist critics. They assume that an adequate constitutivist account must meet the following conditions:

Conceptualism: It must show certain requirements on action to be *analytically contained* in the very concept of agency, a concept that applies to all subjects capable of acting for reasons, however different they may otherwise be.

Formalism: It must show how to *derive* the relevant substantive requirements from a conception of agency, in such a way that a subject who was skeptical of them, but who understood himself to be an agent in the relevant sense, and was capable of appreciating what this implies, would be compelled to accept the requirements on pain of inconsistency.

Absolutism: It must show that certain normative requirement hold for *all possible* agents-capable-of-acting-for-reasons. If a kind of rational agent which is not subject to these requirements were shown to be possible, the relevant constitutivist project would be shown to be a failure.

These assumptions are closely related. Someone who accepts Conceptualism must accept both Formalism and Absolutism, and while a commitment to Formalism or Absolutism may not strictly imply the others, it certainly makes them natural to think. In any

[6]   David Enoch, 'Agency, Shmagency: Why Normativity Won't Come from What Is Constitutive of Action', *The Philosophical Review* **115**(2) (2006): 169–98; Elijah Millgram, 'Practical Reason and the Structure of Actions', *Stanford Encyclopedia of Philosophy*, 2008; Peter Railton, 'On the Hypothetical and Non-Hypothetical in Reasoning About Belief and Action', in *Ethics and Practical Reason*, 53–79; T. M. Scanlon, 'The Appeal and Limits of Constructivism', in *Constructivism in Practical Philosophy*; R. Jay Wallace, 'Constructivism About Normativity: Some Pitfalls', in *Constructivism in Practical Philosophy*.

case, my project here is not to address subtle issues about the logical relations between these commitments, but to ask whether *any* should be accepted.

I raise this question from a standpoint deeply sympathetic to the spirit of constitutivism. I think it is right to see the debate between Hume and Kant as a debate about the kinds of practical requirement to which we are subject in virtue of our capacity to act for reasons. And I agree that understanding the basis of practical normativity in this way would provide a particularly elegant and attractive way of addressing various basic problems in ethics and meta-ethics. My aim is to show that the project of constitutivism can be understood more broadly than its contemporary advocates and opponents typically assume, a way that retains its deepest attractions, while avoiding various difficulties that beset its most prominent contemporary incarnations. If I am right, there is room for a pluralist, non-formalist constitutivism that that does not seek to ground normative requirements on action in the sheer concept of rational agency, but that still presents appealing and distinctive responses to fundamental questions in ethical theory. Moreover, seeing this possibility will shed a revealing light on the debate between Hume and Kant, and the kind of resolution it might admit.

My conviction that such a view is possible grows out of reflection on Aristotelian ethics. Contemporary discussions of constitutivism seldom mention Aristotle and the kind of naturalism he espouses, but he surely deserves to count as a constitutivist in some important sense.[7] His view is, famously, that the fundamental norms governing how to lead our lives are grounded in the fact that we have by nature a certain *ergon* or characterisitic activity, and that the structure of the human soul implies a certain appropriate division of labor in how do what it is our to do. Thus, for Aristotle, the notion of the *nature* of a human being plays a crucial role in explaining practical normativity, or again the good in action: the fact that we, human beings, act well in doing in certain ways is grounded, ultimately, in what we essentially are, where this is characterised in terms of what we

---

[7]   I do not mean to say Aristotle goes entirely unmentioned. See, for example, Stephen Engstrom, 'The Complete Object of Practical Knowledge', in *The Highest Good in Aristotle and Kant*, ed. Joachim Aufderheide and Ralf M. Bader (Oxford University Press, 2015), 129–57; Christine M. Korsgaard, 'Aristotle's Function Argument', in *The Constitution of Agency* and 'How to be an Aristotelian Kantian Constitutivist' (unpublished).

essentially *do*, our characteristic *activity*.[8] In this sense, Aristotle holds that the norms to which we are subject are *constitutive* norms. It seems, however, that his conception of our constitution, of what we are, includes more than the mere fact that we are capable of acting for reasons: he locates the ground of the practical norms to which we are subject, not in our nature as agents, but in our nature as human beings, a certain kind of material being. Moreover, he displays a striking lack of concern with the task of showing that the relevant norms apply to all possible agents, still less with the task of deriving the relevant norms from some abstract or formal characterization of our nature. He famously says that he aims to speak only to persons who have received a sort of upbringing that already equips them to see the point of certain ways of acting, and he seems to allow for the possibility that different life-forms might imply different lists of ethical virtues. I think these features of Aristotle's project are not simply independent commitments, but expressions of a single underlying idea – *hylomorphism*, to give it a name. A central aim in what follows is to bring out the bearing of this idea on the contemporary debate about constitutivism.

3. Absolutist constitutivism: Kantians and anti-Kantians

3.1. Kantian absolutism

It is a brute but inescapable fact that human beings confront the question how to act. We can deliberate about what speaks in favor of acting one way or another another, but the question whether to be agents at all seems not to be one we can coherently regard as open to deliberation. Christine Korsgaard puts the point this way:

> Human beings are *condemned* to choice and action. Maybe you think you can avoid it, by resolutely standing still, refusing to act, refusing to move. But it's no use, for that will be something you have chosen to do, and then you will have acted after all... You have no choice but to choose, and to act on your choice.[9]

Absolutist constitutivists seek to ground practical normativity on this fixed point. If it could be shown that certain normative requirements on action are implied by the very exercise of agency, then, they argue, these requirements would be shown to be inescapable in a special and

---

[8]   Aryeh Kosman, *The Activity of Being: An Essay on Aristotle's Ontology* (Harvard, 2013).
[9]   Korsgaard, *Self-Constitution*, 1.

interesting sense. For we would be committed to them, not in a manner conditional on our having one or another end, but unconditionally, insofar as we act in pursuit of any end whatsoever. Normative requirements grounded in the nature of agency would thus be unconditional requirements on action.

Kant's *Groundwork* is a principal source of inspiration for absolutist constitutivism. On an influential interpretation, Kant there seeks to prove that a certain fundamental norm governing action, the categorical imperative, is implicit in the very idea of a will, conceived a capacity to determine oneself to act on the basis of reasons. *Kantian* constitutivists seek to defend some version of this claim, and thus to vindicate the idea that there are requirements to which we are subject unconditionally, simply as rational agents. *Anti-Kantian* constitutivists deny that any unconditional practical requirements can be wrung from the sheer idea of rational agency. Many stop short of Hume's conclusion that there can be no rational basis for assessing our ultimate ends, but they maintain, in any case, that the very idea of a capacity to act for reasons cannot be the source of the norms governing such an assessment. Surveying this dispute will help to clarify the attractions of absolutist constitutivism, and also to bring out some questionable assumptions on which it rests.

Korsgaard is the leading contemporary advocate of the Kantian position. In a series of influential papers and monographs, she has sought to show that Kant's categorical imperative articulates a necessary norm of agency – a norm to which rational agents are committed by their very exercise of agency, so that in failing to conform to it, they have acted badly by their own lights. For present purposes, the aspect of Korsgaard's argument of interest is not her case for Kant's categorical imperative in particular, but her general strategy for showing that some such unconditional normative requirement holds.

The strategy, very roughly, is to argue that, unless some unconditional normative requirement holds, there can be no distinction between an exercise of agency, attributable to the agent herself, and the mere expression of forces operative in a person, producing behavior that does not constitute the agent's determining herself to do something.

To exercise agency, Korsgaard proposes, is to determine oneself to perform some act A for the sake of some end E. (She reserves the term 'action' for this form of endeavor – doing A for E – and uses the term 'act' to refer to the thing done – do A). But if an agent is to exercise agency in this sense, she argues, there must be a basis for distinguishing the agent's determining to do A for E from some mere impulse determining her to do A for E. If some impulse in the agent, say an irresistible urge for E, determines her to do A for E, then *she* does not determine her action; rather, she is determined to act in a certain way by a force whose efficacy does not depend on her will. There is, however, a basis for distinguishing the agent's determining her own action from her being non-agentially determined to act only if the agent can consider the question whether to do A for E. And this consideration, Korsgaard goes on to argue, must take the form of assessing whether this 'maxim' – do A for E – can be willed as a universal law. So, in effect, to be capable of exercising agency at all, an agent must be capable of assessing whether her maxims satisfy the categorical imperative, and in representing herself as choosing to perform a certain action, she represents herself as taking her maxim to meet this test.

This line of reasoning would be interesting, I think, even if its final steps were judged unsuccessful. Whatever we think of Korsgaard's concluding argument (which I have not tried to reconstruct) for the claim that agents are always already assessing their actions by the categorical imperative, I think we should be intrigued by her strategy for showing that agency requires, not just the capacity to take reasonable means to one's ends, but the capacity to make some sort of unconditional rational assessment of one's action as a whole (one's doing A for E). Korsgaard takes this point by itself to rule out a Humean conception of practical reason. Humeans hold that the proper function of practical reason is simply to consider what means should be taken to realize given ends. But according to Korsgaard, 'the instrumental principle (i.e., the principle that one should take the necessary means to one's ends) cannot stand alone': if there were no supporting rational commitment to pursue some end E, there would be no basis for a distinction between the agent's failing to conform to the instrumental principle (by not taking the necessary means to achieve E) and her simply ceasing to pursue E.[10] For a principle to be a genuine norm governing action, Korsgaard holds, it must be possible for an agent to fail to conform to this principle. In particular, if the instrumental principle is to be genuinely normative, it must be possible for an agent who is pursuing E to know that doing A is necessary for achieving E, and yet fail to do A. But if the agent is not rationally committed to pursuing E, then her not taking what she knows to be the necessary means to E does not exhibit any rational failure, for nothing about the agent's situation requires that she should pursue E at all. Korsgaard concludes that, in the absence of some sort of rational commitment to the pursuit of particular ends, there is no such thing as the agent's being instrumentally irrational.

---

[10] Christine M. Korsgaard, 'The Normativity of Instrumental Reason', in *Ethics and Practical Reason*, 251.

This result, she maintains, is just another manifestation of the point that the applicability of the concept of agency requires a distinction between the agent's determining herself to action and something else determining this:

> [Hume] has no resources for distinguishing a person's ends from what she actually pursues. Another way to put the same point... is to say that Hume has no resources for distinguishing the activity of the person *herself* from the operation of beliefs, desires, and other forces *in her*.[11]

I'm describing these arguments because I think they have undeniable appeal. There is something attractive in the thought that agency requires determining oneself to act in pursuit of a certain end, as opposed to being passively determined to action; and it seems plausible that, if we could not regard certain ends as rational to pursue, the question whether it is rational to take certain means would not have the sort of significance it has for us. Nevertheless, I believe that each of these ideas is in fact question-begging in the context of the debate with anti-Kantians. Explaining why this is so will bring out the need for an alternative account of the appeal of Korsgaard's arguments, one that does not require interpreting them as stating what must be so where there is action at all.

Consider the first idea: that agency requires determining oneself to act in pursuit of a certain end. In arguing from this conception of agency to the existence of unconditional requirements, Korsgaard presupposes that *what* an agent must determine herself to do is of the form: do A for E.[12] This is to conceive of the object of choice, not simply as an act (do A), but a certain principle of action (do A for E). But this is precisely what anti-Kantians should not admit. On their view, the only necessary requirement on agency is the conditional requirement that, given a certain end, the agent should take appropriate means. Hence they should not admit that agents, simply as such, face rationally-assessable choices about whether to act on a certain principle; for this is tantamount to admitting that agents, simply as such, face rationally-assessable choices about whether to pursue certain ends. Anti-Kantians should admit only that, *given the ends* an agent is in fact going after, she faces the choice *whether to take certain means*. On this view, the agent's end does not fall

---

[11]   Ibid., 233.

[12]   Thus Korsgaard takes it to be uncontentious that 'what the will chooses is, strictly speaking, actions', where an 'action' is a doing of A for E. That this assumption is contentious has been discussed by Millgram in 'Pluralism about Action', though he interprets its significance very differently than I do.

within the scope of her choice – or at any rate, the sheer fact that she is an agent does not entail that it do so. And so, if Korsgaard's argument depends on assuming that the object of choice is what *she* calls 'action' – doing A for E – then it takes for granted the very point in dispute. But once this assumption is dropped, there is no direct route to the conclusion that an agent whose ends simply appear and disappear as the result of forces operative in her does not *determine herself* to act. After all, on the anti-Kantian view, the requirement of self-determination applies, not to the agent's principle of *doing A for E*, but only to her act of doing A, and no reason has been given to think that the agent's doing A (rather than, say, B, which she judges to be possible but less conducive to achieving E) cannot be self-determined.

Turn now to the second idea: that, if an agent could not regard certain ends as rational to pursue, the question whether it is rational to take necessary means would lose significance for her. Korsgaard's argument for this presupposes a certain conception of the role that the instrumental principle must play in our practical thought. As we have seen, she assumes that it must be possible for an agent to be pursuing E, and know (or at least believe) that doing A is necessary for E, and yet not do A. Only this, she thinks, would be a genuine failure to respect the instrumental principle, and only a principle that an agent can fail to respect can be a genuine norm of agency. But again, this is precisely what anti-Kantians should not admit. On their view, an agent, considered simply as such, is subject only to the norm that,

(IP$_{AntiK}$) Given the ends she is pursuing, she should: take the necessary means.

Here the 'should' has narrow scope: it applies only to her taking the means that are in fact necessary to achieve her ends.[13] Contrast this with a wide-scope reading of the instrumental principle:

[13] The scope contrast I am drawing here should not be confused with the more familiar contrast between a wide scope reading of practical norms on which they are of the form:

(WS) It ought to be the case that, if p, then the agent does A.

and a narrow scope reading on which their form is:

(NS) If p, then it ought to be the case that the agent does A.

Korsgaard holds that fundamental norms of practical rationality cannot be formulated in the manner of (WS), on pain of their not being genuinely practical norms ('The Activity of Reason', *Proceedings and Addresses of the American Philosophical Association* **83**(2) (2009): 27–29.) It is less clear whether she would accept formulations along the lines of (NS) or hold

(IP$_K$) The agent should: take the necessary means to her ends.

Let it be granted that a principle can only count as a genuine norm of agency if it is possible for an agent to violate it. For an agent to violate (IP$_K$), she would need to choose *not to take the necessary means to her ends*; and this plausibly requires her believing of some act A that it is necessary for achieving her end E and yet not doing A. But for an agent to violate (IP$_{AntiK}$), she would need only to be pursuing a certain end E and choose *not to do A*, which is in fact necessary for E. To impose the additional requirement that she should do this while believing that doing A is necessary to achieve E is to require, not only that she should be capable of voluntarily acting in a manner that is (in fact) not conducive to her end, but that she should be capable of voluntarily flouting the instrumental principle itself – knowing it to apply and yet choosing not to conform to it. But this is again tantamount to assuming the very point in dispute. Anti-Kantians simply should not admit that rational agency requires being 'governed by the instrumental principle' in a sense that would require the possibility of *this* specific sort of violation. For on their view, the only necessary object of practical reason is: whether *to do such-and-such*, not whether *to conform to the principle that requires doing such-and-such*.

The upshot of these criticisms is that Korsgaard has no non-question-begging argument for the conclusion that any agent, simply as an agent, is subject to some unconditional normative requirement. Her arguments apply, at best, only to a certain *form* of agent, one capable of choosing to do A for E – choosing to act on a certain principle, as I have put it. How serious a setback is this for Korsgaard's Kantian constitutivism? It is a decisive defeat *if* the Kantian project must be to derive unconditional normative requirements from the very idea of agency; but is it obvious that Korsgaard's arguments are of interest only if they meet this condition? Whatever may be true of agents simply as such, it seems attractive to hold that human agents are characteristically capable of choosing to act on principles. At any rate, I take myself to be capable of making such

---

out for something else altogether. But whatever the outcome of this dispute, there remains the question whether the scope of the instrumental principle is wide or narrow in the sense I have distinguished: whether it says that we are rationally required to take the means to our ends, or only that, given certain ends, we are rationally required to take certain means. My claim is that, with respect to this latter contrast, Korsgaard's argument presupposes the wide reading.

choices – and I take myself to have this capacity, not on the basis of self-observation, but by reflection on my very ability to understand and deliberate about whether it is right to act on the principle: do *A* for *E*. I don't claim any special success in subjecting my principles of action to such scrutiny: I do not often rise to this level of reflection, nor do I claim any distinction in disciplining my action by its results. But I know myself at least to be *capable* of this sort of self-scrutiny: embarrassment over doing so only here and there expresses a presumption that I could do better.[14] And to this extent, it seems that Korsgaard's reflections – to the extent that they are cogent – might after all get a grip on me even if they do not get a grip on all conceivable agents.

3.2 Kant's anti-Kantianism

Contemporary Kantians like Korsgaard commonly suppose their burden is to show that any conceivable rational agent must accept the categorical imperative as a norm governing her action. One indication that this might not be necessary to comprehend vindication of comes from the historical Kant. For whatever his view might have been at the time of writing the Groundwork, by the time he wrote the *Critique of Practical Reason*, he plainly held that being subject to the moral law is known to us, not as a consequence of some more basic premise about the general nature of rational agency, but as a basic fact of reason – something known to us in virtue of having the sort of power of practical reason that we actually have, together with the capacity to reflect self-consciously on exercises of this power. Indeed, in the *Religion*, Kant says explicitly that the concept of moral 'personality' (i.e. the concept of 'a rational and at the same time responsible being') is not contained in the concept of

---

[14]   Compare Kant's famous remark on how our very recognition of the moral law implies a recognition of our own practical capacities: 'Ask [someone] whether, if his prince demanded, on the threat of the... prompt penalty of death, that he give false testimony against an honest man whom the prince would like to ruin under specious pretenses, he might consider it possible to overcome his love of life, however great it may be. He will perhaps not venture to assure us whether or not he would overcome that love, be he must concede without hesitation that doing so would be possible for him. He judges, therefore, that he can do something because he is conscious that he ought to do it'. Immanuel Kant, *Critique of Practical Reason*, trans. Mary J. Gregor, (Cambridge University Press, 1997), 5:30.

'humanity' (i.e., the concept of 'a living and at the same time rational being'):

> [F]rom the fact that a being has reason, it does not at all follow that, simply by virtue of representing its maxims as suited to universal legislation, this reason contains a faculty of determining the power of choice unconditionally, and hence to be 'practical' on its own; at least, not so far as we can see. The most rational being of this world might still need certain incentives, coming to him from the objects of inclination, to determine his power of choice. He might apply the most rational reflection to these objects – about what concerns their greatest sum as well as the means for attaining the goal determined through them – without thereby even suspecting the possibility of such a thing as the absolutely imperative moral law which announces to be itself an incentive, and, indeed, the highest incentive. Were this law not given to us from within, no amount of subtle reasoning on our part would produce it or win our power of choice over to it.[15]

Kant here appears to admit quite unequivocally that a merely Humean power of practical reason (i.e. one that can and should only reason instrumentally, and perhaps prudentially, on the basis of given sensible inclinations) is conceptually possible, or in any case that we cannot rule it out. If so, the existence of unconditional practical norms cannot be demonstrated by any analytical-deductive argument beginning simply from the idea of a living being with the power of practical reason. Nevertheless, Kant holds that we actual humans know ourselves to be, not merely Humean agents, but morally responsible persons, on the basis of a law 'given to us from within' – namely, the moral law implicit in our very understanding of the unconditional practical 'ought'.[16]

Kant's position suggests the possibility of a non-absolutist constitutivism: one that recognizes the possibility of more than one form of agency, and that seeks to vindicate our subjection to unconditional normative requirements by showing them to belong constitutively

---

[15] Immanuel Kant, *Religion Within the Boundaries of Mere Reason and Other Writings*, trans. George Di Giovanni (Cambridge University Press, 1998), 6:26.

[16] Op. cit. note 145:31. This is commonly supposed to reflect a change in Kant's position. For doubts see Stephen Engstrom, *The Form of Practical Knowledge* (Harvard University Press, 2009). Sergio Tenenbaum, 'Speculative Mistakes and Ordinary Temptations: Kant on Instrumentalist Conceptions of Practical Reason', *History of Philosophy Quarterly* **20**(2) (2003), 203–23 and 'The Idea of Freedom and Moral Cognition in Groundwork III', *Philosophy and Phenomenological Research* **84**(3) (2012), 555–89.

to our specific form of agency, rather than to rational agency *simpliciter*.

3.3. Humean absolutism

The possibility of such a pluralist constitutivism is routinely overlooked, not only by contemporary Kantians aiming to defend unconditional normative requirements, but also by their anti-Kantian opponents. To take just one example, consider[17] which begins by arguing that

> 1. Any rational agent, simply as such, is subject to the instrumental principle.

For, he argues, unless an agent's practical reasoning is governed by this principle, she is incapable of drawing any practical inferences from given aims to determinate actions, and if she is incapable of drawing practical inferences, then nothing can count as a practical reason for her. He then argues that

> 2. The instrumental principle is the only necessary principle of practical reason.

For, he holds, no other putative principle of practical rationality shares the unquestionable necessity of the instrumental principle: it makes no sense to ask for a reason to take the means to your ends, whereas this question at least makes sense for any other putative practical requirement. But it is plausible that

> 3. If compliance with morality were demanded by practical reason, this would require the existence of an unconditional, non-instrumental principle of practical reason.

Thus, Dreier concludes, Hume is vindicated:

> 4. Practical reason does not demand compliance with morality.

Without disputing any premise of this argument, I want to note an ambiguity in its use of the phrase 'practical reason'. It might mean either practical reason, considered simply as such or practical reason as we know it. The considerations Dreier offers in favor of premise (2) – granting their cogency for the sake of argument – establish this premise only if 'practical reason' is read in the former way: they establish that no further principle is required by the very idea of a capacity to reason practically. But the conclusion, (4), is a

---

[17] Dreier, 'Humean Doubts About the Practical Justification of Morality'.

vindication of Hume only if 'practical reason' is read in the latter way, as a claim about our actual power of practical reason – for surely Hume meant to claim, not just that a Humean agent is conceptually possible, but that we are actually Humean agents, whose reason is and ought to be a slave to our passions.

4. The possibility of pluralism

To assume that a vindication of Hume can be inferred from Dreier's premises is, in effect, to assume that if only the instrumental principle is necessitated by the very concept of a capacity to reason practically, then the instrumental principle is the only principle that can belong necessarily to a capacity for practical reason. It is to assume that if no further requirement of practical rationality is conceptually necessary, then no further requirement of practical rationality is actually possible. This is to overlook the possibility of a *pluralist* constitutivism, one which acknowledges that a Humean form of practical reason is conceptually possible, and thus that no unconditional practical requirements can be derived from an analysis of the very concept of a rational agent, but which maintains that other, richer forms of agency are also possible.

Dreier does not give an argument to rule out this possibility: he simply assumes that the debate over constitutivism is a debate about whether there are practical requirements to which all conceivable rational agents are subject. And though I cannot argue the point here, I think this holds true also of other prominent contemporary anti-Kantians: they pass from arguments for the claim that Humean rational agents are conceptually possible to conclusions about what practical reason demands of us, by way of an uncritical assumption that any constitutivist vindication of practical requirements must ground those requirements in the very idea of a rational agent.[18] This absolutist assumption, shared by contemporary Kantians and anti-Kantians, gives their dispute the appearance of a conflict in which only one side can be correct. But once we recognize the possibility of a pluralist constitutivism, we can see that each side might be right about something significant. The anti-Kantians might be right that the very concept of a capacity to act for reasons does not imply any further requirement beyond the instrumental principle, while the Kantians might be right that our actual capacity to act for

---

[18] See, for example, Smith, 'The Magic of Constitutivism', Street, 'Coming to Terms with Contingency', Vogler, *Reasonably Vicious*.

reasons takes a form that implies the existence of unconditional practical norms. So long as neither side frames its point in absolutist terms, their views are consistent.

5. The problem of inescapability

If the discussion of the last section is sound, a pluralist position – one that allows for the possibility of multiple forms of agency, each constitutively subject to its own characteristic requirements of practical rationality – is a dialectically attractive option that is mostly overlooked in contemporary debates over constitutivism. This calls for explanation: if this sort of position is available and attractive, why is it not considered?

To see a reason for this neglect, it will help to consider an influential criticism of the constitutivist program. This criticism brings out that, on some ways of understanding the thesis that being subject to certain norms is 'constitutive of being an agent', this thesis proves too flimsy to support the metaethical results that constitutivists hope to derive from it. It can seem that the only way to avoid this sort of flimsiness is to embrace Absolutism, Conceptualism, and Formalism. I conjecture that it is some – perhaps tacit – recognition of this difficulty that prevents the pluralist alternative from coming into view. But in fact, I will argue, we can avoid the difficulty without embracing these commitments.

The kind of objection to constitutivism I have in mind is exemplified by David Enoch's much discussed essay 'Agency, Shmagency'. He begins by noting that a main attraction of constitutivism, as it is standardly presented, is that it would clarify why certain normative requirements on action are rationally authoritative – why a rational agent cannot coherently ask, concerning such norms, 'Why should I care?' For, constitutivists hold, since the question 'Why should I care?' is asked by an agent considering how to act, and since the relevant norms are implied in the very idea of agency, there can be no genuine question about whether, in the relevant sense of 'should', these norms should be followed. But, Enoch objects, this sort of account of the authority of certain norms simply takes it for granted that one should strive to be what 'an agent' ought to be. If being an agent requires conformity to certain norms to which many people do not actually seek to conform, then it seems coherent to ask 'Why should I be an agent?' But if this question is coherent, then any norms implied by the idea of agency appear to apply to a given subject only conditionally, insofar as she has reason to be an agent. In the absence of such a reason, it is rationally permissible for her to say 'Agency, Shmagency!' And even if there is such a reason, it presumably cannot itself be grounded in norms implied by the very idea of agency, since it is supposed to ground the applicability of those very norms. So in either case, the constitutivist project of grounding the authority of certain norms in the nature of agency fails.

Now, it is not clear that Enoch's question, 'Why should I be an agent?', is genuinely coherent. Constitutivists generally reply that being an agent is not an attribute that a subject can coherently choose to have or not to have. I *am* an agent, not by choice, but simply by virtue of my nature as a free, self-determining being. Any choice I make will inevitably be the choice of an agent. So, arguably, the question 'Why should I be an agent?' presupposes the possibility of a standpoint that no deliberating subject can actually occupy. If this is right, then any norms implied by the very idea of agency are not just conditionally binding; they are binding on any subject who can confront the question what to do, and the constitutivist project is vindicated.

This reply, however, may seem to be available only to a constitutivist who relies in his argument on the most abstract and minimal conception of agency. For it may seem that being an agent is an inescapable attribute of a subject who confronts the question what to do only if 'being an agent' means nothing more than: being such as to be capable of confronting the question what to do. After all, given any richer conception of agency, it is not a necessary truth that a subject who can act for reasons must be 'an agent' in this sense. So given any richer conception of agency, Enoch's question may seem to regain its grip: why should one strive to be 'an agent' in this richer sense, if it is possible to deliberate, choose, and act without being such a thing? But if Enoch's question gets a grip, then Enoch's dilemma for constitutivism applies. So it appears that a principled constitutivism must aim to ground whatever norms it seeks to vindicate in the very concept of agency, a concept that applies to any conceivable subject capable of acting for reasons. And then a pluralist constitutivism is obviously unacceptable: for if a certain form of agency is supposed to be, not the one-and-only form required in any agent capable of acting for reasons, but one of a plurality of possible forms, then the normative requirements implied by that form will be open to Enoch's challenge, and so the relevant form of agency will not provide the basis for a constitutivist vindication of those norms.

I suspect that a more-or-less explicit concern with heading off such a challenge underlies the widespread assumption that a satisfying constitutivism must accept Absolutism. Enoch offers an elaborate version of the challenge, but the basic idea is simple. Constitutivists seek to show that certain norms are unconditionally required by observing that anything you choose to do will be an action, and arguing that any action, as such, is subject to certain normative requirements. But, as Millgram puts it,

> The point that anything you do will be an action is likely to be granted only on the thinnest and most minimal reading of what an action is.[19]

Hence it appears that a satisfying constitutivism must assume only the thinnest and most minimal reading of what an action is. But a pluralist constitutivist would be someone who accepts that there are several possible forms of agency, no one of which is necessarily exhibited by all subjects who can act for reasons. Hence a pluralist constitutivist would seem to deprive herself of the cornerstone on which constitutivist arguments are built: the premise that, necessarily, if you act at all, you must do something that is subject to such-and-such normative requirements.

I have described this challenge because I think it provides an intelligible motivation for the assumption that an acceptable constitutivism must be Absolutist. But while this motivation strikes me as intelligible, I think it actually rests on an unsound inference.

It is true that, if there is a plurality of forms of agency, then no one form of agency is necessarily exhibited by all subjects who can act for reasons. Properly understood, however, the constitutivist project need not rely on the claim that there is a form of agency that is necessarily exhibited by any subject who acts for reasons. The constitutivists' claim need not be:

> **The Form:** There is a form of agency such that, necessarily, any subject who acts for reasons will exhibit that form of agency.

It might rather be:

> **My Form:** For any subject who acts for reasons, there is some one single form of agency such that, necessarily, that subject will exhibit that form of agency.

On the latter reading, the starting-point of the constitutivist argument is not the claim that a certain form of agency is inescapable full stop, but that for a given subject, a certain form of agency is inescapable. If this is true, then that agent is inescapable subject to whatever normative requirements are implied by that form of agency, whether or not it is possible for there to be other kinds of agents subject to other kinds of norms. And that, in effect, is the pluralist's claim: not that there are norms to which any agent, simply *qua* agent, is subject, but that we, *qua* agents of the kind we are, are subject to certain specific norms.

Such a pluralist position will be defensible to the extent that it can be shown that there is a form of agency that is inescapable for us: not an optional refinement that we might choose to exhibit or not to exhibit, but a kind of self-determination that we, being the kind of beings we are, cannot fail to exhibit in our actions. If this condition were satisfied, then we could not coherently ask Enoch's question concerning this form of agency, even if other forms of agency were logically possible.

6. Reason and will: an Aristotelian approach

The preceding section concluded with an abstract description of a possible pluralist constitutivism. But could there actually be a position that met this description? Could we acknowledge that certain fundamental practical norms apply, not to every conceivable agent, but only to agents of a certain form, and yet maintain that, for agents of this form, these norms have an inescapable authority? I think Aristotle's ethics shows the possibility of such a position, and clarifies some of its crucial structural features. My aim in this final section is to sketch – very briefly and programmatically – a reading of Aristotle's ethics along these lines.

It will help to begin by recalling four very familiar features of Aristotelian ethics. First, Aristotle's approach is founded on an appeal to the idea that human beings, as human beings, have a proper work or a function.[20] This, he holds, is what gives determinacy to the inquiry into what human happiness consists in, and thus into how we ought to live. The idea of a human function sounds alien to modern ears, but it becomes clear as the argument proceeds that what Aristotle has in mind is that human beings possess a specific kind of soul, one characterized by certain vital powers or principles, and chiefly, the power of reason. The function of man is to live (and thus to exercise the full complement of these powers) in a manner governed by reason, and Aristotle infers that, since the good of a thing is determined by its function, the human good

---

[20] Aristotle, *Nicomachean Ethics: Translation, Introduction, Commentary*, ed. Sarah Broadie, trans. Christopher Rowe (Oxford University Press, 2002) I.7.

consists in the excellent performance of those activities that belong to a reason-governed life.

This first point dictates the structure of Aristotelian ethics, but it does not yet determine its content. Although the main divisions of Aristotle's investigation are settled by his conception of the structure of the human soul, what falls within these divisions consists – and this is the second point – of an enumeration of various specific virtues. Aristotle makes no attempt to derive these virtues from his abstract characterization of the human function, and this has seemed to some commentators to make the initial appeal to function superfluous. This reaction, however, depends on a questionable view of the role that the notion of function is supposed to play. Apparently it is not supposed to provide a basis from which to derive particular virtues; Aristotle seems to regard it, rather, as a crucial clarification of what sort of thing a virtue is supposed to be. We might say that it is not the principle of their discovery, but the account of their metaphysical basis – of the kind of fact which can make it the case that a certain putative virtue is a genuine and not a merely pretended one.

Third, Aristotle presents his treatise on ethics as addressed, not to people needing to be convinced that the virtues he enumerates are virtues at all, but rather to those who have been 'properly brought up', brought up in such a way that they already are attracted to these ways of living.[21] Aristotle thus does not seek to address the sort of moral skeptic that Plato confronts in the person of Thrasymachus or Callicles: he merely develops a systematic framework in which to clarify and understand the unity of various goods to which his audience is already unreflectively drawn. And this modesty of justificatory ambition seems closely connected to certain other well-known features of Aristotle's view: his insistence that we should not expect the basic principles of ethics to admit of precise codification;[22] his likening of the understanding of the virtuous person to a capacity for accurate perception rather than for sound reasoning;[23] and his identification of the case-by-case judgment of the practically wise person, rather than some abstract formula, as the standard of right action.[24] All these features of Aristotle's view confirm the observation that he does not expect his general account of the human good to supply the principle of a non-question begging deduction or derivation of the soundness of certain ways of

---

[21]   Ibid., I.5.
[22]   Ibid., I.3.
[23]   Ibid., II.9.
[24]   Ibid., II.6, 1107a1-2, VI.12, 1144a34.

life, or of the right thing to do in particular circumstances. This is not to suggest that he would regard such questions as not open to argument, but he does not seem to aspire to offer a certain sort of foundational argument about such matters.

Finally, the fourth point: although the *Nicomachean Ethics* seeks to give a general account of human virtue, Aristotle is notoriously willing to contemplate the idea that different virtues are appropriate to a man, a woman, a child, and a slave. Whatever else we may make of this, it indicates at least that Aristotle thinks of his official system of virtues as characterizing, not norms applying to all possible agents possessing a rational soul, but norms appropriate to a specific sort of rational agent (namely, the patriarchs of free families living together in a political community). Moreover, in a striking passage, Aristotle remarks that, to the extent that we may think of other species of animals as having practical wisdom, it will be right to say that there is 'a different philosophic wisdom about the good of each species.'[25] The apparent implication is that the practical wisdom he characterizes in the Ethics is, not the only possible form of practical wisdom, but the kind pertaining specifically to human beings. We could express the significance of this by saying that, were there another species of rational animal, the fundamental principles of its practical thought might be quite different from those that govern ours. Perhaps the mode of excellent activity that characterized its reason-governed life would not require courage (think of a rational rabbit); perhaps it might not even be a specifically social rational animal, needing the virtue of justice. At any rate, our practical wisdom is the sound capacity for choice of a certain specific form of agent.[26]

I hope these descriptions of familiar aspects of Aristotle's position resonate with the case made earlier for the possibility of a pluralist constitutivism. Aristotle's ethics is evidently open to the possibility of pluralism, and he certainly does not aim to deduce his system of fundamental norms of action from an analysis of rational agency as

---

[25] Ibid., VI.7 1141a32-3.

[26] Michael Thompson brought the passage to my attention. Here and throughout I have been influenced by Thompson's work. See his 'Forms of Nature: 'First', 'Second', 'Living', 'Rational' and 'Phronetic'' (unpublished). Also see the following: Matthias Haase, 'Life and Mind', in *The Freedom of Life: Hegelian Perspectives*, ed. Thomas Khurana (Berlin: August Verlag, 2013), 69–109; Jennifer Whiting, 'Hylomorphic Virtue: Cosmology, Embryology, and Moral Development in Aristotle' (unpublished).

Douglas Lavin

such. He does not aim to deduce these norms at all, but simply (i) to give a clarifying description of them to people who already possess an incipient appreciation of their importance, and (ii) to articulate the metaphysical conditions that make it possible for this description to be sound or unsound.

In what sense is this a constitutivist position? I noted earlier that Aristotle's view can be regarded as constitutivist inasmuch as it seeks to ground the fact that we ought to act in certain ways in what we essentially are – where 'what we essentially are' includes, not just that we are rational agents, but that we are specifically human agents. It may seem, however, that this is a constitutivism in name only; for if it does not seek to show that the relevant sort of constitution has inescapable practical authority over those who bear it, and does not seek to deduce specific practical norms from this constitution, in what sense can it claim to ground these norms in our constitution?

At this point, it is important to recall what made the constitutivist approach attractive in the first place. It was, I take it, not its deductive or analytical aspirations *per se*, but rather what the relevant deductions and analyses were supposed to secure: an account of the source of fundamental practical norms that shows how they can be objective but not alien to our will, and that elucidates why their claim to authority over us is not one we can just shrug off, but one to which we are always already committed in the very exercise of our power to choose and act. The basic attraction of constitutivism, then, lies not in its being specially well placed to prove that certain fundamental practical norms apply to us, but in its giving an especially attractive account of what makes it the case that certain fundamental practical norms apply to us. Or to put it another way: the constitutivist's real contribution to metaethics consists, not in offering an account of the epistemology of normativity that would make its claims especially indubitable, but in offering an account of the metaphysics of normativity that would make the nature and authority of these norms particularly transparent.

It seems to me that Aristotle's approach to ethics can lay claim to these advantages of constitutivism in spite of its pluralist, non-analytical, non-deductivist character. What it offers is not a picture of how we can reason to the relevant practical norms; but that is not the basic sense in which the grounding of these norms needs clarification. What needs clarification is what sort of thing a 'fundamental practical norm' might be such that it could have the relevant combination of objectivity, authority, and capacity to move the will. Aristotle sketches a metaphysics that clarifies this by explaining the relation of the relevant norms to what we essentially are. His account aims to explain why, being the kind of agents we are, and receiving the kind of upbringing that such agents receive in favorable circumstances, we come to find the relevant norms primitively compelling – and also why (i.e., what makes it the case that) we are right to do so. A practically wise Aristotelian agent does not reason from his being (or being committed to being) a human being to specific norms of how he ought to live. His being a human being need not itself come into his practical thought at all, except incidentally. He faces no question about why he should be a human being, or do what human beings, as such, ought to do. It is enough that he is – essentially – a human being, and that this explains why it is sound for the goodness of certain specific ways of living and acting to figure primitively in his thinking about what to do and how to live.

I cannot develop the point here, but I suspect this aspect of Aristotle's ethics reflects much more basic features of his metaphysics. His metaphysics, famously, is hylomorphism: the view that the being of the most basic natural beings (natural substances) consists of a certain type of form being realized in a certain sort of matter. The essence of a natural substance consists, not of its mere form, but of such-and-such-a-form-in-such-and-such matter. In application to human beings, I would argue, this means that our essence is not simply: rational being, or rational animal, but rather: rational-animal-subject-to-such-and-such (specifically human) conditions. And our essence is that sort of being in the absence of we would not be at all. Hence it is not a mode of being one of us might fail to have. The consequence of this point, when brought together with Aristotle's project of explaining good in terms of essence, is that the measure of goodness that flows from our essence is not one that one of us can coherently reject, being what we are. This is not to say that the relevant measure of goodness is unquestionable, but that there is a true and intelligibly well-founded answer to such questions, an answer grounded in what can be called our constitution. We need not accept the substance of Aristotle's ethics to see the structural appeal of such a position. Why should a philosophically significant form of constitutivism claim anything more than this?

University College London
d.lavin@ucl.ac.uk

Action as Downward Causation

HELEN STEWARD

Abstract

In this paper, I try to argue that the recognition that non-human animals are relevant to the free will problem delivers interesting new ways of thinking about the central metaphysical issues at the heart of that problem. Some such dividends, I suggest, are the following: (i) that the problem of free will can be considered to be just a more specific version of a general question concerning how agency is to be fitted into the natural world; (ii) that action can be usefully regarded as an especially interesting form of downward causation; and that (iii) the metaphysical possibility of downward causation, and hence, indirectly, also of free will, can be illuminated in valuable ways by thinking about the hierarchical structure of, and systems of functioning within, biological organisms.

What is the problem of free will? In this paper, I want to argue that an answer to this question which differs in certain important respects from most of the usual articulations would constitute an important step towards actually solving the problem. The reformulation I envisage, moreover, is no mere change of subject; rather, it is an attempt to show that new resources for tackling even the traditional problem can be helpfully brought into view if one conceives of that traditional problem merely as one facet of a more *general* issue about the nature of agency itself – an issue about what it is for something to *act*, as opposed merely to responding in the manner of an inanimate object to the conditions and circumstances in which it finds itself. I contrast agents with inanimate things because life and agency are importantly related. Perhaps we cannot say absolutely that life is a necessary condition of agency – but at any rate, in my view, the only agents we know of *at present* are certainly living ones. And so, I believe, it makes sense to look to biology, the science which deals with the living, and in particular, to the nature of biological complexity, for help with answers to the question how agency is possible – a question which, I shall argue, is simply a more general (and prior) version of the more usual question how free will is possible. My suggestion will be that if there is to be any hope of providing a metaphysically satisfactory answer to the traditional problem of free will, we must learn to see it as simply a specific version of a broader question

doi:10.1017/S1358246117000145   © The Royal Institute of Philosophy and the contributors 2017

about agency and its place in nature. And once we have done so, I argue here, new forms of answer hove into view.

In the first section of the paper, I shall attempt to give a sense of some of the important features of the usual sorts of elucidations of the problem of free will. I have gathered together what I hope is a representative sample of offerings by the simple expedient of sampling the top Google hits which are returned when one searches for the phrase 'The Free Will Problem'. Having drawn out some of the common features of the explanations of the problem which are thus elicited, I shall then move on to suggest, in the second section, that we ought to expand the range of the free will question beyond that assumed by the range of approaches surveyed, so as to encompass all forms of agency and will try to explain why it seems to me indefensible and ultimately incoherent to ask the question only in the limited way in which it has tended to be asked. Then, in the final section of the paper, I shall try to show that thus reconceived, the big metaphysical question at the heart of the free will problem becomes essentially an issue in the philosophy of causation – an issue, specifically, about whether downward causation, understood as the influence of a whole upon its own parts, is possible. I shall try to suggest (though inevitably somewhat speculatively, given the space available) that a proper understanding of the nature of biological organisms gives us reason to think that the answer to this question may be 'yes'.

1. Traditional Free Will

According to *The Information Philosopher*, top of the list of Google hits for 'the Free Will problem', '[t]he classic problem of free will is to *reconcile* an element of freedom with the apparent determinism in a world of causes and effects, a world of events in a great causal chain'.[1] Determinism is usually defined as the idea that everything that happens in the world is determined, or settled, by the way things were beforehand, together with the laws of nature, and although I have my doubts about some aspects of this definition, I shall not quarrel with it for the purposes of this paper. I should like instead to focus, for the moment, on another issue – namely, the question of what is meant exactly, in this account of the classic problem, by 'an element of freedom'? What is the element of

[1]   http://www.informationphilosopher.com/freedom/problem/, accessed 19.07.2016.

freedom which the classic problem requires us to reconcile with determinism? Moving a bit further down the entry in the *Information Philosopher*, we find out that this important freedom has to do with 'our will' and 'our actions' – note that interesting word 'our' - and the site then also goes on to mention the moral responsibility we may be supposed sometimes to have for these actions of ours. Compatibilists, we are told, believe that determinism is compatible with moral responsibility – that even if everything is deterministically caused, we can still be morally responsible for at least some of our actions. Incompatibilists, on the other hand, believe that this is not the case, and that moral responsibility depends on the falsity of determinism.

The next Google result on the list is headed 'The Free Will Problem: A Philosopher's Take' and is written by Justin Caouette. Caouette writes that '"Free Will" is a philosophical term of art for a particular sort of capacity of rational agents to choose a course of action from among various alternatives'[2] and that the problem of free will is that this capacity seems to be incompatible both with determinism and with indeterminism – so that it is impossible to have free will, whether determinism is true or not.

The third result is the Wikipedia entry on free will.[3] According to Wikipedia, 'free will is the ability to choose between different possible courses of action. It is closely linked to the concepts of *responsibility, praise, guilt, sin,* and other judgments which apply only to actions that are freely chosen. It is also connected with the concepts of *advice, persuasion, deliberation, and prohibition'.* The problem of free will is then said to arise for those who believe that free will is the capacity for an agent to make choices in which the outcome has not been determined by past events. For determinism suggests that only one course of events is possible, which looks, on the face of it, to be inconsistent with the existence of such free will.

And then the next Google hit – the last one I'm going to consider – is a Youtube clip of a talk by the philosopher Richard Holton, under which the text announces that 'the problem of free will is the question of whether we human beings decide things for ourselves, or are forced to go one way or another'.[4]

---

[2]   Justin Caouette, 'Free Will: A Philosopher's Take' at https://aphiloso pherstake.com/2012/08/13/the-free-will-problem/, accessed 19.07.2016.

[3]   https://en.wikipedia.org/wiki/Free_will, accessed 19.07.2016.

[4]   Richard Holton, https://www.youtube.com/watch?v=iSfXdNIolQA, accessed 19.07.2016.

Helen Steward

In some respects, of course, these four elucidations of what the free will problem actually is are rather different from one another. The second one, for example, suggests that indeterminism may be just as much of a problem for free will as determinism is, something that the other accounts do not mention. The first and third accounts mention responsibility; the second and fourth do not do so. And there are other differences, too. But I am more interested here in something that the four explanations have in common – and that is this. All four of these explanations either say explicitly, or else imply in one way or another, that the free will problem is a problem which specifically concerns *human beings*, and which has no relevance or application to animals other than ourselves. Let us go through them in turn. *The Information Philosopher*, talks of 'our will' and 'our actions' and the need to reconcile these things with determinism. But who is the 'we' that the possessive adjective 'our' is referencing here? I think it is fairly safe to say that it is a widespread convention in the philosophical literature, that when philosophers use the word 'we', they generally mean 'we human beings'. And any doubts we might have had on this score are in any case soon dispelled by the reference to moral responsibility – for moral responsibility seems to be something we can only really sensibly attribute to human beings.[5] And if this is the case, then the *Information Philosopher* entry seems to be suggesting that the problem of free will is essentially a problem about *human* will and *human* action – and the extent to which the element of freedom we generally suppose to be implicit in these things can be reconciled with the doctrine of determinism.

Let us turn to the next of my four examples. Justin Caouette's stated view is that free will is a capacity of rational agents. This is turn raises the interesting question which *are* the rational agents – perhaps if it were allowed that some animals are rational, Caouette's view would not be straightforwardly inconsistent with the idea that animals might have free will. But traditionally, of course, rationality is thought by philosophers to be the distinguishing mark of the *human being* – for Aristotle, for instance, and hundreds of philosophers since, though humans belong to the *genus* animal, our species is

[5] Of course, we can remonstrate with our pets, and try to train them into behaving as we would wish them to do – but when a puppy chews one's favourite slipper, it isn't really appropriate to think that the puppy is *to blame* in any very deep way. One might punish him, perhaps, to try to stop him doing it in future – but surely no one really thinks that a dog can be *morally* responsible for its actions, even if he can fail to respond as hoped to a training programme.

distinguished from the others by the differentia of rationality.[6] It seems highly probable, then, that Caouette considers the free will problem, once more, to be a problem about reconciling a specifically *human* capacity with determinism and/or indeterminism. This is, moreover, implicitly confirmed further down the page, where Caouette remarks that free will might also be called 'up-to-usness'. For once again, here we must ask the same question we asked in connection with the entry in *The Information Philosopher*: namely, who is this 'us' whom things are being said to be up to? The natural answer to return is that the implicit 'we' of philosophical discourse is generally the 'we' of humanity – and so we are, I think, justified in supposing that this is what Caouette has in mind, too. Once again, then, the free will problem is being implicitly posed as a problem about a capacity of human beings.

The next case is *Wikipedia*. *Wikipedia* says that free will is the capacity to choose between different possible courses of action. Here, one might think, we have a definition potentially more amenable to a more extended application to non-human animals – for it certainly isn't obvious that the capacity to choose between different possible courses of action is peculiar to human beings. For example, I quite often put two bowls of food down for my cat – one wet food, out of a tin, the other dry food, out of a bag. It does not seem totally implausible to say that when she wanders into the kitchen, she has a choice between at least two possible courses of action – eating the wet food or eating the dry. But whatever impression we might have had that the *Wikipedia* definition of free will is liberal in this regard is immediately dispelled by the next sentence, which tells us that free will is closely linked to the concepts of responsibility, praise, guilt and sin – which suggests, once again, a resolutely moral context and a focus exclusively on human beings.

And then finally, there is the YouTube video. At least Richard Holton is absolutely explicit – the problem of free will, he claims, is the problem of whether *we human beings* decide things for ourselves, or are forced to go one way or another. Non-human animals simply do not come into it.

I think, then, that these various websites provide quite a lot of evidence that the traditional free will problem is standardly taken to be a problem exclusively about human beings – a capacity they have which only they have, to choose one course of action over another, and perhaps to do so for reasons, a capacity, moreover, which is very tightly connected to the capacity for moral responsibility. In the

---

[6]   See, for example, *Nicomachean Ethics*, I 13, which develops the Aristotelian view of humanity as the rational animal species.

Helen Steward

rest of this paper, what I want to try to do is to argue that this restriction of the free will problem to human beings has been a serious mistake. Its source, quite probably, is a religious world view, according to which human beings are indeed unique and special creatures, singled out by God for special attention, and given by him a peculiar set of responsibilities, including dominion over the rest of the animal kingdom. We need to try to see, however, whether that view of free will can really survive independently of the support provided by that particular religious context. And I shall be trying to argue that it cannot. I do not wish to deny for a moment that human freedom goes much deeper than the freedoms available to other creatures, because we are the possessors of a range of capacities which enable us to make much more of our freedoms than any other animal can – but we will nevertheless not be able to understand human freedom and its metaphysical requirements properly unless we first think about the animal capacities from which it has evolved.

2. Free Will as Agency

One way to see why we need to think about animals in connection with free will is to think about why free will is supposed to be a problem for philosophy in the first place. The traditional issue, as we have just seen from these various websites, is supposed to arise primarily when we contemplate the thesis of determinism, which we are taking for present purposes to be the idea that the future is settled by the past, together with the laws of nature. Now, speaking for myself, it does not seem too too difficult to imagine that a purely *inanimate* world might be deterministic. I don't in fact believe that the inanimate portions of our world *are* entirely deterministic (considered by themselves, and independently of interference by the animate) – for there appear to be a number of truly random – and hence, indeterministic – phenomena in the inanimate parts of nature. Radioactive decay, for example, as currently understood, appears to be an indeterministic phenomenon. Although there are, of course, overall laws governing the phenomenon of radioactive decay, laws which determine the rate at which the overall process must happen for any given radioactive substance, and hence what is the half-life of any given radioactive element, it appears that the emission of individual particles is a random matter, there being no known way to predict or control when such an individual emission event will occur. So in fact, parts of the inanimate world seem to contain indeterministic events. But there does not appear to be anything particularly difficult, conceptually speaking, about imagining an inanimate universe that is deterministic, even if the actual universe is not in fact an example of one. Mostly, we tend to think that inanimate things do what they do simply as a result of the circumstances in which they find themselves, the events which then impinge upon them, and their own intrinsic natures. For example, suppose I add some potassium to water. What happens is that the potassium zips around on the surface of the water and catches alight. Here, we are seeing, no doubt, the operation of certain chemical laws, which govern the alkaline metals, laws which dictate in general respects what will happen when the potassium contacts the water. And moreover, even though they are doubtless more complicated and difficult to state, most of us would probably think that it was determined not only that the potassium would catch light and zip around, in the manner of the alkaline metals, but also that the precise trajectory of any given, particular piece of potassium was also determined by various prior conditions, in conjunction with more complex and particular laws. Perhaps, for example, the trajectory will be a product of such things as the size and shape of the potassium, the speed at which it hits the surface, the temperature of the water, the shape of the containing vessel, and so on, such that in principle, if we knew all these variables, and how they mattered exactly, we might be able to say where precisely the potassium would go. And this, in turn, is an expression of the conviction that so far as things like bits of potassium are concerned, we more or less expect determinism to be the order of the day, and would be quite surprised if we were to find out that it was not. If the world just consisted of a bit of water and potassium, it seems perfectly conceivable that nothing in the world would be left either to chance or to anything else – that the unfolding of reality through time would be fixed entirely by the properties of those two elements, and the laws which they must obey.

However, the question is, I think, whether this deterministic picture is so readily acceptable once we complicate the nature of the universe we are considering. The traditional philosophical view is, of course, that once human beings enter the picture, there are at least *prima facie* problems about reconciling some of our ordinary beliefs about what human beings are, and the sorts of things they can do, with the thesis of determinism. For we tend to think that on many of the occasions on which we act, more than one course of action is open to us. I could watch TV, or I could go and do some more work. I could walk straight past this homeless person, or bend down to speak to him and try to help. And so on. Whereas if the world is deterministic throughout, it might seem as though these multiple possibilities for action that we think we have are just mirages. The conditions at the beginning of the universe, together with the laws of nature fix or settle exactly what will happen at each subsequent time, rendering free will an illusion, or so the argument goes. Compatibilist philosophers disagree, of course, that determinism would render free will illusory. But for the purposes of this paper, I do not want to go into this debate between compatibilists and incompatibilists. What I want rather to ask is whether the *prima facie* problem of free will must wait for the introduction of human beings into the universe to arise – whether it does not arise already once we add to the world any animals that exceed a certain fairly lowly degree of complexity. Do we really think that absolutely everything that is ever done by a non-human animal is fixed and settled by prior conditions and laws, in just the same way as I suggested we tend to think is the case for things like portions of potassium? Or do we rather think, pre-theoretically, at any rate, that animals are in this respect a bit like humans, with the capacity to choose or decide a certain array of things at the time of action?

I want to suggest that in our everyday thinking, we do not really conceive of many animals in anything like the same way as we think about things like potassium and water. When potassium and water interact, we do not suppose, by and large, that anything is left to be settled at the time of interaction *by the potassium* – it just has the properties it has, and these dictate that it does what it does – and that is that. Whereas so far as the higher animals are concerned, we tend not to think that they do what they do simply as a result of the circumstances in which they find themselves and the relevant laws of nature. In the case of such animals, we tend to posit another factor as well; we are inclined to think that many of the more complex and cognitively sophisticated animals, at any rate, have what one might call a *will*, so that what they do at any given time is partly dependent on *them*, and on decisions or choices they make at the time of action. In talking of decisions and choices, I do not mean to suggest that animals necessarily think things over, weigh alternatives or deliberate, prior to the moment at which they actually act – though there seems in fact to be evidence that some of them do.[7] In the case of many animals, perhaps action is often undertaken without much, or even any prior

---

[7] For sceptics, I recommend watching the problem-solving feat managed by a rather remarkable New Caledonian Crow at https://www.youtube.com/watch?v=cbSu2PXOTOc. It is almost impossible not to ascribe a deliberative thought process to the crow when watching it perform this task.

thought (as indeed is very often true in our own case). But when something acts in one way though it could have acted in another way, that represents a kind of choice, even if the agent does not think about what to do in advance – a kind of choice I have elsewhere called a *settling*.[8] The animal settles which way the world will go in respect of its body and immediate environs, *as* it acts. But a portion of potassium never settles anything. It just does what the circumstances of its positioning dictate that it will do. The higher animals thus have a distinctive place in our conceptual scheme. They are conceptualised by us as entities which *act*, which are true sources of self-motion, which are possessed of that interesting and distinctive form of spontaneity we call a *will*. They are conceptualised by us, that is to say, as agents. The question now is whether in reality they can live up to the demands placed upon them by this exacting conceptual scheme.

I think a very common worry amongst philosophers is that this view of animals as creatures to whom real options are available is biologically unrealistic. Animals, these philosophers might say, are driven by a set of basic forces which are connected with the need to survive – and that means that they are subject to certain laws of nature, just like everything else. Now, at a certain level of description, and in some limited respects, I am actually perfectly happy to accept this. A hungry and healthy dog, for example, presented with a dish of tempting food, will, in the absence of any particular reason to suppose itself in danger, eat that food. I don't wish to deny that – or any similar obvious truths about what animals of different types will do when confronted with certain exigent circumstances. But there are two very important qualifications. The first is that even if the generic type of activity that an animal will perform in certain sorts of circumstances *is* determined, perhaps by some laws relating to its nature, the *specifics* of its activity need not be. Perhaps it is determined, for example, that the hungry dog will attempt to eat the food. But precisely how fast, how often each mouthful will be chewed, whether this or that portion of food will be eaten first, whether to drink some water in the middle of the whole thing, whether to break off eating to exploit the chance of a walk at some point – these, I suggest, are things which are settled by the dog itself at the very time of its activity – they are not things which have been settled years in advance by circumstances and the laws of nature. Part of the surprisingness, the unpredictability and the chanciness of the world derives from these moment-to-moment settlings by animals of how *precisely* the world will evolve in respect of them – where exactly

---

[8]   See my *A Metaphysics for Freedom* (Oxford: Oxford University Press, 2012) for the development of this concept.

Helen Steward

they will move, and how, at what precise speed and direction, and so on. And the second thing is that not all circumstances *are* exigent. Between feeds, searches for mates, sleeps, and so on, many non-human animals seem to engage, like us, in a kind of leisure – engaging in activities such as sunbathing, grooming, playing, and so on. How long precisely these leisurely interludes between more urgent activity will last, what precisely will go on in detailed respects as they happen, and so on, seems to me most unlikely to have been settled since the dawn of time by the initial conditions and the laws of nature. To think that it is would be to turn what animals do into a kind of clockwork – and their activity into something which is not activity at all, but merely what William James memorably called the 'dull rattling off of a chain that was forged innumerable years ago', the tedious and inevitable unwinding of a set of events to which there is no physically possible alternative.

This brings me to a point which I think is of considerable importance in the philosophy of action – and that is that in my view, and for the sorts of reasons I have just given, it is the phenomenon of action *itself* which is in ostensible tension with deterministic visions of the world. It is important to emphasize how different this is from the view which appears now to be standard in the literature on free will. The standard view is that action itself is a widespread phenomenon which is deterministic in many of its manifestations, and in particular is deterministic in all its *non-human* manifestations – but there is a special kind of action – usually referred to as *free* action – which is such that the agent, though she in fact does some particular thing at a given time, could have done something else instead. In other words, the metaphysical picture of the world of actions is something like that pictured in Figure 1:

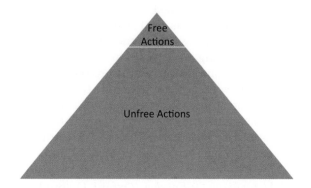

Figure 1. Actions and 'free' actions on the traditional view.

These free actions, according to the standard view, are only ever per-formed by human beings – all other actions (including some human ones) being unfree. But in my view, action is a phenomenon which is *always* indeterministic in its manifestations, because part of what it is for an agent to *act* is to exercise a power at a given time when she needn't have exercised it then. This does not mean that she cannot also be exercising powers which she *has* to exercise then, as a matter of some sort of law, or imperative of nature, perhaps a biological or evolutionary one. Think back to my cat, with her dry food and her wet food. Perhaps, if she is hungry enough, and nothing is putting her off, there is some sense in which she's simply *bound* to eat the food once she notices its presence. But is she also bound to eat the dry food first? Or, if she is, is she bound to chew it by making *precisely* the motions she does in fact make? Is she really determined to go through *precisely* the set of motions she does in fact go through in eating the food, and has the fact that she will go through precisely this set of motions been settled since the dawn of time? My answer to this question is that this is a very unnatural thing to think, and moreover that it seems inconsistent with thinking of the cat as a proper *agent*. This picture transforms the cat from a being with agency into a mere machine, essentially a mere *place* in which various inevitable interactions occur. Part of what is involved in the cat's activity actually being a true action of the cat's in the first place is the thought that the cat didn't have to do exactly what it did. An action, on this view of agency, *just is* the bringing about of some movement or change in the universe *by an agent* – and I think it is very hard to see how an agent could ever be the true *source* of any such movement or change if happenings within her are the en-tirely deterministic causes of those movements or changes, and if those happenings within her are themselves merely the inevitable consequences of the past and the laws.

I think philosophers of action have often had trouble accepting this indeterministic view of agency, because they are operating from the start with an incorrect view of what actions *are*. A very standard view – often called the Causal Theory of Action – holds that actions are just bodily movements caused by certain sorts of mental states – things like beliefs and desires, and intentions. And if this is your view of action then it is unsurprising that there does not seem to be any problem about reconciling the existence of actions with determinism – for on this view, the existence of actions actually *requires* that tight causal relations exist between prior mental states, on the one hand, and bodily movements on the other. Of course, one might wonder whether the causation involved is always

Helen Steward

deterministic – many people accept these days that there can be merely probabilistic forms of causation – but even if we admit that, it is hard to see how an indeterministic nexus between mental states, on the one hand, and bodily movements, on the other, could really help us understand agency. As compatibilist philosophers never tire of pointing out, if my desires and beliefs lead causally to my action but only with a certain high degree of probability, that seems to make things *worse* for freedom, not better; as Laura Ekstrom once put it, that would be a view on which I seem to have to 'wait to see' whether I will act as a result of an intention to do so, and that surely cannot be the right way to ensure that the agent truly gets in on the act when an action occurs.[9] But my worry is that on a standard Causal Theory of Action, it is not clear how an agent can *ever* really get in on the act. The things which seem to be truly causally efficacious, on the Causal Theory of Action are states and events – not agents. On the Causal Theory of Action, when an agent acts, it is only by virtue, as it were, of states and events usually conceived of as being inside her – perhaps inside her head – causally interacting in various ways. But my inclination is to think that this picture of action rather loses the agent altogether, turning her into a mere *place,* a location where various events occur. My desires and intentions aren't *me* – they are merely properties of me – and so *their* causing things needn't be the same thing as *me* causing things. The view of action that I favour offers an alternative to this Causal Theory. On my view, actions are intrinsically linked to agents – they just *are* events (or better still, processes) which are the settlings by agents of a range of questions to which the answers have not yet been settled – questions such as 'where am I going to be at time t_1'? 'at what speed will I be moving at time t_2'? 'Will I be eating or not at time t_3?' etc. (though of course I don't mean to suggest that the agent ever has to explicitly consider any of these questions herself in order to count as having settled them). But if actions are to be such settlings, it is essential that more than one possibility exist for the agent at the relevant moment – how otherwise could it possibly be the case that the agent settles anything *at* that moment? One cannot settle at time t, what has already been settled in advance of time t. So agency requires indeterminism necessarily. There is, though, nothing intrinsically special to *humans* about agency as I have characterised it here. If an action is just the settling by an agent at the time of action of the answers to a range of questions

[9]   Laura Ekstrom, *Free Will: A Philosophical Study* (Boulder, CO: Westview Press): 105.

to which the answers are not yet settled, then there is no reason to think it is a capacity restricted to human beings. Though there are interesting questions about how far down the scale of complexity the phenemenon of agency may be supposed to extend, it seems evident that dogs, horses, dolphins, and many other animals are certainly agents. And that implies, on the view of action I want to embrace, that they having the capacity to settle through the process of their actions, and at the time of those actions, that the world will go one way, when it could have gone another.

There are of course many possible objections to the view I have just tried to outline – and it will not be possible for me to deal with all of them here.[10] What I want to do in the remainder of the paper is just to look at one of them, and to try to explain how this new framing of the free will problem might help to deliver the outlines of a solution to it.

3. Action as Downward Causation

Consider the phenomenon of bodily action. In acting, I make my body move in certain ways – for example, I raise my arm, I bend my leg, etc. – and perhaps by means of these bodily movements, I bring about further effects in the world. But my body cannot move in these various ways unless certain things first happen in my brain and central nervous system – for example, certain neurons must fire in my motor cortex. It would seem, then, that in order to bring about the resultant bodily movement I must either bring about the prior activity in my motor cortex as well – or the activity in my motor cortex must simply *be* (at least part of) the process which constitutes my bringing about the bodily movement in question. If we choose the former answer – that I must bring about the activity in my motor cortex – the question merely arises again how is it possible for me to bring about *this* activity – and the answer would seem, again, to be the disjunctive one that it is possible only if I am able to bring about still *prior* neural activity which produces the activity in the motor cortex; or if the prior neural activity is at least part of a process which *constitutes* my bringing about the activity in the motor cortex. And if we choose the former answer, once again the question will be raised: how on earth is it possible for me to bring about this prior neural activity – and again, the same disjunctive reply seems inevitable. We do not seem to be able to end the

[10] I have dealt in some detail with what seem to me to be the most considerable of them in my *A Metaphysics for Freedom*.

impending regress without at some stage either concluding that the whole chain of neural activity must be initiated ultimately by an ethereal input from something like an immaterial self which sets off a whole chain of physical causes, as in Figure 2; or else that my activity is at the end of the day entirely constituted by the activity of certain of my functionally significant smaller parts on other such parts – neuron on neuron, synapse on synapse, and so on.

Since along with many other philosophers, I take the former dualist solution to be unacceptable for a variety of reasons, *some* version of the latter must be the right thing to say. In some sense or other, my activity must always be realised in the activities of parts of my body – there is no acting on my part, which is not realised in some way by these lower-level events. Action, after all, is not magic – it needs a physical realisation if it is to create physical effects such as bodily movements. But the question is whether it is possible to say this and yet avoid the conclusion that it is not really me but rather my *parts,* and the events that are occurring in them, that are doing all the important causal work. If my actions are simply constituted by neural activity, where am I to be found in the causal story? It is hard to see how, if the story is correct, the agent herself can be anything more than a kind of epiphenomenon, arising out of the hive of activity taking place in the cells, muscles, blood vessels, etc. And it is hard, also, to see how determinism can be avoided. For don't the activities of nerves and muscles have local and deterministic causes? And if they do, how can the actions which result from these activities of nerves and muscles possibly avoid capture in the deterministic web of events?

What seems absolutely essential, if we are to avoid the spectre of a dualistic input at the beginning of the causal chains which in one way or another underlie our actions, is that we avoid thinking of an animal's input into the course of nature as something *prior* to whatever neural processes initiate and then monitor and control the relevant bodily movement or change in the causation of which an action consists. For that just leads to the dilemma already discussed – either the prior input by the animal is itself a neural process, in which case we just face the same question again about how that prior neural process has

Figure 2. Ending the regress: the dualist's picture

been produced by the animal – or it is not, in which case it is hard to see how dualism is to be avoided. The key, if we are going to make proper room for animal agency must be to see the animal's input as a matter not of *prior* intervention but of *top-down* control, control of at least some of the processes taking place within and around certain small physical things (such as neurons and synapses) by a larger one, the animal which those small things partly comprise. What it seems we have to be able to make intelligible to ourselves is the possibility that a whole animal might have top-down effects on its own parts.

But how can a whole thing affect its own parts? Many of us are so used to thinking reductively about complex entities, that this might seem, at first, to be simply impossible. We are used to thinking that the macroscopic behaviour of complex things is ultimately due entirely to the activities of the small bits and pieces of which they are made. This, for example, is how we tend to think about a washing machine, or a TV set. What happens with the drum of the washing machine, or the screen of the TV is, we think, due to events going on inside it of which most of us have only a fairly dim understanding. The behaviour of the whole entity, we tend to think, is dictated by the behaviour of its parts, the whole being an immensely complex mechanism in which overall outputs, given any particular input, are determined by a certain arrangement and disposition of internal circuitry. But we should not allow the importance of this sort of bottom-up determination of large-scale effects by small-scale transactions to blind us to the fact that influence may also flow in the opposite direction. The key to the understanding of how this is possible, I shall argue, lies in the two phenomena of *coincidence* and *ordering*.[11]

In general, a great deal of what happens in our universe is able to do so only because of various forms of spatial and temporal *ordering*. When molecules are connected together in certain spatial arrangements, to form a macroscopic physical object with a distinctive set of powers, it provides us with what is perhaps the simplest example of this sort of phenomenon. Roger Sperry, a neuropsychologist, was a passionate defender of the idea of downward causation which he regarded as essential in order to account for consciousness. In Sperry's view, though, downward causation was not just a phenomenon peculiar to the mental realm – but on the contrary, a quite ubiquitous occurrence. The example of downward causation he often uses is that of a wheel. When a wheel rolls downhill, he notes, 'the molecules and atoms ... are carried along ...regardless of whether the

---

[11] See also my *A Metaphysics for Freedom*, Chapter 8, from which the main lineaments of some aspects the argument which follows is taken.

individual molecules and atoms happen to like it or not'.[12] Sperry's point is that although the wheel is composed of molecules and atoms, whose particular features doubtless determine certain macroscopic features of the wheel (for example, how flexible it is, how strong, and so on) it is also true that certain macroscopic features of the wheel (in particular, its *shape*) determine what will happen to the individual molecules of which it is composed, given that the wheel is placed in certain circumstances (e.g. on an inclined plane). The individual molecules and atoms in the wheel can only move in ways which are enormously constrained by their being bound up into a particular kind of larger whole.

It might be wondered whether this really counts as downward causation. Jaegwon Kim, for example, has argued very forcefully that the idea of downward causation does not, in the end, make sense, because the effects one might be inclined initially to attribute to macroscopic or higher-level phenomena seem on reflection to be re-assignable to the microscopic or lower-level ones which together give rise to the higher level state-of-affairs in the first place.[13] As Kim puts it: 'the difficulties [with downward causation] essentially boil down to the following single argument. If an emergent, M, emerges from basal conditions C, why can't C displace M as a cause of any putative effect of M? Why doesn't C do all the work in bringing about the putative effect of M and suffice as an explanation of why the effect occurred?'[14] Kim's question put in terms of Sperry's particular example, is how on earth the *wheel* can have any causal role to play, over and above the causal role played by the molecules of which it is composed. How, one might ask, can the wheel possibly be an extra causal factor, instead of just being displaced, as a causal player, by the molecules which go to make it up? Those molecules and the bonds between them, one might say, produce the wheel shape in the first place, and so any effects attributable to that shape are actually attributable, in the end, to the molecules arranged wheel-wise. There is therefore no irreducibly downward causation here – all causality flows down inexorably to the lowest level, of which all the rest are revealed merely to be the upwardly determined upshots.

---

[12]   Roger Sperry, 'A modified concept of consciousness', *Psychological Review* **76** (1969), 532–6.

[13]   Jaegwon Kim, 'Making sense of downward causation', in P. Andersen, C. Emmeche, N. O. Finnemann and P. V. Christiansen, *Downward Causation* (Aarhus: Aarhus University Press, 2000), 305–21.

[14]   Kim, 'Making sense of downward causation', 318.

In my view, however, this argument is too quick. Is it really true that the molecules and the bonds between them 'produce the wheel shape in the first place'? It is true that *once the molecules come to be arranged as a wheel*, then of course, wheel-specific effects will follow, which are supervenient of the lower-level arrangements. But of course molecules do not tend spontaneously to form themselves into wheels. Wheels have to be *produced* – and for that, one requires a great many sorts of coincidences and orderings to occur. One requires, for example, a wheelwright with the requisite skills, intentions, tools and raw materials. These things have to come together in the right place at the right time, and then the wheelwright must then use his skills to act upon those raw materials so as to produce a wheel – a process which will in turn require that an enormous number of brain processes take place in the right way and in the right order inside him – processes relating to visual and tactile perception, to motor skills, to memories relating to previous efforts to make similar items, judgements about how to solve difficulties relating to the idiosyncrasies of these particular materials, and so on. In other words, in order for molecules to *become* arranged in such a way that they come to constitute a wheel, an enormous number of separate events must occur together and/or in the right sequential order. But how does the world provide for this coincidence? What is the causal story of its production? The need for such a story puts pressure on the idea that the relevant causation is to be understood wholly as a matter of various forces blindly acting on such things as molecules and atoms, and may thereby simultaneously help to provide us with the answer to Kim's question. For part of the causal story about this particular set of molecules and their journey through the world will involve the telling of the causal story about the coming-into-existence of a wheel – and the causal explanation of *that*, one might argue, cannot be given entirely in terms of lower-level phenomena. In particular, a great many factors are required to *coincide* and thence to *form orderly sequences*, if a wheel is ever to come into being – and it seems very difficult to understand how the requisite coincidences and sequencings have been brought about if we stick doggedly to describing phenomena at the molecular level of resolution. How on earth has it come to be that all the various molecular phenomena which need to coincide in particular, distinctive ways in order to constitute e.g. the existence of a wheelwright with a certain intention, and the existence of various tools, and so on, have so fortuitously arranged themselves! For the answer to this question, I suggest, we need to raise our eyes from the atomic and molecular and look to the realm of the macroscopic – for answers which in this case involve the existence of persons with plans and ideas about how to get them enacted. In Kim's terms, then, M (the wheel) thus displaces C (the basal conditions), because C would never have come about in the first place were it not for the fact that C constitutes M, given that M is the thing that is wanted by an intentional agent.

One might object to this line of thought that the requirement of manufacture is merely a contingent and unnecessary feature of the particular example used by Sperry. If Sperry's example works, someone might suggest, it should work for, e.g. a rounded boulder, just as well as for a wheel – a case in which the sorts of complications rehearsed above, which are to do with intentional creation, would be absent. A boulder, presumably, acquires the eventual shape it does because of a range of historic interactions with other objects and stuffs – things such as glaciers, other rocks, water, and so on. But even in this simple case, the idea that a decent causal account of these interactions can be given without appealing to forces which operate on the *macroscopic* objects in question, in virtue of their strictly macroscopic features seems questionable. A boulder which begins life in the sea when it falls from a sea-cliff might, for example, grow gradually rounder over the course of many years because of the way in which it is dashed against the cliffs by the waves. But how precisely it will wear as a result of this constant dashing seems to be (in part, anyhow) a matter of such macroscopic matters as its original shape, the macroscopic shape of the objects it is dashed against, and so on. It is true, of course, that these shapes 'supervene' on various arrangements of molecular entities. But it is not clear that a *causal* understanding of how the molecular arrangement which constitutes the boulder came to be in the first place can be properly provided entirely at the molecular level. In an admittedly rather 'thin' sense, it appears, even in this simpler case, as though macroscopic features of *the boulder* might matter to the causation of effects on its own parts. The way in which its parts are *ordered* and the way in which the dynamic interactions which produce its eventual shape come about is a story essentially about macroscopic forces, not microscopic ones.

In the case of the boulder, then, I think we could say something like this: that there is a sense in which a very limited sort of top-down causation exists in virtue of the relevance of features of the boulder taken as a whole object to subsequent changes undergone by the boulder, changes which in turn affect what is true of the boulder at the *molecular* level. None of these changes, of course, can take place independently of changes which themselves have molecular descriptions; and there is certainly nothing here to disturb the hypothesis of determinism. The point is merely that the laws and principles in terms of which the changes are to be understood are macro-laws, not micro-ones. No doubt if this is downward causation, it is downward causation of a rather limited sort. But it is a starting point from which we can perhaps begin to see how an understanding of the nature of a whole may be requisite for a full causal account of the trajectory taken through the world by the parts of that whole. It is when we enter the realm of the biological, and in particular, of the psychological, that the phenomenon of top-down causation really comes into its own.

Where animate entities are concerned, the importance of these phenomena of coincidence and ordering becomes much greater than in the case of merely inanimate objects – and the dominance of whole over part is, relatedly, much more significant. It is arguable, indeed, that a certain hierarchical holism is quite ubiquitous in biology. Any animal larger than a single cell is a hierarchically organised entity – cells are organised into tissues, tissues into organs, organs into systems (e.g. the digestive system, the circulatory system, the visual system), and all these systems are organised in their turn so as to operate together for the benefit of the whole organism of which they are the subsystems. And there are ways in which, at every level of this biological hierarchy, entities at the higher level dominate and constrain processes occurring in the lower level ones. Even a single cell is a structure, for example, which, once formed, exercises a certain sort of dominance over the processes which go on inside it.[15] None of the individual processes which constitute the life of a cell is independent of the others – and it is to the functional needs of the tissue, organ, and ultimately the animal, of which the cell is a component that we must look for an explanation of why the particular processes which co-exist together in the cell have thus come to coincide there, and why they take the specific forms they do. The organisation of a cell thus cannot be understood without considering it as embedded in the functional units of a whole organism.[16]

---

[15] See Donald Campbell, '"Downward causation" in hierarchically organised biological systems', in Ayala and Dobzhansky (eds) *Studies in the Philosophy of Biology* (Berkeley and Los Angeles: University of California Press, 179–86).

[16] For detailed accounts of some of these cellular processes, see A. Moreno and J. Umerez, 'Downward Causation at the Core of Living Organisation', in P. Andersen, C. Emmeche, N. O. Finnemann and P. V. Christiansen, *Downward Causation* (Aarhus: Aarhus University Press, 2000), 99–117.

Helen Steward

I believe we should conceive of animal agency as an essential part of this hierarchy of domination-relations – as the power which belongs to certain sorts of whole organisms to organise the operations of certain of the various sub-systems at their disposal, in such a way as to benefit them, as they confront the contingencies of life. Where action is concerned, the requirements for various coincidences and orderings to obtain are vast, and not all of them can be planned for in advance by the instigation of mere instincts and habits. Take, for example, someone's swimming a few lengths of a swimming pool. For a start, the swimmer's arms and legs must be co-ordinated – the movements or each limb must occur at the right time if the stroke is to propel the swimmer forward effectively. Then the swimmer's breathing has to be controlled in such a way that in-breaths occur when the swimmer's head is above the water and out-breaths when it is below. Learning to produce these forms of control and co-ordination habitually is a crucial part of learning to swim for human beings; whereas for other animals, it is part of an instinctive endowment. But not everything needed for swimming can be handed over to these sorts of habitual or instinctive mechanisms. The swimmer must, for example, prepare to turn as she sees the end of the pool approach. She may need to take account of others in the lane: to speed up to overtake someone, or to slow down, to permit someone else to overtake. If she sees a friend in the pool, she may need to break off her swim to say hello, to avoid giving offence. If the fire alarm goes off, she will need to be able to understand what it signifies and abandon the swim altogether. And so on. Sub-systems, in other words, need to be co-ordinated on the spot by an overall co-ordinator which is able to respond to the unexpected, the unpredictable, the contingent, the accidental. *Action* thus emerges when the need for *discretion* enters the biological hierarchy – when a creature itself evolves the power selectively to control certain of its own sub-systems in the light of incoming information, in such a way (roughly) as to optimise its chances of survival and success. In particular, higher animals need to have this kind of discretionary control over their own locomotion – since it is often decisions about where and how to move upon which survival depends – decisions about what to chase, what to flee from, where to hide, and so on. For a mobile creature with many needs, and many competing ends, some way of integrating the operation of these various systems so that the right range of things can be done in a sensible order, must be instigated; nature has found that habits, instincts and tropisms will not always suffice for the survival of a complex and self-moving creature. What it has instead found, I surmise, is that the

214

type of system which best serves those needs is precisely the type that I have here called an agent – a creature that is a settler of matters concerning certain of the movements of its own body, and on whose discretionary settlings its own persistence and flourishing depend.

I have attempted, then, to argue in this paper that action should be thought of as a special form of downward causation. This view has the enormous benefit of placing action into a broadly naturalistic, biological context, which can be seen as in some ways continuous with the other forms of downward causation which are found in hierarchically-organised systems. But the view also gives due recognition to the extreme specialness of action, in that it recognises the discretionary as a genuinely new and emergent phenomenon of life. In that sense, it accepts and respects the presupposition of the traditional free will debate that free will is a metaphysical conundrum – something distinctive in the order of nature which requires a special explanation. Were I to speculate, I should propose that some of philosophy of mind's *other* conundrums – in particular, consciousness and self-hood – also come into being, evolutionarily speaking, alongside the development of discretionary agency. There is thus a prospect, in this biological perspective, I believe, of uniting aspects of the philosophy of mind that tend to be treated entirely in separation, but ought not to be.

University of Leeds
h.steward@leeds.ac.uk

The Representation of Action

ANTON FORD

Abstract

From its inception, the philosophy of action has sought to account for action in terms of an associated kind of explanation. The alternative to this approach was noticed, but not adopted, by G.E.M. Anscombe. Anscombe observed that a series of answers to the reason-requesting question 'Why?' may be read in reverse order as a series of answers to the question 'How?' Unlike answers to the question 'Why?', answers to the question 'How?' are not explanatory of what they are about: they reveal, not reasons for doing something, but ways of doing something, and they have the form of what Aristotle called a practical syllogism. The alternative to theorizing action in terms of explanation, is, thus, to theorize it in terms calculation. In exploring this alternative, I argue for three main theses: first, that (*pace* Anscombe) it is not a matter of indifference whether we theorize action in terms of the question 'Why?' or in terms of the question 'How?'; second, that the question 'Why?' is a question for an observer of action, whereas the question 'How?' is a question for the agent; and finally, that the standpoint of the agent, revealed by the question 'How?', is prior to that of an observer, revealed by the question 'Why?'.

1. Action Explanationism

For as long as there has been anything called 'the philosophy of action' its practitioners have broached their topic through an investigation of *the reasons that explain action*. Anscombe accounted for the nature of action by way of a reflection on 'a certain sense of the question "Why?"', the relevant sense being 'that in which the answer, if positive, gives a reason for acting'.[1] Anscombe's question 'Why?' – like any question 'Why?' – requests an explanation. It asks, of something not understood, that it be made intelligible. For that is what reasons do: they explain. What is characteristic of reasons for action is that they explain action.

Anscombe was not the first to suppose that the question, 'What is action?' ought to be addressed by asking, 'What is an explanation of action?' The opening question of Wittgenstein's *Blue Book*, 'What is

---

[1] G.E.M. Anscombe, *Intention*, 2nd ed. (Cambridge, Mass.: Harvard University Press, 2000), 9.

doi:10.1017/S1358246117000066   © The Royal Institute of Philosophy and the contributors 2017

the meaning of a word?' was followed by a proposal about how to answer it: 'Let us attack this question by asking, first, what is an explanation of the meaning of a word?' Wittgenstein was not proposing a general philosophical method: he did not claim that *every* question of the form, 'What is *x*?' ought to be attacked by asking, first, 'What is an explanation of *x*?' Nevertheless, a dozen pages later, when he took up the topic of action, Wittgenstein began in exactly that way, by inquiring how an action is explained. That was the context of his influential claim that the question 'Why?' is ambiguous:

> The double use of the word 'why', asking for the cause and asking for the motive, together with the idea that we can know, and not only conjecture, our motives, gives rise to the confusion that a motive is a cause of which we are immediately aware, a cause 'seen from the inside', or a cause experience.—Giving a reason is like giving a calculation by which you have arrived at a certain result.[2]

This remark by Wittgenstein set the terms for one of the most controversial questions of twentieth-century action theory: '*How* does a reason for action explain action?'

Like Wittgenstein, Gilbert Ryle argued that not all accounts of why something happened are causal explanations. 'There are', Ryle claimed, 'at least two quite different senses in which an occurrence is said to be "explained"; and there are correspondingly at least two quite different senses in which we ask "why" it occurred. When we ask "Why did someone act in a certain way?" this question might, so far as language goes, either be an inquiry into the cause of his acting in that way, or be an inquiry into the character of the agent which accounts for his having acted in that way on that occasion.'[3] Ryle held that when we explain why a person did something by giving her reason for doing it, we are giving an explanation of the second type, not of the first. According to him, reasons for action explain action otherwise than by citing a cause.

---

[2]   Ludwig Wittgenstein, *The Blue and Brown Books* (London: Basil Blackwell, 1958), 1. In the introduction to his *Essays on Actions and Events* (Oxford: Oxford University Press, 1980), Donald Davidson identifies this text as the source of the view he opposes in 'Actions, Reasons and Causes', xii.
[3]   Gilbert Ryle, *The Concept of Mind* (New York: Routledge, 2009), 74.

This view was opposed by Carl Hempel and Donald Davidson.[4] According to them, an explanation of action adverting to an agent's reasons for acting is a species of causal explanation. In the introduction to his *Essays on Actions and Events*, Davidson identified this as the unifying idea of his work in action theory: 'All the essays in this book... are unified in theme and general thesis. The theme is the role of causal concepts in the description and explanation of human action. The thesis is that the ordinary notion of cause which enters into scientific or common-sense accounts of non-psychological affairs is essential to the understanding of [action]... Cause is the cement of the universe; the concept of cause is what holds together our picture of the universe.'[5]

If in the classical period of action theory – the middle third of the twentieth century – action explanation was the locus of the main doctrinal disputes, and thus also the primary object of inquiry, successive generations have plowed the same field. The view of Hempel and Davidson – that action explanation is causal explanation – soon displaced the one defended by Wittgenstein and Ryle, and for decades it has stood at the center of 'the standard story of action', according to which, in the words of Michael Smith, 'an action is a bodily movement caused in the right way by a belief and a desire'.[6] Nowadays, even the standard story's most radical opponents aspire to replace it with an alternative story of action explanation in terms of which to account for action. Thus, in spite of many relatively superficial differences between followers of Anscombe and followers of Davidson, between anti-causalists and causalists, between event-causalists and agent-causalists, between champions of mechanical explanation and champions of teleology, between defenders of this or that account of an agent's mental states, and between partisans of 'naive' and of 'sophisticated' rationalization – in spite of all such differences, the entire tradition, from Wittgenstein to the present, has taken it for granted that the proper way to account for action is by accounting for an associated kind of explanation.

---

[4]   See Carl Hempel, 'Rational Action', *Proceedings and Addresses of the American Philosophical Association* (1961), 5–23; and Donald Davidson, 'Actions, Reasons, and Causes', *The Journal of Philosophy* **60** (1963), 685–700; reprinted in *Essays on Actions and Events*, 3–19. For a precursor, see C.J. Ducasse, 'Explanation, Mechanism and Teleology', *The Journal of Philosophy* **22** (1925), 150–155.
[5]   Davidson, *Essays on Actions and Events*, xi.
[6]   Michael Smith, 'The Sturcture of Orthonomy', *Royal Institute of Philosophy Supplement* **55** (2004), 165–193.

Anton Ford

I will call this dogma – for that is what it is – *action explanationism.* My aim here is not to refute it, but to expose it to critical scrutiny. In fact, action explanationism is only one expression of a much more general tendency in contemporary philosophy. Philosophers now tend to theorize *any* expression of practical reason in terms of practical reasons, whose office it is to show something to be rational, justified, motivated, caused or otherwise intelligible. Though contemporary practical philosophy is, in general, explanationist, my immediate target is more specific. Here my sites are narrowly set on the species of explanationism that pertains to accounts of intentional action. In the controlled environment of the philosophy of action, where one only considers instrumental connections between ends and means, and where ethical and political questions are temporarily bracketed, it is easier to see, both, that there is an alternative, and what the alternative is.

2. Objective and Subjective Representations of Action

Let us begin by considering why it has seemed so natural, so undoubtedly correct, to address the question, 'What is action?' by asking, first, 'What is an explanation of action?' One apparent rationale begins from a general thought about philosophical method – namely, that the nature of a thing is revealed in an account of its representation.

There are countless expressions of this idea in the history of philosophy, and many within the analytic tradition. To answer the question, 'What is a number?' a philosopher might investigate the structure of our thought about numbers; or, to answer the question, 'What is a cause?' a philosopher might investigate what is involved in representing one thing as being the cause of another; or again, to answer the question, 'What is life?' a philosopher might investigate what it is to represent something as alive. Some of these investigations will exemplify what Strawson called 'descriptive metaphysics', a kind of metaphysics that, according to Strawson, was practiced by both Aristotle and Kant, and whose principal aim is to describe the 'structure of our thought about the world'.[7]

Not every action theorist ascribes to the general principle that the nature of a thing is revealed in an account of its representation, but many do. For those who do, explanationism can seem to be the

[7] P.F. Strawson, *Individuals: An Essay in Descriptive Metaphysics* (New York: Routledge, 1959), 9.

220

natural way, or even perhaps the only way, to bring that principle to bear on the topic of human agency. If we answer the question 'What is a number?' by investigating the structure of our thought about numbers, then, it seems, likewise, we should answer the question, 'What is an action?' by investigating the structure of our thought about actions; and if accounting for the nature of action requires us to investigate the structure of our thought about actions, then, it seems, we ought to follow Anscombe and Davidson in focusing on the question 'Why?' and on the reasons for action that answer that question: for, it is in the structure of action explanation that we see what it is to think about action.

The point of articulating this seeming rationale for action explanationism is not to call into question the methodological principle that the nature of a thing is revealed in an account of its representation. Nor is the point to deny that action explanation is exactly what one should focus on insofar as one wants to understand what it is to represent action. Taking these for granted, what I mean to question is the further idea that this methodological principle dictates that we answer the question, 'What is an action?' as we would the question, 'What is a number?' – by embarking on an investigation of what it is to represent that which is in question. The difficulty lies in seeing how an account of the representation of action could be anything other than an account of what it is to represent action.

To see how it could be something else, consider that, for certain values of x, phrases like 'the representation of x', or 'the consciousness of x', or 'the awareness of x', or 'the thought of x', are ambiguous. Wherever x is a subject of representation, or of consciousness, or of awareness, or of thought, such phrases are ambiguous between an objective interpretation and a subjective interpretation, according as they are taken to employ an objective or a subjective genitive construction. On the subjective interpretation of the phrase, 'the representation of x', x is the subject of representation: it is what does the representing. On the objective interpretation of the very same words, an x is the object of representation: it is what gets represented. Thought belongs to a thinker in two distinct ways: there is, on the one hand, the thinking I do, and, on the other hand, the thinking I suffer; the first is thinking of which I am the subject, the second is thinking to which I am subjected when you grasp me in thought.

In some areas of philosophy, this raises a question of methodology. We have been considering the following principle:

Representationalism: The nature of x is revealed in an account of the representation of x.

Anton Ford

But where x is a subject of representations, the principle is ambiguous. It might be given an 'objective' interpretation:

> *Objective Representationalism:* The nature of x is revealed in an account of the representation of which x is the object.

Alternatively, the principle might be given a 'subjective' interpretation:

> *Subjective Representationalism:* The nature of x is revealed in an account of the representation of which x is the subject.

Both of these interpretations might be thought inadequate, because partial and one-sided. It might be thought that a genuine understanding must comprehend the unity of subjective and objective representations:

> *Absolute Representationalism:* The nature of x is revealed in an account of the unity of, on the one hand, the representation of which x is the object, and, on the other hand, the representation of which x is the subject.

So, in areas of philosophy where the topic of reflection is itself a thinking subject, there is a methodological question that needs to be decided.

This methodological question does not always arise because the topic of reflection is not always a thinking subject. Someone who proposes to explain what a number is by accounting for 'the representation of a number' faces no such question. Thought relates to numbers in only one way: there is such a thing as thinking *about* a number, but no such thing as thinking *as* a number. The representation 'of' a number is always 'of' a number in the objective sense that a number is the object of representation.

But unlike numbers, agents think. As a result, someone who proposes to explain what an agent is by accounting for 'the representation of an agent' faces a decision. The decision is whether to account for (1) the representation of which an agent is the object, (2) the representation of which an agent is the subject, or (3) the unity of these representations.

There is exactly the same array of theoretical options when the topic of reflection is, not an agent, but the activity of an agent, an action. The philosopher who proposes to explain what action is by accounting for 'the representation of action' must decide whether to account for (1) the kind of representation that is 'of' action in the objective sense that it is characteristic of someone who is thinking about action, (2) the kind of representation that is 'of' action in the subjective sense that it is characteristic of someone who is performing an action, or (3) the unity of these representations.

Consider this array of options as it presents itself to a descriptive metaphysician, whose the aim is, again, 'to describe the structure of our thought about the world'.[8] Because we are agents, some of 'our thought about the world' is thought that we think *about* agents, and some of it is thought that we think *as* agents. The practitioner of descriptive metaphysics is therefore faced with the decision whether to account for (1) the structure of our thought about the world insofar as we are thinking about someone acting, (2) the structure of our thought about the world insofar as we are acting, or (3) the unity of these structures of thought.

Or again, suppose that, as Davidson says, 'the concept of cause is what holds together our picture of the universe'. The philosopher who proposes to account for what holds together our picture of the universe must decide whether to account for (1) the picture that is ours insofar we have agents in view, (2) the picture that is ours insofar as we are agents, or (3) the unity of theses pictures.

It is the same for a practitioner of conceptual analysis. Agents both apply concepts and are such to be conceptualized. The analyzer of concepts must therefore decide whether to account for (1) concepts in their application *to* agents, (2) concepts in their application *by* agents, or (3) the unity of these two applications of concepts.

Given that an agent is both a subject and object of thought – both a represent-er and a represent-ee – the methodological question can be put in various ways, but it cannot be avoided, not in the philosophy of action. In their practice, philosophers of action do in fact settle the question one way or the other, even if neither they nor their readers are conscious that a question is being settled. Ryle's example is instructive. His famous discussion of 'knowing how' in the second chapter of *The Concept of Mind* opens as follows:

> In this chapter I try to show that when we describe people as exercising qualities of mind, we are not referring to occult episodes of which their overt acts and utterances are effects; we are referring to those overt acts and utterances themselves.[9]

So, Ryle's stated aim is to account for what is going on 'when we describe people' – that is, when *we* represent *others,* others whom we represent as exercising qualities of mind. His principal thesis is this:

[8]   Strawson, *Individuals,* 9.
[9]   Ryle, *The Concept of Mind,* 14.

Anton Ford

> When a person is described by one or other of the intelligence-epithets such as 'shrewd' or 'silly', 'prudent' or 'imprudent', the description imputes to him not the knowledge, or ignorance of this or that truth, but the ability, or inability, to do certain sorts of things.[10]

What Ryle offers is a theory of ascriptions, or descriptions, or imputations, of intelligence. When I ascribe intelligence to someone – for example, to a baker – I subsume him under concepts of mind. A theory of such ascriptions is, thus, a theory of what one person thinks about another. But the person who is thought about – the one who figures as the object of thought in an ascription of intelligence – that other person is also a thinker, and he has thoughts of his own. While my mind is on the baker, his mind is on the bread. And if there can be a logic to my thought, there must be a logic to his. One might have expected that in a philosophical treatment of 'knowing how' the baker's thought would be the center of attention, since, after all, *he* is the one with know-how: it is he, the baker, not I, the spectator, whose mind is formed in the special way that is under investigation. But in Ryle's treatment of the topic – and in the subsequent literature – the baker's thought is not in fact the center of attention: the center of attention is the thought of someone other than the baker, someone who is thinking about the baker. The baker himself is not in the business of making ascriptions of know-how. Insofar as his mind is on his work, he is concerned with many things, about which he thinks many things: concerning the dough, he may think, for example, that it needs more time to rise, or concerning the stove, that it is too hot. These are ascriptions, but not of know-how. They are imputations, but not of intelligence. They are descriptions, but not of anyone as possessing an ability. In the act of baking bread, the baker applies concepts, but the concepts he applies are not concepts of mind. It was open to Ryle to give an account of the application of concepts *by* knowers-how, but instead he elected to give an account of the application of concepts *to* knowers-how. That is a decision to theorize human agency from the perspective of someone who is thinking about an agent, rather than from the perspective of the thinking agent himself.[11] Such was the general practice in

10 Ibid., 16–17.
11 Ryle maintained that these two perspectives were intimately related – 'the rules which the agent observes and the criteria which he applies are one with those which govern the spectator's applause and jeers' (op. cit., 53–54) – nevertheless, he chose to put the accent on the perspective of the spectator.

224

twentieth-century action theory. Action explanationism is the central manifestation of that practice.

3. Explanation and Calculation

Though Anscombe was not first analytic philosopher to theorize action in terms of explanation, she may have been the first to observe that there is an alternative. On her view, the question 'Why?' is significant because it reveals 'an order that is there wherever actions are done with intentions'[12] – but, as she notices, it is not unique in doing so. The self-same order of ends and means revealed by the question 'Why?' is also revealed by a question 'How?' that an agent confronts in acting.

Anscombe's account of intentional action is built on the observation that, if I am doing A, and someone asks me why, the question may draw out that I am doing A in order to do B. Repeated application of the question 'Why?' may then draw out that I am doing B in order to do C. This gives rise to a series of ends, A–C, in which each action is done for the sake of the next:

> C. replenishing the house water-supply
> B. operating a pump
> A. moving my arm up and down

Anscombe notes that instead of reading this order from bottom to top, as a series of ends, A–C, we can also read it from top to bottom, as a series of means, C–A. She writes: 'if [C] is given as the answer to the question "Why?" about A, B ... can make an appearance in answer to a question "How?" [about C]. When terms are related in this fashion, they constitute a series of means.'[13] Just as successive answers to the question 'Why?' expose that I am doing A in order to do B, and B in order to do C, so, also, successive answers to the question 'How?' reveal that I am doing C by means of doing B, and B by doing A. In drawing out this series of means, the question 'How?' reveals the order of the agent's thought, starting with the end to be achieved and concluding with the means to that end. That is why, near the end of *Intention*, Anscombe claims to have uncovered 'the same order' as is revealed in Aristotle's account of the practical syllogism: 'I did not realize the identity until I had reached my results', she says. The explanatory question 'Why?' and

---

12   Anscombe, *Intention*, 80.
13   Ibid. 46–47, substituting my preferred variables for Anscombe's.

the calculative question 'How?' lead, respectively, up and down the same purposive scale. It is one order, not two, because the way up is the way down.[14]

One might have expected that Anscombe would be alarmed by her discovery that she had approached the topic from the opposite direction of her master, Aristotle. In fact, she is undisturbed: she appears to think that it makes no difference, one way or the other, which way we go at it. That would indeed be the case if the representation of intentional action were sufficiently like the representation of a whole natural number. The arithmetic function '+1' ascends the scale of natural numbers, from 1, to 2, to 3, and the inverse function, '−1', descends the same scale. Just as, in action theory, a single order can be surveyed from bottom to top, as a series or ends, A–C, or, alternatively, from top to bottom, as a series of means, C–A, so, also, in arithmetic, a single order can be surveyed from bottom to top, as a series of addends, 1–3, or, alternatively, from top to bottom, as a series of minuends, 3–1. One might think, as Frege perhaps did, that the most general and fundamental truths about numbers are encoded in arithmetic functions such as these. But whatever might be learned about the nature of a number through reflection on the functions of arithmetic, it could hardly make a difference whether we chose to focus on addition or subtraction, for these two inverse functions stand in the same kind of relation to any natural number. It would be very strange to think that either of them enjoyed theoretical priority relative to the other.[15]

If explanation and calculation differed from each other only in the way that addition differs from subtraction then it would be six of one and half a dozen of the other whether we accounted for intentional action via the question 'Why?' or via the question 'How?' But we are already in position to see that explanation and calculation differ in a much more radical way. We have seen that, since numbers do not think, any representation 'of' a number is 'of' a number in the objective sense that a number is the object of thought. This means that

[14] 'The schema of the practical inference is that of a teleological explanation "turned upside down". The starting point of a teleological explanation (of action) is that someone sets himself to do something or, more commonly, that someone does something. We ask "Why?" The answer often is simply: "In order to bring about p".' Georg Henrik von Wright, *Explanation and Understanding* (Ithica, NY: Cornell University Press, 1971), 96.

[15] For discussion of the parallels between Anscombe's account of action and Frege's account of number in *The Foundations of Arithmetic*, see Anton Ford, 'The Arithmetic of *Intention*', *American Philosophical Quarterly* **52** (2015), 129–143.

addition and subtraction are two different structures of thought about numbers. But that is not the difference between explanation and calculation. The latter do not correspond to two contrasting structures of thought about action. Action explanation reveals the structure of what one thinks insofar as one thinks about action. But its opposite, calculation, reveals the structure of what one thinks insofar as one is acting.

4. Calculation as the Subjective Representation of Action

If I propose to do something – for example, to go home – I need to find the means to my end, and I therefore need to embark on a search. The problem I face, if I want to go home, is that I cannot simply 'go' there: there is no such thing as 'going' home – or for that matter anywhere else – except in some specific way by some specific means. Thus, the first question I must settle, as someone who wants to go home, is how to get there. Am I to walk home? Or to ride my bike? Am I to take a taxi, or a train, or a boat – or perhaps some combination of these? Making this decision may or may not be difficult, but a decision must be made. If I do not make it – if I do not come down on the question how, specifically, to achieve my end – I cannot achieve my end.

Coming to such a decision is not sufficient for discovering the means to an end. If I propose to take a taxi home, I still have to find a taxi: that is, I have to identify something the taking home of which would be the taking home of a taxi. This is no trivial task. (An American visiting London for the first time might search in vain for yellow sedans and arrive at the false conclusion that the city, though full of hearses, is empty of taxi cabs.) If I cannot find a taxi, either because none is available, or because, although one is available, I fail to recognize it as that for which I am searching, then I cannot take a taxi home. In that case, the question from which I began – the question how to get home – remains unanswered.

Or, to take a less mundane example, consider the predicament of Anscombe's gardener, whose ultimate objective is to establish the kingdom of heaven on earth. The Nazis are in power and are prosecuting a murderous war, and his immediate question is how to stop it. One way to stop the war, he thinks, is to get some better leaders in power. But how? One would first need to get the Nazis out, and one can't just run a candidate, not against the Nazis. The gardener decides to assassinate their party chiefs, who happen to be living in the house where he works. But how? With a rifle? With dynamite? No, he thinks: poison. But how? Should the poison be put in their bread-flour? (No, too risky.) It occurs to him that he could poison their water-supply, so he sets about finding a slow-acting poison. He continues in this manner until eventually he is standing in front of the garden water pump, gripping the handle and moving his arm up and down, up and down. The fact that this is a hare-brained scheme is neither here nor there. What matters is its trajectory: it starts from a general end, which could be achieved in various ways, and it proceeds through specifications of that end until it is brought to bear upon the concrete particulars of agent's immediate circumstances.

That is what it is to answer the question 'How?'.[16] In the present context, the most important thing to notice about the answers to this question is that they are not reasons acting. They do not rationalize the action that is in question. They do not justify it, or disclose its motive, or give an interpretation, or situate it in a pattern, or appeal to a 'wider context', or identify a cause. *They are in no way explanatory of what they are about.* And yet, they are the primary concern of an agent as such.

5. Explanation as the Objective Representation of Action

If what speaks to the question 'How?' speaks to the mind of an agent, what speaks to the question 'Why?' speaks to the mind of a spectator. The answer to the question 'Why?' can only enlighten someone whose action is not in question: for, it is a question about the action of someone who already knows the answer to it, and who therefore does not stand to learn anything from the inquiry.

It follows that the poser of the question 'Why?' – the one for whom it is a question – inquires about the action of another. The question may or may not be posed directly to the one whose action is in question. If I care to know why you are setting up a camera, I can try to figure it out without saying a word, and thus without asking anyone, or I can ask a third party, or I can ask you. Whether or not I ask someone, and no matter whom I ask, the question is about someone other than myself.

Anscombe's discussion of the question 'Why?' focuses on the scenario in which the question is posed directly to the one whose action is

---

[16] For a fuller articulation and defense of this account of calculation, see Anton Ford, 'On What is in Front of Your Nose', *Philosophical Topics* **44** (2016).

in question. In what Michael Thompson calls 'the fundamental scene Anscombe is working with throughout [her] book', there is a confrontation between two people:

> One human being comes upon another and perceives her doing something …The enquirer knows by perception, by an intuition or *Anschauung* of the other as other, by observation of her, that the agent is setting up a camera or is crossing a road… The observer moves into what we might call a cognitive relation with the agent herself and asks her why she's doing it. He does not do this with falling trees. The mark of the cognitive relation is the use of the second person, 'Why are *you* doing A?'[17]

The scene here is well-described. When two individuals end up in the cognitive relation marked by the use of the second person – 'Why are *you* doing A?' – it is not on the basis of their mutual consent. One of the two individuals, 'the observer', has imposed himself on the other, 'the agent'. Moreover, what will transpire between them is not the kind of transaction from which both can hope to benefit: it will not be an exchange, but a gift; in answer to the question 'Why?' reasons will be given.

This bears emphasis. In posing the question 'Why?' to an agent I am asking him to explain himself to me. So, I am asking him to do something that he had not been doing before I posed my question. When I tap him on the shoulder and request that he explain himself, he will have been doing something else – setting up a camera, or whatever it was that caught my eye – and answering the question 'Why?' is no contribution whatsoever to what he had been doing. (Explaining why one is setting up a camera is not a step in setting up a camera.) Thus, what I am asking him to do, in asking him to explain himself, is, from his perspective, simply a distraction. He may indulge me, but if he does, that is what he is doing.

A scene like this makes vivid that the concerns of an agent are radically different from those of an observer who is trying to understand what that agent is doing. Prior to the moment of contact when the observer poses the question 'Why?' – there needn't be such moment, but if there is, then prior to it – the agent and the observer are each engaged in rational inquiry, though in rational inquiries of different kinds: on the one hand, the agent is trying to figure out how to set up his camera, wondering, for example, where it should be placed

---

[17]   Michael Thompson, 'Anscombe's *Intention* and Practical Knowledge', in *Essays on Anscombe's* Intention, ed. Ford, A., Hornsby, J., and Stoutland, F. (Cambridge, Mass.: Harvard University Press 2011), 206.

and whether it needs a flash; on the other hand, the observer is trying to figure out why the agent is setting a camera up, wondering, say, whether he plans to take a picture of a building, or, perhaps, of someone passing by (Marilyn Monroe is known to be in the neighborhood), and if the latter, whether it is for journalistic or for merely sensational purposes. While the calculating agent is busily searching for means, the explainer of his action is trying to discern his ends.

6. Calculation as Prior to Explanation

Earlier I claimed that if action explanation were related to calculation in the way that addition is related to subtraction, then it would not matter whether one accounted for action via the question 'Why?' or via the question 'How?' We have already seen one important difference: namely, that while the functions '+1' and '−1' reveal two contrasting ways of thinking about a number, the questions 'Why?' and 'How?' do not reveal contrasting ways of thinking about an action: the question 'Why?' reveals a way of thinking about an action, but the question 'How?' reveals the way an agent thinks in acting. A second important difference is that the symmetry between addition and subtraction differs from the symmetry between explanation and calculation.

To get the relevant contrast in view consider, first, the symmetry between a footprint and a foot. The parties to it are not, as it were, equals: it is the foot's print, not the print's foot. It is similar between a face and its mirror image: the image reflects the face; the face does not reflect the image. What is characteristic of such symmetry is that it is grounded in one of the two symmetrical terms. There is conformity between the terms because one of the terms is such as to conform to the other. Between a face and its mirror image, the face is the prior reality: it and its image are alike, not because the face is like the image, but because the image is like the face. A foot and its footprint have the same contour because the footprint conforms to the foot, not vice versa.

Addition and subtraction are not related in anything like that way. Neither the series of addends, 1–3, nor the series of minuends, 3–1, has any plausible claim to be the prior reality to which the other conforms. There is between them a merely formal symmetry and a symmetry of equals.

By contrast, action explanation is such as to conform to calculation. It is a common trope among action theorists that action explanation *represents* the calculation of the agent whose action is explained. When Wittgenstein remarks that, 'giving a reason is like giving a calculation by which you have arrived at a certain result',[18] he appears to suggest that explaining one's action is a matter of conveying the thought that led one to act as one did. In a passage quoted approvingly by Carl Hempel, William Dray writes that a rational explanation of action is one that offers 'a reconstruction of the agent's *calculation* of means to be adopted toward his chosen end'.[19] In a similar vein, Davidson asserts that 'the explanation of an action [is] the retracing of a course of reasoning on the part of the actor'.[20] The 're-' of 'reconstruction' and of 'retracing' is the 're-' of 'reverse', 'return', and 'reflect'. The prefix indicates that something has been doubled, transposed or bent back to its point of origin. If action explanation represents the calculation of the agent whose action is explained, then it represents a kind of thought that is not only distinct from, but prior to, action explanation.

In fact, calculation is prior to explanation in several different ways. First, calculation is prior in the order of normativity. Insofar as my aim is to understand the reason why you are setting up a camera, your thought, as agent, provides the standard of correctness for my thought, as observer. My thought that you are setting up a camera in order to take a picture of Marilyn Monroe is a good explanation of your action if and only if it is accurate in depicting you as having the aim of taking a picture of Marilyn Monroe, and as having decided to set up a camera as a means conducive to that end. In other words, my answer to the questions 'Why?' is responsible for conforming to your answer to the question 'How?' In general, an explanation portrays the depicted agent as thinking a certain way, and the explanation is evaluated as true or false by reference to the agent's thought – that is, according to whether it portrays the agent's thought accurately or inaccurately.[21] But the reverse is not the case: the agent's calculation does not portray the thought of an explainer. While explanatory thought is evaluated by reference to

---

[18] Wittgenstein, *The Blue and Brown Books*, 1; quoted above.

[19] William Dray, *Laws and Explanation in History* (Cambridge: Cambridge University Press 1957), 122; author's italics. Quoted in Carl Hempel, 'Rational Action', 11.

[20] Davidson, 'Problems in the Explanation of Action', reprinted in *Problems of Rationality* (Oxford: Oxford University Press 2004), 107.

[21] Even when the agent explains her own action, she portrays herself as thinking a certain way. She may portray herself falsely – that is, she may give a false account of her own action, one that does not reflect the calculation that led her to act as she did.

calculative thought, calculative thought is evaluated by reference to the task at hand.

Second, calculation is prior in the order of time. It is only possible to explain what is the case. So, if it is possible to explain why the gardener is operating the water-pump, then it must be the case that he is operating the water-pump. But if he is already operating the water-pump, then he has already chosen this action as a means to his end – his end being, say, to replenish the house water-supply (with poisoned water). Thus, the calculation that is 'reconstructed' or 'retraced' in a sound explanation of why the gardener is operating the water-pump, this calculation has already finished its work by the time that explanation begins.

Third, calculation is prior in the order of being. Calculation produces the explanandum of action explanation. Were it not for the agent's calculation, there would be no action to explain, and thus no conceivable explanation of it. The very possibility of action explanation depends on the actuality of the agent's calculation.

Finally, calculation is prior in the order of account. To rationalize an action is to portray the action as being the product of calculation. So, a philosophical account of rationalization must explain what it is to portray an action as being the product of calculation. So, it must explain what calculation is. This means that an account of rationalization must contain an account of calculation or else be incomplete as an account of rationalization. The reverse is not the case because to calculate is not in itself to portray anyone as rationalizing anything.

None of this is to say that calculation is intelligible in abstraction from explanation. It is not to deny that the subjective representation of action and the objective representation of action can each only be understood in relation to the other. It is rather to observe that, within their relation, explanation and calculation are not on an equal footing: one of them is beholden to the other.

7. Conclusion

To conclude, let us return to Anscombe's claim that an order of ends and means – 'an order that is there wherever actions are done with intentions' – can be looked at in two different ways: either as a series of ends, or as a series of means; either as reasons for doing something, or as ways of doing something; either as answers to the question 'Why?', or as answers to the question 'How?' Given these two possibilities, philosophers of action face a programmatic decision. The decision is whether to theorize action in terms of explanation or in terms of calculation.

Once this programmatic decision is recognized *as* a decision, it is possible to reflect on it. Such reflection is long overdue. Anscombe did not give any reasons for theorizing action in terms of explanation; neither had Wittgenstein or Ryle before her; neither would Hempel or Davidson after her; and neither has anyone since. Upon reflection, the decision to theorize action in terms of explanation appears, at best, questionable. It appears questionable because to privilege the order of explanation, rather than that of calculation, is to theorize action from the standpoint of an observer, rather than from that of an agent, and moreover, because the standpoint of an agent is in various ways prior to that of an observer. In pointing this out, I do not pretend to have settled the question, but only to have raised it.

University of Chicago
antonford@uchicago.edu

Agency and Practical Abilities

WILL SMALL

Abstract

Though everyday life accords a great deal of significance to practical abilities – such as the ability to walk, to speak French, to play the piano – philosophers of action pay surprisingly little attention to them. By contrast, abilities are discussed in various other philosophical projects. From these discussions, a partial theory of abilities emerges. If the partial theory – which is at best adequate only to a few examples of practical abilities – were correct, then philosophers of action would be right to ignore practical abilities, because they could play no fundamental role in an account of human agency. For the idea that practical abilities *do* play a fundamental role in human agency to be worth considering, an alternative conception of them is needed. As a first step, I attempt some of the necessary ground-clearing work.

Introduction

In our everyday thought and conduct, we place great weight on the acquisition, maintenance, and development of practical abilities – such as the ability to walk, the ability to sing, the ability to play the piano, and the ability to speak French. Practical abilities are an object of focus in many developmental, educational, and therapeutic contexts. The evidence of the everyday would thus seem to bear out Randolph Clarke's claim that 'Abilities are fundamental to agency; we don't have a decent comprehension of agency without an understanding of them'.[1] It ought to be striking, then, that contemporary philosophy of action has remarkably little to say about practical abilities.[2] By contrast, philosophers working on other topics have quite a lot to say about them. From their work a partial theory of practical abilities seems to have emerged. But, I will argue, the partial theory is flawed: it at best works for some practical abilities only. Moreover, it presupposes that practical abilities are not, in fact,

---

[1]   R. Clarke, 'Abilities to Act', *Philosophy Compass* **10**(12) (2015), 893.
[2]   For important exceptions, see G. Ryle *The Concept of Mind* (London: Routledge, 1949) especially ch. 5; A. Kenny, *Will, Freedom and Power* (Basil Blackwell, 1975), especially ch. VII); A. Kenny, *The Metaphysics of Mind* (Clarendon Press, 1989), especially ch. 5; A.C. Baier, 'Act and Intent', *The Journal of Philosophy* **67**(19) (1970), 648–58; A.C. Baier, 'Ways and Means', *Canadian Journal of Philosophy* **1**(3) (1972), 275–93.

doi:10.1017/S1358246117000133   © The Royal Institute of Philosophy and the contributors 2017
Royal Institute of Philosophy Supplement **80** 2017   235

fundamental to agency. The partial theory and the status quo in the philosophy of action are thus such as to reinforce each other. My main goal is to bring into view some features of practical abilities the recognition of which may help us to see just what it would be to think that they are fundamental to agency.

Philosophers of action characteristically seek to understand what human action is by examining how it is explained.[3] And what strikes them as distinctive about their subject matter is that we very often explain human actions in terms of the reasons for which the agent acted: human action is such as to admit of this form of explanation. Philosophers disagree about whether the explanation of action in terms of reasons is a kind of non-causal explanation or a distinctive kind of causal explanation, but they agree that the fact that actions can be explained in terms of their agents' reasons for acting distinguishes them from other sorts of phenomena. Many of the questions philosophers of action are interested in concern the nature of these explanations: Are the reasons for which an agent acts facts, or known facts, or believed propositions, or beliefs? Can desires be reasons? Must a reason for φ-ing purport to show that φ-ing is good? And so on. The purpose of a reasons explanation is to lay out which among the various motives and reasons someone *might* have had for so acting were *in fact the agent's*, and thereby to render it intelligible why she should have acted as she did – and, perhaps, not in some other way. Such explanations presuppose that an action has occurred; they do not purport to tell us what it is for someone to have acted.[4] Thus inquiry into the form and elements of reasons explanations of action may reasonably ignore the question whether or not agential abilities are essentially involved in an account of what it is for someone to act. That Amy has the ability to play the piano would not, or at least not usually, figure in a specification of her reasons for playing the piano on an occasion: her reason might have been that she wanted to please Belinda, and knew that Belinda would be pleased if she played the piano for her. The question 'Why are you playing the Moonlight Sonata on the piano?' presupposes that the agent is playing the piano and that she has the ability to play the

---

[3] See A. Ford, 'The Representation of Action', this volume.

[4] Cf. J. Hornsby, 'Agency and Actions', *Royal Institute of Philosophy Supplements* **55** (2004), 19: 'when one has an action-explanation, one knows why someone did something, and that is to know why they played a particular causal role – why *a* brought it about that *p*, say. The explanation does not tell one *what* causal role *a* played: one already knows this when one knows what *a* did.'

piano. That ability is hardly likely to be cited in her response to the *reason-seeking* 'Why?'-question; it is more likely to figure in an answer to some such question as 'How are you making music come out of that piece of furniture?' A reasons explanation tells us why someone acted as she did, but more may belong in an adequate account of why and how some particular action occurred than belongs in an account of why someone φ-ed on an occasion: more may be involved in accounting for the why and how of a particular event than in explaining why an event of some particular type occurred.

By contrast, the so-called 'standard story of action' aims to take the materials of a reasons explanation and fashion them into a reductive account of (intentional) action. According to the standard story, what it is for someone to have raised her arm, say, is for appropriate mental states (for instance, a desire to attract the chair's attention and a belief that raising one's arm is a way to do so) to have appropriately caused her arm's rising. If an arm *rising* has the right kind of causal ancestry, it counts as an arm *raising* (an action, something the agent *did*); if an arm rising has some other kind of causal ancestry, it is a 'mere' arm rising (not an action, but something that merely *happened to* the person whose arm it is). The idea of an arm rising, or a 'bodily movement' more generally, is understood as something intrinsically non-agential and taken as fundamental. The standard story and its variants appeal only to mental states (such as belief, desire, intention), mental processes (such as deliberation or practical reasoning), bodily movements, and event-causation: abilities do not figure among the explanatory elements.[5]

Practical abilities do not figure in the standard story. And it is sometimes objected that neither do agents: the standard story is said by some to 'leave the agent out.'[6] I share Jennifer Hornsby's sense that these issues are conected:

[5] For the origins of the standard story, see D. Davidson, 'Actions, Reasons, and Causes', *The Journal of Philosophy* **60**(23) (1963), 685–700; for a recent defense, M. Smith, 'Four Objections to the Standard Story of Action (and Four Replies)', *Philosophical Issues* **22**(1) 2012, 387–401; for the sorts of variants I have in mind, see e.g. D. Velleman, 'What Happens When Someone Acts?' *Mind* **101**(403) (1992), 461–81, and M. Bratman, 'Two Problems About Human Agency', *Proceedings of the Aristotelian Society* **101**(1) (2001), 309–26.

[6] See e.g. Velleman, 'What Happens When Someone Acts?' and (for a more trenchant version of the criticism) Hornsby, 'Agency and Actions'.

when an account of the causal transaction in a case of agency is given in the claim that a person's believing something and a person's desiring something causes that person's doing something, ... [t]he fact that a person exercises a capacity to bring something about is ... suppressed. It is forgotten that the agent's causal part is taken for granted as soon as she is said to have done something. The species of causality that belongs with the relevant idea of a person's exercising her capacities is concealed.[7]

Once we have in view someone's having done something, we have in view her having exercised some of her agential capacities; in enquiring after *why* she did what she did, we may explicate why she exercised those capacities, but not *what it was* for her to have so exercised them. But if we begin with a bodily movement that, for all we know, may or may not be an action (may or may not have been someone's exercising of some practical abilities of hers), and come to learn that it was an action (because it was appropriately caused by appropriate mental states), then we have not yet said anything about the role of the agent's capacities and their exercise in her acting.

Hornsby suggests that 'the agent's causal part' (her acting, her doing something) resides in her 'exercising her capacities'. But this is not an idea that she further explicates. I think it would be worth explicating. But it will be difficult to do so if we fail to get clear on the basic shape of agential capacities of the relevant sort – what I am calling practical abilities. And the partial theory obscures this basic shape.

The partial theory emerges piecemeal from philosophical work on a variety of topics. For instance, in epistemology, virtue epistemologists such as Ernest Sosa[8] and John Greco[9] have attempted to account for the nature and value of knowledge in terms of its being an exercise of epistemic abilities or competences, while John Hyman[10] has argued that one knows that p if and only if one has the ability to φ for the reason that p. In discussions of free will, moral responsibility, and determinism, something called 'the ability to do otherwise' is

---

[7] J. Hornsby, 'Agency and Actions', 22.
[8] E. Sosa, *Judgment and Agency* (Oxford: Oxford University Press, 2015).
[9] J. Greco, 'The Nature of Ability and the Purpose of Knowledge', *Philosophical Issues* **17**(1) (2007), 57–69.
[10] J. Hyman, 'How Knowledge Works', *The Philosophical Quarterly* **49**(197) (1999), 433–51; J. Hyman, *Action, Knowledge, and Will* (Oxford: Oxford University Press, 2015).

often at issue. Kadri Vihvelin[11] has recently argued that free will and moral responsibility *do* require the ability to do otherwise, but that this is compatible with determinism.[12] These philosophers very often appeal to practical abilities – such as the ability to drive a car, or an archer's ability to hit the bull's-eye – in order to shed light on (what they take to be) abilities that are less familiar to us, but which (they think) share something of the structure of practical abilities.[13] In their attempts to precisify the source of their analogies, elements of the partial theory emerge and coalesce. Another important source of the partial theory comes from work on the metaphysics of dispositions or powers.[14] Though work in this area typically focuses on such dispositions as fragility and solubility, it usually aspires to a systematic account of dispositionality or potentiality that encompasses human qualities such as the habit of smoking, the character trait of irascibility, and the ability to play the piano. The basic structure of an understanding of practical abilities is here taken to be supplied by an understanding of potentiality or the dispositional as such.[15]

Philosophers working on these topics frequently provide a partial account of ability in order to make, or in application of, the claims they're really interested in making. This is, of course, perfectly legitimate: they have their own interests and agendas. But the conception of practical abilities that emerges thereby, and which to my mind seems to be becoming the received view on the matter, is deeply flawed. At the very least, it ought to be recognized as holding for (at best) some practical abilities only, and as embodying

---

[11] K. Vihvelin, *Causes, Laws, and Free Will: Why Determinism Doesn't Matter* (Oxford: Oxford University Press, 2013).

[12] Vihvelin defends a version of the view that for one to have the ability to φ is for one to be disposed to φ if one has the opportunity to φ and tries to φ.

[13] This is a venerable strategy: consider the uses Plato and Aristotle make of the concept of *technē*.

[14] E.g. S. Mumford, *Dispositions* (Oxford: Oxford University Press, 1998); B. Vetter, *Potentiality: From Dispositions to Modality* (Oxford: Oxford University Press, 2015).

[15] Practical abilities are frequently mentioned but rarely examined in recent discussions about the nature of knowledge how, where the following thesis is often discussed: one knows how to φ just in case one has the ability to φ. This thesis is attributed – mistakenly, in my view – to Ryle (*The Concept of Mind*, ch. 2), and rejected by, among others, J. Stanley and T. Williamson ('Knowing How', *The Journal of Philosophy* **98**(8) (2001), 411–44). But neither those who attack nor those who defend the so-called Rylean thesis explain what it is to have the ability to φ.

commitments that philosophers of action should reject. More significantly, it encourages a conception of abilities on which they are *not* 'fundamental to agency' because they play no genuine explanatory role in the theory of action. The claims of the partial theory that I wish to question are these: (1) A practical ability is a disposition of a special kind, distinguished by the fact that its subject is an agent and its manifestation is an action. (2) Practical abilities are to be specified in terms of act-types (that is, the 'φ' in 'ability to φ' ranges over act-types) and their manifestations are tokens of the relevant type.[16] (3) It is possible for an agent to φ despite lacking the ability to φ. This is because possessing the ability to φ requires more than the possibility (or even actuality) of φ-ing on some occasion, namely the possibility of φ-ing in a sufficiently wide range of circumstances; thus (4) an agent's ability to φ improves, or is better than another agent's, when she is such that her attempts to φ succeed more frequently, or across a wider range of circumstances.

1. Preliminaries

Before proceeding, however, two clarifications are in order. My topic is practical abilities, which I introduced by some examples. The

---

[16]   Philosophy of action makes much use of the concept of an act-type or 'thing done' as contrasted with that of a token action or 'doing (of a thing done)'. Much of this use is uncritical (for helpful criticism see S. Rödl, 'Practice and the Unity of Action' in *Social Facts & Collective Intentionality* (ed.) Georg Meggle (Frankfurt: Ontos Verlag, 2002), 323–42; M. Thompson, *Life and Action: Elementary Structures of Practice and Practical Thought* (Cambridge, MA: Harvard University Press, 2008), ch. 8). The conception of an act-type the partial theory's use of which I wish to criticize is broadly Davidsonian. D. Davidson, 'The Logical Form of Action Sentences' in *The Logic of Decision and Action* (Pittsburgh: University of Pittsburgh Press, 1967) argued that action sentences – such as 'Shem kicked Shaun in the forum at noon' – quantify over events. That sentence says that an event occurred, and that it had the properties of being a kicking, of being of Shaun, of being by Shem, of being in the forum, and of being at noon. Any token action exemplifies many act-types: among other things, what Shem did was to kick Shaun, to kick Shaun in the forum at noon, to kick someone, to do something at noon, etc. And any act-type could be (or at least could have been) instantiated by different token actions: Shem might do the same thing every day for a week – kick Shaun in the forum at noon – in which case there would be seven tokens of that act-type.

characteristic exercises of practical abilities are intentional actions: someone exercises her ability to walk in walking to the shops or in going for a stroll, her ability to play the piano in playing Für Elise, and so on. But we ascribe to ourselves and others abilities that are not practical abilities in my sense: for instance, the ability to understand French, the ability to tell a hawk from a handsaw, and the ability to fall asleep on buses.[17] Whereas the ability to *speak* French is exercised in speech acts, which are intentional actions, the 'acts of understanding' in which someone manifests her ability to *understand* French are not intentional actions. The use of 'act' here is that of the contrast between power and act, a contrast which applies to passive powers as much as active ones. The acts of abilities to understand things, like the exercises of recognitional abilities in perception, are in an important sense passive; they are thus not practical abilities in my sense.[18] And though falling asleep on a bus is something one may be said to do, it might equally be said to be something that happens to one. There are various intentional actions one might perform in order to fall asleep, but falling asleep – on a bus or anywhere else – is not an intentional action (though it might be voluntary or involuntary), and the ability to fall asleep on buses is not a practical ability. Moreover, there may be things that someone can do, where her doing them would be an intentional action, but what is exercised is not a practical ability but rather some authority. By virtue of her authority, a registrar can – is able to – institute a marriage by saying things that anybody has the ability to say; but the 'ability' to institute a marriage, if one wishes to speak that way, is not a practical ability. The abilities under discussion in this paper are practical abilities.

[17] For more examples, see J. Hyman, *Action, Knowledge, and Will*, 177–8.

[18] A contrast between active and powers is drawn by Aristotle at the beginning of *Metaphysics* Book Theta. A solvent has the active power to dissolve a solute; a solute has the passive power to be dissolved by a solvent. (Clearly not every active power is a practical ability.) – In saying that acts of recognition and understanding are passive I do not mean to say that they are *wholly* passive; but I doubt that whatever form of activity may be present in them is that of intentional action. Though I distinguish recognitional and intellectual abilities from practical abilities, I do not think they are disjoint. For instance, the ability to recognize a wind shift is internal to the practical ability to sail, and the ability to understand French is internal to the ability to speak French. Crucially, however, whereas the abilities to sail and to speak French are exercised at will, the abilities to recognize a wind shift and to understand French are not – though one can do various things at will (e.g. close one's eyes, block one's ears) to prevent their exercise.

With the scope of my topic thus sketched in some more detail, I pass to the second clarification. Some philosophers distinguish *different kinds of ability* on the basis of different senses or uses of expressions like 'S is able to φ' or 'S has the ability to φ'. A distinction is frequently drawn between 'general abilities' and 'specific abilities'. A tennis player is said to have the 'general ability' to play tennis, something that someone who has never played it lacks; but in the absence of a racquet, or a ball, or an opponent (and so on) she is said to lack the 'specific ability' to play tennis: she can, or is able to, play tennis generally, but she can't, or isn't able to, play tennis *here and now*. An agent who has a specific ability to play tennis needn't actually be playing tennis, but, as John Maier puts it, 'there is, as it were, nothing between her and the deed'.[19] Some philosophers distinguish a third kind of ability that sits between these two that corresponds to an agent's having 'the necessary skills [i.e. the 'general ability'] and the psychological and physical capacity to use those skills'[20] even though she may lack the necessary 'external' factors (such as access to equipment, etc.) required for 'specific ability'.[21]

It is at best misleading to speak of either two or three different kinds of ability on the basis of considerations such as these. There are three different kinds of factors that might explain why someone is not in a position to do something: she may lack the ability to do it, she may lack the opportunity to do it, or she may prevented from exercising her ability by inebriation, injury, fear, phobia, or unconsciousness (and so on). Of course, in ordinary English we may say that she is unable to do it – and perhaps that she lacks that ability to do it – for any of these reasons. But in our thought about the metaphysics of agency, we ought to be more precise: abilities, opportunities, and impediments are quite different sorts of explanatory factors.

---

[19] J. Maier, 'The Agentive Modalities', *Philosophy and Phenomenological Research* **90**(1) (2015), 123.

[20] K. Vihvelin, *Causes, Laws, and Free Will*, 11.

[21] For two-fold distinctions between 'general ability' and 'specific ability', see A. Mele 'Agents' Abilities' *Noûs* **37**(3) (2003), 447–70; A. Whittle, 'Dispositional Abilities', *Philosophers' Imprint* **10**(12) (2010); E. Glick, 'Abilities and Know-How Attributions', in *Knowledge Ascriptions* (Oxford University Press, 2012); J. Maier, 'Abilities' in *The Stanford Encyclopedia of Philosophy*, (ed.) Edward N. Zalta (Spring 2014); J. Maier, 'The Agentive Modalities'. For three-fold distinctions, see Vihvelin, *Causes, Laws, and Free Will*, 7–16; E. Sosa, *Judgment and Agency* (Oxford: Oxford University Press, 2015), 22–23.

Abilities are 'inherently general', in Kenny's phrase,[22] whereas opportunities and impediments are constituted by particular situations, conditions, or occasions. Serena Williams has the ability to hit a forehand winner down the line, on the run. It is the same ability she exercises whenever she hits one, but the opportunities come and go, and some she does not take. When inebriated or injured, Williams does not *lack* a physical ability to exercise her ability to play tennis; rather, she *has* a condition that prevents her from exercising her tennis-playing abilities.[23] Of course, in *saying* that someone is able to do something we may be drawing attention to some combination of ability, opportunity, and lack of impediments to exercising ability; but this does not justify invoking a *kind of ability* that is constituted by the co-presence of these factors.[24] The ideas of 'specific ability' and 'narrow ability' are misnomers; moving forward, then, I shall assume that the only practical abilities are what many call 'general abilities.'[25]

[22]   A. Kenny, *Will, Freedom and Power*, 135.
[23]   Similarly, with psychological impediments to the exercise of one's general abilities: there can be psychological roadblocks to exercising abilities that need to be overcome. But overcoming them is not acquiring an ability to try to φ. Like removing a literal roadblock, removing a psychological roadblock such as grief, depression, anxiety, or a phobia is removing an obstacle to exercising one's abilities. Indeed, Vihvelin's characterization of what she calls 'narrow ability' to φ, or 'having what it takes' to φ – namely, 'the necessary skills [i.e. the 'general ability'] and the psychological and physical capacity to use those skills' – makes it sound as if it consists of the conjunction of two abilities: the ability to φ and the ability (or capacity) to exercise one's ability to φ. This might suggest a regress: if one needs, in addition to the ability to φ, the ability to exercise one's ability to φ, why wouldn't one need the ability to exercise one's ability to exercise one's ability to φ (and so on)?
[24]   We would not expect acquiring or losing the ability to ride a bicycle to affect someone's possession of the ability to recite *The Love Song of J. Alfred Prufrock*. But we might well expect that if someone who can ride a bike and can recite Prufrock gets blind drunk, both abilities will be impaired; and when she sobers up, she will not have gained or regained a kind of ability (a 'narrow ability') to ride a bike – and with it, a 'narrow ability' to recite Prufrock – but she will no longer be impeded from exercising *many* of her 'general abilities'.
[25]   As I noted above, someone may be able to do something because she possesses the authority to do it. Someone else may be unable to do it, because she lacks the relevant authority. But to lack authority is not to lack ability.

Will Small

2. Abilities and dispositions

If anything constitutes a default view about abilities, it is that they are dispositions – probably dispositions of some distinctive kind.[26] To say that Amy has the ability to play the piano, or to run a five-minute mile, or to cook spaghetti bolognese is not to say anything about what she *is currently* doing. Exactly what it *is* to say, on this prevailing view, depends on how dispositions are understood. According to some,[27] dispositions are to be understood in terms of conditionals; thus to say that someone has an ability is to say something about what she *would* do – *if* such-and-such either happened or were the case. For instance, it might be held that to have the ability to φ is to be such that, were you to have the opportunity to φ and try to φ, you would φ.[28] According to others,[29] dispositions are to be understood in terms of restricted possibilities; thus ability ascriptions do not say what an agent *would* do *if* certain conditions obtained, but simply what she *can* or *could* do. The idea is that we understand the claim that it is *possible* for someone to φ in terms of the idea that there is some possible world in which they[30] φ, and then understand the more specific idea that someone has the *ability* to φ (that they can or could 'in the ability

---

[26] Cf. S. Mumford, *Dispositions*, 10: 'I take it that the dispositional is a genus that can accommodate these subclasses [sc. tendencies, capacities and incapacities, powers and forces, potentialities and propensities, abilities and liabilities, etc.] as species'; Vihvelin, *Causes, Laws, and Free Will*, 171: 'To have an ability to act is to have a disposition or bundle of dispositions'; E. Sosa, *Judgment and Agency*, 24: 'Competences are a special case of dispositions....'

[27] E.g. K. Vihvelin, *Causes, Laws, and Free Will*.

[28] This is evidently closely related to the 'Simple Conditional Analysis' of dispositions, which faces well-known counterexamples ('finks' and 'masks' – see e.g. C.B. Martin, 'Dispositions and Conditionals', *The Philosophical Quarterly* **44** (1994); D. Lewis, 'Finkish Dispositions', *The Philosophical Quarterly* **47** (1997); D. Manley and R. Wasserman, 'On Linking Dispositions and Conditionals', *Mind* **117**(465) (2008)) that seem to show that satisfying the proposed conditional is neither necessary nor sufficient for possession of the disposition. There is much dispute over the correct response to such counterexamples: one might give a more complicated conditional analysis, or a non-conditional analysis, or take some conditional to be, not an analysis, but rather some sort of gloss that merely indicates the *sui generis* character of dispositions.

[29] E.g. B. Vetter, *Potentiality*.

[30] Or a counterpart of theirs.

sense' φ) in terms of the idea that there is some possible world *from among a restricted set* of possible worlds in which they φ.[31]

On the restricted possibility view of ability, what distinguishes an ability from a mere disposition is that the subject of an ability is an *agent* – or perhaps an agent *insofar as she is an agent* – and that the manifestation of the ability is an *action.* (More would need to be said, of course, in order to distinguish practical abilities from other sorts of agential dispositions to act – for instance, habits.) The conditional view of ability can appeal in addition to the distinctive role it grants to *trying*. In §5 below, I will return to this difference. But my main concerns abstract from any argument between proponents of conditional and restricted possibility views of ability. No doubt the question whether to prioritize conditionals or possibility in one's thought about dispositions is a significant one. My main focus, however, will be on problems that a conception of ability inherits when it is assumed that an account of dispositions of either of these sorts may be used as it basis: when it inherits what is common to both views.[32]

Kenny writes: 'A skill or ability is always a positive explanatory factor in accounting for the performance of an agent; an opportunity is often no more than a negative factor, the absence of circumstances that would prevent or interfere with that performance'.[33] How would philosophers of action have to conceive – or reconceive – of abilities for them to be candidates to play a genuinely explanatory role? If I'm right, a substantial rethink is in order. I propose to explore three issues, and the connections between them: the robustness or

---

[31] To associate disposition (or ability) ascriptions with conditionals or with restricted possibilities is not to commit oneself to a reductive analysis of dispositions (or abilities) in terms of conditionals or restricted possibilities.

[32] I am not alone in registering such concerns. Millikan writes that: 'The modern philosophical tradition has unreflectively assimilated abilities to capacities and capacities to dispositions. This affords a slippery slope.' R. Millikan, *On Clear and Confused Ideas: An Essay About Substance Concepts* (Cambridge: Cambridge University Press, 2000), 31. See also Baier 'Ways and Means', 285–6: '"Competence" is too pompous a word to use of simple skilled activities such as digging, stirring, walking, but it may be preferable to "ability" which has been debased by philosophical usage until it has lost any discriminatory power. When "x has the ability to φ" is equated with "x is able to φ" and that in turn is equated with "it is possible that x will φ" or "x is not causally necessitated not to φ" then the distinctive features of abilities are hopelessly lost.'

[33] A. Kenny *Will, Freedom and Power*, 133.

reliability of abilities; the gradability of abilities; and the individuation and specification of abilities.

3. Ability and success

Abilities are fallible, as a famous example from J.L. Austin illustrates:

> Consider the case in which I miss a very short putt and kick myself because I could have holed it. It is not that I should have holed it if I had tried: I did try, and missed. It is not that I should have holed it if conditions had been different: that might of course be so, but I am talking about conditions precisely as they were, and asserting that I could have holed it. There is the rub. ... [A] human ability or power or capacity is inherently liable not to produce success, on occasion, and that for no reason (or are bad luck and bad form sometimes reasons?).[34]

An agent may have the ability and opportunity to φ, try to φ, and yet fail to φ. (According to Austin, it seems, this may be so even when nothing interferes.) But though they are fallible, abilities are also supposed to be reliable and robust: it is no accident if someone with the ability to φ succeeds in φ-ing. Thus accounts like the following are common:

> S has the narrow ability at time t to do R as a result of trying [= 'in response to the stimulus of S's trying to do R'] iff, for *some* intrinsic property B that has S has at t, and for some time t' after t, if S had the opportunity at t to do R *and* S tried to do R while retaining property B until time t', then *in a suitable proportion of these cases*, S's trying to do R and S's having of B would be an S-complete cause of S's doing R.[35]

---

[34] J.L. Austin, 'Ifs and Cans', *Proceedings of the British Academy* **42**(1956), 109–132. Cited as reprinted in his *Philosophical Papers* (Oxford University Press, 1961), 166 n. 1.

[35] K. Vihvelin, *Causes, Laws, and Free Will*, 186. 'Narrow ability' is Vihvelin's term for the so-called kind of ability that requires 'the necessary skills and the psychological and physical capacity to use those skills' (*Causes, Laws, and Free Will*, 11) but not the opportunity to use them (see §1 above for criticism). Her account transposes Lewis's 'Finkish Dispositions' conditional analysis of dispositions to the case of abilities. Though most writers prefer a uniform treatment of dispositions and abilities, Lewis himself proposed a restricted possibility view of abilities (D. Lewis, 'The Paradoxes of Time Travel', *American Philosophical Quarterly* **13**(2) (1976), 145–52).

[A]bilities have the following structure: S has an ability $A(R/C)$ relative to environment E = Across the set of relevantly close worlds W where S is in [conditions] C and in E, S has a high rate of success in achieving [result] R.[36]

More straightforwardly, Kenny says that 'There is this much truth in the conditional analysis of ability':

'I can φ' entails: if I have the opportunity to φ, and if I do my best to φ, then I normally will φ.[37]

What makes for a 'suitable proportion of cases' or an appropriately 'high rate of success', and what it takes to 'normally' succeed, will differ for different abilities. In some cases, a 50% rate of success would be evidence of lack of ability: it's luck, not ability, that accounts for my getting heads when I flip a coin.[38] But sport provides many examples of abilities for which a 50% success rate would be evidence of outstanding or even unthinkable ability. The basketball player Stephen Curry, an outstanding three-point shooter, made just over 45% of his three-point shots in 2015–16. The best hitters in Major League Baseball usually hit the ball in play between 29% and 35% of the time. And Dale Steyn – cricket's best bowler – has the ability to take wickets if anyone does, but he takes a wicket only once every 41 balls he bowls. So ability can tolerate quite low probabilities of success, depending on the difficulty of the task; and lack of ability can be consistent with relatively high probabilities of success.[39]

Even though it may be difficult to say what counts as a normal or suitably high rate of success in different cases, views like those of Vihvelin, Greco, and Kenny seem to provide a natural way of saying what it is for an ability to come in degrees. The 'gradability' of abilities is an idea well-entrenched in ordinary thought and practice. Amy is a better runner than Belinda, Brian a more able swimmer than Charles, Chloë shows greater ability at darts than David, and I

---

[36] J. Greco, 'The Nature of Ability and the Purpose of Knowledge', 61.

[37] A. Kenny, *Will, Freedom and Power*, 142.

[38] Cf. A. Kenny: 'I cannot spell "seize"; I am never sure whether it is an exception to the rule about 'i' before 'e'; I just guess, and fifty times out of a hundred I get it right. On each such case…it is the case that I am spelling "seize" correctly but it is not the case that I can spell "seize" correctly' (*Will, Freedom and Power*, 136).

[39] In basketball, making 40% of one's three-point shots would be outstanding, whereas making 60% of one's free-throws would be abysmal: it is much easier to make a free-throw than a three-pointer.

am trying to get better at playing the piano. These accounts provide for at least two dimensions in which one agent's ability might be greater than another's. On the one hand, the more able agent's attempts might succeed at a higher rate (this is what baseball batting averages record, for instance). On the other hand, there might be more circumstances in which her attempts succeed: the more able the agent, the more circumstances constitute opportunities (twenty knot winds may prevent a beginner sailor from going out on the water while providing a more experienced sailor with an opportunity for an exciting sail).[40] Accounts that have a place for *trying* – depending on how it is construed – may provide for another dimension of gradability: Belinda has the ability to run a six-minute mile, but only if she really, really tries, whereas Amy, a better runner, can run a six-minute mile, without really trying. She barely breaks a sweat.

These criteria – *higher rate of success* and *success in more circumstances* – seem well-suited to account for the gradability of dispositions such as fragility and flammability (for 'success' read 'manifestation') and of some abilities. Stephen Curry's extremely high ability to make three-point shots is shown both by his making them at a much higher than average percentange and also by his succeeding with *more difficult* attempts than his peers. But the account looks much less promising when we think about those abilities whose exercises do not have the neat, binary conditions for success or failure (like making a basket, hitting the bull's eye, and so on) that match those of the metaphysicians' favourite dispositions, fragility and solubility (it either breaks or it doesn't, or it dissolves or it doesn't).

Consider: Belinda can run a six-minute mile, but only if she really tries, whereas Amy can run a six-minute mile with ease. It is not that Amy is such as to succeed in running a six-minute mile with a higher rate of success than Belinda. (This might not be true: though Belinda really needs to try, perhaps she always gives 100% in everything she does.) Nor is it that Amy, unlike Belinda, can run a six-minute mile not only when it's warm and dry but when it's cold and wet, on grass, not only on the track, and so on. (This might not be true either: Amy might be unusually sensitive to such things.) Amy's greater ability as a runner doesn't have to do with how frequently, or under what conditions, she runs a six-minute mile. That she, unlike Belinda, can run a six-minute mile *with ease* suggests that she can run a mile in *well under* six minutes. She does not have the

40 Cf. J. Maier, 'The Agentive Modalities', 128.

ability to run a six-minute mile better than Belinda; she is a better *miler* because she, unlike Belinda, can run a five-minute mile – this explains why when she decides to run a six-minute mile she can do so with ease. She is a better *miler* because she runs *faster* miles. Indeed, for many of the 'physical' or athletic abilities that we grade, being better at doing something will be understood in terms of physical magnitude: running *faster*, throwing things *further*, doing *more* push-ups, lifting *heavier* weights. Chloë's ability to do push-ups is greater than David's, not because she is such as to succeed in doing a push-up with a higher degree of success than he is, or because she can do push-ups in a wider range of circumstances, but because she can do *more* push-ups.

There is another way in which the gradability of ability is not captured by the two dimensions provided for by views like Vihvelin's, Greco's, and Kenny's. Evgeny Kissin is a much, much better pianist than me. He can, indeed, play the piano faster than me – but that seems an unpromising way to account for his superiority. No doubt he can play more pieces than me; but more importantly, he can play *more difficult* pieces than me. He can play the Appassionata Sonata; I cannot. If I tried to play the Appassionata, I would fail. But I wouldn't fail to play the piano – the opening bars aren't very difficult. Playing the piano badly is still playing the piano. It's not that Kissin's *ability to play the Appassionata* is greater than mine because when he tries to play it, he succeeds, whereas were I to try, I would fail: I don't have the ability to play the Appassionata. We wanted to understand how my *ability to play the piano* is exceeded by Kissin's, yet it would be a rare occurrence indeed for me to try but fail to play the piano. Kissin is a better pianist than me not because he 'succeeds' in playing the piano with a higher rate of success or in a wider range of circumstances than I do, but because he plays more accurately and more musically than I can, and he can play more challenging pieces. Being better at φ-ing may often be a matter not, or not merely, of one's successes being more frequent or reliable, but of one's successes being better successes. Think of the craftsman or artist who turns out a better product: Brian is better than Charles at making pots, because the pots he makes are better pots. There are evidently normative or evaluative dimensions to the gradability of ability that do not belong to the accounts of what it is for one object to be more fragile than another, one substance to be more flammable than another, and so on.

As well as undermining the thought that the gradability of ability can be understood through those ideas – rate of manifestation in similar conditions, range of conditions of manifestation – that seem suited to accounting for the gradability of dispositions such as fragility and flammability, these examples raise a further question. In each of them, we find it natural to characterize the degree or grade of an agent's ability to φ in terms of whether or not she can exercise that ability by φ-ing in some determinate way. The fact that Amy can run *a five-minute mile* is a reason to praise her ability to run, while the fact that I cannot play *the Appassionata* may figure in a more muted evaluation of my ability to play the piano. But is it that Kissin's ability to play the piano exceeds in degree an ability I possess (the ability to play the piano) because he possesses an ability (the ability to play the Appassionata) that I lack? More generally, how are abilities to be specified or individuated?

4. Individuating and specifying abilities

The proper specification and individuation of abilities is not an issue that has received much philosophical attention. The following list of abilities is representative of the rather relaxed prevailing standards in the literature:

- to move one's limbs;[41]
- to raise my hand; to sink a 3' putt; to dress in a kilt;[42]
- to stand on my head on commuter trains; to row a straight line in a crosswind;[43]
- to sing; to sing when one's aunt is present;[44]
- to read *Emma*; to read *Persuasion*; to read *Werther*;[45]
- to speak French; to ride a bicycle; to sing in tune; to juggle;[46]
- to kiss the Blarney Stone; to know that p;[47]
- to pronounce the name 'Luigi'; to marry for the sake of love; to marry for the sake of money; to φ for the reason that p.[48]

The list contains some highly general abilities (e.g. the ability to move one's limbs – which ones? how?); some extremely specific abilities (e.g. the ability to read *Emma*, the ability to stand on my head on

---

[41]   P. M. S. Hacker, *The Intellectual Powers: A Study of Human Nature* (Chichester, West Sussex: Wiley-Blackwell, 2013).

[42]   A. Mele, 'Agents' Abilities'.

[43]   R. Millikan, *On Clear and Confused*.

[44]   A. Whittle, 'Dispositional Abilities'.

[45]   J.L. Austin, 'Ifs and Cans'.

[46]   K. Vihvelin, *Causes, Laws, and Free Will*.

[47]   J. Spencer 'Able to Do the Impossible', *Mind* (forthcoming).

[48]   J. Hyman, *Action, Knowledge, and Will*.

commuter trains); abilities that require particular objects, not just objects of particular kinds, for their exercise (the ability to kiss the Blarney Stone); and we find the ability to do something for one reason distinguished from the ability to do the same thing for a different reason. And of course we find such humdrum and everyday practical abilities as the ability to speak French, to sing in tune, and so on. Again, I don't propose to legislate on whether or not it is correct speech to ascribe any of these abilities: ordinary language is used for more than metaphysics. But we may ask: is someone who is reading *Emma* exercising an ability to read *Emma* – does an ability to read *Emma* belong in an explanation of her action – or is she reading it by exercising more general abilities, such as the ability to read English? And will the correct account of the abilities exercised in reading *Emma* parallel that of those exercised in playing the Appassionata?

To make progress, let us consider a rare concrete proposal for the individuation of abilities, due to John Hyman:

> for all φ and ψ, the ability to φ and the ability to ψ are different abilities if it is possible to have one without having the other. It follows that the ability to run a mile in four minutes and the ability to run a mile in five minutes are different abilities, since it is possible to have the second without having the first, even though it is not possible to have the first without having the second.[49]

By a continuation of the same reasoning, it would follow that the ability to run a mile is yet a third ability: Belinda has the ability to run a mile, but she can't run a five-, let alone a four-, minute mile; Amy can run a five- but not a four-minute mile; and Alex can run a four-minute (and thus a five-minute) mile. So by Hyman's lights we have three different abilities – of which Belinda possesses one, Amy two, and Alex all three. Parallel reasoning would suggest that we distinguish the ability to play the piano, the ability to play Für Elise, and the ability to play the Appassionata. Someone may have the ability to play the piano without having the ability to play Für Elise or the ability to play the Appassionata, and though possessing either of the more specific abilities entails the ability to play the piano, neither of them entails the other: an average pianist may have the ability to play Für Elise quite well, but not the difficult Appassionata, and a strong pianist who has learnt the Appassionata may simply never have had Für Elise in her repertoire.

[49]   J. Hyman, *Action, Knowledge, and Will*, 177–8.

Though he claims that such abilities are distinct, Hyman acknowledges that they are nevertheless 'related': 'running a mile in five minutes … and … running a mile in four minutes … are both species of the generic act of … running a mile…, and the corresponding abilities are related in the same way'.[50] Presumably he would say the same thing in the other case: the ability to play the Appassionata and the ability to play Für Elise are species of the generic ability to play the piano. But it is not clear that this account of the relations is correct. It is true that running a mile takes time, so any act of running a mile will take a certain period of time; anyone who has the ability to run a mile will possess it to some degree, and that degree may be specified by a time. But the species of a genus, or the determinates of a determinable, *exclude each other*. Nothing can be a mammal without being either a human or a cow or a cat etc.; but equally nothing can be both a cow and cat. Nothing can be uni-coloured all over without red all over or green all over or blue all over, etc.; but equally nothing can be red all over and green all over. Yet Alex has the ability run a four-minute mile and the ability to run a five-minute mile: the 'species abilities' do not exclude each other.[51] Neither the act-types nor the abilities are species of a generic act of running a mile or ability to run a mile.

Hyman might respond that though *biological* species exclude each other, a *logical* conception of the species-genus relation is available, one on which the species of a genus do not exclude each other. So there would be no problem in Alex having multiple species of the generic ability to run a mile: the ability to run a four-minute mile, the ability to run a five-minute mile, the ability to run a six-minute mile, and so on. But such a proposal still seems to multiply abilities unnecessarily, as Don Locke notes:

> I can, for example, walk down Park Street, and I can also walk down State Street: I will succeed in doing these things if I try. But this surely does not mean that I have two abilities, the ability to walk down Park Street and the ability to walk down State Street; there is but one ability, the ability to walk, manifested in two different contexts. Again, the athlete who runs a four minute mile also, in the same performance, runs a five minute mile, but he does not thereby exercise or manifest two

---

[50] Ibid., 178.

[51] A related point is made by B. Vetter, 'Multi-Track Dispositions', *The Philosophical Quarterly* **63**(251) (2013), 346.

abilities. By that token he would be manifesting an infinity of abilities![52]

The ability to walk is something that has to be acquired. Once acquired, one can exercise it walking down a particular street. (Indeed, one cannot exercise it except by walking in some particular place, for some particular amount of time, in particular conditions – but surely there is such a thing as the ability to walk.) The ordinary human acquisition of the ability to walk is the acquisition of an ability that can be exercised in walking down Park Street or State Street or many other streets; on grass or on carpet or on tarmac; at dawn or at dusk; on Monday or on Tuesday. (It is not typically the acquisition of an ability that can be exercised in walking on hot coals or on ice or in space – these, if possessed at all, would usually be developed later. And it is never the acquisition of an ability that can be exercised in walking on water – contrast some insects.) Amy's ability to walk is sufficient to explain how it was possible for her (given the opportunity and motivation) to walk down State Street on Monday: there is no need to ascribe to her the ability to walk down State Street, the ability to walk on Mondays, or the ability to walk down State Street on Mondays in order to account for this; indeed, such 'abilities' would seem to trail after the performances they might be supposed to explain. So though particular streets may belong in the specification of what is done on some occasion when someone exercises her ability to walk (on Monday morning Amy did not merely walk; she walked down State Street from the river to Macy's), the streets do not belong in the *specification* of the abilities that are exercised in walking down them. However, this does not conflict with Hyman's principle for the *individuation* of abilities: one might accept that principle while taking a stricter stance than Hyman on the question of what are legitimate substitution instances for φ in 'the ability to φ'.

Whereas the ordinary acquisition of the ability to walk would put someone in a position to walk down (say) State Street, the ordinary acquisition of the ability to run need not put someone in a position to run a mile, let alone a five-minute mile: stamina, strength, and training will characteristically be required. Going to a new city affords new opportunities for exercising one's ability to walk: there are new streets for one to walk down. It is the same thing that one is doing (walking) and the same ability that one is exercising (the

---

[52]   D. Locke, 'Natural Powers and Human Abilities', *Proceedings of the Aristotelian Society* **74** (1973), 184.

ability to walk) on new and familiar streets alike. But the result of training is not like the result of travel: when, after months of training, Amy can finally run a five-minute mile, there is something she can do that she lacked the ability, and not merely the opportunity, to do before. And this would seem to be a reason for thinking that practice and training enlarge an agent's stock of abilities: Amy acquires the ability to run a five-minute mile, something she lacked before.

Why does Locke reject this? In running a five-minute mile (in running a mile inside of five minutes), Amy ran a six-minute mile (ran a mile inside of six minutes). But though she did many things – though her action exemplified many act-types – it would be absurd, Locke implies, to hold that she exercises or manifests an ability corresponding to each thing done. Of course there is no problem with an action manifesting many – perhaps infinitely many – properties. And there can be no problem with the idea that an agent might exercise more than one ability at the same time: doing so is surely the norm rather than the exception. (In writing this essay I am exercising both my ability to compose English prose and my ability to use a computer.) The problem seems to have to do with the idea that the agent might be exercising too many abilities, or at least too many abilities of the same sort. Though Amy ran a six-minute mile in running a five-minute mile, surely the only mile-running ability she exercised was the ability to run a five-minute mile. So perhaps one could agree with Locke that Amy does not exercise both the ability to run a five-minute mile and the ability to run a six-minute mile, while insisting with Hyman that they are distinct abilities: having recently acquired through training the ability to run a five-minute mile, this and this alone is the mile-running ability that Amy exercises when she sets out to run a (fast) mile.

A difficulty remains, however. If Amy tries to run a five-minute but for some reason succeeds only in running a six-minute mile, which ability did she exercise? One might hold that she exercised her ability to run a six-minute mile, the ability that she possessed prior to, and has retained since, her recent training regime led to her acquisition of the additional ability to run a five-minute mile. But this seems problematic: we seem to be picturing Amy as in the dark about which of her abilities she is exercising while she is acting. Alternatively, one might hold that when she acquired the ability to run a five-minute mile it *replaced* her prior ability to run a six-minute mile, and that it is the new ability that she exercised in running what turned out to be merely a six-minute mile on this occasion (practical abilities are fallible, after all). But this view seems like a less perspicuous notational variant on the idea that, through her training, Amy *developed* her ability *to run*: that ability used to be such that when she tried her best and things went well, she ran a six-minute mile; now it is such that when that happens, she runs a five-minute mile – though she can exercise that ability in running a mere six-minute mile if she so chooses. Amy's ability to run a mile is an ability to run a five-minute (and thereby a six-minute) mile.

Locke's principle for individuating abilities, which does so in a more coarsely-grained way than Hyman's, seems to capture this: 'if those features from an agent's constitution and background which bring it about that he standardly succeeds in doing *x* are also sufficient to bring it about that he standardly succeeds in doing *y*, then we are dealing here not with two separate abilities, but with the one ability, to do *x* and do *y*'.[53] Amy can run a five-minute mile; *a fortiori* she can run a six-minute mile. Those features of Amy's constitution and background that underwrite her standardly succeeding in running a five-minute mile are also sufficient for her standardly succeeding in running a six-minute mile. By Locke's principle, it would seem that we are dealing here not with two separate abilities, but with a single ability: the ability to run a five-minute mile and the ability to run a six-minute mile are the same ability. Belinda, however, can run a six-minute mile but not a five-minute mile. Those features of her constitution and background that underwrite her standardly succeeding in running a six-minute mile are not sufficient for her standardly succeeding in running a five-minute mile: by Locke's principle, we are dealing with two separate abilities. And so when we put these results together, they suggest, absurdly, that the ability to run a five-minute mile both is and is not the same ability as the ability to run a six-minute mile.

The absurdity can be avoided by interpreting Locke's principle as yielding the verdict that *Amy's* ability to run a five-minute mile and her ability to run a six-minute mile are the *same* ability, and that *Belinda's* ability to run a six-minute mile is *not* an ability to run a five-minute mile. On this interpretation of Locke's principle, then, there is no answer to the question whether *the* ability to φ and *the* ability to ψ are the same ability or not; there are answers only to the question whether *so-and-so's* ability to φ and *her* ability to ψ are the same ability or not. But that seems to me just right: practical abilities are acquired, and some particular agent's acquisition of an ability is a particular process that particularizes the ability in her. Perhaps the point is better put like this: Amy and Belinda both have the ability to run, but in each of them that ability is differently specified *in concreto*. Amy's ability to run is such that she can exercise it in running a

53   Ibid., 187.

five-minute mile, whereas Belinda's is not – when Belinda exercises her ability to run in running a mile, she does six-minute miles. It lies within Amy's power to run a five-minute mile, whereas a six-minute mile is the best mile it is within Belinda's power to run. But in each of them it is the power *to run*, rather than a more narrowly specified power, that is exercised when they run a mile in however long it takes. The respective shapes of their abilities to run are different – though Amy is a better middle-distance runner than Belinda, perhaps Belinda is better at sprinting than Amy.[54]

The different shapes taken by an ability in its being possessed by different agents may show themselves in a variety of ways. When the ability is properly specified by an action-type that captures *what was done* in a performance, the shape of the agent's ability *in concreto* may show itself in the proportion of successes to attempts, or in the range of circumstances that constitute opportunities in which the agent succeeds, or in the quality of the success itself (very often, of the product of the performance – whether it is a better or worse one of its kind), or – and surely this will often be the case – in some combination of these. But very often the proper specification of an ability is more coarsely-grained than the specification of what was done on an occasion of its exercise. This is clearly the case when the thing done was to walk down State Street on Monday morning, but the ability exercised was the ability to walk. Other cases are less clear. The ability to play the piano is certainly exercised in a performance of the Appassionata.[55] But is there an ability to play the Appassionata that is also exercised? Whereas someone who has the ability to walk is by that very fact in a position to walk down State Street when presented with the opportunity, it is hardly the case that someone who has the ability to play the piano is by that very fact in a position to play the Appassionata when presented with the opportunity (a working piano and the sheet

[54]   To distinguish again the issue of *individuating* abilities from that of *specifying* them, we should say that if Amy's ability is properly specified as *the ability to run a five-minute mile*, then Hyman's principle of individuation should be rejected, whereas if it is properly specified as *the ability to run*, then his principle may be accepted while acknowledging that what he claims follows from it in fact does not. (This bears on the cogency of Hyman's discussion as a response to the objection – by Hacker (*The Intellectual Powers*, 183) to Hyman's account of knowledge – that animates it.)

[55]   Obviously, in playing the Appassionata the agent is playing the piano. But, in the ordinary case, what is being done is *playing the Appassionata*: it is as a playing of the Appassionata that the agent's activity of piano-playing is evaluated for (among other things) whether or not it was completed.

music, say). A lot of practice is required. I incline to the view that the result of the practice (if it is successful) will be a development and determination of the agent's ability to play the piano, one in virtue of which she is able to play the Appassionata. (Kissin is *able to* play the Appassionata by exercising *his* ability to play the piano; *my* ability to play the piano is not such that I am *able to* play the Appassionata.) On this view, the specific shape of an agent's ability *in concreto* to play the piano or to run may be specified by saying which pieces are within her ability or repertoire, or how far she can run in what time. But such characterizations, of which there will be many for any given ability, are characterizations of the shape taken by a single ability, not the characterization of several different abilities.[56]

I grant that there are other possible views in the vicinity; I hope to have opened up space for discussion of them. But I think that we may at least conclude that a specification of what it is within an agent's abilities to do is not thereby a specification of one of her abilities; or, as Locke puts it, 'it seems possible to specify performances in more detail that is appropriate for abilities'.[57]

This is a way of insisting on the generality of ability, which, though frequently noted, has been underestimated. Kenny and others correctly observe that abilities can be realized in distinct token actions of the type specified by the ability. But I have argued that abilities are more general than this: they can be realized in distinct token actions *of distinct (though related) types*. Therefore, the specification of an ability cannot be arrived at simply by reading it off the act-type exemplified by an concrete performance.[58] But though I have argued that abilities are in one respect more general (less specific) than is usually thought, I have also argued that they are in another respect less general

---

[56] Different such characterizations work in different ways. When we characterize Amy's ability to read English by saying that she has the ability to read *Emma*, we are using Austen's novel as a yardstick of (e.g.) the sort of vocabulary and prose that Amy can read in English – regardless of whether or not she has read *Emma*. But to characterize her piano-playing ability by saying that she has the ability to play the Appassionata would not ordinarily be to use the Appassionata as a mere yardstick of the sorts of technical and expressive demands that Amy can meet, regardless of whether she has played the Appassionata; ordinarily it would be to characterize the particular shape of her piano-playing ability as one that, as it were, contains the Appassionata.

[57] D. Locke, 'Natural Powers and Human Abilities', 184.

[58] The preceding discussion suggests that we need to reflect further on the internal structure of and relations between act-types as well as abilities.

(more particular, not more specific): in acquiring and possessing an ability, an agent particularizes it, thereby giving it a determinate shape.

Indeed, it is quite fundamental to abilities that they are exercised in performances more highly specified than the abilities themselves. It would otherwise be impossible to hold both that we can acquire new and novel abilities and that abilities play a genuine role in the explanation of their exercises. We are in a position to do novel things because we can do them by deploying abilities we already have in new ways, conditions, and combinations. We thus provide for an infinity of possible actions without requiring the postulation of an infinity of abilities. And surely this is required if we are to articulate a conception of ability on which abilities explain the performances in which they are exercised.[59] Fine-grained specifications of abilities make it hard to credit them with a genuine explanatory role.[60]

---

[59] For similar points about the specific cases of our linguistic and conceptual abilities, see D. Davidson 'Theories of Meaning and Learnable Languages' in *Proceedings of the International Congress for Logic, Methodology, and Philosophy of Science*, (ed.) Yehoshua Bar-Hillel (North-Holland, 1965), 3–17 and G. Evans, *The Varieties of Reference*, (ed.) John McDowell (Oxford: Oxford University Press, 1982), 100ff.

[60] Jack Spencer ('Able to Do the Impossible') argues for the provocative claim that 'an agent might be able to do what it is metaphysically impossible *tout court* to do' (msp. 1). A crucial concept in his argument is that of a 'factive ability', for instance the 'abilities' to know or discover or remember that *p*. Factive abilities are cases of 'object-dependent abilities' – 'abilities to perform object-dependent actions, such as *kissing the Blarney Stone* or *seeing the Statue of Liberty*' (msp. 4–5). But taking the concept of ability seriously ought to rule out the idea of object-dependent abilities, in which case Spencer's argument is over before it has begun. Spencer claims that 'Object-dependent actions and abilities are common and familiar' (msp. 5). But though object-dependent *actions* are surely familiar, the contention that object-dependent *abilities* are common seems to depend on the assumption that an ability can be specified by specifying the type(s) of action of which the ability's exercises are tokens – an assumption we have seen fit to reject. Object-dependent abilities are clearly explanatorily idle. To kiss the Blarney Stone, all that is needed, for someone who has the ability to kiss things, is the opportunity – and perhaps whatever is needed to overcome any psychological roadblocks to putting one's mouth on a stone that all and sundry are constantly kissing: no special ability needs to be acquired. And the truth of *p* is a necessary element of the *opportunity* to know that *p*, which opportunity can be taken only by those who have the ability to *think* that *p* (and the abilities to recognize reasons, deal appropriately with evidence, and so on, which may or may not be presupposed by or contained in the ability to think that *p*). Indeed, the ability to *think* that *p* may very well

258

There is some reason, then, to prefer coarsely-grained specifications of abilities. But this is not to say that more coarsely-grained specifications of abilities are always preferable. Sometimes a complex performance (for instance, talking while walking) does not require a correspondingly complex ability (the ability to talk while walking) over and above the constituent abilities (the ability to talk and the ability to walk), but sometimes it does: a child may have the ability to pat her head and the ability to rub her tummy without being in a position to pat her head while rubbing her tummy – here it does seem that she needs to acquire a further ability, the ability to pat her head while rubbing her tummy.[61]

5. Ability and success, again

Opting for more coarsely-grained specifications of abilities makes it easier to see how abilities play an explanatory role: by exercising our abilities in different ways, situations, and combinations we can do more things than we have abilities. We do not postulate an

---

be a pseudo-ability, too: if p is the proposition *that a is F*, then there is no 'ability to think that p' over and above the abilities to think of a and to think F of things (cf. Evans (*The Varieties of Reference*) on what he calls the 'Generality Constraint').

[61]   Though I am sympathetic to the spirit that seems to me to animate Locke's discussion, the actual principle he offers may have to be rejected. It seems possible that one might acquire together two separable abilities the exercises of which involve exploiting the same features of the agent's constitution. Suppose that Sam, who previously lacked any cooking abilities, learns how to cook spaghetti bolognese. In learning how to do this, he learns – let us suppose simultaneously – how to cook bolognese sauce and how to cook and dress spaghetti. It would seem that the same features from Sam's constitution and background which bring it about that he standardly succeeds in cooking spaghetti are also sufficient to bring it about that he standardly succeeds in cooking bolognese sauce, and yet – *pace* Locke's principle – his ability to cook spaghetti and his ability to cook bolognese sauce are not the same ability (nor are they identical with his ability to cook spaghetti bolognese). It is not clear to me that we need or should expect of principle of individuation for abilities. Perhaps Millikan is correct: 'The idea that one might count the number of a person's abilities, or count the abilities that go into a certain activity, often is not really coherent. Like patterns, however, or like patches of ground, abilities can be clearly distinguished and designated even when they have no clear criteria of individuation' (*On Clear and Confused Ideas*, 64).

ability for every thing done, and thus avoid the suspicion that it is the deed that 'explains' the ability, rather than the other way around. But to say only this would be to understate how fundamental abilities are to agency.

As I noted in §3, the fallibility of practical abilities is widely acknowledged. However, many hold not only that ability (in conjunction with opportunity and attempt) does not guarantee success, but also that successfully φ-ing does not suffice to establish the ability to φ – or in other words, that the ability is not necessary for successful action. Indeed, though there is some dissent – Austin says that 'of course it follows merely from the premiss that he does it, that he has the ability to do it, according to ordinary English'[62] – the received view seems to be that one may successfully φ despite lacking the ability to φ.[63] Kenny gives an example that occurs frequently in the literature: 'A hopeless darts player may, once in a lifetime, hit the bull, but be unable to repeat the performance because he does not have the ability to hit the bull'.[64] Even though the hopeless darts player *hit* the bull's eye, he cannot reliably hit it. Hitting it is not within his control: that he *did* hit it on this occasion was down to luck, not ability, as it will be if he ever hits it again. As Kenny notes, 'Counterexamples similar to these will always be imaginable whenever it is possible to do something by luck rather than by skill'.[65]

If it is possible to φ despite lacking the ability to φ, it is easy to see why many philosophers of action should think that the ability to φ plays no essential role in the explanation of an agent's φ-ing on some occasion. The example of the inept dart thrower who flukily hits the bull relies on a conception of what it is to act, or to act successfully, that is restricted to the bringing about of certain states of affairs. Evidently this conception of doing something or succeeding is independent of the idea of ability: a successful deed may be the exercise of an ability, but it may not. What is essential, on this conception, is *that*, but not *how*, the relevant state of affairs is brought about.[66] Vihvelin is quite explicit about this:

[62] 'Ifs and Cans', 175.
[63] See e.g. D. Locke, 'Natural Powers and Human Abilities', 185; A. Kenny, *Will, Freedom and Power*, 136; P.M.S. Hacker, *The Intellectual Powers*, 187–8; K. Vihvelin, *Causes, Laws, and Free Will*, 198; J. Hyman, *Action, Knowledge, and Will*, 180; B. Vetter, *Potentiality*, 222.
[64] A. Kenny, *Will, Freedom and Power*, 136.
[65] Ibid., 136.
[66] Kenny in fact qualifies his claim that successful action does not entail ability: 'a single performance, however successful, is not normally enough to establish the existence of ability. (I say 'not normally' because a single

There are many ways to do something. One way is by having the ability. Another way is by accident or lucky fluke. Yet another way is by having one's brain and body moved, puppetlike, in the appropriate ways by a sorcerer. Doing something by accident or lucky fluke does not entail having the ability to do it; doing something due to direct manipulation by someone else does not entail having the ability to do it. This shows that the fact that S does A does *not* entail that S has the ability to do A.[67]

Most philosophers of action would, I hope, deny that 'having one's brain and body moved, puppetlike, in the appropriate ways by a sorcerer' is a way of *doing* something: it is, rather, a way of *suffering* something – of having something *done to one*.[68] But there is certainly a conception of action on which one's accidental or flukey bringings-about are actions. Consider Davidson's[69] famous example of (unintentionally) alerting the prowler by turning on the light. Davidson illuminated the room,

---

performance may suffice if the task is sufficiently difficult or complicated to rule out lucky success. Pushing one's wife in a wheelbarrow along a tightrope stretched across Niagara Falls would be a case in point)' (*Will, Freedom and Power*, 136). But, to the extent that it is easy to imagine someone pushing his wife in a wheelbarrow along a tightrope stretched across Niagara Falls, it is easy to imagine his doing so being a case of lucky success, in which case the performance would not establish the ability to push his wife in a wheelbarrow along a tightrope stretched across Niagara Falls. What it may well establish (so long as the lucky success was not due to guardian angels, etc.) is that the agent has the ability to walk a tightrope, the ability to manoeuvre a wheelbarrow, and so on. Of course, someone who successfully navigated a short, low-stakes tightrope once would not thereby show herself to have the ability to walk a tightrope (as that is normally understood – which is to say, as that is understood by reference to the standards internal to the practice of tightrope walking). It is a notable feature of Kenny's discussion that his awareness that the concepts of ability and luck come as a package co-exists with his taking for granted the idea of 'doing something' or 'successful performance'; and yet surely that is just what ought to be at issue, if ability is the sort of 'positive explanatory factor' (*Will, Freedom and Power*, 133) he thinks it is.

[67] K. Vihvelin, *Causes, Laws, and Free Will*, 198.

[68] See e.g. M. Alvarez, 'Agency and Two-Way Powers', *Proceedings of the Aristotelian Society* **113**(1) (2013), 101–21.

[69] D. Davidson, 'Agency', in *Agent, Action, and Reason* (University of Toronto Press, 1971).

which caused the prowler to be alerted; his deed could then be described in terms of what he brought about, as his alerting of the prowler. Nevertheless, I think that reflection shows that this conception of action (as the bringing about of results) is secondary or derivative: it depends on a conception of action as essentially the exercise of an ability. For the latter conception of action, but not for the former, Austin was correct: action suffices for ability.

The (not unconnected) influences of utilitarianism and a results-oriented mode of production may make the conception of action as essentially the exercise of an ability difficult to see. It may help to note that certain types of *failures*, as well as successes, may be manifestations of ability – as when an excellent goalkeeper gets a hand on an unstoppable shot that a lesser keeper would not have got near. Even though he failed to make the save, he certainly acted, and his action was an exercise of his goalkeeping abilities. So we cannot capture our concept of ability by relying solely on the thought that it is manifested in successful instances. Some 'successful instances', conceived of as mere 'bringings about', are not manifestations of ability, whereas some failures to bring about the effect that was desired or intended or constitutive of the ability may nevertheless be manifestations of ability. Sometimes all the skill in the world cannot yield success, but that means neither there was no action, nor that skill and ability were not on display.

Though this illustrates the difference between the two conceptions of action – action as the 'successful' bringing about of effects or states of affairs, and action as essentially the exercise of ability – it does not yet show why we should think of the latter conception as more fundamental than the former. But it is clear that to bring it about that p, one must bring p about in some way or other. *Some* ability or competence must be exercised, even if it is not an ability to bring it about that p. It is true that Kenny's hopeless darts player hits the bull without having the ability to hit the bull. But he hits it by doing things he *does* have the ability to do: grasp and grip and aim and throw a smallish object.[70]

---

[70] Cf. Baier's claim that there is an 'asymmetric dependence' of 'effectings' – bringings about – upon exercises of competences (abilities): 'An action description such as "getting the feet wet" is non-specific with respect to how the feet were got wet, but implies that there was a way, either a wading or a washing or a hosing or …By contrast, a [description of an action as the exercise of an ability] need not, although it may, imply an effecting. This guarantees that whenever there is action, there is … exercise of a competence, and that all effectings will depend on competences' ('Ways and Means', 289–90).

If this is right, then the idea that abilities can be distinguished from dispositions simply by characterizing their manifestations as *actions* is undermined. For if action, in the fundamental sense, is essentially the exercise of ability, then we will go around in an unilluminating circle if we appeal to the idea that abilities are manifested in actions to distinguish them from dispositions.

One might hope to break out of the circle by appealing to the idea of *trying* in order to distinguish abilities from dispositions – and thus to opt for the conditional view of ability (see §2 above). But this would be right only if trying were a causal condition on the exercise of ability – if an act of trying were conceived of as a trigger or stimulus of a disposition.[71] Yet this idea is surely misguided, conjuring up as it does an image of my body as a machine the passive operations of which are kick-started by what I *really* do, namely try to act.[72] If – as indeed Kenny holds – it is a mistake to interpret the 'if I tried' in 'I would if I tried' as identifying a causal condition, and so a mistake to interpret the conditional as a causal counterfactual (as it is supposed to be in 'the glass would break if it were struck'), then the point of drawing attention to the role of trying or attempt is not to claim that abilities have a particular triggering stimulus, where the disposition stimulated differs in no fundamental way from (e.g.) fragility, but rather to indicate that abilities are a *formally* distinctive kind of power. Practical abilities are *volitional powers*: they are exercised at will. This idea obviously requires elucidation and defence for which I do not have space here; I hope, however, to have motivated further investigation of it.[73]

---

[71]   Such a view is explicitly advanced by K. Vihvelin, *Causes, Laws, and Free Will*.

[72]   For discussion of different conceptions of trying, see J. Hornsby 'Trying to Act' in *A Companion to the Philosophy of Action*, (eds) Timothy O'Connor and Constantine Sandis (Chichester: Wiley-Blackwell, 2010), 18–25. If trying *were* a causal stimulus of the exercise of abilities, then abilities would differ from many dispositions in having uniform stimuli – Vetter advances a restricted possibility view of dispositions in part because she thinks that '[s]timulus conditions play no part in individuating, or in giving the essence of, a disposition', ('Multi-Track Dispositions', *The Philosophical Quarterly* 63(251) (2013), 349).

[73]   The idea is discussed – unsatisfactorily, in my view – by A. Kenny (*Will, Freedom and Power*, ch. VII); A. Kenny (*The Metaphysics of Mind*, ch. 5); H. Steward, 'Sub-Intentional Actions and the Over-Mentalization of Agency' in *New Essays on the Explanation of Action* (ed.) Constantine Sandis (Houndmills, Basingstoke, Hampshire: Palgrave Macmillan, 2009), 295–312; H. Steward, 'Responses', *Inquiry* 56(6) (2013), 681–706; M. Alvarez, 'Agency and Two-Way Powers'.

Will Small

Conclusion

Everyday thought and practice accords greater significance to the role of practical abilities in human agency than do most philosophers of action, whose accounts are typically oriented around reasons for acting. I share Hornsby's sense that for the philosophy of action to give the agent her due, we must recognize that when an agent acts she exercises her practical abilities. But the conception of practical abilities that emerges piecemeal from a number of contemporary philosophical projects gets in the way of taking this point seriously, and obscures the possibility of crediting practical abilities with a significant role in the explanation of action. To get this possibility in view, an alternative conception of practical abilities is needed. My goal was not to develop this alternative, but to clear some of the ground for its development. It will require giving up the assumption that practical abilities can be distinguished from mere dispositions by virtue of some distinctively practical *element* in the disposition's structure, and instead working out what it is for an ability to be a power of a distinctive *form*. It will also require giving up the assumption that practical abilities are to be specified in terms of act-types, as these are commonly understood: a proper understanding of the acquisition, development, and exercise of practical abilities requires a better grip than we currently have on their specification and individuation.[74]

University of Illinois at Chicago
wsmall@uic.edu

[74] Earlier versions of this paper were presented at the Centre for the Study of Mind in Nature at the University of Oslo, the Royal Institute of Philosophy, and a meeting of the DFG Netzwerk »Praktisches Denken und gutes Handeln« at the University of Leipzig. Thanks to those who participated in those events. And special thanks to John Hyman for comments on a draft, from which I – and I hope the paper – benefitted a great deal.

264

Actions as Prime[1]

LUCY O'BRIEN

Abstract
In this paper I am going to argue that we should take actions to be prime. This will involve clarifying what it means to claim that actions are prime. I will consider Williamson's construal of actions as prime in a way that parallels his treatment of knowledge. I will argue that we need to be careful about treating our actions in the way suggested because of an internal relation between the success condition of an action and the action itself; a parallel relation does not hold for most cases of knowledge.

Philosophers of action very often start with the question: what happens when someone acts? I am going to follow suit. However, I am going to go on to urge that there is a certain kind of answer to that question that is often expected, but that we cannot have, and that we do not need.[2]

Suppose – to start with an unusually simple action – I raise my arm. Two questions immediately arise:

(NEC) What is *needed* for it to be true that I raise my arm?
(SUFF) What is *enough* for it to be true that I raise my arm?

The question that I call (NEC) is a question about what is necessary for me to raise my arm. The question that I call (SUFF) is a question about what, other than that I raise my arm, is sufficient for it to be true that I raise my arm.

Let us set about answering the (NEC) question: what is needed for me to raise my arm? Obviously my material world needs to exist, and the space I move it in, needs to exist. Also my parents needed to have

[1] I owe acknowledgement to a number of people: to Adam Ferner for making sure this paper got written in time for publication, and to Alex, Geddes, Alec Hinshelwood, Jen Hornsby, Mike Martin for very helpful comments and discussion. Particular thanks are due to Doug Lavin for input at all stages, and to Matt Soteriou for crucial last-minute help.
[2] The main contention of this piece – that actions are primitive and not reducible to other psychological and bodily phenomenon – is also argued for in Chapter 8 of my *Self-Knowing Agents*. (L. O'Brien, *Self-Knowing Agents*, Oxford: OUP.) Douglas Lavin in his 'Action as a form of temporal unity: on Anscombe's intention' (*Canadian Journal of Philosophy*, **54**) also sets out a non-reductionist view.

doi:10.1017/S135824611700011X   © The Royal Institute of Philosophy and the contributors 2017

met for me to now be raising my arm. These background conditions are conditions on my acting in virtue of being conditions of more central conditions. What are the more central conditions? I think we can identify four:

Agent Condition. I must exist when I act: I must exist if I raise my arm.

Change Condition. I change things when I act: I change my bodily position when I raise my arm, and change things caused by my changing.

Self-change Condition. I self-change when I act: I change, from having my arm down to having an arm up, when I raise my arm.[3]

Active Condition. The self-change which is my action is up to me: The change from having an arm down to having an arm up is *up to me.*

It seems unarguable that the *Agent Condition* is true: we can agree with Gassendi that 'it is known by the natural light that *whatever acts exists*'.[4] If I act, I, therefore, exist.[5] I am going to assume for the purposes of this paper that I am this human being, this animal writing. On that assumption, if I raise my arm then that is going to require that this human animal exists.

The *Change Condition* is also met in the candidate case. If the act at issue is the act of raising my arm then something needs to change: my muscles need to contract, my bones re-orientate, the position of my arm needs to change. Furthermore, acts like the act of raising my arm are necessarily changes; there are no arm raisings which are not changes. Is change always required for action? Could I act – say 'stand very still' – and not change anything? It seems that in fact

---

[3]   I use the – admittedly clumsy – expression 'self-change' deliberately so as to avoid locutions like 'I change my self' because the latter brings connotations of my taking myself as an object to act on, when what actually happens is that I take myself to be that I act with. The main point is that when I act, I change. I can only change the non-me world by changing. So whenever I change any thing in action, I change.

[4]   J. Bennett (ed.), *Objections to the Meditations and Descartes' Replies*: 'Fifth Objections (Gassendi) and Descartes' replies: Objections to Second Meditation; Objection 1'. www.earlymoderntexts.com/pdfs/descartes1642/pdf, page 86.

[5]   For discussion of this see O'Brien, 'Ambulo Ergo Sum', *Royal Institute of Philosophy Supplement* **76** (2015).

standing very still does require changes – it requires me clenching my muscles and pushing against gravity. Perhaps there are acts such as remaining silent when someone has said 'speak now or I will take it that you agree to the proposal' that are not changes. However, we might think that they are not actions either – but rather deliberate omissions with foreseen and intended effects. To the extent that they *are* actions we can think of them as transitions between similar states – changes in time without change in properties.

Perhaps the more contentious claim here is the *Self-change Condition*. Why must an action that involves change also involve self-change? The simple thought is that any change I bring about must be a change brought about by my doing something and my doing something is my changing. Take those class of acts that involve changes that are not in the first characterization changes to me: acts such as raising a glass, throwing a ball or switching on a light. Let us call the changes constituting such actions changes to the *non-me world*. How are changes to the non-me world brought about by me? They are brought about by, myself, changing. If that is right then *all* actions – even if they involve changes to the non-me world – are also self-changes, or involve self-changes. I don't think I can change anything unless *this thing* – the animal that I am – changes. Anything else I change, I have to change in virtue of changing. I might wish I could actively change things by just hoping for them but I cannot – *I* need to make the change that makes the change to the non-me world.

Note that the claim that all actions that involve changes are self-changes does not mean that in all cases of action the *object* of the action is the self in the same way that the object of an action might be the glass, or ball, or light switch. It is rather the claim that the subject and agent of the action is *always* the self. This is reflected in the fact that when we specify act types we are not required to specify *which subject* it is that is to change in the way determined by carrying out the action. We need specify only what kind of action is to be carried out. In deciding whether to F, or to G, or H, I do not also decide who – me, Harry or someone else – is to F, or to G, or to H. If I am deciding what to do I am already deciding what I, the decider, is to do. It is a given that the subject who determines what she should do is that thing the changes to which are the doing.

The *Active Condition* is extremely hard to state without falling into heavy theorizing very quickly. Some try to capture the active condition by claiming that I change things *on purpose* whenever I act. The thought is not that every change I bring about when I act is a change I bring about on purpose, but whenever I act, I act with purpose.

Lucy O'Brien

Others will try to capture the idea by claiming that all acts are *intentional*; not that everything done by the agent acting is done intentionally but that everything done by the agent acting is done by the agent doing something intentionally. Others claim that actions are self-changes *under the control* of the agent. I have tried to stay away from the more or less technical notions of purpose, intention and control and will instead speak simple of self-changes that are *up to* the agent changing, and then contrast them with self-changes that are not up to the agent.

Consider all the self-changes that an animal undergoes. There are many of them that are not up to the animal: at least not directly. It is not up to the animal to grow: it can eat lots of protein and aid itself in growing upwards, but it cannot *execute* the growing. Similarly, it is not up to an animal to wrinkle, or shrink or heat up, or digest, or produce insulin. These are changes that the animal can bring about indirectly – but, again, they are not changes that are up to them to execute. In contrast there are a large number of self-changes that are directly up to the animal: the animal can run, jump, move its arms, legs, lips, tongue, eyebrows. Relative to each animal in a context there is a large class of movements, that we can call *me-movements*, that the animal can execute directly. They are me-movements that are up to the animal that is acting. Philosophers tend to call the relevant class here 'bodily movements'. This terminology carries with it the unfortunate suggestion that there is on the one hand the agent, and on the other the agent's body that the agent moves when they act – thus making action out to involve some kind of relation between the agent on the one hand and the body to be moved on the other. By calling them me-movements we make it clear that action is a *reflexive or self-conscious* change – agents change by themselves changing – not by changing themselves. As Gareth Evans puts it, such self-consciousness is manifested in action 'not in knowing which object to act upon, but in acting. (I do not move myself, I myself move.)'[6]

In answer to the initial question: 'what happens when I act?' we have the answer: I, myself, change in a way that is up to me. We have given some sense of the category of self-changes that are up to me, and contrasted them with self-changes that are not up to me, but can we say anything more about the difference? What do we mean when we say that someone has brought about a self-change in a way that is up to them?

[6] G. Evans, *The Varieties of Reference* (Oxford: Clarendon Press, 1982), 207.

One way to approach the question is to look more carefully at two cases which on the surface involve a similar change, but where one is up to me, and where the other is not.

Consider the standard case of my moving my arm up. In such a case my arm moves from being down to being up – and it so moving is my moving it up. In contrast consider a case where my arm moves from being down to being up because it was blown up by a strong wind from below. If we are trying to understand what is it for my moving my hand up *to be up to me*, in contrast to be caused by the wind, we may be led to set ourselves a certain kind of subtraction problem. We may ask Wittgenstein's question 'What is left over if I subtract the fact that my arm moves up from the fact that I raise my arm?'[7]

We may start to note that it is not just that my arm went up when I moved it up – I also *wanted* it to go up, *knew how* to make it go up, *intended* it to go and *willed* it to go up. We may then, having identified things that do go on when I raise my arm in a way that is up to me, be tempted to make the further move of thinking that it is these extras make it the case that I move my arm in a way that is up to me, in contrast to a case where my arm moves up due to the wind.

We started by asking 'what is needed for me to raise my arm?'. We have answered: well, one of the things you need is the agent who self-changes – I could not have raised my arm without me. We have also acknowledged that I might need to want my arm to go up, and need to know how to make it go up. Perhaps I also need to intend for it to go up, and to will for it to go up. This list of things that are required for me to raise my arm is very contentious – but for the purposes of this discussion let us assume that we are happy to accept that an instance of each of this list of things needs to be in place when I act – raise my arm, for example.

We have not said anything about whether these things are independent of my arm going up, or whether they are things I can understand without already understanding what it is to move my arm up in a way that is up to me. I have just agreed that we can assume that these things have to be in place when I act. That is, we have assumed that our answer to (NEC) is, at least partly, answered by that list.

The trouble, however, starts when we take two further steps. First, when we take the list that is our best attempt to answer (NEC) as an answer to (SUFF). (SUFF) was the question what is enough for it to be true that I acted. Second, when we take the resulting answer to (SUFF) to be a reductive answer to what my acting is. If we say

[7]   L. Wittgenstein, *Philosophical Investigations* (1953), §621.

that not only does the list (of my arm going up, my wanting it to go up by knowing how to make it go up, my intending it etc.) give me an account of what is *needed* to act, and a list of what is *enough* to act – it also tells us what my acting is, we have embarked on an attempt to analyse my action in other terms. If the attempt were successful it would imply that the act - my raising of my arm - is not actually a single unified element in my psychological life but is *psychologically molecular*. It is composed of all, or some, of the 'more basic' elements we have on the list we gave in an answer to (NEC).

There are two sort of reasons that might make us worry about whether an answer to (NEC) is going to add up to anything like an answer to (SUFF), or anything like an answer to what an action is that is stated in these more basic terms.

The first sort of worry is a circularity worry. You might think it is true that you need to want, know how to, intend, will, when you act. But what is it you need to want, know how to, intend or will *to do*? The answer, in our case, is 'to raise my arm'. But to raise one's arm *is* the action we are trying to understand, so to know what all those other conditions are, we need to know what an action is. If we are involved in an explanatory project that is going to try to say what an action is, and build it out of the components we identify in our answer to (NEC), those components would need to be understood *independently* of our knowing what an action is. But it does not, at first sight, look as though they are. To want to raise my arm, know how to raise my arm, intend to raise my arm, to will to raise my arm are all things that may need to be in place when I raise my arm but they do not seem to be things we can understand independently of knowing what it is to raise my arm. As Lavin and Boyle point out, it is a 'striking fact' about the reductionist who tries to give an account of what an action is that:

> they tend to insist of re-writing desire ascriptions which we would colloquially express by saying:
> (1) S wants to do A
> By transforming what follows 'wants' into a proposition, as in
> (2) S wants that S does A.[8]

In such re-writing we hide, to some extent, the fact that you already have the action type embedded in the description of what the agent

---

[8]   M. Boyle and D. Lavin, 'Goodness and Desire' in S. Tenenbaum, (ed.), *Desire, Practical Reason, and the Good* (Oxford: Oxford University Press, 2010), 170.

wants when she acts, and thereby hide the fact that we need already to know what is for the agent to raise her arm if we are to know what it is for her to want to raise her arm. The same would be true of attempts to re-write what the agent knows, or intends, or wills.

The second, and more commonly discussed, sort of worry about the attempt at reduction is an insufficiency worry. The insufficiency worry amounts to the worry that one could have a case where you have an agent who wants to do something, knows how to do it, intends to do it, wills to do it, and indeed does it – but where the thing that she does is not an action that was up to her. Here is a case, adapted from a famous case of Davidson's to match the conditions we have identified as candidate states that may be required for action:

> Suppose a climber wants to rid himself of the weight and danger of holding another man on rope. Suppose he knows that by loosening his hold he could rid himself of the weight and danger, intends to drop the climber, and wills to do so. But suppose at the moment of willing he becomes so unnerved and shocked by what he is doing that it causes him involuntarily to loosen his hold and drop the other man. Here, he didn't have a choice about loosening his hold, nor did he do it intentionally. You can have all these things going on, but still not have an action.

Many resourceful philosophers have expended huge effort in trying to give a reductionist theory of action only to face further counterexamples. Davidson himself declared that he 'despair[ed] of spelling out…the way in which attitudes must cause actions if they are to rationalize the action.'[9]

These worries invite the hypothesis that actions are prime: if actions are psychological phenomenon not to be analysed in terms of other psychological attitudes it would be clear why we face the circularity and insufficiency worries.

To assess, and indeed understand, the hypothesis we need to ask what we mean when we claim that some phenomena is prime? The dominant association that philosophers currently have when faced with the claim that some phenomenon is prime is Williamson's claim that knowledge is prime.

'Prime' is a word that has two distinct uses, and Williamson picked the word advisedly, meaning to make claims relative to both. However, we need here to untangle those uses if we are to be clear

---

[9]   D. Davidson, *Essays on Actions and Events* (Oxford: Clarendon Press, 1980), 79.

Lucy O'Brien

about what we are claiming when we consider whether actions are prime, and what we are not.

What are the two things we might be saying when we say that something is prime?

When we say that X is prime we may mean that X is *BASIC* in some way and *not factorizable into other phenomena*. It is prime in the sense that a prime number is prime. It is what it is, and not reducible to another thing. It is important to note that lots of things can be basic.

When we say that X is prime we may also mean that X is *FIRST in some ordering*. It is prime in the sense of Prime Minister, or prime cut. It is *primary*. Only ONE thing in a given class or ordering can be first.

I want to pursue the question as to whether we should treat actions as prime, by thinking about whether we should take action to be prime a way that mirrors Williamson's claim that knowledge is prime. So, what is involved in Williamson's claim that knowledge is prime? Williamson claims that knowledge is prime in, more or less, both the senses that we have identified. So, for him, both the following are true:

Knowledge is BASIC: Knowledge is a basic epistemic and psychological phenomenon that is not to be reduced or fully analysed in more basic psychological or epistemic terms.[10]

Knowledge comes FIRST: Knowledge has a claim to primacy over other other epistemic and psychological phenomenon. We should understand other epistemic and psychological phenomenon in terms in terms of knowledge.

So, correlatively we may take the claim that action is prime to involve the following two claims:

Action is BASIC: Actions are basic psychological phenomena are not to be reduced to, or fully analysed in more basic terms.

Action comes FIRST: Action has a claim to primacy over other practical and psychological phenomena. In particular, action has primacy in explanation over belief, desire, intention, bodily movement.

---

[10] Williamson in fact intends something a bit narrower, construing primeness as non-factorisability in to specifically a conjunction of a purely internal condition and a purely external condition. Thanks to Aidan McGlynn for reminding me of this.

When deciding which, if any, claims to the effect that action is prime are true it is worth noting just how strong primitiveness claims are when they are of the form 'X comes first' rather than 'X is basic'. For a start claims to the effect that 'X comes first' are in competition with each other. If, for example, both action and knowledge are elements of the ordering relative to which we are making a primacy claim it cannot be that both action and knowledge come first: it cannot be that action has primacy over knowledge, in such a way that the latter is to be explained in terms of action *and* that knowledge has primacy over action, and that action be explained in terms of knowledge. Williamson's claim that knowledge is prime is a claim about both senses. This means that he is committed, not just to the idea that knowledge is basic, but to there being a significant class of phenomenon – evidence, belief, action, justification and so on – which are to be explained in terms of knowledge. This makes it clear straightaway that Williamson would have to deny that action is prime in the sense that action comes first.

Not only are 'action first' and 'knowledge first' claims in competition with each other, they are independently very ambitious claims. They demand that a whole array of phenomena come to be explained by one primary one. To that extent such claims are claims of systematic philosophy. They are also forms of reductionism about explanatory resources, governed by the idea that philosophical explanations in epistemology or philosophy of mind have to bottom out in a way that refers to just a few basic phenomena. In contrast, claims to the effect that something is basic – and not factorizable in to other more basic phenomenon within a class – are relatively philosophically, and explanatorily, ecumenical.

In suggesting that actions may be prime I mean to be suggesting, not that we take on a philosophical programme in which actions play a primary explanatory role – in contrast to knowledge, evidence, reason, belief or desire and so on – but only that actions may be prime in being basic, and not reducible to other more basic psychological notions. There are interesting questions to raise about the relations between actions and what we want, know how to do, intend or will. The circularity point made above with reference to Boyle and Lavin – that we specify what we want, know how to do, intend or will in terms of the action to which they are directed suggests that action may have a primary explanatory role in relation to a restricted set of phenomenon. However, the task for now is to set out what the claim of basicness amounts to and argue that we have reason to take it to be true.

So, what does the claim of basicness amount to? What are we saying when we say that actions are basic? A claim of basicness of a psychological phenomenon is, for my purposes, to be understood as a claim about the relation of that phenomenon to other personal level psychological phenomenon (PPPs). The class of PPPs is supposed to be the class of familiar psychological states and occurrences that we take to be correctly ascribed to psychological subjects. The class will include desires, beliefs, intentions, perceptions, emotions, suspicions, guesses, judgments, thinkings, deliberatings etc.

When we claim that actions are basic, what we are doing is denying that they are a personal level psychological phenomena that are composed of, or analysed in terms of, more basic PPPs, our bodies and their relations. Within the class of PPPs there will be those that are more basic, and that are not capable of being fully understood with reference to the others. The claim is that actions are more basic. The claim is a relative claim, and indeed not a very strong one in the broader context of philosophical reductionism.

It is important to emphasise that the claim that actions are prime, in the sense of basic, is not a claim to the effect that actions are basic particulars in the final and most fundamental inventory of the universe. It may be that the basic elements of the universe are microphysical particles perhaps not yet identified by any human science. If that is so, then only those particles will be basic in a non-relativized way. In claiming that actions are basic I am not denying that the facts about them will be fixed by the fundamental facts of the universe, if it turns out that there are any. Nor am I claiming that actions are explanatorily or metaphysically independent either of other PPPs, or of other non-PPPs. Facts about whether a creature can act may be importantly interdependent with facts about whether she can intend or desire and so on. Similarly, the actions of an agent bear dependence relations to the movements of its body, to contractions of its, to its neural activities such as its motor commands, and a whole host of sub-personal, physiological and others facts. In claiming that actions are basic, we are certainly making no claim to the effect that an animal could act without the organism and its parts doing various things, and without various low level physiological activities taking place.

The claim that actions are basic is really little more than the claim that actions are (a) psychological phenomena and (b) that, despite the tendency of philosophers to treat them otherwise, *they are no less basic* than beliefs, desires, intentions, tryings, willings and so on.

Does that mean that if actions are prime there is no work to be done by a philosopher of action? No. There are a number of explanatory tasks for a philosopher of action without her undertaking the task of trying given an account of actions in terms of other PPPs, our bodies, and the relations between them. We can give normal conditions on actions; we can give necessary conditions on actions. We can clarify the nature and consequences of those conditions, and give an account of the relation between actions and other psychological phenomenon. We can learn more about the neural and physiological occurrences and structures that ground or realise our actions. We can try to understand how it is that we can change, and thereby change other objects, in a way that is up to us. We can explore how active reflexive changes are possible. We can explain our particular epistemic relation to actions understood as self-changes that are up to us; we can offer a semantics for action ascriptions that respects the reflexive nature of action. These are all tasks for other occasions. What I want to do now is move beyond setting out what it means to say that actions are basic, and offering the hypothesis that actions are be basic in that sense, and consider a couple of positive arguments in favour of the hypothesis. So far all we have done is appeal to the fact that the task is a tricky one, and stated Davidson's own scepticism and despair in the face of it.

The first argument to consider is one we can call *the argument from multiple sources*. The reductionist about actions that I have been opposing tends, as we saw, to proceed as follows. They consider a movement a human subject might make – a movement of arm rising, for example. They then note that there are occasions where an arm rising is not an action, because they are not up to the agent. They then ask what pattern of psychological states or occurrences precedes the arm risings in the cases where the arm rising is an action that is up to the subject. The hope is that they can thereby find the difference maker: that they can identify the unique pattern of prior states and occurrences in virtue of which the arm rising is an action that is up to the agent.

A naïve first reaction to this way of proceeding is to point out that when we look at human action we see that the aetiologies, and aims, of human action seem to be as *various and unpredictable* as the aetiologies of human belief, desire, and intention. We should, therefore, not expect to find a unique kind of aetiology distinctive of those arm risings that are *actions*, in contrast to those that are *mere movements*.

Prima facie it seems that I can φ, where φ-ing is something I do intentionally, in very, very different ways with different causal histories and different goals. Take an everyday case of acting: suppose I drink a glass of beer. The psychological reality that can precede my drinking a beer may, it seems, come in many different forms. I might be drinking because I love the taste of beer, I might be drinking automatically from habit, I might be drinking from addiction, I might be drinking because a week ago I planned to have a beer at this time, I might be drinking spontaneously, perhaps out of thirst, maybe out of a desire for the sugar. Perhaps I am drinking for joy, or out of embarrassment, social nerves, or excitement. Perhaps I hate beer, but have resolved to drink so that I confirm to the desires of my host, or to conform to the rule I have set myself to drink at least one beer a week in order that I do my bit to keep hop growers in business. And note that the concern is not just that that there are multiple dispositions, states and occurrences that might be relevant to the fact that I drink beer, but that they may be *present at the same time.* Even if I am drinking out of thirst, I may *also* have a desire to fit in, or have planned to have a beer a week ago, or love the sugar, or be resolved to drink one beer a day. Actions spring from many sources of motivation, habit, compulsion and resolve that can all be in place at once, whether or not they are directly operative in the action at issue. Perhaps there will be one source – or one disjoint set – that is *the* source of the action at any time? Well, it is clear that there may be potential sources that are inoperative – but it is not obvious that we can make good sense of identifying *precisely* what the psychological source of the action was *this time.* There may be background motivations, for example, that the action does not seem to be an action for the sake of, but they might be motivations that, had they not been in place, the agent would have not acted on the distinct motivation that lead her to act. So I may not have drunk the beer to fit in, but rather out of my love of beer, but it may be true that I would not have drunk the beer had drinking it, for example, put me at odds with those around me.

Our fixed point seems to be that, whatever the prelude or purpose of an action, we end up with an agent who self-changes in such a way that she moves, and thereby moves her glass towards her mouth pouring the beer into it, and swallowing. We end up with me drinking beer in a way that is up to me. The prospects of giving a tidy account, that is true to the phenomenon, of what kinds of sources, and what kinds of links between those sources and my movement, makes the movement an action of mine look foggy. Of course, we can as Davidson did, try to conceptualise the preceding states and occurrences at a level of abstractness that brings some order to these myriad of sources. We might, for example, look for a way to construe my drinking as drinking rationalised by the belief-pro-attitude pair of (desiring the consequences of drinking, and believing that drinking is a way to secure those consequences). But the prospects of such an attempt are not my primary concern: my primary concern is to point out that the salient thing in common between all these different possible beer drinkings – and indeed in the supposed rationalising reason – is my *action of drinking the beer.* Without a decisive reason to talk about actions of that kind in other terms, the fact that our actions have multiple sources gives us a good reason to admit them as basic.

The second kind of argument in favour of the basicness of action we can call *the argument from explanatory* role. The first thing to note is the *ubiquity* of appeal to actions in explanations. If we look at patterns of explanations for why things are as they are we will find them laced through with appeals to human action. We will also find them laced through with appeals to human wants, knowledge, intentions and movements but not to the same extent and the explanations that appeal to human action cannot in general be inter-substituted for explanations that appeal to other PPPs and bodily movement. I make this point and give an example in O'Brien 2007:

> Suppose I am angry with Elmore for making a V-sign at me, in the presence of those I respect. Suppose that I am angry with him because he acted in a way that humiliated me and showed a failure to respect me. I am not angry with him merely for trying to act in such a way. Although I might be angry for someone for trying to do this, in this case I am angry with him in part for the humiliation he has caused. Nor am I angry with him for moving his body in a certain way. If he had moved his body, but inadvertently, I would not have been angry. I might have been embarrassed, but I would not have been angry having accepted that he merely moved his body without acting. Nor it seems need my anger be explained by the fact that he tried to produce a V-sign at me *and* that his body moved in a certain way. Nor by the fact that he tried to produce a V-sign at me *and* that his body moved in a certain way *and* that there was causal connection between the two. Rather we can reasonably suppose that in this case my anger is explained and justified by he has done, for the way he has acted to humiliate me, and not by these conjunctions of more basic facts.[11]

There is nothing particularly special about this case. Explanations will very often appeal at some point of another to an action of another: How come you are late? I went to buy milk on the way home. Why are house prices going down – because more people are selling their homes due to personal debt. Where has the dog gone? He ran out the gate an hour ago. Are you hungry? No, I ate. Why haven't you sent me your paper? I was writing a referee's report.

Perhaps we could in some cases give a sufficing explanation by appealing to what the agent wants, knows, or intends, or wills and how

[11] O'Brien, *Self-Knowing Agents*, 137.

she moves. I am not optimistic about doing so across the board. However, even if I could, the proffered explanation seems to get its target of explanation wrong. If I am explaining my anger at Elmore it is important to record that my anger is with him for doing what he did when what he did was up to him – my concern is not his intention, or his movement, but his *action*. Human actions – changes that are up to the agent – seem to sit at the centre of our explanatory concerns. This fact is reflected in what is perhaps *the* central theme of many novels and dramas. Oedipus is punished because he killed the man that was his father. Had he accidently fallen from the chariot, sword raised, desiring his father dead, planning his father's death, and willing him to kill him we would have a comedy on our hands and his punishment would be unintelligible and unspeakable. Hamlet views to seek his revenge on Claudius because he killed his father – not because he wished him dead, caused poison to drip into his ear and whatever else – but because his father died by his action. The lodestone of the story is the act of killing.

Again any force this positive argument has comes not from its having established that it is *impossible* to do the explanatory work needed if we do not appeal to actions. There may be a sophisticated philosophical framework that will allow us to see how the act of the other is usually our primary concern, even when the act of the other is not basic. Rather, the point is that without serious pressure to give up appealing to actions in our explanations of our interactions with each other we should take actions to be basic elements of our explanatory resources. Our everyday common sense appeal to actions in our explanations are both ubiquitous and central: it would be costly to give them up.

The real question is, given that actions are just as embedded in our explanatory and ascriptive practices as beliefs, intentions and desires, why are philosophers lead so much more easily into thinking that we need to give a reduction of actions in terms of other PPPs and bodily movements?

It is not because a successful reduction has been given that has convinced us that what seemed to be basic turned out not to be. Nor can it simply be because actions are physically realised, whereas beliefs and desires are not: most philosophers of mind will take actions to be no more, and no less, physical that beliefs and desires. They are all as much candidates for being grounded in, realised by, or identical to physical states and occurrences.

One explanation of the tendency to take actions as analysable in terms of supposedly more basic psychological and physical states and occurrences might come from looking at the parallel between knowledge and action. The resistance to taking knowledge to be a basic psychological phenomenon seems to lie in a kind of human *individualism* about the mental. Knowledge seems to be relational – it relates a subject to the truth – a truth which is usually independent of the individual who knows. Is action similarly relational, and so subject to the same worry, when treated as a basic psychological phenomenon? And if action is relational what is it a relation to?

In *Knowledge and its Limits* Williamson starts with the suggestion that there is an analogy between knowledge and action – claiming that both need to be treated as key *relations* between mind and world.[12] Williamson goes on to argue there, and in a more recent paper, that this relationality is no impediment to us treating knowledge or actions as mental phenomena. As he puts it in the recent paper:

> What is fundamental to mind is not a bunch of monadic 'qualitative' properties making up an inner world, but a network of relations between an agent and the environment: relations such as seeing, referring, loving hating, and all sorts of ways of acting intentionally on things. It is an illusion that the way to pure mind is by abstracting from such relations, as wrong headed as the idea that the way to play soccer is by abstracting from the other team.[13]

In this paper Williamson further explores the suggested parallel between the knowledge case and the action case. He sets up the parallel roughly as follows:

KNOWLEDGE
Knowledge: One knows that P
Belief: One believes that P
Truth: P
Falsity: not-P

ACTION
Action: One intentionally φs
Intention: One intends to φ
Success: One φs
Failure: One does not φ

---

[12]   T. Williamson. *Knowledge and its Limits* (Oxford: OUP, 2000), 1 and 6–8.
[13]   Williamson, T. in Carter, J.A., Gordon, E. and Jarvis, B. (eds), *Knowledge-First* (Oxford: OUP, *forthcoming*). See 22–23 of online draft: http://www.philosophy.ox.ac.uk/__data/assets/pdf_file/0005/35834/KfirstCarter.pdf

Lucy O'Brien

Williamson sees the reductionist about knowledge as aiming, and failing, to complete the formula: Knowledge = Belief + Truth + X in such a way that it is true that A knows that P *iff* A believes P, P, and A satisfies condition X with respect to P. In parallel he sees the reductionist about action as aiming, but failing, to complete the formula: Action = Intention + Success + Y in such a way that it is true that A intentionally φs *iff* A intends to φ, Aφs, and A satisfies condition Y with respect to A φs.

I have argued, in agreement with Williamson, that the task of trying to complete the action formula is mistaken, and that we have default reasons to take actions to be prime. However, I want to point to important differences between action and knowledge, and suggest that there is a way in which pursuing the analogy between the two may be problematic.

In particular, I want to argue that while we can plausibly construe a subject's knowledge in a given case as a relation between relata – the subject and the fact that P – that exist independently of the subject's knowledge, we cannot construe an action as primarily a relation between an agent and an independent condition. So, to the extent that the objection to treating a mental phenomena as basic, comes from its being understood as a relation between subject and an independent world, actions will be easier to swallow candidates for basicness than knowledge.

Why do I suggest that action may not be as easily thought of as relational in the way knowledge is? Suppose that we react to the dissatisfaction with the reductionist by making the following claims:

Knowledge is a basic relation between a subject and a truth: P
Action is a basic relation between a subject and a success: one φs

To understand the claim being made we need at least understand what a subject is, what a truth, P is, and what a success, one φs, is?

We have assumed for the purposes of this paper that a subject is a human animal.

What of the truth, P? Our choice here is to take knowledge to be a relation between a subject and a proposition that has the property of being true, or taking it to be a relation between a subject and a state of affairs of worldly condition. I will assume that it is agreed between both parties – the reductionist and the non-reductionist – that at least in a particular case of knowing the truth P is to be construed as a particular fact, state of affairs, or worldly condition. On this assumption, in the table above, we are comparing a belief that is true, to a case of knowledge. (P, as it figures in ascriptions of false beliefs with the content P, will be have to construed somewhat differently.) The non-reductionist holds that in a particular case of knowing there is a worldly condition that the knower stands in the knowledge relation to, and that the knower so standing in that relation cannot be reduced to, or explained in terms of, her standing in a belief relation, justification or other relation to that condition. The reductionist denies this.[14] If we understood P as, for example, merely a propositional object, or a sentence, that also has the additional property of being true, then we would have little reason to deny that the states of mind involved when a subject stands in the belief relation, and when she stands in the knowledge relation are fundamentally different. They need differ only to the extent that the belief relation can obtain when the propositional object the subject stands in a relation to, is not true, whereas the knowledge relation must meet the extra constraint of the propositional object being true. For, there to be something substantial that the reductionist and the non-reductionist are arguing about: for knowledge to be thought to be *fundamentally* a different relation to a truth we need to think of it, in a particular case of knowledge, as a relation between a subject and a fact, state of affairs or worldly condition – not a propositional object that also happens to be true.[15]

So, if P is a truth that a subject stands in relation to when she knows, what, in parallel, does a subject stand in relation to when she acts? The analogy between knowledge and action suggests that we should take an action to be a relation to the success condition appropriate to the action. But how should we understand the success

---

[14]   Perhaps, we are wrong to think that the kinds of account being offered – of knowledge, or action – are supposed to be applied in this way to the particular case? Perhaps they are accounts only of the general kinds *knowledge* and *action* – not directly applicable to particular knowings and actions? (Thanks to Jen Hornsby for this question.) If that is so then the question we started with cannot be understood to engage *these* forms of non-reductionism. Our starting question was whether, when a particular agent – *me* – acts at a particular time, we can understand the agent's action in terms of more basic psychological and worldly conditions. My non-reductionism was intended to answer *that* question in the negative. Correlatively, my understanding of the non-reductionist about knowledge is intended to be a non-reductionist about particular acts of knowing – and as such permitting this assumption. Perhaps Williamson himself is not this kind of reductionist.

[15]   If we thought propositions that were true were different in *kind* from propositions that are false this may not seem as plausible – but why would be think that, unless we took true propositions to involve facts?

condition such that a subject stands in relation to it when she acts? Williamson suggests that the success condition of an action is that 'one φs'.[16] But now, in order to know what the correlative claim about action is would be I need to know how to understand the condition that 'one φs'.

First let us suppose – as Williamson's unpacking of the condition suggests – that the success condition that 'one φs' is such that if A is acting, then the success condition is that Aφs.

How should we understand Aφs? Williamson's guidance is that 'the range of the variable 'φ' is not limited to paradigmatic actions' (page 8): there are a range of act types – φings – which A can carry out intentionally or not. It can be true of A that she φs on an occasion when she does not intentionally φ, and also be true of her on another occasion that she φs when she does intentionally φ. However, consider a particular case when A φs intentionally, and suppose that her intentional action is a relation between A and Aφs. Should we understand Aφs in such a case as picking put an action of A's? Given that we know that in that case A φs intentionally it seems natural to do so.

But let's consider more carefully the consequences of taking Aφs to be an action of A's in this framework. In such a case, we are taking the intentional action, A intentionally φs, as a relation between A and Aφs, where Aφs is an action. The question now arises: what is the relation between *that* action of A's – Aφs – which is the success

---

[16]   Williamson notes that 'An apparent asymmetry between the two columns is that the contents on the knowledge side were just treated as propositional while those on the action side were not' but he considers 'this asymmetry is largely an artefact of presentation'. In one way this is true – the decision to represent the contents of actions and intentions as incomplete but the decision to present the objects of knowledge and beliefs as complete is a presentational decision. However, the decision is not a superficial one: the contents of actions – and the contents of intentions – are usefully presented as non-propositional to capture the fact that the subject *must* stand in a reflexive relation to herself in acting. This relation is distinct from the relation she stands in when she acts on another – or to indeed her herself when she acts on herself as she might act on another. The object of an act or intention needs to be reflexively bound to the agent. That is economically effected by removing the specification of the agent from the object of the action or intention altogether – and thus removing both the suggestion that the subject needs to single herself out as the thing to be changed when she acts, and the suggestion that someone other than the agent could be in the subject place. But to argue for this is a job for another occasion.

condition and the intentional action of A's that is the relation between A and the success condition. We have two choices. Either, the actions are the same and A does *one* thing: Aφs is the same action as the intentional action we are seeking to understand. Or they are different and A does *two* things: Aφs, but also distinctly, A intentionally φs.

But it cannot be that A does one thing. Aφs cannot be the same action as A intentionally Aφs. A intentionally Aφs cannot be a *relation* between A and Aφs, as we have assumed, and be *identical* to Aφs, which is one of its relata. A relation cannot both be one of its relata, and the relation to it.

The other option is that when A acts intentionally, A acts twice. A intentionally φs and Aφs. But that is also absurd. It cannot be that our account of an action as a relation has it that, whenever A acts, she acts twice. Apart from the implausibility of thinking of all action as duplex, we are likely to face regress. Suppose Aφs is itself as action distinct from the action A intentionally φs that it is a relation to. We have to either stop there and say that our account of intentional action as a relation to success conditions depends on accepting a class of actions as those success conditions – which are not themselves to be understood in the same way. But, this would be like suggesting that we had made progress in understanding knowledge by suggesting that we construe 'A has believed knowledge' as a relation between A and 'A knows that P'. More plausibly we will then be led to consider the action 'Aφs' – the success condition of A intentionally φs – as itself a relation between A and a success condition, and ask how we should understand *that* success condition – as Aφs? We will then have a regress on our hands.

I think that these considerations suggest that *if* the analogy between action and knowledge is to hold, that we cannot without absurdity hold that the success condition Aφs is also an action of A's. We need to take the predicate 'one φs' – as it ranges overs the set of particular independent success conditions that actions are supposed to stand in a relation to – to be a *non-active predicate* – as 'something that happens with or to A'.

To mirror the situation in the knowledge case we need to be able specify a non-active success condition of the form 'Aφs', which both the reductionist and non-reductionist can agree is not itself an action but is an independent success condition for A's action. We would need to establish that there are individual occurrences that: (a) are properly construed as being of the form Aφs, (b) are non-actions (c) which are distinct from, but necessary for, actions of the corresponding type, (d) can plausibly function as something an individual always stands in relation to when she acts intentionally.

Lucy O'Brien

I am not confident that this is a task that either needs to be, or can be, successfully completed. It implies – against the grain of the anti-reductionist picture – that we will be able to specify a change A undergoes that is *necessary*, but distinct from her action, that is of a kind that A could have undergone without acting, and in relation to which we can ask what the difference is when A is related to it when A acts, in contrast to when she does not, but it occurs. It suggests that we will have a class of changes A can undergo – perhaps, changes such as A's arm rising – which are in each case distinct from the change that is A's action – A's raising her arm. The anti-reductionist may complain that when A acts the changes she undergoes *just are her* actions: A's arm rising is *identical* with A raising her arm – and to take another view is to take us perilously close to resuming the Wittgensteinian arithmetical task we wanted to move away from.

It is beyond the scope of this paper properly to explore the question of whether we will be able to given a plausible account of non-active success conditions of the form Aφs for our actions.[17] *Prima facie* any success condition of the form Aφs of an action of the form 'A intentionally φs' is just the action itself; *prima facie* the reflexive-changes to A when she acts are just her actions not something that her actions stand in relation to. Again, that is not enough to establish that there is no class of non-active success conditions that the non-reductionist could acknowledge and welcome. The point for now is that it not a *given common ground* between the reductionist and the non-reductionist that there is a neutral and independently construable relatum – Aφs – that a subject might be argued to stand in relation to when she acts. It *is* a given common ground that there exists an independent truth, P, the relation to which the reductionist and the non-reductionist disagree about in the case of knowledge.

I want to end by suggesting that we should not be surprised to find a disanalogy here. The breakdown of the analogy between knowledge and action is telling. In the case of knowledge the identity of the thing known of is quite independent of the knowing of it, and the agent who knows. We can therefore quite sensibly think of knowledge as a

---

[17]   It is more plausible that there are success conditions, not of the form Aφs, for transactional actions – actions in which an agent acts on an object distinct from herself. If an agent A acts on a patient P, P having a certain property may be a candidate for a success condition independent of A's action: If Polly puts the kettle on the stove, the kettle being on the stove is plausibly a success condition which is not just Polly's action – but is the result of Polly's action.

Exploring this is a job for another occasion.

284

relation between these independently existing relata. In the case of action, however, the identity of the thing *done* not independent of the *doing* of it, and the *doing* of it is not independent of the thing *done*: 'I do what happens' as Anscombe puts it.

This is not how we consider knowledge. The thing known – what is true – is in general independent of my knowing of it. Of course, if knowing P, in general, was what *made* P so – as is supposed to be the case for God – then the supposed disanalogy would break down. But so, I think, would the claim that knowledge is a relation between God and the truth: God's knowledge would be the truth. If God's knowing P made P so, then God's knowledge could not be thought of as simply a relation to P – for the relation would have to be such that it produced one of its relata. God's knowledge would instead be both God's creation and the truth. It is interesting to note that this construal explains why a commitment to God's productive knowledge often comes with a commitment to God *being that which he produced*. If God's knowing creates what is so, and if what God creates is an act of God, and if acts of God are self-changes – as we have argued they are – then the changes God creates must be changes to him – so he must be the truths he creates.

Once we appreciate there is no obvious way of stating the success condition of an action without appealing to the action itself we can come to see why a certain kind of action first philosophy of mind may not suggest itself. Consider the case of knowledge. We start with the following materials – the subject and the truth, P. We propose a knowledge relation between the subject and the truth – and we then note that many weaker relations might relate the subject to the truth – evidential relations, belief relations, justification relations, guessing relations and so on – without the knowledge relation being in place. When we then ask which of these relations is the primary one – which comes first in the order of explanation – it is attractive to see these weaker relations as intelligible in terms of the basic knowledge relation. But now consider the case with action. We cannot obviously suggest starting with the following materials: the agent and the success – and then go on to note the many weaker relations of intention, trying, desiring and so on – relations that might hold without the action relation holding. If the action relation did not hold the success condition would not exist.

University College London
l.o'brien@ucl.ac.uk

Index of Names

Alvarez, M. 127,
134ff., 261n.
Annas, J. 139n., 141–3,
146
Anscombe, G.E.M.
1n., 90n., 106, 118,
128n., 136, 217ff.,
265n., 285
Aristotle 71n., 78n.,
139, 141, 164, 175–6,
189–93, 198, 217,
220, 225–6, 239,
241n.
Audi, R. 119
Aune, B. 131
Austen, J. 76, 257n.
Austin, J.L. 118n.,
246, 250n., 260,
262

Bard, C. 149, 150n.,
151n.
Bennet, J. 111, 266n.
Bennett, E. (fictional)
76
Blum, L. 141,
161–3
Boyle, M. 171, 270,
273
Brandt, R. 81

Calicles 190
Caouette, J. 58n.,
197–9
Clarke, R. 52n., 235
Claudius 278
Cohen, L. 109
Cook Wilson, J. 128–9
Curry, S. 247–8

Dancy, J. 116–17
Davidson, D. 7n.,
28–9, 89, 108,
109n., 115, 218n.,
219–23, 231–33,
237n., 240n., 258n.,
261, 271, 275–6
Davies, D. 123, 125
DeGroot, A.D. 153,
154
Dray, W. 231
Dreier, J. 173n., 184,
185
Dretske, F. 169
Dworkin, R. 125
Dylan, B. 123

Ekstrom, L. 206
Enoch, D. 174n.,
186–9
Evans, G. 268, 258n.,
259n.
Ewing, A.C. 106

Fleury, M. 149, 150n.,
151n.
Frege, G. 226
Frankfurt, H. 35,
51n., 62n.

Gassendi, P. 266
Gettier, E. 121
God 58, 113n, 118,
200, 285
Greco, J. 238, 247, 249
Grice, H.P. 28n., 99

Hamlet (fictional) 278
Hanser, M. 115–16

Harman, G. 30, 121n.,
122
Hempel, C. 219, 231,
233
Holton, R. 32n., 197,
199
Hornsby, J. 108, 130,
237, 281n.
Hume, D. 171–5,
177ff.
Hursthouse, R. 106n.,
116–17
Hyman, J. 127, 134ff.,
238, 251ff.

Jacobsen, D. 142, 146
James, W. 204
Jones, C.M. 157

Kane, R. 49ff.
Kant, I. 1, 13, 18, 21–2,
118, 120, 171–2,
175ff., 182ff.
Kenny, A. 235n., 243,
245, 247, 249, 257,
260, 261n., 262, 263
Kim, J. 210–12
Kissin, E. 249–250, 257
Korsgaard, C. 27n,
171n., 173n., 175n.,
176–82

Lavin, D. 270
Lenin, V. 108
Littlejohn, C. 121
Locke, D. 252, 253n.,
254–5, 257, 259n.,
260n.
Lowe, E.J. 132–3

Index of Names

MacMurray, J. 106–8,
    114n., 123
Maier, J. 242, 248n.
Mann, D. 149 152n.,
    153n., 158
McCarthy, M. 124
McDowell, J. 139n.,
    142, 143–6, 163n.,
    258n.
Miles, T.R. 157
Mill, J.S. 119, 124n.
Miller, C. 70n., 80
Millgram, E. 36n.,
    172n., 174n., 179n.,
    188
Molière 74
Molnar, G. 71n., 72,
    73n.
Monroe, M. 230–1
Murdoch, I. 113–14,
    141n., 161

Nagel, T. 117–19
Nehamas, A. 125
Nichols, S. 166
Nietzsche, F. 124–5
Nussbaum, M. 113–14

Obama, B. 117
Oedipus 122, 278

Parfit, D., 113n., 122

Paul, S. 33, 48n.
Plato 190, 239n.
Pollock, J. 123, 124
Prichard, H.A. 111,
    127ff.
Prinz, J. 110, 166–9
Proust, M. 108, 109n.,
    117
Pylyshyn, Z. 159,
    160n.

Railton, P. 166, 169n.,
    174n.
Rawls, J. 30
Riceour, P. 107, 124
Rosenberg, H. 123–5
Ross, W.D. 10n.,
    18n., 111, 120–1
Ryle, G. 75–76, 82,
    83n., 87, 93, 96,
    218–19, 223–3, 233,
    235n., 239n.

Sartre, J-P. 43, 125
Smart, J.J.C. 29–30
Smith, M. 35n.,
    173n., 185n., 219,
    237n.
Sosa, E. 238, 242n.,
    244n.
Sperry, R. 209–10,
    212

Stanley, J. 87ff., 239n.
Steyn, D. 247
Swann (fictional) 117

Thompson, M. 171n.,
    191n., 229, 240n.
Thrasymachus 190
Tyldesley, D.A. 150

Velleman, J.D. 27n.,
    34n., 40, 173n,
    237n.
Vihvelin, K. 239,
    242n., 243n., 244n.,
    246n., 247, 249,
    250n., 260, 261n.,
    263n.

Wallace, R.J. 34,
    174n.
Williams, A.M. 151ff.
Williams, B. 31n.,
    122
Williams, S. 243
Williamson, T. 87ff.
    239n., 265ff.
Wisneiwski, J.J.
    145–6
Wittgenstein, L.
    125n., 217–19, 231,
    233, 269
Wu, W. 148